CONTENTS

PREFACE

Each of us has taught social psychology for several years now. In that time, we have each gone through the annual ritual of deciding on a textbook, knowing that none of the ones on offer really covers all the material we want to address in our courses. We moaned about this long and loud enough that we eventually talked ourselves into the position of having to put our typing fingers where our mouths were; that is, to write the book we always wished someone else would write.

Why was it that we could not find a satisfactory book? After all, there is anything but a shortage of social psychology texts on the market. Although there is a seemingly endless supply of such books, they are, by and large, interchangeable. Further, with but a couple of exceptions, they are all North American. Not that that is bad, necessarily. But most available texts present uncritically a social psychology which is predominantly North American, cognitivistic, and individualistic. There are, to be sure, a few texts written by Europeans, and even a couple by Australians, and these do at least acknowledge social psychological research and theory outside the cognitivistic and individualistic mainstream. But none was satisfactory, at least to us. What we wanted was a text which, in a figurative sense, worked both sides of the Atlantic, but from a neutral southern hemispheric corner. We wanted to take the best of North American social cognition and integrate it with the broader frameworks provided by European work on social identity, social representations, and ideology. Possibly this reflects our own intellectual upbringing in Australia, where we have been invariably exposed to both North American and European traditions.

In writing this book, however, we wanted to do more than write a text for undergraduates. We also wanted the book to inform and stimulate and challenge our colleagues, to do more than rehash what they already know. In the embryonic days of the work, we were told more than once we were daft to try to write both a text and a monograph, that to attempt both would inevitably result in

SOCIAL COGNITION

An Integrated Introduction

Martha Augoustinos
and Iain Walker

SAGE Publications
London • Thousand Oaks • New Delhi

First published 1995, Reprinted 1996, 1999, 2000, 2001, 2002

SAGE Publications Ltd
6 Bonhill Street
London EC2A 4PU

SAGE Publications Inc
2455 Teller Road
Thousand Oaks, California 91320

SAGE Publications India Pvt Ltd
32, M-Block Market
Greater Kailash – I
New Delhi 110 048

British Library Cataloguing in Publication data

A catalogue record for this book is
available from the British Library

ISBN 0 8039 8989 X
ISBN 0 8039 8990 3   pbk

Library of Congress catalog card number 95–69398

Typeset by Photoprint, Torquay, S. Devon
Printed in Great Britain by The Bath Press, Bath

achieving neither. Perhaps we were foolish to persist, but we believe and hope that we have managed to achieve both. Only you, the reader, can judge though. In the spirit of open academic exchange, we invite you to let us know what you think.

In writing this book our friendship has not been strained as much as we feared it might be. There were fewer major disagreements than we expected. However, we do not always agree entirely with one another, and there are places in the book where this may be evident. In the end, we decided not to try to remove or gloss over all the things we disagree about, but instead to let them stand. Social psychology, after all, is not without its internal wranglings and contradictions. Why should a text reflect a false harmony and unanimity? Similarly, it will probably be obvious to those who know us and our respective styles who wrote which chapters. For the same reasons that we did not remove all our disagreements, we did not attempt to impose a standard style on the chapters.

A glance at the outline of the chapters makes it apparent that the book is organized in a 'bottom-up' fashion, in which we start at an individualistic level and proceed to consider the broader areas of social identity, social representations, and ideology. This is deliberate, but perhaps not ideal. We did consider arranging the book in the opposite direction, and one of us taught a whole course in that way in 1994. Students in that course were, however, more bemused and befuddled than informed and educated. It seems that most psychology students are more comfortable with, and can more easily grasp, an approach which starts with what is familiar to them – the individual. So we have retained the 'bottom-up' approach.

Finally, we would like to acknowledge our debts to the many people who have helped us write this book. First and foremost we thank Willem Doise, who, in discussions with Martha Augoustinos at the First International Conference on Social Representations in Ravello in 1992, enthusiastically encouraged the writing of this book. We also extend many thanks to Miles Hewstone who commented on the initial outline. His continual support and encouragement is greatly appreciated. Neil Macrae and Tom Pettigrew also commented on outlines of the book. Thanks also to John Soyland who, despite his anti-cognitivist bent, saw some merit in the writing of a book on social cognition. Jonathan Potter provided invaluable comments and points of clarification for Chapter 10, as did Ian John and Richard Pank. Thanks also to the Meta-theory Discussion Group in the Department of Psychology at the University of Adelaide for comments on Chapter 11. Special thanks to Dave Taylor for his insightful comments on most chapters of this book and to Jill Barlow who helped with the preparation of the manuscript. At Murdoch

University, Sally Ensor, Andrew Guilfoyle, Kerry Kretzschmar, Vance Locke, Gail Moloney, Maree Stirling, Anita Tan and Peter Warren have all read drafts of various chapters, and provided helpful comments gently suggesting ways to improve the text. Keith Gibbins at Murdoch has been a constant source of ideas, enthusiasm, and difficult questions. Ziyad Marar at Sage has been a tremendous help and source of encouragement, prodding and extensions. Also at Sage, Nicola Harris has provided invaluable editorial guidance. Grants to each of us from the Australian Research Council have supported some of our own research described in the book, and have also supported some of the research needed in the course of writing. But our biggest debts are owed to our respective families, to whom we dedicate this book: Dave and Dylan, and Jane, Alex, and Joel. Thank you.

1

INTRODUCTION

THE CRISIS IN SOCIAL PSYCHOLOGY

A quarter of a century ago, Kenneth Ring (1967) published a provocative article taking to task the social psychology of his time for being frivolous, and for being more concerned with demonstrating a cute, clever experimental manipulation of the latest theoretical toy than with making serious progress in the task of building a body of worthwhile knowledge. Ring's article heralded the start of what came to be known as the 'crisis' in social psychology (Cartwright, 1979; Elms, 1975; Gergen, 1973; McGuire, 1973; Pepitone, 1976, 1981; Ring, 1967; Sampson, 1977, 1981; Tajfel, 1972; Taylor and Brown, 1979). The enthusiasm with which an earlier experimental social psychology was met became dampened by critics who described a general feeling of discontent with the discipline's course of direction. While experimentation deliberately and purposively controls for 'contaminating variables' of the real world, it was argued that the artificiality of this contrived environment did not and could not adequately simulate human social experience. Furthermore, experimentation led to its own class of problem, such as demand characteristics (Orne, 1969) and experimenter bias (Rosenthal, 1969). Other possible sources of bias were identified, such as the political ideologies, cultural backgrounds and biographical characteristics of researchers (Innes and Fraser, 1971).

Expressions of discontent were not only directed at the fetishism of laboratory experimentation. On a more epistemological level, Gergen (1973) claimed that social psychology could never be a science because the subject matter with which it deals (human social behaviour) is largely culturally and historically specific. Unlike the physical sciences, general laws of human behaviour cannot be established definitively, because these fluctuate with changing cultural and historical circumstances. Social psychology is, therefore, predominantly an 'historic inquiry'. For some, the location of the crisis was in the unchallenged epistemological assumption that the individual is 'the centre of all things', and thus should be the principal unit of research and analysis. In particular, Hogan and Emler (1978), Pepitone (1976, 1981) and Sampson (1977, 1988) argued how most of social psychology's theories (dissonance theory, game theory, equity theory, attitude theories and theories of personality and socialization) are imbued with the thesis of self-contained individualism.

The individualization of social psychology is largely attributed to the joint forces of experimentation and positivism which came to dominate the discipline and cloak it in scientific respectability. These forces also led to the demise of interest in collective phenomena with which early psychologists such as Wundt and McDougall had been interested (Farr, 1989). Along with the sociologist Durkheim (1898) these early psychologists believed that cultural phenomena such as language, myths, religion and nationalism could not be reduced to the individual level of analysis. In particular, Wundt believed that such higher cognitive processes could not be adequately studied by the experimental tradition which he founded.

The conflict and tension between the individual (psychological) and collective (sociological) levels of analysis has had a long history and is documented in the famous debate between Tarde and Durkheim (Doise, 1986). Those who have provided a critical history of social psychology are in agreement that the dominance of the former tradition over the latter can partly be attributed to the behaviourist views of F. H. Allport, who was highly critical of collective concepts such as McDougall's notion of 'group mind' (Cartwright, 1979; Farr, 1989; Graumann, 1986; Pepitone, 1981). Allport's methodological individualism is contained in his famous statement: 'There is no psychology of groups which is not essentially and entirely a psychology of the individual. Social psychology . . . is a part of the psychology of the individual' (1924: 4). Allport was insistent that collective phenomena such as crowd behaviour and public opinion were nothing more than the sum total of actions and attitudes of the individuals who comprise the collectivity. His methodological individualism was a powerful force which helped shape the subsequent nature of the most dominant theories and methods in North American social psychology.

Crisis? What crisis?

Little has been written of the 'crisis' since the late 1970s. For some, it was a minor distraction in the normal course of business (for example, Jones, 1985). For others, it has brought to the fore the limitations of social psychology's methods, its epistemology, and even its questions (Gergen, 1985; Manicas and Secord, 1983). One of Ring's criticisms was that debates and issues in social psychology are never really resolved. Rather, they just fade away from centre-stage because people lose interest in them, not because we now know more than before. Indeed, in many ways, the crisis itself faded from centre-stage not because the questions being raised about the enterprise of social psychology received any satisfactory answers, but simply because the discipline lost interest. We believe that the crisis was of epistemology, not just confidence, and that the epistemological problems of the 1960s and 1970s are just as problematic in the 1990s, particularly with respect to the most dominant perspective of the moment – social cognition.

SOCIAL COGNITION

Social psychology has always prided itself on never succumbing to the behaviourist revolution which so debased and derailed the rest of psychology. During the heydays of behaviourism, social psychologists were researching internal mental constructs such as attitudes, values and stereotypes. But in avoiding the excesses and pitfalls of behaviourism during the 1960s and 1970s, social psychology became increasingly drawn to the information processing metaphor of the person which came to dominate cognitive science. Just as with behaviourism, cognitivism is associated with its own excesses. Today, the dominant perspective in North American social psychology is known as *social cognition*. Some have argued that the 'social' is a misnomer and that the only thing social about social cognition is that it is about social objects – people, groups, events. It has an impressive armament of mini theories, concepts and experimental procedures borrowed from cognitive psychology. But despite all its hardware, for many it has been unable to satisfy the doubts and the questions that the crisis raised.

Currently, research and theory in social cognition is driven by an overwhelming individualistic orientation which forgets that the contents of cognition originate in social life, in human interaction and communication. The information processing models central to social cognition study cognitive processes at the expense of content and context. As such, societal, collective and symbolic features of human thought are often ignored and forgotten. Contemporary social cognition research is individualistic because it searches within the person for the causes of behaviour. Social cognition will never explain adequately the totality of socio-cognitive experience so long as it remains at the individual level of analysis. However, unlike some critics of the mainstream, we also argue that mainstream social cognition research is not completely irrelevant and does have much to offer alternative social psychologies which have emerged and gained momentum more recently. Indeed, we will argue that a reconciliation and integration of individual and social accounts can perhaps lead to a more reflexive and dynamic understanding of human experience.

What is this 'social' with which we suggest social cognition ought to be integrated? It comes largely from European social psychology, and is typified by three approaches, each of which will be described in this book. First is the approach provided by social identity theory (Tajfel and Turner, 1986). Social identity theory provides an analysis of identity based on group belongingness. In contrast to North American social psychology, the group has been more valorized than the individual in European social psychology. People are conceptualized first and foremost as social beings, who derive a sense of who they are, how they should behave and what they should believe on the basis of their group membership. Society, as a collectivity, is comprised of the complex web of intergroup relations which characterize any socio-historical period. As social identity theorists are so keen to emphasize, social identity theory reinstates the social (or group) within the individual. The second of the European perspectives we discuss, social representations theory (Moscovici, 1984a), also emphasizes the centrality of social group membership, but focuses more upon how this membership shapes and constitutes an individual's consciousness. Social representations refer to the stock of common-sense theories and knowledge people have of the social world. The theory is interested not only in mapping the contents of this common sense and how this may differ between different social groups, but also in studying how representations are used by individuals and groups to understand and construct a common and shared reality. Third, and most recent of the predominantly European perspectives, is discourse analysis. Having its origins in the postmodern and social constructionist critique of positivist science, discourse analysis emphasizes the centrality of discourse and rhetoric in human interaction. By focusing on what people say rather than on what people think, discursive psychology challenges the cognitivist assumptions underlying not only the social cognition mainstream, but also social identity theory and the theory of social representations.

ORGANIZATION OF THIS BOOK

This book is organized into two parts. Part I – 'Theoretical Perspectives in Social Cognition' – details five major conceptual frameworks which have been influential within social psychology: attitudes, social schemas, attributions, social identity and social representations. All five chapters are primarily descriptive in content, and are designed to familiarize the reader with conceptual and empirical developments in each area. While the chapters in Part I stand alone, we hope that readers will be interested enough to read Part II of the book, which aims to extend these theoretical perspectives further through critique and integration.

Chapter 2 deals with social psychology's perhaps most theorized and researched concept – attitudes. In this chapter we detail the way in which the attitude construct has been defined and how it has been theorized within social psychology. We consider the functional approach to attitudes, and discuss how various theoretical perspectives such as cognitive dissonance theory, self-perception theory and the theory of reasoned action, have dealt with one of the most problematic issues in the field – the relationship between attitudes and behaviour. Following this, we discuss research which has investigated the cognitive organization of attitudes, including how attitudes are activated and accessed. Finally, we criticize attitude research for its very individualized and asocial treatment of the attitude construct.

Chapter 3 reviews the work on social schemas, a more recently developed theoretical perspective which proliferated with the advent of the information processing paradigm central to social cognition. In this chapter we discuss Rosch's pioneering work on categorization. Indeed, the process of categorization forms the backbone of all the theoretical perspectives we discuss in the book. Even postmodern perspectives such as discursive psychology acknowledge the significance and importance of the categories people use to construct meaning. We then go on to consider the research which has been conducted into the four major schema types: person schemas, self schemas, role schemas and event schemas. Following this we discuss how schemas function as generic knowledge structures. Finally, we point to some of the anomalies and contradictions which have been documented within this body of research and hint at the limits of this individualistic and highly cognitive account of how we come to understand the world around us. Chapter 7 resumes this critique in more detail.

Another central and dominant perspective within social psychology has been attribution theory. Attributions are the subject matter of Chapter 4. We outline the three major theoretical contributions to attribution theory, Heider's (1958) pioneering work, Jones and Davis's (1965) theory of correspondent inferences and Kelley's (1967) covariation model. We spend considerable time detailing and discussing the various attributional biases which have been documented within the literature and canvass various perspectives as to why these biases occur. Finally, we point to some of the limits of attribution research; a theme to which we return in Chapter 8.

In Chapter 5 we discuss the notion of social identity, which has had significant impact and influence in European social psychology. Of course, Henri Tajfel's work, and the theory it gave rise to – social identity theory (SIT) – forms the cornerstone of this chapter. Beginning with the minimal group studies, we document the theoretical principles and the empirical work associated with SIT. We go on to consider how SIT deals with 'real' intergroup phenomena like threats to social identity. We also discuss more recent theoretical developments to SIT, namely the work on multiple group membership and self-categorization theory (Turner, Hogg, Oakes, Reicher, and Wetherell, 1987). Lastly, we take a more critical look at SIT.

Chapter 6 deals with Serge Moscovici's theory of social representations. Like SIT, social representations theory has been largely an European intellectual endeavour. We begin the chapter by documenting the basic tenets of social representations theory, as detailed by Moscovici (1981, 1984a, 1988). This includes the phenomenal aspects of the theory which define social representations as socially created, shared and communicated branches of knowledge which people construct to organize and understand aspects of everyday reality. The processes by which social representations are generated are also described, as are aspects of the meta-theory; the status of knowledge and thinking in the scientific and consensual universes. This chapter also reviews representative examples of empirical research in the social representation tradition. Finally Chapter 6 reviews some of the critical evaluations to which social representations theory and research has been subjected.

Part II of the book extends our discussions of the theoretical perspectives dealt with in Part I and subjects them to more rigorous scrutiny through integration, application and critique. Chapter 7 examines the conceptual similarities between social representations theory and social schema theory. Despite advances made within social schema research, it remains a highly individualistic and mechanistic account of the way in which people understand the social world. By emphasizing the shared and interactional nature of social knowledge, social representations theory has the potential to revolutionize the social schema approach by contributing a much needed social perspective. Chapter 7 essentially compares the theoretical approaches, documenting the points of similarity, but also the important divergences between the two theories. Both approaches remain distinct at present and, many would say, contradictory. Even so, at some minimal level at least, the two theories essentially deal with a similar subject matter: the phenomenon of internalized social knowledge.[1]

Chapter 8 continues the theme of conceptual and theoretical integration by making links between social representations theory and attribution theory. While both theories emphasize the import- ance of explanation in social life, they are articulated at different levels of analysis. Attribution theory focuses primarily on the indi- vidual cognitive processes involved in making causal explanations, while social representations theory emphasizes the social and collective nature of explanations. Where do lay explanations for societal and individual events come from if not from the stock of common knowledge and widespread beliefs within a collectivity? This social knowledge, therefore, forms the basis upon which attributions are made. In this chapter, we not only discuss and argue for a cultural and social explanation for the fundamental attribution error, but also discuss the research on lay explanations for a range of social issues such as poverty, unemployment, riots, health and illness, success and failure.[2]

Chapter 9 applies many of the constructs dealt with in Part I to the study of intergroup relations. It critically reviews the extensive work on stereotypes and stereotyping. As role schemas, stereotypes serve certain cognitive functions. They direct attention to cues in the environment, they guide encoding and retrieval of information, and they serve as energy-saving devices. This highly cognitive account of stereotypes and stereotyping, however, is severely misleading, and we argue for a more social analysis of stereotypes, defining them as the quintessential social representation. Moreover, in Chapter 11 we go further, and define stereotypes as *ideological* representations. Chapter 9 also considers social psychological theories of prejudice, the theorized link between personality and prejudice, and the relation- ship between stereotypes and prejudicial beliefs and behavioural expectancies. Lastly, we review the literature on intergroup attri- butions which demonstrate the impact of stereotypical group representations on attributions.

Chapter 10 discusses the recent uptake of discourse analysis as a postmodern and critical approach to understanding how people construct meaning and versions of reality for themselves and for others. The 'turn to language' which discourse analysis epitomizes challenges not only the very notion of cognition itself, but also the realist epistemology with which it is associated. We focus primarily on Potter and Wetherell's (1987) work in this area which introduces non-cognitive, discursive reconceptualizations of some of social psychology's most central constructs: attitudes, representations, categories, stereotypes and social groups. We also outline their discursive approach to understanding prejudice and racism (Wetherell and Potter, 1992), which contrasts with the socio-cognitive perspectives we presented in Chapter 9. We detail some of the reservations we have about the discursive approach and consider whether it is appropriate to abandon the notion of cognition altogether.

In Chapter 11 we consider one of the most contested concepts in the social sciences, that of ideology. We define the social psychological study of ideology as the study of the social psychological processes and mechanisms by which certain representations and constructions of the world serve to legitimate, rationalize and reproduce the existing institutional, social and power relations within any society. Given the reluctance of social psychological theories to consider collective and societal explanations for a range of cognitive phenomena, we feel that the system-serving and justificatory functions of certain values, beliefs, stereotypes, representations and attributions have been seriously neglected. Ideology, however, should not be viewed solely as a cognitive construct. More recently, ideology has been located in linguistic and discursive repertoires as well as in certain material and behavioural practices. The study of ideology is perhaps social psychology's greatest challenge.[3]

Throughout this book, we will be presenting conflicting models of the thinking person that have been proposed not only within the field of social cognition, but also in theories of ideology. On the one hand we have the cognitive miser, the lazy and slothful information processor, who, given any opportunity, will use short-cuts and heuristics when drawing inferences and making judgements. This necessarily leads to distortions, errors and biases in everyday human thinking. Some of these cognitive strategies may lead to costly and socially embarrassing mistakes, but most of the time many of these pre-judgements are benign and inconsequential. More than this, thought and judgement is sometimes automatically and spontaneously activated. These unintentional thoughts are sometimes beyond volitional control, being dominated and shaped by dominant expectations, schemas and stereotypes (Fiske and Taylor, 1991). These themes within the social cognition literature bear remarkable similarities to some theories of ideology which suggest that we are all subject to and dominated by the ideological undercurrents of the society in which we live. As with theories in social cognition, these approaches to ideology emphasize the distorted and mistaken perceptions and beliefs that are shaped by ideology (Althusser, 1970). This is perhaps best exemplified by the Marxist notion of 'false consciousness' in which beliefs and values held by individuals and groups conceal and mystify what is really going on in the world.

In contrast to this we have the image of the person as a moral philosopher (Gramsci, 1971) or ideological dilemmatician (Billig, Condor, Edwards, Middleton and Radley, 1988). This version emphasizes the constructive and reflexive cognitive capacities of human thought and emphasizes our ability to think critically outside existing ideological discourses and representations.

Thus we have two distinct, and possibly contradictory, metaphorical conceptualizations of human cognition. The normal reaction of protagonists in such a situation is to dismiss the other side as foolish, pig-headed or immoral. The normal reaction of a social psychological 'scientist' would be to design the crucial experiment to assess the two competing views empirically. Our position is that human thought, under certain conditions, may be slothful, but at other times will be reflexive. Unfortunately, the cognitive miser view has taken over at the expense of studying the more critical and reflexive subject. Laboratory experiments and questionnaire studies conspire towards such a view given the decontextualized and often meaningless tasks people are asked to perform in such studies. Social psychology must embrace both conceptualizations, recognizing that both can't operate simultaneously, but not dismissing the possibility that the two may co-exist in a dialectical fashion.

CONCLUDING COMMENTS

Many readers will find it strange to see a book on social cognition dealing with theoretical perspectives such as social representations, discourse analysis, postmodernism and ideology. Indeed, in canvassing areas beyond the mainstream, many people will find this book confusing. We make no apologies for the confusion. Uncertainty is, after all, part of the postmodern condition. Some will be horrified to see these critical perspectives being included in a book purported to be about 'social cognition'. Many of these traditions have been at pains to differentiate themselves from the social cognition school. All perspectives contained in this book have one fundamental thing in common, however: they all attempt to understand how we orient ourselves in the social world we inhabit, how we come to understand and construct our world, and what consequences these understandings and constructions have for us. Moreover, all these critical perspectives have themselves been a response to the crisis in social psychology which we described earlier. While many in the discipline largely ignored the crisis, others have been busily developing alternative conceptual and methodological frameworks.

When we were planning this book and submitted proposals for review, a common concern was that the reconciliation and integration of a predominantly North American, individualistic, social cognitive framework and a predominantly European, collectivist and social framework would lead students to believe that there was some figurative trans-Atlantic intellectual war taking place. This is certainly not our intention, and we don't think our arguments reflect such a binary and oppositional approach. We don't believe there is any fundamental trans-Atlantic conflict. Not all European social psychologists are interested in social representations, social constructionism or discourse analysis. Likewise, not all American social psychologists are staunch cognitivists and positivists. We believe that individualistic social cognition research and theorizing can be enriched by social identity, social representations and discursive perspectives. Likewise, many of the phenomena described in social cognition research should be of interest and significance to those espousing alternative perspectives. If there is any fundamental opposition, we hope it is dialectical, eventually leading to some form of synthesis. In presenting an integration, we hope to preserve the value of all approaches, and hope to avoid the peril of destroying them all in the process of creating a drab grey admixture of everything.

Another concern expressed by some reviewers was that the project proposed was fundamentally flawed, that in integrating, say, social representations theory with theorizing about social schemas and attributions we would destroy the nature of the theory by individualizing it. This is a genuine risk, but we hope we have avoided doing so.

NOTES

1 Some of the material in Chapter 7 has been published in Augoustinos and Innes (1990).
2 Some of the material in Chapter 8 can be found in Hewstone and Augoustinos (1995).
3 Some of the material in Chapter 11 is based on Augoustinos (1995).

PART I

THEORETICAL PERSPECTIVES IN SOCIAL COGNITION

2

ATTITUDES

One of the problems in doing social psychology is that many of its constructs and terms are shared with the vernacular. A glance at the index of any standard social psychology textbook reveals terms such as aggression, altruism, androgyny, anxiety, arousal and attitude, to mention only the a's. This is both a boon and a bane: the former because it makes easier the task of 'giving psychology away' (Miller, 1969), and perhaps also because it may reflect the absorption of social psychology into everyday thinking; the latter because it makes more difficult the task of pinning down precisely what is meant by any of these terms. So it is – perhaps especially so – with 'attitudes'.

In the vernacular, we talk of people 'having' an attitude, sometimes of people 'having attitude', and sometimes even of people having an 'attitude problem'. We talk as though people have an attitude in the same way they have an ear, nose or toe. We confer upon 'attitude' the status of noun, denoting implicitly something real and tangible, something which influences the way the attitude-owner behaves. Indeed, so common is our usage of 'attitude' that the word 'has become almost invisible from familiarity' (Fleming, 1967: 290). We don't stop to think what it is we mean when we so often invoke attitude. But it has not always been so. Fleming (1967) intriguingly traces the concept of attitude from its entry to the English language around 1710, through its use by the sociologist Herbert Spencer and the biologist Charles Darwin, and its use earlier this century to refer to a physiological state or physical orientation, to its current meaning. 'Attitude' has not always been a part of the 'common sense' we take it to be now.

The everyday use of 'attitude' is loose. So too in social psychology. Definitions, models and theories of attitudes abound. Although attitudes have been the single most researched topic in social psychology, what is meant precisely by the term is more often than not left tacit, vague and inconsistent. In this chapter we attempt to make precise what *we* mean by the attitude construct. After considering what an attitude might be, we consider briefly the functions of attitudes, the relationship between attitudes and behaviours, and the cognitive organization of attitudes. Finally, we discuss the forgotten but inherent social nature of attitudes, criticize the way in which the attitude construct has been individualized within contemporary social psychology and touch upon the relationships between attitudes and the broader constructs of social representations and ideology.

One final caveat should be mentioned. We talk in this chapter of attitudes as nouns – people have an attitude. This is misleading. We believe that the construct attitude is better construed as an adjective. It refers to a summary description of a set of covert behaviours which are inferred from more overt behaviours. The fact that we choose to summarize a variety of behaviours, both verbal and non-verbal, with the label 'attitude' does not mean that 'attitude' exists. It is no more than a summary, a description, a hypothetical construct, with more or less use in helping us understand the world around us.

WHAT IS AN ATTITUDE?

> . . . attitudes are defined at least implicitly as responses that locate 'objects of thought' on 'dimensions of judgement'. (McGuire, 1985: 239)

> We regard an attitude as the categorization of a stimulus object along an evaluative dimension based upon, or generated from, three general classes of information: (1) cognitive information, (2) affective/emotional information, and/or (3) information concerning past behaviors or behavioral intentions. (Zanna and Rempel, 1988: 319)

We concur with both McGuire and Zanna and Rempel: attitudes are evaluations. They denote a person's orientation to some object, or attitude referent. All attitudes have a referent, an 'object of thought', a 'stimulus object'. Referents may be specific and tangible: Margaret Thatcher, brussels sprouts and Jameson's whiskey may each be the object of an attitude. But so too may referents be esoteric, abstract and intangible; liberalism, equality and social psychology are the objects of attitudes as much and as often as are Thatcher, sprouts and Jameson's. By denoting the attitude-holder's 'orientation' to the referent, an attitude conveys that person's evaluation of the referent. Attitudes are expressed in the language of 'like/dislike', 'approach/ avoid' and 'good/bad'; they are evaluative. When the object of the attitude is important to the person, the evaluation of the object produces an affective, or emotional, reaction in that person.

The two definitions above are essentially the same, but include different emphases. Two features are important here. The first is that attitudes are *categorizations*. Categorization refers 'to a process with at least some minimal cognitive activity' (Zanna and Rempel, 1988: 319). Although Zanna and Rempel take this to mean that attitudes are effortful, there is evidence that the required effort is minimal; so minimal, in fact, that attitudes can be activated and can function automatically. The view of Zanna and Rempel is similar to that of Pratkanis and Greenwald, who, in their socio-cognitive model of attitudes, argue that 'an attitude is represented in memory by (1) an object label and rules for applying that label, (2) an evaluative summary of that object, and (3) a knowledge structure supporting that evaluation' (1989: 249).

The second important feature is that attitudes are 'responses that locate'. This means that attitudes are communicative; they only have sense in as much as they convey information from one person to another; attitudes are *social*. Together, these two points suggest that attitudes are, at the same time, a part of cognitive life and a part of social discourse.

The dimensions of judgement upon which attitudes fall may be universal or specific, persistent or transitory. Some dimensions may apply, or in principle be applicable, to all referents. All referents – Thatcher, sprouts, Jameson's, liberalism, equality and social psychology – can be placed somewhere on a dimension ranging from bad to good. Not all referents, though, can be located on a dimension from stupid to smart.

The definition of attitude as evaluation is becoming increasingly common in social psychology, though still not universal. It replaces a previously widespread 'tripartite' definition of attitude: the so-called 'ABC model' of attitudes. Stemming originally from the Yale Communication and Attitude Change Program at Yale University through the 1950s and 1960s, but sharing a fundamental viewpoint with many other philosophical traditions (Hilgard, 1980), the ABC model divides attitudes into three components: affect, behaviour and cognition. For this model, 'attitudes are predispositions to respond to some classes of stimuli with certain classes of responses'. The three major classes of response are cognitive, affective and behavioural (Rosenberg and Hovland, 1960: 3). Cognitive responses to a particular stimulus are the knowledge and beliefs the person has about the stimulus object; affective responses are simply how the person feels about the object; and behavioural responses are simply overt behaviours. The model allows for these three responses to be inconsistent with one another, which is just as well, because more often than not they are (for example, Breckler, 1984; Kothandapani, 1971; Ostrom, 1969). The degree of discrepancy between empirical measures of the three presumed components of the same attitude held by one person toward a single object is usually so large that the tricomponential model has largely been dismissed (for example, Eagly and Chaiken, 1993: 12–14; Pratkanis, 1989: 73). And furthermore, by defining behaviour as a *component* of attitude, the problem of any putative relationship between attitude and behaviour is simply defined away. This is not a helpful resolution of one of social psychology's major perennial problems – do attitudes predict behaviour?

FUNCTIONS OF ATTITUDES

Attitudes serve a function. They are useful to the person who has an attitude. It is hard to imagine why a person would have a reasonably consistent evaluation of some referent, be it Thatcher or sprouts, if such an attitude served no purpose. What are the functions of attitudes? Social psychology has furnished answers to this question in two different epochs, one in the 1950s and the other starting from the mid-1980s. In between, little was written about attitude function. Regardless of time, though, social psychology has focused on the functions attitudes serve for the individual attitude-holder, and has ignored any social functions.

The 1950s saw two separate, independent research programmes each focus on a functional analysis of attitudes, and each converge upon similar sorts of answers to the question of why we have attitudes (Katz, 1960; Smith, 1947; Smith, Bruner and White, 1956). The 1980s witnessed a return to functional analyses, and recast the earlier work into more contemporary forms. The newer work has been informed by, but has not departed radically from, the earlier work.

Katz (1960) articulated four functions of attitudes. The *knowledge* function is similar to the common understanding of what an attitude does. Attitudes help us explain and understand the world around us. In the Pratkanis and Greenwald (1989) definition, an attitude is a memorial representation of an object, and associated with that representation are rules about the labelling of the object, an evaluative summary of the object and a knowledge structure about the object. The knowledge function of attitudes helps us know the world.

Second, for Katz, attitudes serve a *utilitarian* function, by which is meant that they help us gain rewards and avoid punishments. To be 'politically correct' or 'ideologically sound' is to hold and display attitudes for utilitarian reasons. People are attitudinally labile to an extraordinary degree, altering their 'attitude' to the same object according to the social context they are in.

The third function is the *value-expressive* one. The expression of an attitude can sometimes be no more than a public statement of what a person believes or identifies with (probably strongly). Political statements painted on bus shelters (eat the rich, ban nuclear warships), stickers placed on car windows (Save the Planet), T-shirts adorned with group labels (Twisted Sister, Greenpeace, Youth for Christ, The Grateful Dead, Amnesty International), uniforms or sporting teams (Glasgow Celtic, LA Lakers, Fremantle Dockers), and clothing with manufacturers' labels displayed (Jag, Levis, Lacoste); these are all public signs intended to convey a message about the owner. They signal to the world that you support Celtic and not Rangers, that you're a Deadhead and not a rap freak, that you can afford designer clothing and don't buy from the local K-Mart, and so on. There is no real point to such expressions, other than to tell the world something about who you are. You are what you wear, or at least what is adorned upon what you wear.

Finally, and less obviously, attitudes can serve an *ego-defensive* function. Such attitudes are usually deep-seated, difficult to change and hostile to the attitude object. The classic examples are homophobia and xenophobia. Each of these expresses strong hostility to some outgroup. According to Katz, at least some people who hold such attitudes do so because they are unconsciously denying some aspect of their own self. Homophobics, for example, are perhaps so hostile to homosexuals and homosexuality because they deny and do not wish to confront aspects of their own sexuality. Attitudes that serve this function thus project outward what are really internal, intrapsychic conflicts. A less dramatic example is provided by Mills (1958), who gave subjects – sixth grade students – a chance to cheat without being detected, or so they thought. The next day he measured their attitude to cheating. Those who were most strongly opposed to cheating were those who had resisted the great temptation the previous day to cheat. As all smokers and sinners know, the worst people in the world are reformed smokers and sinners. The moral high ground belongs to those who project onto the world a persona built upon a falsely righteous self-image.

Attitudes may simultaneously serve more than one function, and may be held or expressed for different reasons at different times. For example, a person's attitude to medically assisted reproduction may largely serve a knowledge function, being based upon what that person knows about IVF, donor insemination, and so on, and depending on how much that person needs to formulate an attitude to assisted reproduction. But the same attitude may also aid that person's relationship with an infertile relative, or it may also be the expression of more deeply held beliefs about God's will and the

Church's position on procreation, or it may also reflect that person's own, perhaps unconscious, conflicted sense of their own sexuality and fecundity.

The typology developed by Smith et al. (1956) closely resembles that of Katz, but describes only three functions: the *object-appraisal* function is the same as Katz's knowledge function, and the *externalization* function mirrors Katz's ego-defensive function. The value-expressive and utilitarian functions described by Katz are combined by Smith et al. into the single *social adjustment* function.

More recently, Herek (1986, 1987) and Shavitt (1989, 1990) have rejuvenated interest in the functions that attitudes serve, by reinterpreting and recasting the earlier analyses. Shavitt's contribution combines the taxonomies of Katz and Smith et al. into a more parsimonious account. Thus, she describes attitudes as having a *utilitarian* function, which includes Katz's knowledge and utilitarian functions and Smith et al.'s object-appraisal function; a *social identity* function, which combines Katz's value-expressive function and Smith et al.'s social adjustment function; and a *self-esteem maintenance* function, which incorporates Katz's ego-defensive function and Smith et al.'s externalization function. Shavitt succeeds in making more stark the ties between attitudes and individual and social identities, and has also demonstrated how the success of attempts to change an attitude depends on the function that attitude serves for its owner.

Herek's reanalysis of attitude function breaks more with tradition, and leads him to propose two different kinds of attitudes: *evaluative* and *expressive*. The former are attitudes in which the attitude object is an end in itself, and the attitude functions to allow the individual access to the object itself. In contrast, expressive (or symbolic) attitudes are those in which the attitude object is a means to an end, by providing social support, increasing self-esteem or reducing anxiety. Evaluative attitudes may be *experiential and specific* (based on and restricted to a single object), *experiential and schematic* (based on experience with particular objects, but generalized to a class of objects) or *anticipatory* (based on expected, rather than direct, experience). Expressive attitudes may be social-expressive (based on the individual's need to be accepted by others), value-expressive (based on the individual's need to define self by expressing important values and aligning self with important reference groups) or defensive (based on the individual's need to reduce anxiety associated with intrapsychic conflicts). As with Shavitt's analysis, Herek suggests that strategies to change attitudes must consider whether attitudes are held for evaluative or expressive/symbolic reasons.

Herek's empirical work has focused on attitudes to homosexuality, but it has much wider relevance. For example, in the domain of racial prejudice (discussed in detail in Chapter 9), a distinction is commonly drawn between whites' anti-black prejudice which is based in self-interest and that which is based on symbolic beliefs. Further, attitudes formed for different functional reasons are likely to be more or less resilient. For example, few white Australians have much direct contact with Aborigines, but this does not prevent them from forming strong anti-black sentiments. Because these sentiments are based on anticipatory rather than experiential factors, they are hard to disconfirm through direct experience, and hence are hard to change.

Note that in the above analyses of attitude function, the emphasis is very much on the functions for the individual attitude-holder. To be sure, some of the attitude functions do refer to social aspects (for example, the social adjustment function), but by and large the functions are theorized at an *individual* level. Attitudes also serve *social* functions, though. There is basically no research on the social functions attitudes serve, but we can speculatively suggest a few.

First, attitudes serve to locate an individual within the social matrix. When earlier theorists talked of the value-expressive function, it was from the point of view of the attitude-holder. But viewed from the other side, the expression of values through attitudes is required for social cohesion and evaluation (Dornbusch, 1987). A group member who is reticent about expressing an attitude on a matter of importance to the group will not usually be allowed by the group to remain silent on the issue. The group will enforce or extract an expression of attitude. This expression is an important marker of the individual's position relative to the group. It is important to the group that such positions not be far from the group's 'prototypical' position. Enforcing or extracting attitudes can be a potent form of social control, requiring a demonstration of group allegiance from the individual.

A second social function of attitudes is that they are a mechanism for the transmission of social beliefs and attitudes, social representations and ideologies, to the individual. The public expression of an attitude by an individual usually provokes some form of reaction from those around – attitudes are not usually expressed only to the gods, then to disappear in the social ether. The public reaction to an expressed attitude engages both the individual and the public in a rhetorical dialogue. Positions, views, beliefs, doubts, inconsistencies, related issues, and so on, are exchanged and debated upon. These processes force the individual, perhaps unwittingly, to resolve inconsistencies, to consider one attitude in relation to many, to figure out what he or she believes in and how strongly, to commit publicly to a position – in short, to think about his or her attitude and its object.

A third and final social function of attitudes is that they play an explanatory, and hence justificatory, role in orienting the individual to the social world. An attitude of dislike and disdain of the poor, of the unemployed, of people of a different class, of people of a different colour, serves not only to orient the individual to that particular social object, but also to position that social object, be it a person or a group, in social space. This helps to explain, as well as justify and reproduce, the social system which produced those social positions, and to defend the individual's own social position. We return to many of these ideological functions and consequences in more depth in Chapter 11.

ATTITUDES AND BEHAVIOURS

One of the most enduring enigmas social psychologists have been concerned with is the relationship between attitudes and behaviours. The common-sense view of attitudes has it that attitudes directly cause a person to act in a particular way. If you know that someone feels strongly that cheating in exams is immoral and wrong, you can safely predict that person's cheating behaviour across time and context, or so the story goes. Social psychology has known for a long time that the relationship between attitude and behaviour is not as simple as this, that as often as not behaviours appear to be quite unrelated to attitudes, and that behaviours can 'cause' attitudes as much as the other way around.

An early American sociologist, Richard LaPiere (1934), was perhaps the first to present evidence that the expressed attitudes of a set of people to a particular object do not particularly correspond to their behaviour toward the same object. In the early 1930s, LaPiere and a Chinese couple travelled the US west coast, staying at inns and campsites. This was a time of strong anti-Chinese feelings throughout the US, yet the trio were refused accommodation on only one occasion. After their trip, LaPiere wrote to all the managers of the establishments they had visited, and others they hadn't stayed at, asking if they would accept Chinese guests. Many (more than 90 per cent) claimed they would not. There is a disparity between the expressed attitudes of the managers of the inns and auto camps and their overt behaviours.

This disparity has been noted in many studies over the years. Wicker (1969) summarized the results of 32 different studies, each of which contained a measure of individuals' attitudes to a particular object and a direct (not self-report) measure of behaviour toward the same object. The attitude–behaviour correlations reported in these studies rarely exceeded +.3, were often close to zero, and were even negative on some occasions. Thus, at best, attitudes appear to explain (in a statistical sense) up to, but no more than, 10 per cent of the variance in behaviour. So much for a simple, direct and strong link between attitudes and behaviour. Where does this leave the attitude construct? Of what use is such a construct if it doesn't help explain behaviour? The years after Wicker's widely cited review saw social psychology endeavour to refine attitude measurement techniques, on the assumption that perhaps the low correlations were a product of measurement error, and to specify more clearly under what conditions we do expect attitudes to be related to behaviour and under what conditions the two ought to be unrelated. Issues of attitude measurement are beyond the scope of this book, but excellent reviews are provided by Dawes and Smith (1985) and by Himmelfarb (1993). We turn now to a brief consideration of the conditions under which attitudes and behaviours should be related, and to the processes by which behaviours can affect attitudes.

Social psychology produced two broad classes of response to the challenge laid down by Wicker: many have attempted to work with the relationship between a single attitude–behaviour couplet, attempting to find when the link is strong and when it is not; others have attempted to formulate and test a more elaborate model of the general link between attitudes and behaviour. We consider each in turn.

Strengthening the attitude–behaviour link

Many variables influencing the strength of the attitude–behaviour link have been identified. Some of the more important ones are listed here. First, attitudes about an object which have been formed through direct experience of that object appear to be more strongly associated with behaviour related to that object than are attitudes which do not rely on any direct experience (for example, Regan and Fazio, 1977). It has been suggested that the link between behaviours and attitudes formed through direct experience is stronger because such attitudes are held with more clarity, confidence and certainty (for example, Fazio and Zanna, 1978a, 1978b, 1981), because such attitudes are more accessible (able to be brought into consciousness easily) and stronger (Fazio, 1989), and because such attitudes are automatically activated upon presentation of the attitude object (for example, Fazio, Sanbonmatsu, Powell and Kardes, 1986).

Second, it has been suggested that attitudes which are more stable will show greater attitude–behaviour consistency than attitudes which are unstable (for example, Ajzen and Fishbein, 1980). This proposal has two components. First, the greater the time between measuring the attitude and measuring the behaviour, the less strong will be the attitude–behaviour link (in LaPiere's case it was six months). This makes good sense, in that attitudes change, and the behaviour may be susceptible to the influence of many non-attitudinal factors. But second, even when the attitude and the behaviour are measured fairly well together, the link will still be stronger for stable – often more general rather than more specific – attitudes (for example, Schwartz, 1978). Stability of self-esteem, which is one's attitude to self, has other consequences too, in terms of how defensive people are to negative and positive feedback (for example, Kernis, Cornell, Sun, Berry and Harlow, 1993).

Finally, several individual differences have been found which affect the strength of the attitude–behaviour link. People who have been made self-aware (usually by placing a mirror next to them while they complete attitude scales) typically display much greater attitude–behaviour consistency than do people not made self-aware (for example, Gibbons, 1978). People who are described as high self-monitors (that is, who monitor and regulate their own reactions through the reactions of others) typically show lower attitude–behaviour consistency than those people who are described as low self-monitors (who monitor internal reactions, rather than others' reactions – for example, Zanna, Olson and Fazio, 1980), although the strength of the effect may also depend on variables such as attitude accessibility (for example, Snyder and Kendzierski, 1982). Being asked to provide reasons for their attitudes may lower the consistency of people's attitudes and behaviours (for example, Wilson, Kraft and Dunn, 1989). There is also teasing, but scant, evidence of cross-cultural differences in the tendency to believe that attitudes *should* correspond to behaviours (Kashima, Siegal, Tanaka and Kashima, 1992).

These lists of variables affecting the attitude–behaviour link are not intended to be exhaustive. They merely hint at a large literature pertaining to the problem. The point for present purposes is simply that the pessimism of Wicker (1969) may be allayed somewhat by a more detailed consideration of the many other factors which may be implicated in the relationship between attitudes and behaviour. Whereas the evidence demonstrating that attitudes lead to behaviour has often been weak, the evidence demonstrating that attitudes *follow* behaviours is much stronger.

Cognitive dissonance theory

Festinger's (1957) theory of cognitive dissonance is simple, but helps explain how it is that people change their attitudes in accord with their behaviour, rather than the other way around. The theory simply states that if a person holds two cognitions that are psycho-logically (not necessarily logically) discrepant, that discrepancy (dissonance) is uncomfortable, and the person is motivated to reduce the dissonance. Dissonance may be reduced by changing either or both of the cognitions, or by introducing a new cognition. For example, if I smoke and if I also know that smoking is bad for my health I ought to experience dissonance because these two cog-nitions are psychologically discrepant from one another. Note that there is nothing *logically* inconsistent between them; there is just a psycho-logical discrepancy. The dissonance I experience can be alleviated by changing one of the two cognitions or by introducing some new cognition. For example, I could give up smoking, but that's a difficult and unlikely thing to happen. Alternatively, I could alter my cognition that smoking is bad for my health. It is not unusual for smokers to argue that the evidence against smoking is not as strong as public health campaigns make out. Or, I could introduce some new cognition. I could, for example, accept that I smoke, and that smoking is bad for my health, but then get out of it by claiming that I smoke to relieve stress and gain pleasure.

Applying the principles of cognitive dissonance theory to the relationship between attitudes and behaviour, we can see that if people engage in a particular behaviour, for whatever reason, they are likely to alter their attitudes to correspond to the just committed action. Suppose, for example, that a young child attending a mostly white primary school with a handful of Aboriginal children joins in with a group of older children to tease one particular Aboriginal child. The young child may not have had any attitude at all to Aborigines before teasing this one Aboriginal child, but it is unlikely that that child will remain agnostic regarding Aborigines, especially if the unpleasantness of the behaviour is pointed out by a teacher or parent or another child. Rather, the child will alter (or, in this case, invent) his or her attitude to correspond to the behaviour. The child can hardly deny or change the cognition regarding his or her behaviour (although outright denial is not uncommon in children, and the child may argue that the event was not really as bad as it seemed). Any dissonance will be displaced by another cognitive change – in this case, by developing a negative attitude to the Aboriginal child, and perhaps to Aborigines in general. To borrow the title of a chapter on a similar process, but one on a much grander scale – the dehumanization of the Viet Cong by American soldiers and the massacre of Vietnamese civilians at My Lai by American infantrymen – 'It never happened and besides they deserved it' (Opton, 1971).

Attitudes follow behaviour, not the other way around. This principle applies, according to the proponents of cognitive dissonance theory anyway (Aronson, 1968, 1989; Festinger, 1957), to any instance where a person engages in a behaviour which does not correspond with any pertinent attitude held before that behaviour. Cognitive dissonance is especially aroused when one of the cognitions in the syllogism is about *self*.

Cognitive dissonance theory is one of a family of *consistency* theories: it assumes that inconsistency is unpleasant, and that people are motivated to achieve consistency and balance. This assumption has been challenged by several authors (for example, Billig, 1987), who argue that the desire to achieve and maintain consistency is a peculiar cultural construction and that people are far more tolerant of cognitive and interpersonal inconsistencies than cognitive dissonance theory assumes.

Self-perception theory

Cognitive dissonance theory has not gone unchallenged in its explanation of attitude change and the relationship between attitude and behaviour. In particular, self-perception theory was developed by Daryl Bem (1967, 1972) to explain precisely the same events as those cognitive dissonance theory purports to explain, but without recourse to elaborate, and in Bem's eyes unnecessary, psychological processes. Bem argued that we deduce our own attitudes to objects in the same way we deduce others' attitudes – by the processes of attribution, to be discussed in Chapter 4. Attribution theory suggests that observers attribute attitudes to an actor which correspond with the actor's behaviour, and that this tendency is stronger when the action is chosen freely by the actor. Bem proposes a similar process in inferring our own attitudes. In Bem's words, the major hypothesis of self perception theory is that 'in identifying his [or her] own internal states, an individual partially relies on the same external cues that others use when they infer his [or her] internal states' (1970: 50).

How is this theoretical stand-off resolved? Here we have two quite different theories, each purporting to explain precisely the same set of events. Which, if either, is right? It may appear to you, as it did to any number of researchers in the late 1960s and 1970s, that the thing to do is design and conduct an experiment which pits both theories against one another to see which one works. Unfortunately, it is impossible to design such a definitive, crucial experiment. Several tried, but each time there was always more than one possible explanation for the observed results. That's not how science – broadly defined to include social psychology and the other 'softer' social sciences – works. So it goes.

The picture painted by the accumulation of research on attitude change has been neatly summarized by Fazio, Zanna and Cooper (1977). Self perception processes seem to operate when behaviour falls within the 'latitude of acceptance'; but when the behaviour falls outside that latitude, cognitive dissonance processes appear to operate. 'Latitude of acceptance' and 'latitude of rejection' are terms from social judgement theory (Sherif, Sherif and Nebergall, 1965). Social judgement theory suggests that the dimension characterizing the range of possible attitudes to a particular object may be divided into these two latitudes. Any one person's latitude of acceptance comprises all those attitudes that person finds acceptable. All those attitudes the person finds unacceptable constitute the latitude of rejection. (A third, but usually ignored, area is called the 'latitude of non-commitment', and is made up of those attitudes the person does not care about either way.) Thus, according to social judgement theory, it is more fruitful to position a person within a range of possible attitudinal positions relative to some object than it is to argue that a precise single position represents that person's attitude.

The theory of reasoned action

The second reaction to Wicker's (1969) damning review attempted to theorize the attitude–behaviour relationship more fully than had been the case, rather than search for the conditions under which attitudes do and do not predict behaviour. The major representative of this work is Fishbein and Ajzen's theory of reasoned action (Ajzen and Fishbein, 1980; Fishbein and Ajzen, 1975).

Fishbein and Ajzen argued that attitudes do not predict behaviours *per se*, but rather *behavioural intentions*. It is behavioural intentions which directly predict behaviour. Behavioural intentions themselves are a function of attitudes to the behaviour and what Fishbein and Ajzen called *subjective norms*. Subjective norms refer to what the individual actor believes his or her significant others believe he or she *should* do. The theory of reasoned action is really only applicable to behaviours under *volitional control*.

The theory of reasoned action has been used widely and has received considerable empirical support, in areas ranging from the

decision to abort (Smetana and Adler, 1980) to the decision to breast-
or bottle-feed a baby (Manstead, Proffitt and Smart, 1983), from
smoking marijuana (Ajzen, Timko and White, 1982) to attending
church (King, 1975). Meta-analytic summaries of the size of the
association between attitudes and subjective norms, on the one
hand, and behavioural intentions, on the other, show the average
correlations ranging from .53 to .68, and between behavioural
intentions and behaviour of just over .50 (Sheppard, Hartwick and
Warshaw, 1988). These associations are considerably larger than the
maximum of .30 reported by Wicker (1969).

Despite its empirical support, the model is not without its critics. It
has been argued, for example, that personal norms (individual
beliefs about the appropriateness of particular behaviours) and
behavioural norms (what everyone else does, rather than what it is
believed they expect to be done) are as important in the formation of
behaviour as are subjective norms (for example, Schwartz and
Tessler, 1972).

Another criticism has been that even behaviour under volitional
control does not necessarily conform to the model. Some behavioural
routines are so scripted (Abelson, 1981) and rehearsed that they are
adhered to mindlessly (Langer, 1989). Similarly, Bentler and Speckart
(1979) have argued, and demonstrated empirically, that behaviours
which have been performed in the past are more likely to happen
again, simply because they have been performed and despite the
actor's intentions to behave otherwise. New Year's resolutions are
perhaps a good example of how difficult it is to cease certain
behaviours despite all the best intentions to change.

Finally, one of the authors of the original model, Icek Ajzen, has
revised the model to become the theory of planned behaviour
(Ajzen, 1988, 1989, 1991; Ajzen and Madden, 1986), to accommodate
the fact that behaviours are often not under the volitional control
assumed by the theory of reasoned action. The theory of planned
behaviour retains behavioural intentions as central in the link
between attitudes and behaviour, and still holds that behavioural
intentions are the product of attitudes toward the behaviour and
subjective norms. However, an important third factor is added –
perceived behavioural control. This factor refers to the actor's perception of the ease or difficulty of performing the behaviours.
Some behaviours are easy to do once you decide to do them, others
are harder. Some behaviours are easy not to do once that has been
decided, other behaviours are much harder not to do. Perceived
behavioural control affects the formation of behavioural intentions,
and also, importantly, directly affects the production of behaviour
itself, independently of behavioural intentions. Ajzen (1991) reviews

several studies which show that the theory of planned behaviour predicts behavioural intentions better than does the theory of reasoned action – that is, perceived behavioural control adds to the prediction of behavioural intentions over and above the effects of attitudes to the behaviour and subjective norms.

THE COGNITIVE ORGANIZATION OF ATTITUDES

Attitudes can have definite structure. The mental representation of an object often has a form consistent with the mental representation of other objects, and which directs the functioning of the attitude. Furthermore, attitudes do not exist in isolation from one another – there is structure across attitudes. In this section we consider the cognitive organization of attitudes, how they operate as cognitive systems, and how they are usually structured.

Chapter 3 discusses the notion of schema. A schema is a mental structure of some referent which consists of knowledge and examples of that referent, and which selects and processes information pertinent to that referent. In many ways a schema is like an attitude, except that an attitude has *evaluation* of that referent as its defining and central element. Two features of attitude as schemas are important structural properties: the *activation* of attitudes, and the *accessibility* of attitudes.

Not all our attitudes are active at any one time. It almost goes without saying that only a small set of our repository of attitudes is ever active at one time. Attitudes must be *activated*, or turned on somehow. The processes of attitude activation have received considerable research attention. Much of this work has drawn from principles of cognitive psychology. Attitudes are conceived of as nodes in memory, connected in an associative network. Nodes become connected through experience, and the more any connection is experienced the stronger the connection becomes. Some connections become so well rehearsed that when one node is activated, the other is *automatically* activated also. A node, or an attitude, is accepted as automatically activated if its activation is unavoidable, if the person cannot deliberately inhibit the attitude from being activated when a relevant stimulus is present. Not all nodes, or attitudes, are automatically activated, though. Whether automatic or not, attitudes become activated by stimuli in the environment. Once activated, attitudes influence what we pay attention to, how we interpret what we attend to (Friedrich, Kierniesky and Cardon, 1989), and how we recall certain events (Echabe and Rovira, 1989).

Attitudes vary in their *accessibility*, or the ease with which they may be retrieved from memory (Fazio, 1989). Strong and important attitudes are more accessible (more easily and more quickly activated) than weaker attitudes (Krosnick, 1989), and accessible attitudes govern behaviour more strongly than do less accessible attitudes (for example, Fazio and Williams, 1986).

Work on the spread of activation of attitudes largely assumes that each attitude exists as a discrete node in an associative network which has no structure other than horizontal associations formed through rehearsal. Using different approaches, several researchers have examined the vertical, rather than horizontal, structure of attitudes. There is nothing necessarily conflicting or incompatible between these two approaches. It is quite plausible to imagine nodes (attitudes) having vertical structure, as well as associative or horizontal structure.

Attitudinal structure can have two senses. First, it can refer to the structure of elements within a single attitude. The early work on the ABC, or tricomponential, model of attitudes is an example. Second, and to be discussed here, it can refer to the pattern of relatively stable relations across different individual attitudes. We consider here Kerlinger's (1984) work on the structure of political attitudes as an example of the hierarchical structure of attitudes.

Kerlinger was concerned with how social and political attitudes are organized. Work prior to his had suggested that such attitudes could be arranged in a *bipolar* way, ranging from liberal to conservative (for example, Eysenck, 1975; Eysenck and Wilson, 1978; Ferguson, 1973). In this view, liberalism is the *opposite* of conservatism, and someone who agrees strongly with a liberal item in an attitude scale is also presumed to disagree strongly with a conservative item in a scale. The bipolar assumption undergirds much work in the analysis of social and political attitudes (for example, attitudes to women are usually assumed to range from 'traditional' to 'liberal', and for these two poles to be opposed to one another – for example, Spence and Helmreich, 1972; Smith and Walker, 1991). Kerlinger suggested that the two ideologies of liberalism and conservatism do not exist in opposition to one another, but rather are independent from one another.

Kerlinger's model starts with social referents – the objects of social and political attitudes, such as abortion, real estate, trade unions, money, racial equality and patriotism. Some of these referents are said to be *criterial* for liberals, and some are criterial for conservatives. A referent is said to be criterial for someone if it is significant, or salient, to that person. Whereas bipolar models would assume that referents criterial for liberals are also negatively criterial for conservatives, and vice versa, Kerlinger argues that liberals do not care about conservative referents and conservatives are indifferent about liberal referents. In other words, criteriality is generally positive or neutral, not negative. As an ideology, liberalism has one set of criterial referents and conservatism another, and the two are independent.

The evidence Kerlinger marshals in support of his theory relies on the factor analysis of criterial ratings (both liberal and conservative) of a large number of referents by a large number of people. That is, the structure Kerlinger talks about is identified *across*, not *within*, people, although it may be paralleled as a structure within one person. Factor analysis of criterial ratings typically produces about a dozen first-order factors, identifiable as things like religiosity, racial equality, civil rights, morality, and so on. When these first-order factors are themselves factor analysed, they produce two orthogonal second-order factors – liberalism and conservatism.

Smith and Walker (1992) adapted and expanded Kerlinger's model to accommodate a third ideology, and to focus on the structure of attitudes to a single social object ('woman') rather than attitudes to many objects. Kerlinger deliberately focuses on only two ideologies – liberalism and conservatism. Radical or revolutionary ideologies are ignored, as are reactionary ones. In the domain of attitudes to women, there are well-articulated ideological positions centred on equality and tradition, which equate to Kerlinger's use of liberal and conservative. But there is also a strong position built around independence, or autonomy, of women from men. This was included as a third ideology in Smith and Walker's study. Their results confirm the independence of three ideologies about women and women's social position as coherent, but deep, attitudinal structures, which are related to the evaluation of particular behaviours (attitude referents) through prescribed identities. It is possible that criterial referents theory could be expanded to be a general account capable of relating all ideologies to particular attitudes.

An ideology is usually defined as a collection of beliefs, attitudes and values organized around some coherent core and associated with a particular group in a social structure (Scarborough, 1990; we challenge this definition later in Chapter 11). Ideologies are *shared*: it is not possible for one person to 'have' an ideology. They do not 'exist' or 'reside' within any one person. Rather, they are bodies of thought themselves. They only have life to the extent they are shared, and hence can be said to be truly and only social – they are a product of social relations. Not all sets of shared beliefs, attitudes and values, though, can be said to constitute an ideology. There is an identifiable set of beliefs, attitudes and values concerning the paucity of cricketing talent in England, and that set is shared among many people living in England as well as in Australia, the West Indies, India, Pakistan, South Africa and even New Zealand. But that set does not constitute an ideology. An ideology is characterized by a core which is explanatory and generative. Ideologies explain a given range of social phenomena. Usually that range is large. They explain how and why it is that crime occurs, and/or how and why it is that 'races' of people are ostensibly different, and/or how and why it is that the workers of the world have failed to unite to throw off their chains, despite their universal exploitation. This is different from everyone believing that the English cricket team is no good. In addition, ideologies are generative. This means that they can accommodate and explain any *new* phenomenon, as well as extant ones. Ideologies may themselves be the referent or object of an attitude. Thus, people may have an attitude to Marxism, or to Maoism, or to apartheid, or to egalitarianism, as those ideologies manifest themselves in popular culture, in specific others and in themselves.

Considering the structure of social and political attitudes as being built upon ideologies returns us to issues raised at the start of this chapter. Most of the work in social psychology and sociology on attitudes has concerned the intra-individual structure of attitudes – their accessibility, whether they function automatically or can be controlled by conscious processes, how they are changed to maintain intrapsychic consistency, and so on – and how, if at all, attitudes are related to behaviours. Work on the ideological nature of attitudes is relatively scarce, but no less important. These two traditions of research are not incompatible with one another; instead, they are complementary. Work on the intra-individual, or micro-, level focuses on how attitudes work. Macro-level concerns place attitudes in a social context, and illustrate their fundamental *social* character. Attitudes are *social*, in origin, in function, and in consequence. They originate in social life, they communicate meaning, they are shared, and they have social consequence.

THE SOCIAL NATURE OF ATTITUDES

Throughout this chapter, it should be clear that contemporary social psychology treats the attitude construct as an *individual* phenomenon. Attitudes have primarily been conceptualized as individual and internal cognitive and affective states, or as behavioural intentions and predispositions. This belies how attitudes were originally construed when the construct entered the social sciences.

Earlier this century, the sociologists Thomas and Znaniecki (1918–20) introduced attitudes as an explanatory concept to the social sciences. They argued that attitudes provide the links that tie individuals to their social groups, giving them a social position and social heritage, and allowing them to live socially. The sociological tradition of symbolic interactionism (Stryker and Statham, 1985) accepted this view and extended it to argue that attitudes, like all forms of meaning, arise through social interaction and communication. Throughout this century, mainstream social psychology has increasingly individualized the attitude construct (Jaspars and Fraser, 1984). Only recently have analyses emerged which re-establish the social nature of attitudes (Eiser, 1994; Fraser and Gaskell, 1990; Lalljee, Brown and Ginsburg, 1984). Consistent with the earlier views of Thomas and Znaniecki and of the symbolic interactionists, an increasing number of theorists are again emphasizing that attitudes originate and emerge from social life itself, through our everyday interactions and communications with others. Further, some attitudes are widely shared, providing cultural meaning and substance to everyday life. Shared attitudes are relied on to make sense of the social world and to orient ourselves to that world. Attitudes can also be group-defining, with individuals deriving their sense of identity from the shared attitudes of the social groups to which they belong. As such, attitudes can also have important social and behavioural consequences.

Historians of social psychology and its constructs have attributed the increasing individualization of the attitude construct to Gordon Allport's classic and influential contribution to this topic in the original edition of the *Handbook of Social Psychology* (1935). Allport defined an attitude as a global stimulus–response disposition for the purpose of explaining differences in behaviour to objectively similar situations. This view of attitudes resembled the behaviourist tenor of the times much more than it resembled the sociological origins of the construct. Allport's view, coupled with the important development of techniques to measure attitudes (Thurstone, 1928), signalled the beginning of the dominant positivist position, marked by a fetishistic desire to measure individuals' attitudes to just about any and every topic, and to search for individual differences in attitude which could predict differences in behaviour. Attitudes had become objectified, reified cognitive entities with a life of their own inside people's heads. As an individual cognitive and emotional predisposition, the attitude construct took on a methodological individualism which shaped the subsequent nature of attitude theories in social psychology. In Graumann's (1986) view, this led not only to the 'individualization of the social' but also to the 'desocialization of the individual'.

Contemporary theories of attitude can be contrasted with the more recent emergence of social representations theory, an approach to be covered in detail in Chapter 6. Social representations theory, as developed by Moscovici (1984a), attempts to reinstate the collective and social nature of cognitive constructs like attitudes, beliefs and values. Social representations refer to the shared stock of common sense knowledge and beliefs people within a collectivity use to orient themselves toward the social world. Having a social constructionist emphasis, social representations are the building blocks used to construct and thereby understand social reality. However, Moscovici warns that social representations are not simply 'attitudes' to social objects. As will become clear in Chapter 6, the concept of social representations has been endowed with a different epistemological status to that of the traditional attitude construct, a status which recaptures a social, cultural and collective emphasis. In the last two chapters of the book, we will address a more radical critique of the attitude construct which has been articulated by proponents of a radically different kind of social psychology – discursive social psychology. Following that, we will attempt to conceptualize the notion of attitude within a critical perspective of the study of ideology.

SUMMARY

This chapter has presented an overview of how attitudes are defined in contemporary social psychology, the functions attitudes serve, how attitudes are related to behaviours, and the cognitive organization of attitudes. We have argued that the attitude construct has lost its original and inherent social nature, that it has become 'individualized'. Finally, we have suggested links between attitudes and social representations and ideology which will be explored more fully in later chapters.

3

SOCIAL SCHEMAS

Social schemas are cognitive structures which contain knowledge of the social world. Schema theory is an information processing model of perception and cognition which attempts to isolate the mechanisms by which people come to understand the complex social world in which they live. Many of the ideas and concepts within this theoretical approach have been borrowed from work in mainstream cognitive science. While cognitive science has concerned itself with the way in which people perceive, understand, store and remember physical stimuli and objects, the emphasis within social schema theory and research has been on the perception and processing of social information, that is, information about people, groups and events.

WHAT IS A SCHEMA?

A schema is conceptualized as a mental structure which contains general expectations and knowledge of the world. This may include general expectations about people, social roles, events and how to behave in certain situations. Schema theory suggests that we use such mental structures to select and process incoming information from the social environment. In Taylor and Crocker's words, a

> schema is a cognitive structure that consists in part of a representation of some defined stimulus domain. The schema contains general knowledge about that domain, including specification of the relationships among its attributes, as well as specific examples or instances of the stimulus domain. . . . The schema provides hypotheses about incoming stimuli, which include plans for interpreting and gathering schema-related information. (1981: 91)

Schemas take the form of general expectations learned through experience or socialization. It would be very difficult to function if we went about our everyday life without prior knowledge or expectations about the people and events around us, so schemas give us some sense of prediction and control of the social world. As such, schemas are theorized to be functional and essential for our well-being. As existing mental structures, they help us to understand the complexity of social life. The schema concept, therefore, emphasizes our active construction of social reality. Schemas help guide what we attend to, what we perceive, what we remember and what we infer. They are a kind of mental short-hand that people use to simplify reality. Indeed a dominant theme associated with schema models is that people are 'cognitive misers', economizing as much as they can on the effort they need to expend when processing information. Many judgements, evaluations, opinions and decisions we make in our everyday lives are said to be 'top of the head' phenomena (Taylor and Fiske, 1978), made with little thought and considered deliberation.

Schema research aims to understand how people represent social information in memory and how new information is assimilated with existing knowledge; that is, how people are able to process, interpret and understand complex social information. In most cases our expectations and knowledge serve us well, but sometimes our preconceptions may be rigid and knowledge limited. In such circumstances our schemas can be dysfunctional and may require reassessment.

As mental structures, schemas contain abstract and general knowledge about a particular area. For example, as an organizing framework for a social event, a party schema would contain ideas about parties that are true in most cases. Parties are social events aimed at bringing people together for the pursuit of fun and entertainment. Behaviours which are expected at parties include drinking, talking, eating and dancing. This schema would be used as a general organizing framework and would guide our interactions and behaviour at such events. We may not always plan to drink or dance at a party, but it is generally assumed that one should be, at the very least, sociable (if not polite) at such functions. Certainly, reading a book in the corner, or requesting that the music be turned off, would not go down well at such occasions. Of course, this organizing schema may not apply equally to all parties, but as a general framework it would probably be functional in most cases.

The concept of schema has appeared in various psychological writings but the most influential tradition of research which preceded the work on social schema theory was Bartlett's research on non-social memory (1932a). Bartlett was an English psychologist whose research in the 1930s concerned human memory for pictures, figures and stories. He argued that people organize images and information into meaningful patterns and these patterns facilitate later memory recall. This view was different to the most dominant view at the time which argued that people perceived and represented information as isolated elements. As with Bartlett's work, contemporary research in social schema theory clearly shows that people are better able to remember information when it is organized around a theme compared to when it is not. In contrast to the elemental view of perception, Bartlett's work suggested that the processing and recall of information is facilitated by the imposition of a meaningful and organizing structure.

CATEGORIZATION

Before we can apply a schema to a social object we need first to categorize the object. Historically, within the areas of philosophy and linguistics, categorization has long been considered a central and fundamental human cognitive tendency (Lakoff, 1987). The process of categorization is central to schema theory and to other theoretical approaches we will be discussing in this book. Borrowed from cognitive psychology and the pioneering work of Eleanor Rosch, the process of categorization refers to how we identify stimuli and group them as members of one category, similar to others in that category and different from members of other categories. Categorization is seen to be fundamental to perception, thought, language and action. Most of the time we employ categories automatically and with little conscious effort. Whenever we identify or label an object as something (a book, tree, animal) we are categorizing. Categories impose order on the complexity of the stimulus world, and by doing so allow us to communicate about the world effectively and efficiently.

Rosch's (1975) experimental work found that some members of a category act as cognitive reference points in that people consider them to be more representative of a category than other members. Rosch referred to these as prototypes. For example, people judged robins and sparrows to be better examples of the category 'bird' than emus and penguins. Thus some instances contained within the category are considered more typical than others. Instances can therefore range from being quite typical to atypical. The most typical or prototypical instance would best represent the category. The prototype is the 'central tendency' or average of the category members. Rosch found that subjects identified stimuli which were judged to be more prototypical significantly faster as members of a category compared to stimuli judged as less prototypical. Essentially, when we categorize we compare the new instance or object to the category prototype. If it is relatively similar we would conclude that the instance fits the category. The more features an instance shares with other category members, the more quickly and confidently it is identified as a category member (Rosch, 1978).

Rosch found that some categories, like 'bird', have very clear boundaries, whereas other categories have 'fuzzy' boundaries. To classify an object as belonging to a particular category doesn't necessarily require that the object contain all the attributes of that category. However, the object must share some common features with other category members so that members of a category are related by 'family resemblance'. This is especially the case for social objects such as people and events where the boundaries for category inclusion are less clear. Social categorization is assumed to be a more complex process than object categorization in that social objects are variable, dynamic, interactive and therefore less predictable. As with non-social categories, members of a social category share common features, though some members are more prototypical than others. For example, consider our tendency to categorize or classify the people we know in terms of their dominant personality traits – John is 'neurotic', Sue is 'easy-going', Jane is 'shy'. Each of us has some representation of what it is to be 'neurotic', 'easy-going' and 'shy', though we may differ in what we consider to be a typical or representative instance of such behaviour. Similarly, social situations are categorized in terms of representative features so that certain behaviour is anticipated and expected in certain contexts. For example, one generally knows what range of behaviours and social interactions characterizes a party which may be totally inappropriate in other social contexts. On the whole, however, category inclusion in the social world is a more variable process which is shaped and influenced by a multitude of factors. Categorizing people and events allows us to simplify and structure the social world and thus anticipate future behaviour and experiences. Some predictability and coherence is thereby given to our everyday social interactions.

The work by Rosch and her colleagues on natural object taxonomies (Rosch, Mervis, Gray, Johnson and Boyes-Braem, 1976) also found that categories at different levels of abstraction varied in the richness of information which could be deduced from the category. Middle-level categories are the most optimal in that objects can be described in terms of characteristic features which differentiate them from objects in closely related categories. More abstract categories tend to be over-inclusive and do not provide the same richness of information, and lower-level categories are too detailed, requiring considerable cognitive effort. For example, consider the category 'chair'. This object category contains characteristic attributes in defining the appearance and function of a wide variety of objects which could be confidently classified as chairs. We would have little difficulty in describing the prototypic features and functions of a chair. However, it is more difficult specifying the necessary or sufficient features of the category 'furniture', which is a more superordinate and over-inclusive category. At more specific levels, the differentiations required to discriminate between types of chairs such as kitchen chairs, office chairs, wheelchairs, dental chairs, are numerous and may obscure differentiations between objects in other closely related categories.

The prototype approach to category representation has been a very influential account of how social stimuli are stored and represented in memory. However, more recently it has been suggested that categories may not only be represented by some averaged abstraction but by a number of specific and concrete instances or 'exemplars' of the category which have been encountered. The exemplar approach to category representation has considerable advantages over the prototypic view in that it is able to account for the variability and diversity of instances contained within a general category. As such, exemplars serve as more specific and concrete reference points. Most theorists have suggested that people probably rely on a combination of prototype and exemplar-based representations, depending on the conditions under which the information is processed (see Fiske and Taylor, 1991).

SCHEMA TYPES

The schema concept has been applied empirically to four main content areas: person schemas, self schemas, role schemas and event schemas (Fiske and Taylor, 1991; Taylor and Crocker, 1981). All schemas serve similar functions – they all influence the encoding (taking in and interpretation) of new information, memory for old information and inferences about missing information. We consider each of these four content areas in turn and familiarize the reader with some of the most widely cited empirical studies in the literature. Our aim is to document some of the central theoretical issues within this approach as well as to illustrate the experimental methods and designs used in this empirical tradition.[1]

Person schemas

Person schemas deal with abstracted conceptual structures of personality traits or person prototypes that enable a person to categorize and make inferences from the experience of interactions with other people (Cantor and Mischel, 1977). In most research these person schemas are actually referred to as trait prototypes, so we will use the terms interchangeably. We have already introduced the notion that we may categorize individuals in terms of their dominant personality traits. For example, we are more likely to categorize Woody Allen as a prototypical 'neurotic', whereas Robin Williams evokes images of the prototypical 'extrovert'. Trait or person schemas enable us to answer the question: 'what kind of person is he or she?' (Cantor and Mischel, 1979), and thus help us anticipate the nature of our interactions with specific individuals, giving us a sense of control and predictability in social interactions.

Cantor and Mischel (1977) were among the first researchers to generalize findings in cognitive psychology on prototype research to the area of personality traits. They argued that personality traits may serve as conceptual prototypes which people use to process information about others. They devised a recognition memory task in which subjects were presented with four fictional characters: a prototypic extrovert, a prototypic introvert, a non-extrovert and a non-introvert. The latter two characters served as controls. The extrovert and introvert characters were described by six sentences containing traits words which had been previously judged to be moderately related to extroversion and introversion. In addition, four descriptive sentences contained words unrelated to extroversion/ introversion. The control characters were described by 10 sentences containing words which were unrelated to extroversion or introversion. Before presentation of the characters, subjects were asked to remember as many as possible of the descriptions for each character. After presentation of the characters subjects were required to rate the characters along six trait scales, one of which included an extroversion/introversion dimension. In addition, subjects were asked to indicate from among a list of 64 randomly presented words which of these they recognized from the character descriptions.

Consistent with expectations, Cantor and Mischel found that subjects rated the target characters highly on extroversion and introversion respectively, whereas the control characters were less likely to be attributed the extroversion/introversion trait. In the recognition memory task, subjects were significantly more likely to indicate recognizing previously presented words for the target characters which were extrovert/introvert-related, words which, in actual fact, were not presented. For example, subjects were likely to indicate having recognized extrovert-related words such as 'spirited' and 'outgoing' for the extrovert character, and introvert-related words like 'quiet' and 'shy' for the introvert character. In contrast, these effects were not found for the control characters. Cantor and Mischel argue that subjects used an abstracted conceptual proto- type of an extrovert and introvert and used this as a basis for remembering subsequent material. The memory bias in recognizing prototype-related but non-presented words indicates that subjects use this conceptual schema as a unifying category.

Self schemas

Self schema research examines the conceptual structures people have of themselves, and the degree to which such structures may affect the speed and efficiency of processing information which is relevant or irrelevant to the self (Higgins and Bargh, 1987; Markus, 1977; Markus and Wurf, 1987). Markus describes self schemas as 'cognitive generalisations about the self, derived from past experi- ence, that organise and guide the processing of self-related infor- mation contained in the individual's social experiences' (1977: 64). Individuals are said to be 'schematic' on a particular dimension if they regard the dimension as a central and salient feature of their self-concept and 'aschematic' if they do not regard the dimension as central to the self. For example, if you have a clear recognition and conception of how ambitious you are, then you would be classified as being self-schematic along this trait dimension. If you are unsure or ambivalent about how you would rate yourself along this dimension, then you would be classified as aschematic on this characteristic.

In one of the first studies to investigate the utility of the self schema concept and the implications it has for processing infor- mation about the self, Markus (1977) compared the self-descriptive, behavioural and predictive ratings of a sample of female students who were classified as either schematic or aschematic on the dimension of independence. She found that the schematic subjects (who rated themselves as high on either independence or depen- dence) were significantly more likely to endorse schema-related adjectives as self-descriptive and to respond to these significantly faster. Thus, schematic-independents were more likely to endorse independent-related adjectives and to endorse these significantly faster than the dependent words. Conversely, schematic-dependent subjects were more likely to endorse the dependent-related descrip- tions and to respond to these significantly faster than the independent words. While aschematic subjects endorsed more of the dependent than independent words as self-descriptive, response latencies did not differ between these two sets of words, suggesting that they did not differentiate these as readily as did schematic-dependents. In further cognitive tasks which required subjects to describe instances of past behaviour and make predictions about future behaviour, Markus found consistent response patterns which differentiated between independent, dependent and aschematic subjects. Together, these results were interpreted as providing empirical evidence for the operation of a generalized cognitive structure which organized, selected and interpreted information about the self along an independence–dependence dimension for schematic subjects.

Self-schemas are conceptualized as well-elaborated structures which are linked to salient and largely stable individual traits and behaviour. They are components of the self-concept which are central to identity and self-definition. The self schema concept is consistent with various psychological conceptions of the self which emphasize the static, enduring and self-protecting nature of the self-concept (for example, Greenwald and Pratkanis, 1984; Swann and Read, 1981). Alternatively, the self-concept has been conceptualized as multiple, dynamic and flexible, changing with the affective and situational needs of the individual (Gergen, 1967). Subsequent work by Markus and her colleagues (Markus and Kunda, 1986; Markus and Nurius, 1986) has emphasized the more malleable and situationally variant notion of the self.

Role schemas

Role schemas refer to the knowledge structures people have of the norms and expected behaviours of specific role positions in society. These can refer to achieved and ascribed roles. The former include roles which are acquired through effort and training, such as the doctor role or psychologist role, while the latter refer to roles which we have little control over such as age, sex and race. Achieved roles are usually occupationally related, and provide us with a set of normative expectations about the behaviour of individuals occupying certain positions.

Social cognitive research on ascribed roles has been prolific, especially in the areas of gender and racial stereotypes. Stereotypes are a type of schema which organize information and knowledge about people from different social categories. Hamilton defines a stereotype as 'a cognitive structural concept, referring to a set of expectations held by the perceiver regarding members of a social group' (1979: 65). Consistent with most of the theorizing in schema theory, stereotype research sees the process of categorizing individuals into their respective social group memberships (gender, race, class, etc.) as highly functional in that it simplifies the inherent complexity of the social world for the perceiver. Indeed, ascribed roles in society, such as man/woman, rich/poor, black/white, are viewed by this cognitive approach to be highly salient and prior to any other kind of person categorization which may take place. On meeting someone for the first time, we are more likely to attend to obvious and salient cues such as sex, race, age, physical appearance, dress and speech in guiding our interactions with the individual. With increased familiarity, these cues become less important and we may subsequently employ trait-based schemas in our interactions.

In distinguishing between trait schemas and social stereotypes in person perception, Andersen and Klatzky (1987) found social stereotypes to be associatively richer in structure and able to elicit more concrete and specific attributes than trait prototypes. The salience of social group membership over more individualized person schemas when processing information is also attested to by an early study by Taylor and her colleagues (Taylor, Fiske, Etcoff and Ruderman, 1978). Subjects were asked to listen to a taped group discussion involving six male participants, three of whom were black and three white. When each individual spoke, his picture was presented on the screen. Subsequently, subjects were asked to match the individual comments to the participants. Taylor et al. found that subjects were better at recalling the racial background of the individual making the comment than identifying which particular person within the racial group had made the comment. Similar results were obtained in another study in which half of the all-white group were female and half male. Subjects were more likely to remember the sex of the contributor than which particular female or male had made the comment.

As with any other kind of schema, in some instances our expectations linked to a social stereotype may be inappropriate and require reappraisal. Indeed, much of the research on stereotyping points to the prejudicial and negative consequences which are linked to stereotyping, especially for members of marginalized groups in society. Most prolific within the general area of social psychology has been the research on race stereotypes, though only the most recent of this research has used schema theory as a theoretical framework. The literature on race stereotypes and the specific attitudinal and behavioural consequences of such stereotypes will be documented in more detail when we consider the literature on intergroup relations in Chapter 9.

As with racial stereotypes, stereotypes related to gender have also generated a great deal of empirical research (Ruble and Stangor, 1986). Of particular importance in this area has been Sandra Bem's

(1981) gender schema theory. In accounting for the considerable evidence pointing to the early development of gender role stereotypes in children as young as 18 to 20 months, Bem argued that gender role stereotypes act as organizing schemas for gender-related information in the developing child. The young child uses this framework to evaluate incoming information as appropriate or inappropriate for his or her own gender. In this way children develop schemas for both male and female stereotypes. Bem argued that the child's self-concept becomes assimilated to the gender schema, though there are marked individual variations in the extent to which the gender schema is important for self-identity. For highly sex-typed individuals, gender is a very salient component of personal identity. Markus, Crane, Bernstein and Siladi (1982), for example, found that subjects who scored high on masculinity on the Bem Sex Role Inventory (BSRI) later recalled significantly more masculine than feminine trait descriptions. Likewise, highly sex-typed feminine subjects recalled significantly more feminine than masculine traits. A further study found that masculine subjects judged masculine traits to be self-descriptive significantly faster than other trait words, and feminine subjects judged feminine traits to be self-descriptive significantly faster than non-feminine traits listed in the BSRI. Markus et al. (1982) present this research as evidence for the salience of gender as a self-defining schema for sex-typed individuals.

Event schemas

Event schemas have been conceptualized as cognitive scripts that describe the sequential organization of events in everyday activities (Schank and Abelson, 1977). Thus, event schemas provide the basis for anticipating the future, setting goals and making plans. They enable the individual to set strategies to achieve such goals, by specifying the appropriate behavioural sequences through which the individual must move to attain the desired state. So we know that the appropriate behavioural sequence for eating at a restaurant is to enter, wait to be seated by a waiter, order a drink, look at the menu, order the meal, eat, pay the bill and leave.

Schank and Abelson (1977) argue that our common-sense understanding of behaviour in particular situations is characterized by a large repertoire of unconscious knowledge and assumptions – a kind of behavioural pragmatics which orients us in everyday life. This repertoire is stored in memory and activated unconsciously whenever it is needed. Indeed, Schank and Abelson argue that 'memory is organised around personal experiences or episodes rather than around abstract semantic categories' (1977: 17). This allows us to generalize from repeated experiences so that we do not need to process information from scratch every time we encounter a similar situation.

Scripts as background knowledge and causal chains provide 'connectivity' so that a simple statement like 'Sue went to the library' tells us much more than is relayed by these five words alone. From previous experience we know what libraries are for, why people go to libraries and how to behave in them. All this knowledge is activated upon hearing 'Sue went to the library'. Thus 'new information is understood in terms of old information' (Schank and Abelson, 1977: 67). Indeed, a study by Bower, Black and Turner (1979) found that people were more likely to understand, recognize and recall conventional event sequences than unconventional sequences.

However, scripts and plans are not simply stereotyped sequences of events. To accurately predict the world around us we need also to know something of people's intentions and goals. Predicting other people's and our own behaviour depends on knowing what goals motivate behaviour. We are able to infer a lot more from the statement 'Sue went to the library' if we know that Sue is a student studying for exams. Schank and Abelson suggest that goal-oriented knowledge forms the background from which we infer and understand behaviour. Of course, it is impossible to know what goals and motivations drive every individual as many goals are linked to particular social and cultural beliefs. However, Schank and Abelson suggest that there are a number of universal goals which we use to understand most people's intentions and future actions, irrespective of their cultural and social location. These include the satisfaction of basic needs such as hunger, sex and sleep, and avoiding negative physical and psychological experiences.

HOW DO SCHEMAS FUNCTION?

Thus far we have considered four major types of schemas central to social cognition research. We want now to consider in more detail what schemas do in information processing terms: that is, how they function as organizing structures which influence the encoding, storing and recall of complex social information.

Schemas as theory-driven structures

The most central function of schemas is to lend organization to experience. The internal cognitive mechanisms through which this is achieved are generally not known though hypothetical processes have been postulated. A schema is matched against an incoming stimulus configuration, so that the relationship between the elements of the schema are compared to the incoming information. If the information is a good match to the schema, then the constitutive elements of the schema are imposed upon the information. Thus, a schema guides identification of the elements of the incoming stimulus, thereby providing a context for its meaning, organization and internal representation. Information processing is therefore conceptualized as theory-driven rather than data-driven; that is, it relies on people's prior expectations, preconceptions and knowledge about the social world in order to make sense of new situations and encounters.

An inherent feature of theory-driven or schematic processing is that often it can lead to biased judgements. As existing cognitive structures, schemas can 'fill in' data that are missing from incoming social information. In such ambiguous situations, schemas can either direct a search for the relevant information to complete the stimulus more fully, or they can fill in the missing values with 'default options' or 'best guesses'. These are usually based on previous experiences with the particular stimulus. For example, consider an Australian university student who was about to meet someone for the first time, and the only information she had about this person is that he is a male college student from the United States, holidaying in Australia. If her previous experience with American college students was rather limited, then she may (erroneously) rely on limited assumptions and preconceptions about American college students to guide her. These preconceptions may have been drawn largely from popular films about American college students. With insufficient or ambiguous information she may 'fill in' the missing details with stereotypes drawn from such films. These film portrayals suggest that he is likely to be tall, blond, a good athlete, likes to drink and hang around with the boys, is preoccupied with sex, and drives a flash car paid for by his middle-class parents. However, if she learned that he was short, dull, clumsy and wore glasses, she may apply an entirely different schema – perhaps one borrowed from American college films once again – that of the college 'nerd'. However, if she then learned he was black, the schema is likely to change again. So with ambiguous data the blanks are filled in with pre-existing assumptions and knowledge.

Schemas can also provide short-cuts when processing information by the use of heuristics. For example, with limited information people use the representativeness heuristic (Kahneman and Tversky, 1972, 1973) to determine to what degree a specific stimulus is representative of a more general category. Is Sue, who is shy and mild-mannered, more likely to be an accountant or a business executive? In schema models, people are viewed as 'cognitive misers' who simplify reality 'by interpreting specific instances in light of the general case' (Fiske and Taylor, 1984: 141).

Schemas as memory traces

Schemas influence and guide what social information will be encoded and retrieved from memory. As mentioned previously, schemas which are based on highly salient visual cues such as gender, age and race often have a determining influence on what is encoded and later remembered. Early memory research in the schema literature generally found that schemas facilitate the recall of information, so that a good stimulus match to a schema facilitates overall recall and that schema-consistent material is better remembered than schema-inconsistent material. For example, Cohen (1981) presented subjects with a videotape of a woman having dinner with her husband. Half the subjects were told that she was a waitress; the other half were told she was a librarian. Those who were told she was a librarian were more likely to remember features and behaviour of the woman which previously had been judged by another group of subjects to be prototypical of librarians (for example, wore glasses, drank wine). Likewise, subjects who had been told she was a waitress were more likely to remember 'prototypical waitress behaviour' like drinking beer. Such studies tell us that we are more likely to notice, encode and subsequently remember information which is consistent with our initial expectations (see also Hastie, 1981; Rothbart, Evans and Fulero, 1979).[2]

Furthermore, some research has indicated that subjects can have distorted memories of information which is schema-inconsistent. That is, when asked to recall information, people sometimes unconsciously change atypical data so that it is more typical. Cordua, McGraw and Drabman (1979) exposed 5- and 6-year old children to a counter-stereotypical image: a video of a female doctor and male nurse. When asked to later recall the gender of the actors, over half the children reversed the genders, making the doctor the male and the nurse female. The children distorted their recollection of the film to make it more in line with their usual gender-role expectations.[3]

Overall, schema-based judgements do not evoke exhaustive cognitive processing. People's prior expectations and knowledge will determine for what incoming social information they will need to engage greater cognitive activity. Schema- or representation-consistent information will not require in-depth processing, given that the information is expected and, therefore, automatically processed. However, schema- or representation-inconsistent information may take longer to process (Devine and Ostrom, 1988; Hastie and Park, 1986). Thus schemas also influence processing time, with the research literature predominantly indicating faster processing times for schema-relevant as opposed to schema-irrelevant information. People take less time to process, interpret and remember information which is consistent with their general expectations.

Theory-driven vs data-driven strategies

While schema theory conceptualizes social cognition as predominantly theory-driven, this view of human information processing has been challenged (for example, Higgins and Bargh, 1987). In a person memory experiment, Hastie and Kumar (1979) found that subjects were significantly more likely to recall information about the person which was incongruent with the character's personality description. These findings are largely inconsistent with schema models, as well as with a number of previously mentioned empirical findings pointing to the superior recall of schema-consistent information. Thus, in some instances people *are* influenced by the nature of the stimulus information itself. People do not apply their schemas and ignore the data at all costs. According to Hastie and Kumar (1979), information which is inconsistent with expectations because of its novelty and distinctiveness is potentially more informative to the individual. The person is therefore more likely to attend to this information and perhaps process it more thoroughly. In turn, information which is processed more thoroughly is more likely to be recalled (Craik and Lockhart, 1972).

Forgas's (1985) research on the processing of person prototypes which vary in cultural salience attempts to resolve the apparent contradiction between 'depth-of-processing' (data-driven) and schematic (theory-driven) models of information processing. Forgas found both models to be ecologically valid in that subjects adopted different processing strategies depending on the nature of the stimulus information. He found that the more culturally salient and consensual the stimulus, the more likely schematic processing was to be activated, whereas information with low cultural salience, because of its distinctiveness, is more likely to be data-driven. This suggests that people use either of two strategies depending on the nature of the information to be processed. Forgas's research is a timely reminder that cognitive factors may not be the only influences upon information processing and that cultural influences may also play a significant role: a theme to which we will return in subsequent chapters.

In contrast to the dual processing model (theory- vs data-driven) suggested by the above research (Brewer, 1988), Fiske and Neuberg (1990) suggest that social information processing can be conceptualized as a continuum, moving from schema- or category-based processing to a more individuating data-based approach. Schematic processing is used when the data are unambiguous and relatively unimportant to the person. However, if the data are less clear and are of considerable importance and relevance to the person, then a more individuating and piecemeal approach is used. People are more likely to use data-driven strategies as opposed to schema-driven strategies when there is a strong motivation for accuracy. What is clear is that in-depth processing requires attention and effort whereas category-based processing is automatic and sometimes unconscious. For example, the time and effort we spend forming impressions of others depends very much on their relative importance to us and our motivation in 'getting to know' them. Everyday superficial encounters often do not require us to go much further than to base our impressions of others around people's salient social group memberships, such as gender, race, age and occupation. Thus, social categorization is always the initial step in impression formation. Social categories access for the individual a range of preconceptions or stereotypes which are linked to the category. The individual may move beyond this stereotypic content if the target person's behaviour is in some respects ambiguous or incongruent with expectations. The social perceiver may then recategorize the target, by searching for and applying a more appropriate category or subcategory. If, however, the target defies categorization, or the social perceiver is motivated to pay detailed attention to the person, then information about the person is integrated in a more piecemeal fashion. This latter approach leads to a more intimate and individuated knowledge of the person (Fiske and Neuberg, 1990; Fiske and Taylor, 1991).

While processing can take place anywhere along the schema vs data end of the continuum, Fiske and Neuberg (1990) emphasize that most person impressions are primarily and initially category-based. In their words, category-based processing is always the 'default option'. We simply do not have the time nor the capacity to employ more individuating strategies. As a consequence, many of our day-to-day judgements are category-based judgements which are associatively linked to stereotypes about the social categories, as we elaborate in Chapter 9.

The 'energy-saving' effect of schematic processing has always been a central assumption in social cognition theory and research. However, it was not until recently that this effect was demonstrated empirically. In a series of studies, Macrae, Milne and Bodenhausen (1994) found that when subjects were engaged in two concurrent cognitive tasks, forming person impressions based on the presentation of a number of personality traits for four target persons while simultaneously listening to a passage, performance on both tasks (memory recall) was significantly facilitated for subjects who were presented with stereotype labels for the four target persons. Moreover, this effect was found when the stereotype labels were presented subliminally, that is, outside conscious awareness. Macrae et al. suggest that the use of stereotypes and their probable unconscious activation (see also Devine, 1989a) frees up valuable cognitive resources which can be utilized elsewhere. In most day-to-day superficial interactions this kind of automatic category or stereotype-based processing is not only economical but also functional in some contexts.

The necessity to simplify information and to reduce cognitive effort through the use of 'energy-saving' devices such as stereotypes has often been lamented by social psychologists. Macrae et al. suggest that stereotype activation has perhaps been too maligned. Stereotype activation specifically, and inferential thinking more generally (Gilbert, 1989), may have evolved not because humans are cognitively lazy and slothful, but because we need to deploy our limited cognitive resources economically and functionally. Even so, such a functional approach to stereotyping does not explain and account for the content of social stereotypes and why some groups rather than others are more likely to be stereotyped negatively and to be discriminated against. Cognitive models alone can never account for socio-structural and historical forces which shape specific intergroup relations. We will have more to say about the limits of cognitivism in stereotyping research in Chapters 9 and 11.

Schemas as evaluative and affective structures

One of the major criticisms of social schema theory is that it is a highly cognitive account of how people process social information which too often ignores the evaluative and affective components involved in processing social information. Schema theorists themselves have recognized this deficiency (Higgins, Kuiper and Olson, 1981). Since Zajonc (1980) argued for the distinctiveness of affect and cognition as separate systems, there has been increasing interest in the affective dimension in information processing models. After all, one of the reasons why research on stereotypes as schemas is so prolific is because of the highly evaluative (prejudicial) consequences of stereotyping people, especially those from minority groups.

Conceptually, at least, schemas represent normative structures and thus provide a basis for evaluating one's experience. Importantly, this normative function can also access a rapid, almost automatic, affective or evaluative reaction to incoming information.[4] Fiske's (1982) work on schema-triggered affect is central here. Fiske argues that some schemas are characterized by an affective/evaluative component, and that when an instance is matched against a schema, the affect/evaluation stored within the schema structure is cued. So, for example, we may experience automatic negative arousal at the sight of a prototypical politician, or fear and anxiety in the presence of a dentist. There is no doubt that many racial schemas have a strong affective component, so that the mere sight of a person from a particular group may trigger emotions like fear and suspicion and evaluative judgements which are negative and derogatory.

Fiske argues that affect and evaluation may not be determined in a piecemeal on-line fashion, but may be accessed rapidly via their associative links to the schema as a whole. Thus, 'affect is available immediately upon categorization, so evaluations and affect are cued by categorization, that is by fitting an instance to a schema. In this view, a perceiver first comprehends an input, by assimilating it to an existing knowledge structure, and then evaluates the instance on the basis of the affect linked to the schema' (Fiske, 1982: 60).

This rapid affective response does not require an attribute-by-attribute analysis and hence saves time and processing. The category label is theorized to have an 'affective tag' which is the average or sum of the affective tags associated with the constituent attributes at the lower levels of the schema. Thus an affective or evaluative response can be made without necessary reference to the lower-level attributes (Fiske and Pavelchak, 1986); provided, however, that the categorized instance is a good match to the category or schema. If the categorization process is unsuccessful and the instance proves to be complex and ambiguous, then this can lead to piecemeal processing which is more likely to involve an attribute-by-attribute evaluative and affective response. This is consistent with our previous discussion of theory-driven vs data-driven processing. Whether processing is configural or elemental, rapid or slow, is determined largely by the complexity and previous familiarity of the stimulus itself and by time constraints, as well as by the motivational and attentional needs of the perceiver (Fiske and Pavelchak, 1986).

Fiske (1982) reports a series of studies testing the notion of schema- or category-based affect. After ascertaining the consensual stereotype of the typical politician in the form of trait attributes, personality descriptions (supposedly based on intimate knowledge of the political front-runners for the American Presidency at the time these were Carter, Reagan, Bush, Kennedy and Brown) were manipulated so that some of the candidates were described according to this typical portrait (for example, extroverted, extremely ambitious, occasionally untrustworthy) while others were described in terms not typically associated with politicians. As expected, politicians who were described in prototypical terms evoked more negative and less positive affect in subjects. The politician schema, therefore, appears to contain considerable negative affect so that individuals who are a good match to the schema may be significantly disadvantaged.

Internal organization of schemas

Consistent with the work by Rosch and her colleagues on natural object categories, schemas are theorized to be hierarchically structured with more abstract and general categories of information at the top of a pyramid structure and more specific categories at the bottom. This enables the person to move from the concrete instance to a more general level of inference. Thus information can be processed at different levels of abstraction as one moves through the schema structure.

For example, a music schema could be structured as follows. First, there would be the general over-inclusive category of 'music', subdivided by four major subcategories of 'rock', 'pop', 'jazz' and 'classical'. Depending on our knowledge and familiarity with these music genres, these could be further subdivided into lower-level categories. Some subcategories of music may be poorly differentiated, so that, for example, all kinds of classical music might be 'lumped' together indiscriminately. In contrast, the 'rock' and 'pop' subcategories may be differentiated further by various subtypes. The former might include, for example, heavy metal, rhythm and blues, country rock, jazz rock, etc. Concrete exemplars are associated with each of these subtypes, some of which may be prototypically representative. AC/DC may be prototypically representative of a heavy metal band, and the Rolling Stones may be prototypic of rhythm and blues rock. We could go through the same process with the pop music category, subdividing it into more concrete and specific levels at which prototypic contemporary popular music would be represented by the likes of Kylie Minogue and Madonna.

Different schemas can also be linked to one another in a hierarchical manner where higher-order schemas subsume more concrete, lower-order ones. So, for example, our music schema may be linked to a more general schema of personal interests or an 'entertainment' schema.

However, a strict hierarchical structure for organizing information, as in the music example above, is not the only way to structure social information. Structures which are simplistically linear or a complex web of associations also may be used. The organizational elements of a schema reveal the way in which an individual organizes information about particular social domains. For example, a balanced structure is a preferred mode of schema organization for personal relationships, whereas schemas in which dominance relations prevail are primarily characterized by a linear structure (see Taylor and Crocker, 1981). Social event schemas are comprised of action scenes which are organized in a temporal fashion. This temporal organization basically reflects the goal-directed nature of the behaviour contained within the event schema (Schank and Abelson, 1977). Many everyday events such as seeing a doctor, attending a party or cooking a meal are highly consensual 'scripts' which organize behaviour in a temporal sequence. Inferences and predictions about future and intended behaviour are often predicated on the temporal actions contained within event schemas.

The way in which a schema is organized therefore depends upon its content and the degree of personal knowledge and relevance associated with the content. As with natural object categories, Cantor and Mischel (1979) found that middle-level categories in person taxonomies (for example, comic joker) are richer in information than that contained in superordinate categories (extroverted person) and contain less overlap with objects in related categories (circus clown). In turn, schemas based on role stereotypes are much richer and more complexly organized than schemas based on trait prototypes (Andersen and Klatzky, 1987). The former are characterized by a more complex network of associative links. Social stereotypes are therefore better articulated and are more predictive knowledge schemas than are trait prototypes. Information processing is also significantly faster for category-based structures than for trait-based structures (Andersen, Klatzky and Murray, 1990).

Like natural object categories, social stereotypes have been found to be differentiated into lower-order subcategories or subtypes. If you were asked to think of the 'typical' woman, and to list the characteristics and behaviour which come to mind, this would not be such an easy task. A superordinate category such as 'woman' may comprise a number of subtypes such as career woman, housewife, mother, feminist, etc. Listing the prototypical features of these subtypes is a considerably easier task than to attribute characteristics to a much broader category. Brewer, Dull and Lui (1981) found this to be the case amongst young people's representations of the elderly. The elderly category was differentiated further into three elderly subtypes, the 'senior citizen', the 'elderly statesman' and the 'grandmotherly' type. Each of these subtypes was associated with distinctive characteristics and traits. For example, at least half of the sample described the 'grandmotherly' type as helpful, cheerful and kindly, whereas the 'elder statesman' was described as intelligent, dignified and conservative.

The origins and development of schemas

While there has been considerable empirical research delineating the processing functions of schemas, social schema theory says very little about the origins of schemas. After all, where do schemas come from (Eiser, 1986)? Schemas are seen as cognitive structures which reside in individuals' heads, but how these schemas get there or where they originate from in the first place has rarely been the object of research.

Generally, schema theory states that schemas are learned or are acquired over time from direct and indirect experience with the social environment. Through experience, we are said to build up a large repertoire of schemas (Rumelhart, 1984). While it is generally agreed that little is known about the process of schema acquisition (Higgins et al., 1981; Rumelhart, 1984), tentative and hypothetical processes of acquisition have been outlined. For example, Rumelhart and Norman (1978) refer to three processes involved in the learning of schemas. The first process is called 'accretion', a sort of fact learning from which memory traces are formed and stored for later retrieval. The second process is referred to as 'tuning', in which existing schemas are refined and adapted to align them more closely with experience. Finally, 'restructuring' is a process by which new schemas are created via patterned generation. Other theorists (Higgins et al., 1981) have concerned themselves with the question of whether the mode of acquisition (induction vs propositional transmission; simultaneous vs successive instances; partial vs continuous congruent instances, and concentrated vs dispersed instances) may influence the interaction between stored social information and subsequent incoming information. Is subsequent incoming information assimilated to existing social information, or does it lead to a modification or accommodation of the stored information?

More recently, Fiske and Dyer (1985) demonstrated the generalizability of Hayes-Roth's (1977) non-monotonic learning theory for nonsense syllables to meaningful social stimuli. The obtained learning effects suggested that schema development proceeds from an initial learning of a number of independent and unintegrated components to a single and integrated schematic unit with strong associative links between the components. These associative links become strengthened through experience and use, so that the entire structure is activated by triggering any of its components. So, for example, a young child's developing gender schema for 'female' in the first 18 months of life may begin with isolated and unintegrated bits and pieces of information and observations like girls play with dolls and are dressed in pink. Other features are added to this with experience and age, such as the genital characteristics of females, expected behaviour, preferred activities and interests and occupational preferences. Over time these different dimensions become integrated to such an extent that when the 'female' gender schema is used, all of the associated links in the structure are automatically activated.

As they develop, schemas also become richer and more complex, containing more dimensions and detail. Well-developed and highly complex schemas are also more likely to incorporate exceptions or contradictions to the schema. For example, it has been found that people who have highly expert political schemas are more likely to notice and tolerate ambiguities and information which is inconsistent with the schema (Fiske, Kinder and Larter, 1983). Similarly, children's gender schemas become less rigid during middle childhood when they realize that gender stereotypes are culturally relative (Huston, 1983). In short, with experience, schemas become more organized and detailed, but also more flexible in accounting for contradictions. In other words, with experience schemas become more accurate and reflective of the complexity of social reality (Fiske and Taylor, 1991).

Schema stability and change

Generally, it has been assumed that social schemas, once developed and strengthened through use, are stable and static structures. As a unified structure, a social schema is activated as a unitary whole, even when only one of its components is accessed (Fiske and Dyer, 1985). In fact, research has indicated that well developed schemas generally resist change and continue to exist even in the face of inconsistent and contradictory evidence. This is especially the case for strongly entrenched social stereotypes. A chauvinist's well-developed schema that women are genetically inferior is rarely convinced otherwise even when confronted with evidence to the contrary.

There are conditions, however, when well-established schemas such as stereotypes are forced to change. If a person is confronted with many disconfirming instances of the stereotype, or if experience suggests that the schema is ceasing to be functional and adaptive, then changes and accommodations may be made. Weber and Crocker (1983) describe three possible models of schema change. The first is the bookkeeping model (Rumelhart and Norman, 1978), which suggests that people fine-tune the schema with each piece of information. Information contradicting the schema will lead to small gradual changes, but the experience of many contradictions and extreme deviations will lead to considerable change to the schema. The second is the conversion model, which argues that while minor inconsistencies are tolerated, schemas can undergo dramatic and sudden change in response to salient instances which clearly disconfirm the schema (Rothbart, 1981). Finally, the subtyping model suggests that disconfirming instances of the schema are relegated to subcategories. This model recognizes the hierarchical structure of schemas, characterized by the presence of more general and superordinate categories at the top, with more concrete and specific subcategories (types) at the bottom. Thus a schema can be differentiated hierarchically by the development of subtypes which accommodate exceptions to the schema, but by and large leave the overall schema intact. This model is therefore one which emphasizes the maintenance and perseverance of schemas rather than schema change (Weber and Crocker, 1983).

In a series of experiments Weber and Crocker (1983) attempted to differentiate the conditions under which stereotype change was most likely to occur. Overall, they found that when disconfirming evidence of a stereotype (in this case, the occupational stereotypes of lawyers and librarians) is dispersed across many instances, the bookkeeping model is more likely to explain the process of change, whereas when disconfirming evidence is concentrated over a few instances, subtyping is more likely to occur. Individuals who deviated either moderately or extremely from the 'lawyer' stereotype were equally likely to be subtyped, though exposure to the latter led to greater stereotype change. Furthermore, representative and unrepresentative instances of lawyers (that is, white men earning more than $30,000/year vs black men earning less than $15,000/year) who disconfirmed the group stereotype were also likely to be subtyped, though the former produced more stereotype change.

Overall, it appears that the less representative the member is of a group and the more extreme the disconfirming behaviour, the greater the tendency to treat the individual as an exception to the group, and therefore to subtype. In turn, this leaves the stereotype unchanged and unchallenged. Together, Weber and Crocker's studies provided most support for the subtyping model of schema change and some, though limited, evidence for the bookkeeping model. Little evidence was found for any dramatic change in the face of concentrated disconfirming instances, suggested by the conversion model.

In an interesting real-world study of stereotype change Hewstone, Hopkins and Routh (1992) evaluated secondary-school students' representations of the police after a one-year implementation of a police–schools liaison programme. To improve relations and increase contact between young people and the police, a programme was introduced in which a police liaison officer was assigned to a particular school. Hewstone, Hopkins and Routh (1992) found that the concentrated exposure and contact with the police liaison officers did little to change the students' stereotypes of the police. The liaison officers were, however, evaluated more favourably than the police in general but were also judged to be atypical of the group. Indeed, in a similarities rating task, students differentiated the school police officer from other police categories, such as a foot patrol officer and a mounted police officer. Furthermore, they tended to view the school police officer as sharing characteristics with other helping professionals such as teachers and social workers. In contrast, the other police categories tended to be perceived as relatively similar and to share characteristics with law and order professionals such as lawyers, shop security guards and traffic wardens. Again, what this real-world research suggests is that people who are exposed to and come into contact with individuals who disconfirm a group stereotype are less likely to change their stereotype of the group and are more likely to subtype the individual. Thus by isolating disconfirming instances, the stereotype remains intact.

Hewstone and his colleagues have found further support for the subtyping model (Hewstone, Johnston and Aird, 1992; Johnston and Hewstone, 1992), though importantly they have also found that the amount and kind of stereotype change which takes place depends on the variability of the social group in question. Concentrated salient instances which contradict a stereotype are more likely to bring about stereotype change for social groups which are perceived to be homogeneous rather than heterogeneous. Disconfirming instances in the latter are more likely to be absorbed or tolerated because variability is expected. In contrast, because homogeneous groups are perceived as less variable, any instances which disconfirm expectations are more likely to be noticed and given more weight. This suggests that stereotype change is more likely to occur for homogeneous groups under concentrated conditions. However, while Hewstone, Johnston and Aird (1992) found evidence suggesting that disconfirming evidence was more likely to be noticed in homogeneous compared to heterogeneous groups, this did not result in significant stereotype change. While there is still much research yet to be done identifying the conditions and parameters associated with stereotype change, it is clear that there is a strong tendency to treat stereotype-inconsistent information, especially if extreme, as an isolated case. This may explain the oft-quoted lament by social psychologists that, despite interventions, social stereotypes are extraordinarily resilient and continue to persist (for example, Lippmann, 1922).

CRITICISMS OF SCHEMA THEORY AND RESEARCH

Thus far we have presented schema theory and research in a relatively uncritical manner which may lead you to think that much of what constitutes this field is not problematic. Indeed, much of what constitutes schema theory makes considerable intuitive sense and many students find that as an information processing paradigm it accords well with how they go about dealing with complex social information in their everyday busy lives. We will be detailing our views regarding the limitations of schema theory and research in considerable detail in Chapter 7 where we contrast this approach with social representations theory. For now, we point out that whereas the schema concept has been a dominant perspective within social cognition research, it has been subject to a number of criticisms. Most notable has been the cry that while schema theory has considerable heuristic value as an explanatory concept, as a theory it is very general and non-specific. For example, the schema concept is able to account for contradictory findings. As we noted earlier in this chapter, some research has found a memory bias in favour of schema-consistent information while other research has found better recall for schema-inconsistent information. The latter finding challenges whether information processing is always theory-driven or a 'top-down' phenomenon, as schema theory implies. More recently these contradictory findings have been explained within a continuum model of information processing (Fiske and Neuberg, 1990) which is able to accommodate the range of empirical findings. While such accommodation perhaps reflects the complexities of processing social information, it is clear that it is difficult to falsify the schema concept since it 'can be evoked to explain any result and its opposite' (Fiske and Linville, 1980: 545). Within the tradition of positivist science, a theory which is conceptually unfalsifiable is not a good theory.

On an important methodological note, it has been suggested that the superior memory for schema-consistent material particularly evident in some of the earlier studies may be accounted for by response bias. Take the Markus et al. (1982) study on gender schema, which found that highly feminine subjects recalled significantly more feminine traits than masculine traits on the BSRI, and masculine subjects recalled more masculine than feminine traits. While this finding was presented as evidence for the salience of gender as a self-defining schema for highly sex-typed individuals, the better memory of the respective BSRI items may simply have been due to the prior act of endorsing particular traits as self-descriptive. That is, the act of endorsing particular items gives those items a memory advantage which may have little to do with the activation of a self schema (Ruble and Stangor, 1986).[5] Ruble and Stangor (1986) also make the more general point that in memory studies findings which point to schema-consistent memory effects may emerge largely as a result of subjects invoking a guessing strategy – one which produces a higher hit rate for schema-consistent items. Studies which measure memory effects through recognition tasks are significantly more prone to such response bias than recall studies. A recent meta-analytic review of 60 memory studies in the schema literature by Rojahn and Pettigrew (1992) found that when the recognition research is corrected for the possibility of guessing, and is considered together with the memory studies utilizing recall measures, the weight of the evidence suggests that memory is facilitated for schema-inconsistent compared to schema-consistent material. However, a similar meta-analytic review of this research, by Stangor and McMillan (1992), concluded otherwise: that memory was better for schema-consistent information. Recently, Fyock and Stangor (1994) have resolved this contradiction by suggesting that a memory consistency effect is more likely to occur when the information is linked to a person's social group membership than with trait descriptions of the individual. That is, expectancies associated with group stereotypes are stronger than expectancies associated with person types.

Further inconsistencies and problems in the schema literature abound. The empirical research related to the self schema concept is often presented in textbooks as a coherent body of findings providing clear evidence for the facilitation of self-reference effects. However, a recent review by Macrae and Foddy (1993) found inconsistent and contradictory findings across 21 studies. Indeed, only half of the reviewed studies found better recall for self-related stimuli. Furthermore, not all studies have found faster response latencies to self-relevant stimuli, and of those that do, some report only between-subjects comparisons and do not conduct within-subjects analyses of the data (Macrae and Foddy, 1993).

Fiedler (1982) has argued that the schema concept is also potentially circular. As a knowledge structure a schema should exist independently and prior to any individual's participation in an experiment. He suggests that in the case of research on causal schemas the stimulus materials used in experiments are so highly structured that the results which are eventually obtained are sometimes a *fait accompli* and by no means warrant being accepted as evidence for causal schemas. In a similar vein, consider the study by Brewer et al. (1981) on the existence of subcategories of the stereo-type of the elderly. There is little empirical evidence that the three subcategories used in the study existed 'in the minds' of the subjects prior to the experiment. There was no spontaneous and unstruc-tured method to elicit these subcategories from the respondents. The stimulus materials included in both the picture and trait sorting task were chosen specifically because they reflected the authors' a priori categorizations. While not disputing the possible ecological validity of the subcategories chosen for analysis, it could be argued that the fact that subjects elicited these subcategories in their clustering sorts is not surprising given the highly structured nature of the stimulus materials used in the research.

SUMMARY

Essentially, schemas are cognitive structures which organize com-plex information in a meaningful way so that we can access the information readily when needed. Schemas help us to make sense of the world, they lend structure to our perceptions and experience, and they are stored in memory for later retrieval. Schemas as knowledge structures help guide a number of central cognitive processes such as perception, memory, inference and evaluation. Empirical research has primarily focused on person schemas, role schemas, self schemas and event schemas.

The schema concept is embedded within a cognitive process model (Fiske and Linville, 1980) which borrows heavily from much of the work in cognitive science. Before a schema can be applied, stimuli need to be identified and categorized. Categorization is a fundamental human cognitive process central to perception, thought, language and action. Schemas have been conceptualized as theory-driven structures which are based on people's prior expectations and experiences. These are used to make sense of new situations and encounters. Schemas are organized structures stored in memory. They are also evaluative and affective in nature influencing our judgements and preferences. These structures are learned and acquired over time, becoming more complex in content and structure with experience. As a unified structure, all elements of the schema are activated when used for processing information. Schemas are highly resistant to change, though certain conditions may facilitate change.

Schema theory has been criticized for being too general and conceptually able to account for many contradictory and inconsistent findings. The theory is clearly embedded within a cognitive model of human information processing. In fact, many critics view this as one of its major handicaps. The question often asked is 'what is social about social schema theory?' Schema theory has been criticized for being too cognitive in nature and lacking a dynamic social and contextual perspective. We will have more to say about this in Chapter 7, where we contrast social schema theory with the theory of social representations.

NOTES

1 Intuitively, the schema concept can be applied to any knowledge domain. Indeed, there have been applications of the schema concept beyond the four main content areas. For example, Conover and Feldman (1984) apply a schema model to investigate how political knowledge is structured around certain themes, one of the most central being a conservative–liberal political framework.

2 However, a recent meta-analytic review of 60 memory studies in the schema literature by Rojahn and Pettigrew (1992) found that memory for schema-inconsistent information is more likely to be facilitated than for schema-consistent information. See discussion in the section of this chapter on Criticisms of Schema Theory and Research.

3 While other studies have found similar memory distortions for gender-inconsistent behaviour amongst 5- to 7-year-old children, this tendency decreases among older children (Drabman, Robertson, Patterson, Jarvie, Hammer and Cordua, 1981). Ruble and Stangor (1986) suggest that such memory distortions may be due less to any schematic effects that gender may have in young children, and due more to the rigid moral conformity younger children demonstrate toward gender-appropriate behaviour. This conformity declines with age once gender constancy has been achieved and children realize that departures from these standards are acceptable.

4 Much of the work on schemas does not differentiate clearly between evaluation and affect. While the evaluation of an object and the affect it evokes may be intricately linked, it is clear that in many cases evaluation can operate in the absence of any affective reaction. Moreover, a strong affective reaction to an object may make an

independent contribution to the evaluation of the object (see Breckler and Wiggins, 1989).

5 Likewise, Markus's (1977) research on the independence dimension as a self schema provides no clear evidence that anything like a specific 'independence' schema *per se* exists for some individuals. It may be that a trait such as independence is one of many others that contribute to some construction of a more general and multidimensional self schema.

4

ATTRIBUTIONS

Things happen. Cars break down, people fail exams, sports teams win and lose, people fall in love, marriages end in divorce, children beat up their siblings, people lose their job, loved ones die, people fight in the streets, people kill others in war, ethnic groups try to eliminate other groups. Most people, most of the time, do not accept that the world in which they live is capricious, whimsical or random. For most people, most of the time, things happen for a reason. Events are caused. For life to be orderly and predictable, people attribute causes to events. The ways in which people do this, the reasons why they attribute, how they attribute, the conditions under which they do and don't attribute, all constitute the subject matter of *attribution theory*. Attribution theory has dominated mainstream North American social psychology for the past 25 years and in that time a massive body of research has accumulated. We will not even attempt to review it all in this chapter. Rather, we will focus on the major theories of attribution, biases in attributional processes, and some of the reasons for those biases. Throughout the chapter we will mention some of the limits of social psychology's understanding of causal attribution.

THEORIES OF ATTRIBUTION

Despite the enormous attention devoted to the study of attribution over the last quarter century, social psychology has failed to develop a single, unifying, integrating theory of attribution. Rather, there are several 'mini-theories' of attributional processes. Historically, three of these are considered central – the contributions of Heider, Jones and Davis, and Kelley – and it is these which are considered here. There are also other accounts which could be considered mini-theories of attribution (for example, Hilton, 1990; Hilton and Slugoski, 1986; Kruglanski, 1975, 1979, 1989; McClure, 1991; McClure, Lalljee, Jaspars and Abelson, 1989; Trope, 1986; Trope and Cohen, 1989; Weiner, 1985, 1986), but space prohibits us from reviewing these. The accounts of Heider, Jones and Davis, and Kelley are not in any real sense competing theories. They are not offered as rival abstract accounts of the same social phenomena. The three complement, rather than compete against, one another. It is likely that they could, and probably should, be integrated into a single over-arching theory of attribution.

Heider's naïve scientist

Fritz Heider was an Austrian Jew who fled the horrors of wartime Europe to the relative safety of the United States. Heider and Kurt Lewin, another Jewish refugee, have probably had a more significant and long-lasting influence on the development of modern social psychology – especially in North America – than any other figures this century. Heider's most important work is his 1958 book *The Psychology of Interpersonal Relations*, in which he presages most of the work on attribution to follow. In this book, and in an earlier article (Heider, 1944), Heider articulates a 'common sense psychology' or a 'naïve psychology of action'.

Heider's common-sense psychology views people as naïve scientists. People intuitively, or in a common-sense way, infer or deduce the causes of events around them. They naturally view the world as sets of cause and effect relations, even in an anthropomorphic way, when there is no causal relationship at all (Heider and Simmel, 1944; Michotte, 1963). The arrangement of objects and events into cause and effect relations constitutes a *causal system* in our cognitive architecture (Krech, Krutchfield and Ballachey, 1962). The question of which of the many available objects and events shall be taken as cause and which as effect is crucial; it almost defines the attributional process. Heider claimed that we tend to perceive a cause and its effect as a perceptual unit. Some objects and events combine more easily than others to form a causal unit, especially when the object or cause is a human actor and the event or effect is a social behaviour. Two prime determinants of 'unit perception' are similarity and proximity. In our intuitive causal systems, two events are more likely to be seen as causally related if they are proximal rather than distal. Temporal proximity is especially potent at influencing perceived causality. Likewise, greater similarity between two events makes them more likely to be perceived as a causal unit than is the case for dissimilar events.

Two further principles of causal inference are important. First, people tend to attribute behaviour to a single cause rather than to multiple coterminous causes; and second, causes of behaviour can be thought of as residing either within the actor or outside the actor somewhere in the situation. Causes within the actor are said to be *dispositional* causes, and those outside the actor are *situational*. According to Heider, these two broad classes of cause are ipsative – the more one is favoured as an explanation of a particular behaviour the less likely the other will also be used. Heider also noticed that actors tend to see their own behaviour as driven by situational causes, but observers tend to attribute the behaviour of an actor to factors internal to the actor.

Much of Heider's work was discursive and lacked empirical support. Others formulated more systematic theoretical accounts and provided empirical tests of Heider's ideas. His ideas, though, have proven to be remarkably insightful.

Correspondent inferences

The start of the ascendancy of attribution theory in North American social psychology is marked by the publication in 1965 of a paper by Edward Jones and Keith Davis, outlining their theory of correspondent inferences. This theory is the first systematization of some of Heider's earlier ideas. The basic premise of the theory is that, under certain conditions, people display a strong tendency to *infer* that people's intentions and dispositions *correspond* to their actions.

Consider the general problem facing a perceiver when confronted by a behaviour performed by some actor. First, the perceiver must decide if the behaviour, or at least some of the effects of the behaviour, was *intended* by the actor. If a behaviour and its effects are judged to be accidental, they are uninformative; they tell the perceiver nothing about the actor. Assuming, though, that the perceiver decides that the behaviour and/or some of the effects of the behaviour were intended, the perceiver must then engage in an inferential process to decide what can be concluded about the actor on the basis of the behaviour and its effects. In doing this, according to Jones and Davis, the perceiver attempts to extract as much information as possible about the actor from the observed behaviour. The informativeness of a behaviour is defined by the extent to which the amount of uncertainty (about the actor) is reduced by knowledge of that behaviour. In other words, Jones and Davis, like Heider before them, view the perceiver as an intuitive scientist, systematically (though perhaps unwittingly) extracting abstract theoretical information from observed behavioural data, testing and eliminating alternative theoretical explanations for the data before settling on one theoretical explanation best supported by the data.

In the domain of professional science, not all data are useful. Some data (from badly designed experiments, for example) are incapable of favouring one theoretical interpretation over another. They are uninformative. They don't help to reduce uncertainty. So too in the domain of everyday intuitive science. Not all data are equal. Some data are more informative than others. So what are the situations under which data (behaviours performed by actors) are maximally informative (reduce uncertainty about the causes of those behaviours)? Jones and Davis (1965) outline three major factors affecting the process of making correspondent inferences: desirability of outcomes, the principle of non-common effects, and the motivational variables of hedonic relevance and personalism.

Behaviours judged to be *socially desirable* are less informative than behaviours judged to be socially undesirable. When a behaviour is socially desirable – desirable in the context in which it occurs, that is – it is normative or expected. Observing such behaviour is not informative to the perceiver because there are several alternative, equally probable, reasons why the behaviour occurred. The behaviour may have occurred because the actor is intrinsically a good person, chronically prone to commit such socially desirable behaviours (that is, a dispositional or internal attribution). But the behaviour may have occurred simply because it was expected; it was the right thing to do (a situational or external attribution). Either explanation is equally likely. The behaviour is uninformative because it does not help the perceiver adjudicate between the two competing explanations of the good, desirable, expected, normative behaviour.

This is not the case for socially undesirable behaviour. Such behaviours are counter-normative; they are not what is expected. Precisely for this reason they are more informative than socially desirable behaviours. In the latter case, dispositional and situational explanations for the behaviour are equally probable. For undesirable behaviours, the situational explanation has been eliminated; it is less probable than the dispositional explanation. Thus, the perceiver, the intuitive scientist, has data which reduce uncertainty, which help arbitrate between competing explanations. Undesirable behaviours are more informative than desirable behaviours, and allow the perceiver to make a dispositional attribution about the actor with confidence. The attribution about the actor's disposition is likely to be as negative as the observed behaviour.

A second important determinant of correspondent inferences is *the principle of non-common effects*. The principle applies particularly when an actor has, or at least is perceived to have, free choice in action between several behavioural alternatives. Again, the principle works because under these conditions the behaviour is informative; it reduces uncertainty by implicitly favouring one explanation for the behaviour over other, competing explanations.

A non-common effect is a distinctive outcome that follows from an act. When an actor can select one behaviour from a set of many possible behaviours, the characteristics and effects which are unique, or non-common, to that chosen behaviour – the things that set that behaviour apart from the non-chosen alternatives – provide important and powerful information about the actor, from which correspondent inferences are easily made about the actor's disposition. Whatever it is about the alternative that is chosen which distinguishes it from the other alternatives provides information about the actor, and that information is taken as a sign of the actor's disposition. The fewer the non-common effects associated with an act, the more likely an inference will be made about the actor which corresponds to the non-common effects.

The desirability of outcomes and the principle of non-common effects are both cognitive factors influencing the attributional process. The final factor in the Jones and Davis theory of correspondent inferences is motivational, and includes two related constructs – *hedonic relevance* and *personalism*. An action is said to be hedonically relevant for a perceiver if the consequences of the action affect the perceiver; the welfare of the perceiver is either harmed or benefited by the action. Personalistic actions are a subset of hedonically relevant actions, and are characterized by the *intention* of an actor for the action to have hedonic relevance for the perceiver. Actions which are perceived to be hedonically relevant or personalistic are more likely to produce correspondent inference about the actor than are other actions.

The principle of covariation

The analogy between the professional scientist and the everyday perceiver, first articulated by Heider, is brought to the fore in Harold Kelley's covariation model of attribution. The model rests on the principle of covariation, which asserts that before two events can be accepted as causally linked they must covary with one another. If two events do not covary, they cannot be causally connected.

The principle of covariation was used by Kelley as an analogy for the way in which people infer causation in their everyday lives. Kelley (1967) suggested that three factors are crucial in assessing covariation, and that different constellations of positions on these three factors lead to different types of causal conclusions regarding the specific behaviour in question. The three factors are *consistency, distinctiveness* and *consensus*. If they are thought of as independent of one another, the three dimensions constitute a cube – hence Kelley's model is often referred to as an attributional cube. The general context in which these three dimensions are applied is one where a perceiver attributes a cause to a person's response to a particular stimulus at a particular time. Consistency refers to whether that person responds in the same way to the same stimulus or similar stimuli at different times. Distinctiveness concerns whether the actor acts in the same way to other, different stimuli, or whether the actor's response distinguishes between different stimuli. Consensus is not a feature of the actor's behaviour, but of the behaviour of others: is there consensus across actors in response to the same stimulus, or do people vary in response? According to the covariation model, perceivers will decide, almost in a dichotomous way, that the actor acts either in the same way at different times (consistency is high) or in different ways (consistency is low), that the actor either shows similar responses to different stimuli (distinctiveness is low) or acts this way only in response to this particular stimulus (distinctiveness is high), and that the actor either acts in the same way as most other people (consensus is high) or acts differently (consensus is low).

Different constellations of positions on the three dimensions lead to different attributions about the causes of behaviour. An internal or dispositional attribution is most likely when consistency is high, distinctiveness is low and consensus is low. An external or situational attribution is most likely when consistency is high, distinctiveness is high and consensus is low. Other constellations lead to less clear attributions.

Two important factors were added to the covariation model by Kelley five years after his original formulation (Kelley, 1972) – *discounting* and *augmentation*. An event can have many causes. It sometimes happens that several plausible causes co-occur, but some would be expected to augment, or make more likely, the given effect, and some would be expected to inhibit, or make less likely, the given effect. If the effect occurs even in the presence of inhibitory causes, then the augmenting cause will be judged as stronger than if the augmenting cause and its effect had occurred without the inhibitory cause. Any single factor is discounted as a cause of an event if there are also other plausible causes present (Kelley, 1972).

Kelley's covariation model has one important requirement of perceivers which is not included in either Heider's or Jones and Davis's models – namely, that perceivers utilize information from across times, situations and actors. Without such information it is impossible to make consistency, distinctiveness and consensus judgements. In contrast, the perceiver in the naïve scientist model or in the correspondent inference model makes causal attributions based on a single action performed by a single actor on a single instance. The point is an important one when attempting to evaluate how well the theory relates to everyday practice. People do not approach the problem of assigning cause to an action as though they are unaware or ignorant of the likelihood that other people would perform the same action in response to the same stimulus, or the same person would repeat the behaviour, or how that actor would perform in response to other stimuli. People do not consider each event as if it were new. On the other hand, people do not engage in the complex mental calculus described by Kelley's covariation model every time they assign a cause to an action. A resolution to this dilemma is offered by the concept of *causal schemas* (Kelley, 1972, 1973). We discussed the notion of a schema in Chapter 3. Kelley's concept can be taken to refer to a set of stored knowledge about the relations between causes and effects. We each of us acquire through socialization an implicit causal theory of events. This implicit theory provides us with a ready-made attributional account of most events we encounter from one day to the next. It allows us to run on default most of the time, and we only have to devote attention to unusual, exceptional or important cases. The concept of a causal schema is similar to Heider's earlier notion of a causal system.

The writings of Heider, Jones and Davis, and Kelley constitute the major theoretical foundations of attribution theory. They complement one another, rather than vie for the trophy of best attribution theory. Whereas Heider writes generally and with little recourse to experimental data, Jones and Davis are precise and marshal evidence in their support. Whereas Jones and Davis deal principally with the production of single, one-off attributions, Kelley requires perceivers to have knowledge spanning times, situations and actors. Together, the three accounts provide a wide-ranging view of how people go about the business of making causal sense of their worlds. Each of these three theorists adopts, explicitly more than implicitly, the professional scientist systematically seeking the causes of events in Nature as an analogy of the layperson seeking causal understanding of the surrounding world. A consequence of this analogy is a view of the human perceiver as rational, as going about the attributional process in a fairly systematic, logical fashion. A moment's reflection is all that is needed to acknowledge that people typically do not act in this way – not even scientists. It is reasonable to think of attribution theory as being prescriptive – it describes how attributions perhaps should be made. We may think of systematic divergences from this prescription as constituting biases in the attributional process, and we turn now to consider what these attributional biases are and what their origin is.

ATTRIBUTIONAL BIASES

If attribution theories are prescriptive rather than descriptive – that is, they describe what should be rather than what necessarily is – then do attribution theories have any relationship with the real world at all? If indeed no one in the real world goes about making causal attributions, then it is either moot or redundant to have a theory about how attributions should or may be made. Do people spontaneously engage in processes leading to causal attributions, and if so, under what conditions do they make causal attributions and under what conditions do they fail to do so? Two studies address these questions directly.

Lau and Russell (1980) examined newspaper reports of 33 sporting events – the six baseball games in the 1977 World Series, and a number of college and professional football games. Although the primary intention of this study was to examine *kinds* of attributions for victory and defeat, the authors reported that more causal attributions were made after an unexpected outcome than an expected one. On a more serious matter, Taylor (1982) reported a study which found that 95 per cent of a sample of cancer victims spontaneously made attributions about the cause of their cancer, and 70 per cent of close family members of cancer victims made such attributions. These two studies suggest that people do in fact spontaneously make causal attributions about events around them, at least when those events are either unexpected or negative. Weiner (1985) concludes likewise in his review of spontaneous attributions. No doubt many events in social life are common, routine, everyday, and give no rise to the need for any sort of attributional analysis. For such events, people probably function *mindlessly* (Langer, 1989), or essentially run on automatic. However, people *do* make causal attributions under some conditions, and even when operating mindlessly people probably could generate causal attributions for the events passing them by if they were required to. Attribution theory, then, is not a well-formulated theory of an imaginary phenomenon.

In the correspondent inference theory of Jones and Davis, the more hedonically relevant or personalistic an action is, the more likely a correspondence inference about the actor will follow. Hedonic relevance and personalism are motivational factors, and, as such, give rise to the possibility that subsequent attributions will not be made following the normal, prescribed, rational rules of attributing cause to an action. When an attribution deviates from the prescribed model, it is thought of as a biased attribution. Some attribution researchers refer to biases as *errors*. This implies that those researchers know the *true* causes of behaviour. In all probability they don't. There are no validity benchmarks for assessing the veracity of an attribution. It is better, then, to refer simply to attributional biases, not errors.

The fundamental attribution error

[The *fundamental* attribution error] is the tendency for attributers to underestimate the impact of situational factors and to overestimate the role of dispositional factors in controlling behavior. (Ross, 1977: 183, original emphasis)

The earliest empirical demonstration of the fundamental attribution error (FAE) was produced by Jones and Harris (1967), in which subjects were shown to make correspondent inferences about an actor's attitudes based on the actor's statements about an issue. These inferences occurred even when the subjects knew the actor had no choice in making the statement. In their first experiment, subjects read a short essay on Castro's Cuba and then indicated what they thought was the true attitude of the essay writer to Castro's Cuba. Each subject read just one essay, but half of the essays were pro-Castro; the other half were anti-Castro. Given the time and the place of the study, the direction of the essay (pro- or anti-) constituted a manipulation of the prior probability of the behaviour – there simply weren't many Castro advocates in North Carolina in the mid-1960s, making the pro-Castro essay inherently an improbable, and hence more informative, behaviour. Layered over the manipulation of essay direction was the second manipulation, of choice. Subjects were told that the essay they were to read was written as an answer in a political science exam. Half of the subjects were also told that the essay writer was instructed to write an essay either defending or criticizing Castro's Cuba; the other half were told either that the essay writer was instructed to write a criticism of Castro's Cuba or that the writer was instructed to write a defence of Castro's Cuba. In other words, subjects were led to believe that the essay's position had been either assigned (no choice, uninformative) or chosen by the writer (choice, informative). After reading the 200-word essay subjects answered questions about what they thought

Table 4.1 Mean attributed attitude scores (and variances in parentheses), according to essay direction and degree of choice

	Essay direction			
	Pro-Castro		Anti-Castro	
Choice condition				
Choice	59.62	(13.59)	17.38	(8.92)
No choice	44.10	(147.65)	22.87	(17.55)

Source: Jones and Harris, 1967: 6

the essay writer's true attitude was towards Castro's Cuba, and then indicated their own attitude towards Castro's Cuba.

If the informativeness of the behaviour were the most important factor determining whether or not a correspondent inference were made by the observer subjects, then such inferences should be most evident among those subjects who read a pro-Castro essay written by someone who could have chosen to write an essay criticizing or defending Castro's Cuba, and should be least evident among those subjects who read the anti-Castro essay written by someone who was instructed what to write. The mean 'attributed attitude scores', where scores can range from 10 (anti-Castro) to 70 (pro-Castro), are reproduced in Table 4.1. There is indeed evidence here that subjects made correspondent inferences – the inferred attitude matched the essay direction, and inferences are stronger in the choice conditions than in the no-choice conditions. But – and this is the important part for the FAE – correspondent inferences are still evident in the no-choice conditions. Even when subjects were told that the essay writer was instructed to write either a pro- or an anti-Castro essay, they still infer that the essay writer has an attitude consonant with the views expressed in the essay. This is the FAE: attributers (subjects in the experiment) have apparently underestimated the impact of situational factors and overestimated the role of dispositional factors in determining behaviour.[1]

The Jones and Harris (1967) study contains two more experiments. Experiment 2 demonstrated that emphasizing the choice manipulation did not diminish the attitude attribution effect, even under no-choice conditions, that subjects were correctly aware of the essayist's choice or lack of choice, and that making the essay ambivalent did not much alter subjects' attributions either. The third experiment changed some procedural details of the first two experiments. The topic in this experiment was racial segregation, subjects listened to tape-recorded speeches rather than read essays, and the speakers were either from the North or the South of the United States. This last variable was presumed to represent prior probability – the experimenters assumed Northerners were likely to be judged by the subjects as being more likely to be anti-segregationist, and vice versa for Southerners. As it turned out, this apparently was not the case, especially for the Southern target person. The speakers' degree of choice was also manipulated, as before. Despite these changes, the attribution effects were reproduced, suggesting that the earlier results were not due to some quirk of Fidel Castro or of reading essays.[2]

The Jones and Harris experiments establish the phenomenon of correspondent inference (the FAE). How pervasive and tenacious is this phenomenon? Does it warrant the rather grand title of *fundamental* attribution error? What are the boundary conditions of the phenomenon? And where is the self in all of this? The Jones and Harris experiments show that people make attributional inferences about others, but what of the actor in the actor–observer effect?

The Jones and Harris research demonstrates the attribution of *attitudes* to others in accord with their behaviour. Researchers have shown that people make analogous inferences about others' *abilities* (for example, Reeder and Fulks, 1980) and even *personalities* (for example, Miller, Jones and Hinkle, 1981). The FAE is by no means universal or even consistently strong, though. For example, Reeder and Fulks (1980; experiments 1 and 3) showed that inferences about others' abilities (pool-playing and artistic abilities in this case) are stronger when the behaviours being portrayed by actors and being witnessed by observers are overt and visible rather than covert and implied. They also showed that skilful and unskilful performances lead to different kinds of attributions about the actor's abilities. Earlier, Reeder and Brewer (1979) proposed a model of attributional schemas which talked of partially restrictive, hierarchically restrictive and fully restrictive schemas. This model claims that different kinds of behaviours can be produced by different networks of dispositions. Skilful behaviour is an example of behaviour which is interpreted by most people in terms of a hierarchically restrictive implicational schema. Behaviour which is skilful (such as playing pool well or sketching an impressive portrait) *must* mean that the actor is skilled, and hence leads to a strong, confident attribution of competence to the actor. Behaviour which is unskilful, though, is not very informative. It may mean that the actor does not possess the requisite competencies to produce a skilful performance; but it may also mean that the actor was not motivated or that situational factors inhibited the performance of the behaviour. Situations like this, in which a behaviour high on a dimension (such as skill) must mean that the actor possesses a lot of the corresponding underlying disposition but a behaviour low or middling on a dimension could indicate the actor possesses a lot of or a little of the disposition, are referred to as hierarchically restrictive implicational schemas. Partially restrictive and fully restrictive schemas represent different patterns of relationship between observed behaviour and presumed disposition. The experiments by Reeder and Fulks, using skilful and unskilful examples of behaviours, show, among other things, that observers make attributions of skill following a skilled performance, but tend not to make a dispositional attribution (either that the actor is skilled or not) following an unskilful performance – except when the situation requires a skilful performance. Presumably an actor who behaves unskilfully when skill is required must be unskilful, at least in the eyes of attributing observers.

So, in terms of the original Jonesian formulation of the FAE, making a correspondent inference appears to be easy, and people seem ready to infer attitudes, abilities and personalities. Occasionally, research is reported which shows a failure to produce the FAE. One such piece of research was a study by Ajzen, Dalto and Blyth (1979). Working again with the attribution of attitudes (this time to abortion), Ajzen and his colleagues argued that observers are likely to make a correspondent inference only when the observed behaviour is consistent with other information about the actor available to the observer. When there is inconsistency, no correspondent inference will be made. This is indeed what they found. When subjects were presented with an essay, either pro- or anti-abortion, purportedly written under choice or no-choice conditions, and with no other consistent information about the essayist, subjects failed to make a correspondent inference. Subjects who read a pro-abortion essay in the no-choice condition judged the essayist's attitude to be 57 on a scale from 0 to 100; those who read an anti-abortion essay gave a judged attitude score of 50. The difference between the two is not statistically significant, and both hover around the scale's midpoint, indicating that subjects were not inclined to impute any attitude to the essayist. Thus, the FAE failed to occur. It is not a fundamental error, in the sense that it is a *necessary* characteristic of making attributions about an other.

The actor–observer effect

There is a pervasive tendency for actors to attribute their actions to situational requirements, whereas observers tend to attribute the same actions to stable personal dispositions. (Jones and Nisbett, 1972: 80)

Fritz Heider noted that actors and observers have different views of behaviour, of the situation, and of the causes of behaviours in situations. 'The person tends to attribute his own reactions to the object world, and those of another, when they differ from his own, to personal characteristics in [the other]' (Heider, 1958: 157). Heider referred to this as a 'polar tendency in attribution'; Jones and Nisbett (1972) called it the 'actor–observer effect' (AOE). The fundamental attribution error discussed above is essentially an elaboration of one half of the AOE. The FAE claims that attributers (that is, actors) underestimate the strength of situational factors and overestimate the strength of dispositional factors in controlling others' behaviour. According to Heider, Jones and Nisbett, and Ross, situational and dispositional factors are ipsatively related. Thus, the FAE restates the second half of the AOE – observers tend to attribute the actions of others to stable personal dispositions.

Many studies claim to have demonstrated the AOE. Two 'classics' will be described here in some detail: the first experiment of three reported by Nisbett, Caputo, Legant and Maracek (1973), and an experiment by Ross, Amabile and Steinmetz (1977). In reviewing these two classic studies, we will arrive at two conclusions. First, that situational and dispositional attributions do *not* vary inversely with one another – both can be, and often are, seen as important causes of behaviour by both actors and observers. And second, that while many experiments have demonstrated a *difference* between actors and observers in their attributions, they have *not* demonstrated that actors favour situational causes and observers dispositional causes, that is, there is no evidence for the AOE as formulated by Jones and Nisbett.

A session in the first experiment by Nisbett et al. (1973) consisted of two experimenters, two real subjects and two confederates of the experimenters posing as real subjects. When the two subjects and the two confederates (all of whom were women) arrived in the laboratory, one of the real subjects was chosen 'randomly' to be an observer. Experimenter 1 took the observer aside and explained that, although the study was on decision making, she would not be asked to make any decisions. Rather, her job was 'to watch one of the participants carefully throughout the entire session' (Nisbett et al., 1973: 155). The one she was told to watch was the other real subject. The actor and the two confederates were taken to another room and seated facing Experimenter 2, who described the decision-making experiment about to follow. Then Experimenter 2 slipped in a request to the other three 'subjects' in front of her. This constituted the real experimental procedure, but from the point of view of the subjects it was unconnected to the experiment they expected was about to commence. This request asked subjects to volunteer some

Table 4.2 Mean estimates of the likelihood the actor
would volunteer on a subsequent request

| | Ratings of | | | |
	Actors who volunteered	Actors who did not volunteer	Actors offered $1.50	50 cents
Ratings by				
Actors	3.31	3.91	3.73	3.38
Observers	4.27	2.78	4.25	2.71

Scores could range from 0 (not at all likely) through 4 (neither
likely nor unlikely) to 8 (very likely).
Source: Nisbett et al., 1973: 157

time on the weekend to help entertain the 'wives of businessmen'
attending a meeting of prospective backers of the corporate board of
the Human Development Institute at Yale University. Participants in
one condition were offered 50 cents per hour as an incentive; those in
another were offered $1.50 per hour. Experimenter 2 then asked each
of the confederates and the actor subject if they would volunteer.
The actor subject was always asked last, after the first confederate
had volunteered four hours and the second 12 hours. After giving
their responses, the two subjects and the two confederates were each
taken to a separate cubicle. The actor subject was interviewed by
Experimenter 1 and the observer subject by Experimenter 2. Each
was asked to rate the importance of six different reasons why the
actor had chosen to volunteer, and to estimate how likely it was that
the actor would also volunteer time to help a charity. The six reasons
covered a range of possible situational and dispositional motives for
volunteering – wanting to help the Institute; it sounded interesting; a
chance to earn money; meeting people would be fun; it seemed
worthwhile; and social pressure to volunteer.

The size of the monetary incentive made a big difference to
subjects' decisions to volunteer or not, but that is hardly surprising.
Only four of the 17 subjects in the 50 cents condition volunteered,
but 11 of the subjects in the $1.50 condition volunteered. Among the
volunteers, though, the number of hours volunteered was not
significantly different between the two conditions (5.6 hours and 6.7
hours in the 50 cents and $1.50 conditions, respectively).

It may be obvious that money made a difference to volunteering
rates, but it wasn't so obvious to the subjects themselves. The mean
ratings of the likelihood the actor would volunteer time to help
another charity are given in Table 4.2. Unfortunately, we don't know
what the standard deviations are in each of the eight conditions. But
we do know that there is a reliable, statistically significant difference

between observers' ratings of actors who volunteered and observers' ratings of actors who did not volunteer. We also know that observers made more extreme judgements than did the actors: observers thought that volunteers were more likely to volunteer again than did the volunteers themselves, and observers thought that non-volunteers were less likely to volunteer if given another request than did the non-volunteers themselves. If we take the judged likelihood of volunteering in response to a second request as an indication of how the actors and observers each see the actor – of how *dispositionally* inclined the actor is to help or not to help – then the results of this experiment fairly clearly demonstrate that actors and observers diverge in their dispositional inferences.

At least, that is how Nisbett et al. and social psychological lore interpret these results. 'It therefore appears that observers are inclined to make dispositional inferences from behavior under circumstances in which actors infer nothing about their general inclinations' (Nisbett et al., 1973: 157). But are observers so inclined? There *are* differences, to be sure, between the ratings provided by actors and observers. But do the observers make such dispositional inferences? Look again at the means in Table 4.2. These mean scores are subjects' responses to the question 'How likely do you think it is that you (or the girl you watched) would also volunteer to canvass for the United Fund?' Subjects indicated what they thought by circling a number on a nine-point scale, where 0 was marked 'not at all likely', 4 was marked 'neither likely nor unlikely' and 8 was marked 'very likely'. The means in the left-hand side of the table (actors' and observers' ratings of volunteers and non-volunteers, regardless of monetary incentive) range from 2.78 to 4.27. These extremes are the observers' ratings, and the difference between the two means, which is statistically significant, is certainly larger than the difference between the actors' mean ratings (3.31 and 3.91; the significance of this difference is not reported) – this is the actor–observer effect. The midpoint of the rating scale is 4, representing an ambivalent response by subjects. It is unlikely that the mean rating by observers of volunteers (4.27) differs significantly from the scale midpoint, and even if it does differ statistically the difference is not theoretically significant. It is also unlikely that the mean rating by actors who did volunteer (3.31) differs from the scale midpoint. In other words, ratings close to the scale midpoint do not represent dispositional attributions. While it is correct for the authors to claim that 'observers of volunteers saw them as *more likely* to help the United Fund than did the volunteers themselves . . . and observers of nonvolunteers tended to see them as *less likely* to help the United Fund than did the volunteers themselves' (Nisbett et al., 1973: 157, emphasis added), it is *not* correct to say that observers of volunteers made a dispositional attribution about the actors. *None* of the actors appeared to make any sort of dispositional attribution; indeed, volunteer actors rated themselves as *less* likely (though perhaps not significantly less likely) to help than did the non-volunteer actors. The only condition which produced dispositional attributions was the observers of non-volunteers. Thus, while it is true that the actors and observers diverged in the views of the likelihood of future behaviours, observers did not demonstrate an unconditional tendency to make dispositional attributions of actors – *more* dispositional than the actors' attributions, but not dispositional in an absolute sense.

Subjects' ratings of the reasons why the actors performed as they did may have shed more light on the differing tendencies of actors and observers to make dispositional attributions. But, unfortunately, all that is reported of these results is that 'best' indications are that neither volunteers offered $1.50 nor the observers fully realized the importance of money in eliciting actors' cooperation. Volunteers offered $1.50 and their observers were agreed in rating the importance of money lower than they rated the importance of three other reasons – the desire to help, the interest of the activities, and the fun of meeting the people (Nisbett et al., 1973: 157). This does not help much in elucidating subjects' causal attributions for the behaviour they witnessed.

The other two experiments reported in Nisbett et al. (1973) confirm the *relative* difference between actors' and observers' tendencies to make dispositional attributions, but still do not establish an *absolute* preference of observers for dispositional attributions and of actors for situational attributions. We turn now to an experiment by Ross, Amabile and Steinmetz (1977), which more directly addresses the heart of the AOE and which demonstrates it more clearly.

The Ross, Amabile and Steinmetz experiment adopted the format of a quiz game. Pairs of same-sex subjects participated in the experiment together. One member of the pair was randomly allocated to the role of questioner, the other to the role of contestant. The randomness of the allocation was explicit to the subjects. Twelve pairs of subjects were in the experimental condition and six pairs were in the control condition.

In the experimental condition, questioners were told to make up 10 'challenging but not impossible' general knowledge questions to ask of the contestant. While the questioner did this, the contestant was told to compose 10 easy general knowledge questions, just to 'get into the spirit of the study'. In the control condition, questioner and contestant alike produced 10 easy questions, after being told that

Table 4.3   Mean ratings of self's and other's general knowledge by questioners and contestant in a quiz game experiment

| | Ratings of | |
	Self	Other
Ratings by		
Experimental condition		
Questioner	53.5	50.6
Contestant	41.3	66.8
Control condition		
Questioner	54.1	52.5
Contestant	47.0	50.3

Source: Ross, Amabile and Steinmetz, 1977

during the quiz game itself the questioner would ask the contestant to answer 10 questions compiled before the experiment by someone else.

After subjects had composed their respective sets of questions, they took part in a quiz game. During the 'game', questioners in the experimental condition asked the contestants their 10 difficult but not impossible questions; questioners in the control condition were given 10 questions to ask of the contestants. The number of questions answered correctly was recorded by the experimenter. In testimony to the diligence of the questioners, the average number right was only 4 out of 10. After completing the quiz game, questioners and contestants rated self and partner on a number of dimensions, the most important of which for our discussion was 'general knowledge compared to the average Stanford student' (the experiment was conducted at Stanford University). Subjects rated self and other on this dimension on a scale from 0 to 100, with 50 marked as 'the average Stanford student'. The mean ratings provided by subjects are given in Table 4.3.

In the control condition, questioners and contestants did not really distinguish between self and other in terms of general knowledge relative to the average Stanford student – everyone rated self and other as about average. It would be hard for these control subjects to have done anything else. They knew they had been randomly assigned to conditions, and they knew the questions had been prepared by the experimenter in advance. Neither the questions nor the contestant's answers could reasonably be taken, by either subject in each pair, to indicate either the questioner's or the contestant's 'general knowledge'.

In the experimental condition, on the other hand, there are big differences in how each member of the pair sees self and other. The questioner does not really distinguish between self and other, rating both around average. The contestant, though, devalues self relative to average (presumably in response to getting only 4 out of 10 right, on average) and increases the rating of the questioner relative to average (presumably acknowledging the difficulty of the general knowledge questions produced by the questioner).

What is startling about the results? Allocation to the role of questioner or contestant was random, and subjects were aware it was random. So presumably, if the roles were reversed, the erstwhile contestant would have made up 10 difficult questions and the former questioner would have got about 4 of them right. There is an asymmetry between the roles in terms of ability to express 'smart' behaviour. The questioner gets to call the tune; the contestant merely plays along. The role of the questioner confers an advantage to the questioner over the contestant. Questioners apparently recognize this, and neither elevate their own status nor lower the contestant's. But contestants appear to be unaware of, or to under-correct for, the advantage conferred upon the questioner.

In a second part of the experiment, Ross, Amabile and Steinmetz had confederates re-enact some of the questioner–contestant performances. Real subjects witnessed these interactions under the apprehension that they were authentic. These subjects then rated both questioner and contestant on general knowledge ability, relative to the average Stanford student. These subjects, acting purely as observers, apparently saw the quiz game through the eyes of the contestant. The average rating given to the questioner was 82.08 and that for the contestant was 48.92, thus mirroring the ratings provided earlier by the contestants themselves.

Let us take it then that there is something to the actor–observer effect and the fundamental attribution error. These phenomena appear to be easy to demonstrate in many domains, meaning perhaps that they reflect a part of common thinking. They are probably not 'fundamental', essential or universal; and they are probably better thought of as biases rather than errors, although the simple term 'effect' may be best. But they are not methodological artefacts either.

Explanations of the fundamental attribution error and the actor–observer effect

A small handful of explanations of the FAE and the AOE have been suggested, many with few or no data to support them. These explanations tend to belong to one of two types. The first are explanations based on psychological processes and mechanisms which differ in content or perspective between the actor and the observer. The second are explanations which seek the origins of the AOE and the FAE in broad, social, cultural and ideological processes, arguing that these and other attributional effects rely on, are a product of and are limited to modern, western, industrialized constructions of the 'individual' as the source of behaviour. We will consider each of these classes of explanation, bearing in mind that there is nothing inherently contradictory or exclusive between them.

Individualistic explanations   Following Jones and Nisbett's (1972) and Nisbett et al.'s (1973) reasoning, Storms (1973) suggested that actors and observers may explain the same behaviour differently either because the information available to each about the behaviour is different, or because actors and observers process the same available information differently. Jones and Nisbett, Nisbett et al. and Storms all plump for the former explanation. Storms provides evidence for their preference by showing that attributions made by actors and observers change if they are provided with information about the behaviour from a different point of view.

Two actors and two observers were seated round a table. The two actors sat opposite each other, and interacted to become acquainted (all four subjects were strangers to one another prior to the experiment). Each observer observed one of the two actors. Two video cameras recorded the interaction, one camera focused on each actor. After the interaction had lasted about five minutes, the actors stopped conversing, and the video cameras were stopped and the tapes rewound. For the four subjects in the control condition, the experimenter explained that the tapes were no good, and asked each subject to complete a questionnaire. In the experimental condition, though, the experimenter explained that one of the tapes was no good, and so all four subjects would have to watch only the one tape of the one subject. After watching this tape, all four subjects completed the same questionnaire as the control-group subjects. The questionnaire asked actor subjects to rate the dispositional and the situational causes of their own behaviour during the interaction, and asked observer subjects to make the same ratings of the actors they were watching. Thus, at the end of the experiment, Storms had ratings of the perceived strength of dispositional and situational forces from actors about their own behaviour, from actors who had just seen a videotape of the other actor (that is, whose point of view during the interaction was the same as that shown on the videotape), and from actors who had just seen a videotape of their own behaviour (that is, whose point of view during the interaction was different from that shown on the videotape). He also had similar ratings from the observers of the interaction.

What did Storms find? First, in the no-videotape control condition and in the same orientation condition, there was some evidence of the AOE, but it wasn't very strong: actors placed relatively more emphasis on situational causes than did observers, but actors and observers did not differ in their use of dispositional causes. Further, observers favoured dispositional explanations more than situational explanations, but actors were more or less equally reliant on dispositional and situational explanations. And finally it should be noted that actors and observers in these conditions rated both dispositional and situational factors to have been important in the interaction: differences between conditions were due to subjects in one condition or the other rating one type of cause as even more important, not due to subjects in either role in either condition rating one type of cause as *unimportant*. Thus, once again, we have some evidence of the AOE, but it is certainly not strong or absolute, and it is certainly not as clear as is usually described in most social psychology textbooks.

But what of the subjects who saw a videotape of themselves? The videotape provided them with a new and different point of view from which to witness their own behaviour. How were their attributions affected? In brief, the new orientation reversed the relative attributional preferences of actors and observers. Whereas in the control conditions actors provided stronger situational attributions than did observers, the new orientation furnished by the videotape resulted in observers producing stronger situational attributions than actors. This is an important effect, commonly known as Storms' reversal, and has gone into the store of social psychological knowledge as a 'classic' demonstration of the importance of perspective in producing the actor–observer effect. It shows that the AOE is due to actors and observers having different information available to them. But a closer examination of the source of the significant effects in Storms' analysis – and, more importantly, of the things which are *not* different – gives some cause for doubting Storms' interpretation of what is happening.

In the videotape and same orientation conditions, observers consistently favoured dispositional over situational explanations (the mean ratings were 27.20 for dispositional and 22.35 for situational, both on a scale ranging from 4 [extremely unimportant] to 36 [extremely important] and with a 'moderately important' midpoint of 20). This divergence of about five points in favour of dispositional explanations disappears in the new orientation condition, where the means are 25.75 and 24.15, respectively. This difference (1.6) is probably not significant. Thus, for observers the new orientation has tended to increase their rated importance of situational causes and has tended to decrease their rated importance of dispositional causes, but dispositional causes are still rated as marginally (non-significantly) more important than situational causes. Observers' ratings converge; they don't reverse. And importantly, the mean rating for both dispositional and situational factors is above the scale midpoint of 20 – observers don't see either cause as unimportant. The convergence in observers' ratings is not apparent in actors' ratings. In the two control conditions, actors tended to see dispositional and situational factors as about equally important (means of 26.7 and 25.5, respectively, on the same scale from 4 to 36 as before). In the new perspective condition, the respective means were 27.5 and 20.7. Thus, presenting new information to actors by making them watch a videotape of their own behaviour did not alter the judged importance of dispositional factors. It did reduce the rated importance of situational factors, but only to a point where such factors were seen to be 'moderately important'.

A precise phrasing of the Storms' effect does not state that a new perspective *reverses* the actor–observer effect so that actors prefer dispositional explanations of their own behaviour and observers attribute the same behaviour to the situation surrounding the actor. Rather both actors and observers see both situational and dispositional factors as 'moderately' important, actors tending not to distinguish between the two and observers favouring dispositions. After being presented with a new perspective, observers reduce the disparity between their ratings of the importance of dispositions, but reduce the importance of situations, though not to the point where they are judged 'unimportant'.

Changing the point of view of attributers by providing actors with a view of themselves acting and observers with a view of the actor's situation *does* change the sorts of attributions that are made. The experiment by Storms provides some evidence of this. Much stronger evidence comes from an experiment by Taylor and Fiske (1975). Jones and Nisbett (1972) argued that the different perceptions of behaviour furnished by actors and observers are due to different perceptual orientations. Taylor and Fiske expanded this argument to the more general position that 'point of view or attention determines what information is salient; perceptually salient information is then overrepresented in subsequent causal explanations' (1975: 440). Their experiment to test this was clever, and the results compelling.

Two male confederates were seated opposite one another, and conversed for five minutes. Seated behind confederate A were two observers, each with confederate B, but not A, in their visual field. Two other observers were behind B watching A. And two further observers were seated at the side of the table in between A and B, and with both in sight. After witnessing A and B interact for five minutes, all observers were asked to rate each confederate on the dimensions of friendliness, talkativeness and nervousness, and the extent to which each confederate's behaviour was caused by dispositional qualities and by situational factors. They also rated how much each confederate set the conversation's tone, determined the kind of information exchanged in the conversation and caused the other's behaviour. If Taylor and Fiske are right, the two observers behind A watching B should see B as more causal than A, the observers behind B watching A should see A as more causal than B, and the observers in between A and B should see A and B as about equally influential. This is exactly what they found. In a similar experiment. McArthur and Post (1977) manipulated actors' relative salience using strong lighting, and again attributions about an actor's behaviour were influenced by the actor's salience.

Although Taylor and Fiske found that viewpoint influenced perceptions of causal agency, they did not find that observers made any sort of correspondent inference about either of the conversing confederates. A second experiment reported in the same paper failed to unravel why correspondent inferences were not made by observers, when Jones' theory says they should.

An interesting extension of the point of view effect is provided by Frank and Gilovich (1989). In this study, subjects took part in a get-acquainted conversation with another subject of the same sex. Immediately after this conversation, each subject completed an attribution questionnaire which contained questions based on Storms' (1973) earlier questions. Each subject completed the same questionnaire again three weeks later, along with a question assessing how they viewed the original interaction – did they recall the conversation from the point of view of an outside observer (that is, they were watching their self converse with the other subject) or did they recall the scene as they had originally experienced it? Most of the subjects (71 per cent) reported remembering the scene through their own eyes as they had originally experienced the interaction, but a sizeable minority (29 per cent) claimed a memory perspective of an observer witnessing self and other interact. All subjects, regardless of their memory perspective, gave stronger dispositional than situational attributions, although the mean situational attribution scores were always above the scale midpoint on a range from 'not at all important' to 'very important'. On the first set of ratings straight after the interaction, those with an 'observer' memory perspective and those with an 'actor' memory perspective equally endorsed dispositional attributions, but the former gave stronger situational attributions than the latter. Over time, though, the strength of dispositional ratings increased in those with an observer memory perspective but decreased in those with an actor memory perspective. The pattern of change was the opposite for situational attributions: observers decreased and actors increased the strength of their situational attributions. In a second experiment, the same pattern of results was obtained when memory perspective was experimentally induced rather than allowed to vary naturally.

The results of the experiments by Storms, Taylor and Fiske, McArthur and Post, and Frank and Gilovich all support a perceptual salience explanation of the actor–observer effect. In this, behaviour 'engulfs the field' (Heider, 1958) for observers. Observers see the actor acting, but usually don't see a situation. The actor is salient; the situation is not. Actors, though, don't see themselves acting. They see the situation around them, and are aware of responding to invisible situational forces. Thus, when actors and observers are asked to explain the same event, they give different accounts because different facets of the same event are salient to them.

Using the different points of view of actors and observers to explain their different attributional preferences is an example of an individualistic explanation. Several other individualistic explanations of the same phenomenon have been suggested. For example, Jones and Nisbett (1972) originally suggested, but discounted, the possibility that actors and observers possess different information about events and it is this that leads to the different attributions. Actors have access to their own feelings, desires, motivations, as well as their own cross-situational behavioural history. Observers are unaware of, or at best can only assume, what lies within the actor, but can detect behavioural patterns and regularities which perhaps actors are unaware of. Some evidence of informational differences between actors and observers is provided by Eisen (1979) and White and Younger (1988).

Another individualistic (although more social and interactive) possibility hinges on the linguistic practices of actors and observers (Guerin, 1993; Semin and Fiedler, 1988, 1989; Slugoski, Lalljee, Lamb and Ginsburg, 1993). Different linguistic categories convey different information about an event. Semin and Fiedler (1988) suggest there are four linguistic categories referring to interpersonal relations: descriptive action verbs (for example, A is talking to B); interpretative action verbs (for example, A is helping B); state verbs (for example, A likes B); and adjectives (for example, A is an extroverted person). Adjectives convey more information about a person than do, say, descriptive action verbs, and hence lead to more dispositional inferences. It is hard to imagine making any sort of correspondent inference at all based on the statement 'A is talking to B', but it is hard to avoid doing so when presented with 'A is an extroverted person'. Indeed, the latter presumes a disposition. Semin and Fiedler (1989) showed, in a replication of the second experiment by Nisbett et al. (1973), that actors tended to use the more concrete linguistic forms (descriptive and interpretative verbs) and observers tended to use the abstract forms (state verbs and adjectives) which permitted and conveyed dispositional assumptions.

A third and final kind of individualistic explanation of the AOE refers to motivational factors. Recall that in their theory of correspondent inferences, Jones and Davis (1965) claimed that actions judged to be hedonically relevant or personalistic to the observer are more likely to produce correspondent inferences than are other actions. Hedonic relevance and personalism are motivational characteristics. Similarly, Miller and Norman (1975) have suggested that dispositional attributions are more likely to be made by an active rather than a passive observer, possibly because of a greater desire or need to predict the behaviours of the actor. Little research has been done on motivational factors in attribution.

Ideology Individualistic explanations of the actor–observer effect often assume that the effect is a necessary consequence of our cognitive hardware; that human beings are constitutionally built in such a way that observers will always see the actor as the causal origin of behaviour and that actors themselves will see their own actions as reacting to the situational moment impinging upon them. Perceptual salience and informational explanations are especially prone to this theoretical premise. There are many reasons why it would be imprudent to assume that either the actor–observer effect or the fundamental attribution error are necessary consequences of the human cognitive make-up.

The first comes from cross-cultural research. Fletcher and Ward (1988) have reviewed this research, and concluded that actor–observer divergences are far from ubiquitous. As but one example, Miller (1984) compared samples of middle-class Americans and middle-class Indian Hindus. Her samples included adults and 8-, 11- and 15-year-old children. The American adults favoured dispositional over situational explanations for a variety of others' everyday behaviours. Indian Hindu adults, on the other hand, favoured situational over dispositional explanations. So the tendency to rely on dispositional explanations so frequently observed in the research literature is far from universal. Miller also found that attributional preference – dispositional for Americans and situational for Indians – increased with age. This, then, is the second reason why the AOE is not universal.

If the AOE were a necessary consequence, it would be present at birth, and, presumably, detectable in neonates if only they could complete questionnaires. Miller's (1984) study shows that attributional preferences change from age 8 to age 15, and change in different directions depending on culture. This suggests that people must learn – directly or tacitly – how to attribute, how to make causal sense of the events around them. Other (American) evidence shows that young children rarely make dispositional attributions (White, 1988). The influence of socio-cultural factors on attributions is dealt with extensively in Chapter 8.

Third, there are individual differences in the tendency to display the FAE (Block and Funder, 1986; see footnote 1), suggesting that personality and motivational differences between people limit the generalizability of the phenomenon. The role of individual differences in the AOE and the FAE has rarely been investigated. Furthermore, there are well-documented *group* differences in attributions, again suggesting that effects such as the FAE and the AOE are far from necessary consequences of individual cognitive factors. The literature on intergroup attributions is reviewed extensively in Chapter 9.

The actor–observer effect and the fundamental attribution error are two of the most vigorously investigated attributional biases. As we have seen, actors and observers diverge, sometimes quite markedly, in the inferences they draw from and the attributions they make about ostensibly the same event. However, the evidence reviewed in this section cannot support a strong form of either the AOE or the FAE. It appears that attributers do not make *either* a dispositional *or* a situational attribution. Rather, a weak form of the AOE and the FAE is more consistent with a wide variety of data. In this, attributers use *both* dispositional *and* situational factors in constructing causal sense of the events surrounding them, but tend to rely on one relatively more than the other depending on their perspective on events. While there is evidence that changing people's point of view alters their attributional accounts of events in that view, this does not imply any hard-wired, innate, psychologically or cognitively necessary attributional mechanisms. Developmental and cross-cultural evidence suggests that people must learn the attributional accounts favoured by their social milieu. This learning is likely to be so efficient that particular attributional accounts become automatic and unthinking. The AOE and the FAE can be considered biases in the sense that the same event is attributed differently depending upon the attributers' position relative to that event. We turn now to consider another class of attributional biases, the so-called 'self-serving biases'.

Self-serving biases

Theories of attribution tend to view the attributer as a dispassionate bystander of events, coldly processing information available to him or her. This is, of course, far removed from the warmth of normal human interaction. People *are* involved, passionately or not, in the events around them. They, and their attributions, affect and are affected by others and by events. Often people make attributions which are self-serving, designed, consciously or not, to enhance their esteem in their own eyes and in the eyes of others. Self-serving biases take a number of forms, some of which are described in this section.

The false consensus effect   The tendency of people to overestimate the commonality of their beliefs, opinions and attitudes is known as the *false consensus effect* (FCE), and has long been acknowledged in social psychology. Floyd Allport (1924), for example, talked of the illusion of universality, by which he meant that people often assume that the way they react to a particular situation is the same way others would react. But it wasn't until the publication of studies by Ross, Greene and House (1977) that interest in, and research on, the false consensus effect gained momentum.

In the most compelling of three studies reported by Ross, Greene and House (1977), passers-by on the campus of Stanford University were asked if they would walk around the campus for half an hour wearing a sandwich-board sign extolling witnesses to 'Eat at Joe's'. Of 80 subjects asked, 48 agreed to do so and 32 declined. All subjects were then asked to estimate what percentage of other people would make the same decision they had just made. The results provide a revealing symmetry between those who would and those who would not wear the sandwich-board sign. Refusers thought, on average, that two-thirds of all other people would also refuse. Likewise, acquiescers also thought that, on average, about two-thirds (62 per cent) of all other people would agree. Subjects were also asked to make trait inferences about a fictitious other who agreed to wear the sign and an other who refused to wear the sign. Those subjects who agreed to wear the sign made stronger inferences about the fictitious other who refused, and subjects who refused to wear the sign made stronger inferences about the fictitious other who agreed. Thus, in keeping with Jones and Davis's theory of correspondent inferences, behaviours which are counter-normative – in the sense that they are not what perceivers expect most other people would do in the same situation – lead to stronger trait inferences about the actor.

A sizeable body of evidence demonstrates that, on matters of opinion, we overestimate the commonality of our own position (Marks and Miller, 1987; Mullen and Goethals, 1990). Marks and Miller (1987) describe four mechanisms which might account for the FCE. The first two mechanisms are similar to one another and are both heavily cognitive. An argument based on the *availability* of information from memory (for example, Ross, 1977; Tversky and Kahneman, 1973) suggests that memories of interactions with others who are similar to ourselves or who agree with us are more readily accessible from memory than are instances of interactions with dissimilar others or disagreeing others. Thus, when asked to estimate the commonality of our opinions, instances of similarity and agreement are weighted disproportionately in our mental calculations, leading us to overestimate the commonality of our opinions. Related to this explanation is the second, which relies on the notion of *salience*. Salience refers to the extent to which a stimulus, or referent object in the surrounding situation, stands out from other stimuli, or from other aspects of the situation. A salience explanation of the FCE posits that when we focus on our own position or opinion other positions or opinions are necessarily relegated to the attentional backstage and therefore are considered less when formulating an estimate of commonality of the opinion.

Both the availability and salience explanations resort to the notion of distortions or biases in cognitive information processing to explain the FCE. The third explanation is just as cognitive, but suggests that the FCE is a rational, not a biased, outcome of information processing. In this explanation, the FCE is but another manifestation of the actor–observer effect. If it is the case that actors tend to attribute their behaviour to situational factors, then it is quite reasonable to expect a high degree of behavioural consensus when others are subject to the same situational forces.

Finally, the fourth explanation of the FCE gets away from cognitive mechanisms altogether, focusing instead upon motivation and self-esteem. According to this argument, it is psychologically valuable to believe that one's opinions are common. Social consensus on such matters provides social support and validation. Contrariwise, there is a psychological cost to pay for believing one's opinions to be rare or deviant.

Marks and Miller (1987) review the support provided for each of these four explanations by over 45 studies. Although they conclude that there is some evidence for each explanation, and that the four mechanisms perhaps all operate but each under different conditions, Marks and Miller tend in the end to favour the two cognitive mechanisms of availability and salience over the others. We think this emphasis is misplaced, and suggest instead that a motivational account is more convincing, more social, and theoretically both more integrative and simpler and neater. As we will see, availability and salience cannot explain simultaneously both the false consensus effect and the false uniqueness effect. A social motivational account can. One motivational explanation of two related phenomena is better than two cognitive ones. Apart from satisfying Occam's razor principle, the motivational mechanism involved is encompassed within social comparison theory.

The false uniqueness effect   If we overestimate the frequency of occurrence of our opinions in the population, so too do we underestimate the commonality of our *abilities*. This is the *false uniqueness effect* (FUE). Apparently, we like to believe that our abilities are unique and our opinions common (Marks, 1984). Perceived uniqueness is not restricted to judgements of our own ability, though. On almost any dimension which ranges in bipolar fashion from 'good' to 'bad', we tend to see ourselves closer to the 'good' pole than are most other people. Consider some examples. Svenson (1981) showed that most drivers think they are safer and more skilled than most others. This holds true even among drivers hospitalized after a car accident (Preston and Harris, 1965). Weinstein (1980) found that subjects were unrealistically optimistic about what life held in store for them; they believed they were much more likely than average to experience a range of positive events (to like their job, to secure a high-paying job, to live past 80, and so on) and much less likely than average to suffer a range of negative events (to have a drinking problem, to get divorced, to have a heart attack before 40, to get venereal disease, to be sterile, and so on). Headey and Wearing (1987) found that 86 per cent of a sample of Australian workers believe they work better than average, and only 1 per cent believe they are worse than average. Ross and Sicoly (1979), in a series of experiments, found consistent evidence from naturally occurring discussion groups, married couples, basketball teams and laboratory groups that individuals working with other people in a group claim more responsibility for a group product than the others attribute to them. This bias was reduced, but still present, when the group product was evaluated negatively.

As with the false consensus effect, the false uniqueness effect appears to be a stable, widespread and well-documented phenomenon. The question, of course, is why does it happen? Two broad explanations can be considered; both are also explanations of the false consensus effect. The first is cognitive, and focuses on the availability and salience of certain kinds of information; the second is motivational, and uses the notion of self-esteem and how self-esteem is enhanced and maintained through social comparisons between self and others.

Ross and Sicoly (1979) conclude, after their five experiments, that a cognitive explanation relying on differential availability of information, or selective retrieval of information from memory, is most strongly supported by their data. They argue that when a person works with others to produce some joint product, and that person is then asked to estimate his or her contribution to the product, he or she will attempt to recall the contributions each group member made. Each member's recollections of the group's efforts will be biased, though, so that a greater proportion of his or her own efforts are recalled than of the others. This happens because his or her own efforts are cognitively more available in memory; they are easier to recall. This is the same mechanism favoured by Marks and Miller (1987) as an explanation of the false consensus effect.

The second explanation proposes that people selectively encode and retrieve information because the favoured information enhances their self-esteem, not because of any other cognitive mechanism. Some evidence for this is furnished by Ross and Sicoly's (1979) second experiment, which showed that subjects attributed a greater proportion of statements from a prior dyadic interaction to themselves following dyadic success than they did following dyadic failure. However, this is hardly strong evidence, and, besides, the subjects in their third experiment (basketball players) did not differ in their accounts of 'turning points in a ball game' depending on whether their team won or lost, as would be expected from a motivational explanation. For stronger evidence, we turn to recent work by George Goethals and his colleagues, on what they label the 'uniqueness bias'.

The *uniqueness bias* refers to 'the tendency for people to underestimate the proportion of people who can or will perform socially desirable actions' (Goethals, Messick and Allison, 1991: 149). It is closely related to, but operationally different from, the false consensus effect. Over many studies with different types of subjects, the uniqueness bias has been found to be as pervasive as the false consensus and false uniqueness effects, and, importantly, the size of the bias correlates positively with self-esteem. Self-esteem is not correlated with actual status on any given dimension, but rather with the judged difference between self and others.

To explain the uniqueness bias, Goethals et al. (1991) draw upon and elaborate Festinger's (1954) social comparison theory, to which we devote more consideration in Chapter 5 on social identity. Briefly for now, Festinger's social comparison theory suggests that all people attempt to evaluate their abilities and performances, beliefs and opinions. Some human characteristics are easy to evaluate against objective, physical benchmarks; others have no such benchmarks for evaluation. Festinger proposed that in the absence of such benchmarks people evaluate their abilities and opinions through social comparison with relevant others. In the case of abilities, Festinger proposed a universal drive upward, such that marginally more able others are selected as the comparison other. In the case of opinions, though, it makes no sense to think of one person's opinion as better than another, and so comparison others are selected according to criteria such as their degree of similarity to the comparer. The central motive underlying all social comparisons, for Festinger, is the desire and the need to evaluate one's abilities and opinions accurately, for accurate *self-evaluation*. But if we did engage in social comparisons the way Festinger said we do, especially when evaluating our abilities, we would always come out of the comparison worse off than the comparison other, and a vast literature on self-esteem suggests that this is unlikely behaviour. Other social comparison theorists have recognized this (for example, Hakmiller, 1966; Wills, 1981), and have adapted social comparison theory to accommodate downward comparisons with less able others.

Goethals et al. (1991) distinguish between realistic and constructive social comparison. The motive underlying realistic social comparison is accurate self-evaluation, and this sort of comparison is what is described in Festinger's original theory. Constructive social comparisons are driven, on the other hand, by a self-enhancement motive. These sorts of comparisons are characterized by a construction or fabrication of social reality. The comparison other is not a tangible person or defined, real benchmark, as in realistic social comparison, but rather is an imagined, generalized other or distribution of others. Applying the principle of social construction to the false uniqueness effect and to the uniqueness bias, it is easy to see how these two phenomena are the consequence of a constructed social reality, invented in such a way that the self is relatively well positioned and this relative positioning of self and a constructed, generalized other serves a self-enhancement motive.

It is no doubt the case that cognitive mechanisms such as availability *and* motivational processes such as the drive for self-enhancement underlie the false consensus and false uniqueness effects. It makes no sense that cognitive mechanisms operate without some energizing or motivating force impelling them. Neither does it make sense that a self-enhancement motive can describe and explain the phenotypic expression of informational biases and distortions.

Attributions for success and failure   It is an all too common phenomenon that people accept credit for success and deny responsibility for failure. Students do it after passing or failing a course; athletes do it after winning or losing an event; even academics do it after having a manuscript accepted or rejected for publication (Wiley, Crittenden and Birg, 1979). Although the strength of the effect varies across cultures, the attributional asymmetry following success or failure has been noted from around the globe (Fletcher and Ward, 1988; Kashima and Triandis, 1986; Zuckerman, 1979).

Once again, both cognitive and motivational explanations have been promulgated to account for this attributional asymmetry. Weary (1981), for example, suggested that focus of attention toward self or away from self (Duval and Wicklund, 1973) and informational availability may be two cognitive mechanisms implicated in the phenomenon. However, most researchers advocate a motivational explanation in accord with an almost self-evident, common-sense explanation – people accept credit for success and deflect responsibility for failure because doing so makes them feel good and look good; it serves a self-enhancement motive. For example, Miller (1976) showed that the attributional asymmetry is accentuated when the task subjects succeed or fail on is important. Schlenker and Miller (1977) likewise showed that attributional egocentrism among majority and minority group members in groups that succeeded or failed could be explained by a self-enhancement explanation and not by information processing biases.

Attributing egocentrically not only bolsters self-esteem, but also influences the impressions others have of the attributer. The evidence of the latter effect, though, is clearer than for the former. As but one example, Schlenker and Leary (1982) showed that audiences were generally most favourably impressed by actors who made 'accurate' attributional claims for their success, that actors who underclaim superior performance were liked more than actors who performed the same but who apparently boasted, and that audiences disliked actors who predicted that they would not do well, even when that prediction turned out to be accurate. It is clear that different attributional patterns following success or failure create different impressions on an audience: some kinds of attributions do seem to make the actor look good. Whether they also make the actor feel good is another matter.

Central to any self-enhancement explanation of attributional biases must be the predictions that self-esteem will increase following a self-serving attribution (an internal attribution following success or an external attribution following failure) and that self-esteem will decrease following a self-deprecating attribution (an external attribution following success or an internal attribution following failure). There is strong evidence (Maracek and Metee, 1972; Shrauger, 1975) that people chronically high in self-esteem make more self-serving attributions than do people chronically low in self-esteem, who tend to make more self-deprecating attributions. This is an important finding with clinical implications for the aetiology and treatment of depression, but it is not quite the same thing as evidence that changes in self-esteem follow particular attributions, which is the core of any self-enhancement explanation.

The absence of studies documenting attribution effects on self-esteem is curious, and perhaps due to two factors. First, many researchers appear to accept such effects as obvious and hence not needing empirical verification or falsification. Second, it is methodologically difficult to design an unconfounded experiment to test the hypothesis. A pure, experimental investigation would require the experimenter to allocate subjects randomly to either an internal or an external attribution condition following either success or failure and to observe consequent effects on self-esteem. But subjects make their own attributions; they cannot be allocated to an internal or an external attribution condition in the same way as they can to a success or failure condition. So direction of attribution cannot be experimentally controlled. It can only be investigated by allowing subjects to make their own attributions. But allowing this automatically introduces a confound between subjects' attributional direction and their prior self-esteem, since we know that people with chronic high self-esteem accept credit for success and deflect blame for failure and people with chronically low self-esteem tend to do the opposite. And who knows if these attributional styles cause or reflect differences in chronic self-esteem. There is thus no direct test of the central hypothesis of a self-enhancement explanation. None the less, the indirect evidence provided by tracking changes in self-esteem following particular types of attributions, perhaps separated by subjects' prior chronic self-esteem, would be valuable.

Depression   Implicit in the self-enhancement account of attributional biases is the notion that it is normal, functional and
biologically adaptive to make such biased attributions because they
help to create and maintain a positive self-esteem. It is assumed that
a positive self-esteem, or evaluation of self, is good, and that a
negative self-esteem is bad, abnormal, dysfunctional and maladapt-
ive. One of the severe consequences of a chronically low self-esteem
may be depression. Such a self-esteem is one of several characteristics of depression. Depression is more than just feeling low or blue,
which happens to almost everyone at some time. Depression, in its
severe or clinical form, is marked by listlessness, flattened affect,
hopelessness, helplessness, disrupted sleep and reduced appetites.
It can last a long time.

Several attribution theorists have applied attribution principles to
an understanding of depression, both severe and mild (for example,
Abramson, Seligman and Teasdale, 1978; Kuiper, 1978; Lewinsohn,
Mischel, Chaplin and Barton, 1980; Peterson and Seligman, 1984).
The notion was developed that depressives possess a particular
attributional style in which failures and other negative events are
attributed to internal, stable and global causes. A large body of
research has now firmly established a link between attributional style
and depression (Sweeney, Anderson and Bailey, 1986). Attributional
retraining programmes have been devised for use in clinical
interventions with depressed people, in which people are taught
how to make more self-serving attributions for their successes and
failures (for example, Wilson and Linville, 1985).

Some interesting evidence has accumulated that, relative to high
self-esteeming or non-depressed people, those who have low self-
esteem or who are depressed make more realistic attributions about
their performances. For example, Lewinsohn et al. (1980) collected
two sets of ratings of social competence: from individuals about
themselves; and about those individuals from others. Ratings from
and about three different groups of people were collected: depressives (at the time receiving clinical treatment for their depression), a
psychiatric control group (with a variety of problems, but none of
whom was depressed), and a normal (that is, non-clinical) control
group. Subjects met for a group session. Each group (usually) had six
members, and always had at least one representative from each of
the experimental conditions. During the course of the group
sessions, subjects rated self and others on 17 different dimensions of
social competence (for example, friendly, assertive, warm, reasonable, trusting). To begin with, depressives rated themselves lower on
each dimension than they rated the others, and the others agreed
with this relative positioning. Over the course of the experiment the

depressives' self-views improved, presumably because of the treat ment they were receiving. The depressives were more accurate or realistic in their self-ratings than were either the normal or the psychiatric control subjects – if the criterion for accuracy or realism is concordance of self's ratings of self and others' ratings of self. In other words, depressed subjects saw themselves as the others saw them. On the other hand, the non-depressed subjects saw themselves more favourably than the others saw them. Along with the improvement in self-view in the depressed subjects through the course of the experiment, the realism of their self-view diminished. Lewinsohn et al. suggest that normal functioning is characterized by an illusory warm glow in which 'one sees oneself more positively than others see one' (1980: 210), and this warm glow may generally be functionally advantageous for most people.

We started this section with the idea that the self-enhancement account of attributional biases posits that such biases are normal and persist because they help to create and maintain a positive self-esteem. The research on attribution and depression supports this basic premise, and shows that, although non-depressives (that is, high self-esteem people, with or without some clinical malady of the psyche) may be 'unrealistic' in the view they have of themselves compared to the view others have of them, this is perhaps only a small price to pay for the purchase of a generally positive sense of self-worth.

CRITICISMS OF ATTRIBUTION THEORIES

We have made critical comments about attribution theories and attribution effects throughout this chapter, and we briefly reiterate them here. First, the evidence supporting attributional effects such as the AOE and the FAE is not as strong or clear as is generally assumed. Second, attribution theories are articulated at the individual and interpersonal levels only. Thus, Kelley's covariation model, for example, focuses on the mental judgements individuals make on the dimensions of consistency, distinctiveness and consensus. The model ignores how individuals may differ in how they attribute, and ignores how interpersonal relations, affect and evaluation, the language of causation, the dominant social representation of the individual, and the relative group memberships of the attributer and the object of attribution all might affect the attribution process. The model assumes the interchangeability of individuals, and the universality of the attribution process. These comments are not confined only to Kelley's model, but apply equally to the Jones and Davis model of correspondent inference, and to the research which attempts to explain phenomena such as the FAE and the AOE. Attribution theories are overwhelmingly individualistic and cognitive. There is suggestive evidence that individuals are not interchangeable (for example, Block and Funder, 1986). There is also strong evidence that people in non-western cultures do not attribute in the ways described by dominant attribution theories, and that patterns of intergroup relations affect attributions for success and failure as well as for cause. There is evidence that the process of seeking causal understanding of the world is deeply rooted in cultural practices, and that phenomena such as the FAE and the AOE are restricted to, and are a product of, the dominant ideology of individualism in western societies. These limitations of attribution theory are developed more fully in later chapters: attributions are tied to the more social construct of social representations in Chapter 8, and group effects are discussed in Chapter 9.

SUMMARY

In this chapter we reviewed how the major, classical attribution theorists proposed that people function in their day-to-day lives as though they were intuitive scientists, constructing implicit theories of everyday behaviour if they follow Heider's ideas, busily partitioning the variance of behaviour into main effects due to consistency, consensus and distinctiveness if they accept Kelley, or attempting to make the best dispositional inference they can from some actor's constrained or unconstrained behaviour if they are a Jonesian. Research on attributional biases shows just how bad we are as intuitive scientists, especially when it comes to discerning our own behaviour and its causes. We apparently bend and shape, distort and construe information from our ambient social environments so that, in the end, we look good both to ourselves and to others. We overestimate the rarity of our abilities, we overestimate the commonality of our opinions, we accept credit for our successes and deny or deflect blame for failures, and we tend to see ourselves in a much more flattering light than others see us. It is fairly clear that cognitive mechanisms operate to produce these rosy effects. It is also clear that a solely cognitive explanation of these effects is inadequate. The motive that drives the cognitive apparatus is the desire to think well of one's self.

NOTES

1 An often forgotten finding of this experiment is that the variance of attributed attitude scores is much greater in the pro-Castro/no-choice condition than in any other condition, suggesting that some subjects in this condition attributed very pro-Castro attitudes to the essay writer and other subjects attributed very anti-Castro attitudes. This bifurcation in attributed attitudes was stronger in this condition than the other three, indicating perhaps that subjects in this condition resolved the ambiguous information – an unlikely event and no-choice – either by discounting the low prior probability and focusing on the lack of choice (leading to a pro-Castro attributed attitude), or by discounting the lack of choice and focusing on the rarity of the expressed attitude (leading to an anti-Castro attributed attitude). But a number of individual differences which lead some people to resolve the ambiguity one way or the other. The issue of individual differences in attributions has largely been ignored, but one study demonstrates their role in the FAE. Block and Funder (1986) showed that 14-year old subjects failed to consider appropriately the strength of situational forces and were led to 'overattribute' to the actor. But a number of individual difference variables were found to be related to the strength of the attributional effect. The effect was stronger for girls than for boys; there was a small and positive association between the size of the effect and IQ scores for boys, but not for girls; self-esteem was positively associated with the attributional effect for boys and girls; and a number of personality attributes – most noticeably the tendency to be more socially engaged, competent and emotionally well adjusted – were associated with the effect. Thus, the FAE does not seem to be a universal, unvarying phenomenon. It is stronger in some people than others, and is related to other dimensions of difference among people.

   Also concerning the greater variance in the pro Castro/no choice condition, Jones and Harris report the correlations between subjects' own attitude and their attributed attitude, separately for the four experimental conditions. Among subjects in the pro-Castro/no-choice condition, this correlation was .50. In the other three conditions the correlations ranged from −.12 to .05. Although none of these four correlations is statistically significant because of the small numbers of subjects in each condition, the correlation of .50 in the pro-Castro/no-choice condition is teasing evidence of an attributional phenomenon subsequently named the false consensus effect, which we describe more fully later in the chapter (Ross, Greene and House, 1977). Briefly, this effect refers to the tendency to overestimate the prevalence of our own attitudes and beliefs in the general community – we mistakenly think more people share our attitudes than is actually the case. We can apply the false consensus effect to what may have been happening in the heads of the pro-Castro/no-choice subjects. Faced with having to answer an experimenter's questions about some putative essay writer, and with only really two bits of information – the knowledge that the writer was asked to write a particular kind of essay and the essay itself – subjects managed to resolve the ambiguity between the two bits of information, and to answer the experimenter's questions, by projecting their own attitudes toward Castro's Cuba onto the target person. This points to the important lesson that people actively construe their worlds. Attribution theories tend to portray people as cognitive automata, coldly following a mental calculus to deduce a presumed cause of an observed effect. Sometimes, to be sure, people do act this way – perhaps more often inside social psychology laboratories than outside them, but they do so none the less. But the construal process runs hot and cold, and sometimes 'hot' (or at least, tepid) cognitions intrude upon theoretically 'cold' processes (as in projecting one's own attitude onto others).

2   In the second experiment the variance of scores in the pro-Castro/no choice condition was again much larger than in the other conditions, and again there was a correlation between subjects' own attitude and their attributed attitude in this condition (this time significant, and a massive .93). In the third experiment, although Jones and Harris don't discuss it, the variance in attributed attitude scores was much larger in the no-choice than in the choice conditions. The correlation between subjects' own attitude and attributed attitude was significant in three of the four conditions when judging the Northern target person (the choice/pro-segregation condition being the exception), but was significant in none of the conditions when judging the Southern target person.

5

SOCIAL IDENTITY

Who are you? The question of identity is one of the most central questions facing people throughout their lives. The ways to answer the question are close to infinite, but, at least in contemporary western societies, there are just a few, reasonably consistent ways of thinking about who we are. In the tradition of symbolic interactionism, an influential stream of micro-sociological thought originating with George Herbert Mead, Charles Horton Cooley and others at the University of Chicago in the early years of the twentieth century, Manford Kuhn developed the Twenty Statements Test (Kuhn, 1960, Kuhn and McPartland, 1954). The Twenty Statements Test is perhaps one of the simplest psychological tests ever constructed. It consists of one page, headed by the question 'Who are you?', and 20 blank lines for respondents to provide answers.

Following Kuhn, Zurcher (1977) proposed that answers to the 'Who are you?' question can be sorted into one of four categories, representing different modes of viewing self. The *physical self* includes responses which identify the self only in terms of physical attributes (for example, 'I am male', 'I am dark-haired'). The *social self* locates the self in a social structure, identifying the self with a particular social position or status (for example, 'I am a psychology student', 'I am a daughter', as well as 'I am a lover of poetry'). The *reflexive self* describes attributes which are not tied to a particular social position, but which only have meaning in a social sense (for example, 'I am a happy person', 'I am tolerant of other people'). Finally, the *oceanic self* includes statements which are global and which fail to differentiate one self from another (for example, 'I am a human being', 'I am a child of God'). These modes of viewing self are not fixed, but are contextual, and it is assumed that most people are able to express all four modes. Zurcher presents an interesting argument that the prevalence of *reflexive self* responses greatly increased in the United States through the 1960s and 1970s, in response to accelerated social and cultural change. Those changes made it increasingly difficult to define self in terms of social positions, since doing so requires a relatively stable social structure. Whether or not reflexive self responses become more modal during times of rapid social change, the important lesson is that individuals' views of self are tied inexorably to social forces and social structures. Even when individuals do not define self explicitly in terms of social positions (the social self), their views of *self* still depend on, and are qualified by, the *social*.

It is useful to distinguish between *personal identity* and *social identity*, bearing in mind that the distinction is forced and arbitrary. Personal identity refers to those qualities and characteristics we see in ourselves which are strictly individual. If someone answers the 'Who are you?' question with statements such as 'I am bored', 'I worry a lot' and 'I am highly strung', then they are revealing aspects of what would normally be called their personal identity. On the other hand, if the answers were 'I am a psychology student', 'I am Australian' or 'I am in group A in this experiment', then that person is revealing aspects of their social identity. Social identity is defined as 'that *part* of the individual's self-concept which derives from their knowledge of their membership of a social group (or groups) together with the value and emotional significance of that membership' (Tajfel, 1981: 255; original emphasis). Social identity normally locates an individual in relation to a social category, social position or social status. Our social identities are normally attached to, and derive from, the groups to which we belong. But we can also identify with groups to which we do not belong (these are called reference groups), and with particular individuals. Roger Brown's 'test of being a fan' (of the Boston Celtics or the soprano Renata Scotto, in his examples) is simple: your own self-esteem must rise and fall with the successes and failures of your object of admiration (1986: 555–6). The same test applies more generally as a test of social identity. Social identity is always attached to some social referent, usually a social group. If your psychological fortunes wax and wane with the fortunes of that social referent, then you identify with the referent.

Contemporary social psychology has tended to be over-enthusiastic and uncritical in viewing the self from the standpoint of the individual and individualism, and some writings on the subject relegate social identity to a minor position in the analysis of self (see Brewer, 1991, for an extension of this argument). Social identity is *not* just another aspect of individual identity. Social identity is not reducible to personal identity, or any other form of identity. Indeed, strictly speaking, the notion of 'personal' identity is a fiction – all identity, all forms of self-construal, must be social. To say, for example, that 'I am bored' is to say something about me as an individual, to be sure. But the statement only makes sense through its implicit comparison between my state of mental alertness just now and, at the very least, my mental alertness at some prior or imagined other time. In other words, the statement *necessarily* contains a social comparison between my self now and my self as represented memorially or as imagined in some other alternative setting. Although the example may be trite, the point is important – strictly speaking, *all* forms of identity are social. And, to extend Zurcher's point, even apparently asocial self descriptions subtly depend on particular forms of social organization. The notion of a solely personal identity is fictional, as is the distinction between personal and social.

One further preliminary point must be made before we proceed to consider social identity theory. When we say that the distinction between personal and social is forced and fictional, we mean that the social is forever and always reproduced within the individual. The distinction between personal and social, between individual and group, has been problematic throughout the history of social psychology. Early on, debates were waged over the issue of whether the idea of a 'group mind' was sensible. On the one hand were those who argued that all groups, and all group psychology, were ultimately reducible to the individuals constituting those groups and to their individual psychology (for example, Allport, 1924). On the other were those who argued that such reducibility was impossible, that as individuals were aggregated into groups, properties emerged from that aggregation which were not reducible to the constituent elements (for example, McDougall, 1921). Our position is that social psychology is genuinely *social* (Hogg and Abrams, 1988: 10–14; Taylor and Brown, 1979), that the phenomena social psychology seeks to understand are not explicable in terms of subsidiary, individual, elemental properties.

SOCIAL IDENTITY THEORY

The most all-encompassing approach to the study of social identity is known as social identity theory (SIT: Abrams and Hogg, 1990a; Hogg and Abrams, 1988; Tajfel and Turner, 1986). SIT has been developing since Tajfel's first formulations in the early 1970s, and represents both a *movement* in European social psychology away from the individualistic excesses of North American social psychology (Jaspars, 1986) and a more narrowly defined set of postulates and explanatory principles.

SIT is explicitly a theory of *intergroup behaviour*. A distinction is commonly drawn between *interindividual* behaviour and *intergroup* behaviour (Tajfel and Turner, 1986: 8). The former involves individuals interacting with one another solely on the basis of their respective qualities as individuals. Any groups they may belong to are irrelevant to the interaction. Just as there are no forms of identity which are strictly personal (asocial), there are no forms of strictly interpersonal behaviour. Intergroup behaviour is exemplified by interactions among people which are governed solely by their respective group memberships and not at all by any individual qualities they may display. All behaviour is seen as falling somewhere on a *continuum* from interindividual to intergroup.

The notion of a continuum from interpersonal to intergroup is not straightforward, and ought to be replaced with an alternative conceptualization in which interpersonal behaviour and intergroup behaviour are *independent* dimensions, rather than opposite poles of the same dimension. Stephenson (1981: 190–7) was perhaps the first to suggest this argument. The notion of a continuum implies that interpersonal and intergroup forms of behaviour must function as *alternatives* in any particular situation. Stephenson argues, and suggests evidence from studies on negotiation and bargaining, that *both* can operate simultaneously. This then allows for conflict between the two to occur, both within a social context and within a particular individual. It also suggests a mechanism whereby the relative dominance of each, either in a given situation or in a particular individual, can change. And it allows the possibility of other dimensions, representing other forms of social behaviour. The continuum implies that interpersonal and intergroup are *opposed* to one another. But such a conceptualization makes little sense, especially when one tries to relate intragroup behaviours to the continuum. Are intragroup behaviours opposed to interpersonal or to intergroup behaviours, or to both or neither? It is better to conceptualize interpersonal and intergroup, and perhaps also intragroup, behaviours as constituting separate and independent dimensions. But regardless, the point for present purposes is simply that it is conceptually useful to distinguish between interpersonal and intergroup behaviours.

An early experiment

Prior to SIT, the dominant theory of intergroup behaviour was realistic conflict theory (RCT: Sherif, 1966). RCT is premised on the appealing notion that intergroup conflict is always based upon *real* competition between groups over scarce resources. There is ample evidence, both social psychological (for example, Brewer and

Campbell, 1976; Campbell, 1967; Sherif, 1966; Sherif and Sherif, 1956; Sherif, Harvey, White, Hood and Sherif, 1961) and anecdotal, to support this simple premise. But it is possible to question whether competition over scarce resources is either a *necessary* or a *sufficient* condition to produce intergroup conflict. Is it possible that some instances of such competition do *not* generate intergroup conflict, and is it possible that some forms of intergroup conflict occur in the *absence* of competition and scarcity? It is possible to find examples from real life which show that real conflict is neither a necessary nor a sufficient cause of intergroup conflict (see, for example, Tajfel and Turner, 1986) – although undoubtedly it is a major and prevalent cause. However, to investigate the individual effects of the many possible causes of intergroup conflict it would be ideal to create a 'minimal' group in an experimental laboratory – a group which is stripped of all that we take as normally characterizing what it is to be a group, such as real social and economic relations, interaction among ingroup members, structural divisions within the group to create different roles, interdependency among ingroup members, and so on. If such a minimal group could be created in the laboratory, then further characteristics of 'groupness' could then be layered on top in such a way that the effects of each could be experimentally evaluated. This is the research programme that Henri Tajfel initiated in his now famous minimal group experiments, and which led directly to the development of SIT (Tajfel, 1970; Tajfel, Billig, Bundy and Flament, 1971).

The aim of the original minimal group experiment was to examine whether '[intergroup categorization] can, *on its own*, determine differential intergroup behaviour' (Tajfel et al., 1971: 153; original emphasis). To do this, experimental groups were created in which group members were alone and anonymous. Subjects were 14- and 15-year old schoolboys in a state school in Bristol, England. Each estimated the number of dots which were projected quickly on a screen in successive clusters. After doing so, subjects were allocated to either a group of 'overestimators' or 'underestimators' (the allocation was done randomly, though). While the first experimenter was apparently marking the answer sheets, another experimenter announced that a second experiment was also going to be conducted, involving rewards and penalties, and that the existing groups of over- and underestimators would continue to be used. Subjects were then seated in a cubicle, and asked to complete a series of 'payoff matrices' which appeared in a booklet. They were told that they were about to allocate points to two people. Sometimes the two people would be from the same group, sometimes the two would be from different groups, and sometimes there would be one person

Table 5.1 Example of an 'intergroup differential' payoff matrix used in a minimal categorization experiment

Member 26 of the overestimators	7	8	9	10	11	12	13	14	15	16	17	18	19
Member 17 of the underestimators	1	3	5	7	9	11	13	15	17	19	21	23	25

Source: Tafjel et al., 1971: 157

from each group. At the end of the experiment, the number of points allocated by all the subjects to each person would be added up, and that person would receive an amount of money proportional to the number of points. To eliminate self-interest, subjects never made an allocation decision involving themselves. The booklet consisted of one payoff matrix on each of 18 pages. Each matrix had two rows of numbers, as shown in Table 5.1. What is of interest is what happens when the two recipients belong to different groups.

Suppose that a subject had been told he was an 'overestimator', and was faced with the matrix in Table 5.1. He knows that one of the recipients is also an overestimator. This group is, then, the ingroup. The other recipient is an underestimator, and hence belongs to the outgroup. How would the subject decide which allocation to make? He could follow a strategy of maximizing joint profit, and choose the 19:25 response. He would also choose the 19:25 response if he followed a strategy of maximizing ingroup profit. Or he could follow a strategy of maximum difference in payoff to the two groups, and choose the 7:1 response. Different payoff matrices can be constructed to assess the relative strengths of each of these allocation strategies.

What did the schoolboy subjects do in the original minimal group study? For the matrix in Table 5.1, subjects who were told they were overestimators settled, on average, on the 12:11 response choice. What does this mean? It means that subjects did not follow a communal strategy of maximizing joint profit, nor did they attempt to maximize ingroup profit, nor did they allocate strictly fairly. Rather, they seemed to resolve a conflict between a fairness strategy and a maximum ingroup profit strategy by choosing the fairest response which also allowed the ingroup to receive more points than the outgroup – even though doing so meant that the ingroup member received fewer points than had the subject followed a maximum joint profit strategy.

Real-life parallels with these subjects' behaviour are easy to find. It is reported that Placido Domingo once agreed to sing at a concert at Wembley Stadium only if he was paid just one pound more than

Pavarotti was paid (Litson, 1990). He wasn't particularly concerned with how much he earned in absolute terms, only with the distinction of earning more than his rival.

An artefact?

It is possible that the results described above may be due not to any social psychology of groups, but rather to a methodological artefact. There are at least three artefactual explanations of the experiment just described; two plausible, one less so. The less plausible artefactual explanation holds that there is something about the way the two groups – overestimators and underestimators – were created which also produced the intergroup differentiation in the subjects' responses. The easy way to discount this as an explanation of the results is simply to use another categorization procedure. Tajfel et al. (1971: experiment 2) did just that. Instead of creating two groups of over- and underestimators, subjects were classified upon their supposed preference for abstract paintings by Klee or Kandinsky (classification was still random, though). The results were the same as before. Billig and Tajfel (1973) produced the same results again, even though they made the classification explicitly random to subjects – subjects saw the experimenter toss a coin to decide whether they were in one group or the other. This experiment also eliminates the possibility that subjects were more attracted to ingroup members than to outgroup members because they are more similar to one another on the basis of their shared preference for paintings by Klee than Kandinsky. The explanation of the results does not lie in the way in which the groups are created.

Another, and more plausible, artefactual explanation of the results relies on a notion that there is something about schoolboy culture, perhaps especially in English state schools, which compels the behaviour of the subjects. Schoolboys are, more than most, concerned with group memberships, with belonging and exclusion, and with conflict. Perhaps Tajfel and his colleagues had created a sort of *Lord of the Flies* in the laboratory. And if so, the results are hardly surprising and are probably not typical of other people. This explanation is open to empirical examination, and several studies have shown it to be wanting. Although the strength of the intergroup differentiation effect varies, it has been found with Maori and Polynesian children (Vaughan, 1978a, 1978b; Wetherell, 1982), and with adults in the United States (Brewer and Silver, 1978; Locksley, Borgida, Brekke and Hepburn, 1980) and in Switzerland (Doise and Sinclair, 1973). A recent meta-analytic review of 137 tests of the ingroup bias phenomenon in 37 different studies concluded that the effect is robust (Mullen, Brown and Smith, 1992). It is thus unlikely that Tajfel et al.'s results are due to the peculiarities of English schoolboys.

A third possible artefactual explanation suggests that the results are due to the demand characteristics latent in the experimental situation; that is, that the subjects acted in the way they thought the experimenter wanted (Rosenthal, 1966). In this argument, subjects somehow divine the hypotheses being investigated by the experi-menters, translate this knowledge into expectations about how they ought to behave, and then behave accordingly. Several factors mitigate against this as an explanation of the results. First, in the original experiment Tajfel et al. did not expect to find the group favouritism effect – they were attempting to create a 'minimal' situation in which no group effects were present (see Brown, 1986: 545; Oakes, Haslam and Turner, 1994: 41; Tajfel, 1978b). So if subjects were behaving according to what they thought the experimenter's expectations were, they misconstrued those expec-tations. Second, the array of matrices allows for several different allocation strategies to be followed by subjects. Even if they surmised that the experiment was about groups and between-group rewards, they could have followed any number of payoff strategies, such as maximizing ingroup profit regardless of the outgroup's result. Why did they follow a strategy of maximizing intergroup difference?

St Claire and Turner (1982) report the only experiment designed explicitly to evaluate the demand characteristics explanation. This experiment involved three groups: a Control condition, which mimicked a standard minimal group procedure; a Prediction con-dition; and a Prejudice condition. Subjects in the Prediction condition were treated as though they were in a standard minimal group experiment, up to the point where they would have been asked to allocate rewards. Instead of doing so, they were asked to predict how other subjects would allocate rewards after having gone through the same experimental procedure. If subjects were following the demand characteristics of the experimental setting, these subjects in the Prediction condition ought to have been able to predict accurately how the other subjects would behave. Subjects in the Prejudice condition were treated exactly the same as subjects in the Control condition, except that they were provided with an explicit cue about expected behaviour. This was done by openly describing the study as one investigating prejudice. St Claire and Turner argue that if the demand characteristics explanation is correct, subjects in the Control condition will display the usual ingroup bias effect, subjects in the Prediction condition will predict the ingroup biased behaviour, and subjects in the Prejudice condition will show the ingroup bias effect even more strongly than subjects in the Control condition. Contrary to these predictions, St Claire and Turner report that subjects in the Control and Prejudice conditions show the same degree of bias, and subjects in the Prediction condition failed to predict any bias in others' allocation behaviours. St Claire and Turner accept these results as indicating that the ingroup bias effect is genuine and not the product of subjects' compliance with the demand characteristics of the experimental setting.

This study fails to put to rest the demand characteristics argument, for two reasons. First, the Prejudice condition failed to make the demand characteristics more salient, as was intended. The crucial manipulation was in the title of the study described at the top of the response booklets. Yet most subjects in this condition (and in the Control condition) could not remember the study's title when they were asked at the end of the experiment. And second, St Claire and Turner assume that the demand cues in the Prediction condition were the same as those in the Control condition. However, if the cues are latent in the allocation task itself, which the Prediction subjects did not do, then it is not surprising that subjects in the Prediction condition would not be able to predict how *bona fide* subjects would perform. In a similar vein, Hartstone and Augoustinos (in press) suggest that the minimal group setting itself may unconsciously prime intergroup competitiveness. The fact that the Prediction subjects were not consciously aware of demand cues does not deny their operation.

An explanation

Although the role of demand characteristics cannot be completely excluded, it appears that the results of the Tajfel et al. (1971) experiments, and those of many other minimal group studies since, constitute a genuine intergroup phenomenon. But how can the results be explained? Realistic conflict theory can't explain the results, since there is no real competition between the groups – subjects could have followed a maximum joint profit strategy, for example. These minimal groups lack all the characteristics normally associated with groups. There is no history or culture within and between the groups, there is no interaction among group members, there is no intragroup structure, there is no common fate among group members, there is nothing. The groups are truly minimal. In a sense, there are no 'groups' at all. Yet subjects still acted in a way which is inexplicable in terms of solely intrapersonal or interpersonal processes. The subjects acted as though the groups were real for them, and the way in which they acted – to create positive intergroup differentiation – can only be thought of as intergroup behaviour in search of an explanation.

How are the results of the Tajfel et al. (1971) experiments to be explained? SIT was developed very much to account for the minimal group phenomenon. The theory has undergone several transformations in its lifetime, and indeed was originally given another moniker – categorization–identity–comparison (CIC) theory (Tajfel, 1982). But the core structure and premises of all versions of SIT are the same, and it is these that are described here.

Categorization   It is an undeniable fact that the social world is carved up into many social categories. Some of these are large, such as class, race, religion, ethnicity and gender. Others are smaller, more localized, more transient, and perhaps more idiosyncratic, such as hobby groups, minor political groups and groups created by an experimenter in a laboratory. For any person, though, some of these categories will be ingroups, or membership groups, and some will be outgroups. Most, but not all, social categories stand in real status or power relation to one another.

The simple fact of categorization has important cognitive consequences. The *accentuation effect* asserts that when stimulus objects are categorized, similarities among members of one category are perceived as greater than they actually are, and differences between members of different categories are perceived as greater than they actually are – in other words, intercategory differences and intracategory similarities are accentuated. The accentuation effect has been demonstrated in the judgement of lines as well as in the judgement of social stimuli. Tajfel and Wilkes (1963) showed that when eight lines of different length were presented to subjects who had to estimate their length, and when the four shortest lines were always presented with a letter A and the four longest lines were always presented with a letter B, subjects overestimated the difference between the A lines and the B lines. Some evidence, though not statistically significant, was also found that subjects overestimated the similarity of lines within each group. The accentuation effect has been demonstrated using all sorts of physical stimuli (see Doise, 1978; Doise, Deschamps and Meyer, 1978; and McGarty and Penny, 1988, for reviews).

The accentuation effect also operates in the judgement of social stimuli. One set of studies, for example, showed that white subjects in the United States who were asked to rate the degree of 'negroness' of a series of pictures of faces imposed their own classification onto the faces so that some were judged to be 'white' and others were judged to be 'black'. Once so classified, the similarities among the faces within one category and the differences between categories were accentuated (Secord, 1959; Secord, Bevan and Katz, 1956). Other examples of categorization effects with ethnicity are provided by Tajfel, Sheikh and Gardner (1964) and Doise (reported in Doise et al., 1978).

McGarty and Penny (1988) note that many studies related to the accentuation effect report either intracategory or intercategory accentuation, but rarely both. The reason, they argue, is the failure to heed part of Tajfel's original theoretical analysis. Not all categorizations produce accentuated judgements. The accentuation effect is only to be expected when the categorizations are salient to the person judging the stimuli and when the categorizations are useful to the person in the judgement task. McGarty and Penny go on to provide empirical support for their argument. One can begin to see how the basic, and probably unavoidable, perceptual process of categorizing the social world can lead to the formation of stereotypes.

The categories used to apprehend the world, especially the social world, do not reside within the objects of perception. There is no innate, divinely given or 'natural' set of categories to be used in perceiving the world, waiting there for social psychologists to discover, if only they try hard enough with the right methods. The categories which form the basis of our perceptual grasp of the world around us are imposed by us upon the world. They are construals. This is not to say that each and every one of us must continually reinvent the way in which we perceive the world every time we wake up in the morning. Perception is ordered and reasonably consistent. It is also shared. Although the categories of perception reside within the perceiver rather than the perceived, this does not mean that each perceiver has an entirely unique or idiosyncratic set of perceptual categories. The categories of perception are very much given to us by the culture we are born into. This is what we mean when we say that perception is shared, or social. At a broad level, the forms and processes, and even the content, of perceptions of the social world are structured and limited by the dominant social representations surrounding us. Knowledge of these consensual, social knowledge structures is apparently acquired early in life, although it also changes through life (for example, Augoustinos, 1990).

One of the most basic categorizations – perhaps *the* most basic – is the distinction between *self* and *other*, and its more social corollary, the distinction between *us* and *them*. The acquisition of the disjunction between self and other is an early and necessary part of socialization. Some – notably the symbolic interactionists – argue that the distinction only arises through social interaction, and that a necessary consequence is the distinction between self as subject and self as object (see Mead, 1934, and Stryker and Statham, 1985). One interesting empirical example which supports this view comes from work by Gallup (1977) on self-recognition in apes. Gallup has shown that, apart from humans, apes and chimpanzees are the only animals who behave in front of a mirror in such a way that they appear to recognize the reflected image as their own – but only apes and chimps reared from birth in the company of other apes and chimps show this behaviour. When reared from birth in isolation, the apes and chimps never act as though they recognize the mirrored image as their own. In other words, the sense of self, and the knowledge that self is not non-self, and the ability to have reflexive self-awareness, are all products of social interaction. This is another example of the fallacy of the individual–society distinction. The two are not nearly as separable as the distinction implies.

The category of *self* appears to have prime potency in memory. Work reviewed in Chapter 3 on schemas has demonstrated that information relevant to the self is more easily activated than other information, and that it has a strong influence on the encoding of new information and the retrieval of old information. The self's social analogue, *us*, appears to have similar potency in our cognitive processing. Perdue, Dovidio, Gurtman and Tyler (1990), for example, show that words paired repeatedly with ingroup pronouns come to acquire a more positive evaluation than do words which are paired with outgroup pronouns, and that ingroup designators facilitate response times to positive trait words (but outgroup designators do not facilitate negative trait word accessibility). Thus, even at the level of unconscious information processing, self and 'us' attract more of our mental resources and are associated with positivity. We elaborate these issues in Chapter 9.

To sum up, then, the most elemental part of SIT is the simple and obvious proposition that the social world is perceived in categories which are socially constructed. We each belong to some categories and not to others. In the minimal group experiments, the categorizations available for subjects are, literally, minimal. There exist only two categories: underestimators or overestimators, Klee or Kandinsky preferers, group X or group Y, depending on the experimental procedure. In and of themselves, these are empty, meaningless categories (purposely so). Any meaning they have for subjects, who always are assigned to one or the other category, is imposed by the subjects themselves. Some evidence exists that the most elementary social categorization, into us and them, automatically produces ingroup favouritism. However, SIT argues for another source of the ingroup favouritism so often seen in minimal group experiments (and outside them, too). That source is identity.

Identity   We already intimated at the beginning of this chapter that the question of who we are, of our identity, is one of the most important questions we face. Our identity can be defined as our self-image or self-concept. Our attitude to self as object, or how we evaluate our self-concept, is self-esteem. Identity is central to SIT.

A powerful and perhaps universal motive is the motive to think well of one's self, to have a positive evaluation of identity; or, in the parlance of pop psychology, and also in a vast amount of research in individual psychology, to have a positive self-esteem (for example, Tesser, 1986, 1988). Failure to enact this motive successfully is often considered psychologically unhealthy. But the motive operates at the social as well as the individual level. There is as strong a motive to evaluate one's social identity positively as there is to evaluate one's personal identity positively. This motive for a positive social identity propels much social behaviour, and is expressed as a tendency to evaluate one's ingroup memberships, the social categories one belongs to, positively.

SIT assumes that a person's social identity is constituted by the vast number of social identifications that person has with various social categories. Not all those identifications are primed, or activated, or salient, at any one time. Rather, social identity at any one time is made up of a few identifications selected to suit the particular social context.

Knowledge of social identifications on its own is not sufficient to form an evaluation of those identifications. For a person to know he or she is Australian, or a psychology student, or a parent, is not enough, and inherently can never be enough, on its own for that person to evaluate those category memberships. Evaluation of category memberships can only be made through processes of social comparison.

Comparison   At an individual level, to have a positive self-esteem means that one thinks well of one's self. For most dimensions on which self is evaluated – from the broad to the specific, from 'am I a good person?' to 'am I a good driver?' – to have a positive self-esteem means that one thinks one is better than average, or better than most other people. It is not possible to answer most of the evaluative questions posed of self without reference to the general distribution of the relevant property among all other people. It is, by definition, not possible for most people to be better than average, but that does not prevent most people from thinking well, or reasonably well, of themselves on most dimensions. Most people do not think they are a schmuck; most people have a positive self-esteem.

In evaluating self on any dimension, an implicit social comparison with others is necessary. So it is also, only perhaps more so, with the evaluation of social identifications of self with social categories. Any particular social category membership can inform a positive social identity only through social comparison between the ingroup and some relevant outgroup. The value of being Australian, or a psychology student, or a parent, can only be evaluated through comparison with other social categories.

How people evaluate personal and social attributes through social comparison has been theorized and studied since the 1950s. The theory of social comparison processes, which forms the backbone of this last part of SIT, has undergone major changes over the years. We present in this section just a skeletal outline of the major tenets of social comparison processes.

The original version of the theory was formulated by Festinger (1954), and was largely a theory of how individuals evaluate individual qualities. It suggested that people prefer to evaluate self and its qualities against some 'objective' criterion or other. When such objective criteria are unavailable, people turn to social comparison – comparison with others – for evaluative standards. Festinger distinguished between comparison of abilities and opinions, and suggested that the motives driving comparisons of each were different: accuracy and self-improvement in the case of abilities; gaining social consensus in the case of opinions. In the case of abilities, Festinger proposed a *universal drive upward*, in which a person selected as the comparison other someone who displayed a greater amount of the ability in question. The principle of *similarity* asserts that, all other things being equal, a person will select as a comparison other someone who is more similar than dissimilar. Joining the universal drive upward with the similarity principle leads to the prediction that, when evaluating abilities, a comparison other will be selected who is only slightly better than the comparer.

The motive underlying all comparisons, according to Festinger, is the desire for an accurate self-evaluation. Plenty of evidence has amassed since the 1950s that this is not the case. Rather, people appear to engage in social comparisons mostly for reasons of *self-enhancement*. The proposition that people compare upward to evaluate their self and their abilities conflicts with much research on self-esteem, which suggests that people selectively attend to information which bolsters their self view. Self-evaluation and self-enhancement are usually conflicting and competing motives, and, usually, people follow a self-enhancement strategy. This is the position taken by SIT, and is the cornerstone of SIT's use of social comparison.

Evaluating social category memberships is akin to evaluating opinions. There are no 'objective' criteria for right and wrong or good and bad. It makes as little 'objective' sense to say 'my group is better than your group' as it does to say 'my opinion is better than yours'. There are no benchmarks to establish the meaning of 'better'. But this is not to say that people do not act as if their category memberships or their opinions are better than those of others. On the contrary, they do so act, and in a sense, for them, their claims are 'true'.

To make a social comparison between an ingroup and an outgroup, two problems must first be resolved. First, the ingroup member must decide which outgroup of the many available should be chosen as the comparison other. This is known as the problem of *referent* selection. And second, along which dimension should the comparison be made? This is the problem of *dimension selection*. These twin problems have plagued social comparison theory for four decades (Kawakami and Dion, 1993, 1994; Pettigrew, 1967; Wheeler, 1991).

Regardless of *how* people engage in social comparisons between ingroups and outgroups, it is the *consequences*, rather than the mechanisms, of such comparisons that are most important to SIT. It may well be the case that it is the consequences of social comparison that are of prime importance to those doing the comparing too, inasmuch as people select referent targets and dimensions according to the anticipated (positive) outcome of the comparison.

As mentioned earlier, SIT proposes that people are motivated to achieve a positive social identity, just as they are motivated to achieve a positive self-esteem. Most of the time, social category memberships, on their own, can neither enhance nor degrade social identity. Category memberships are only of value in relation to other categories. It is only the relative status positions of an ingroup and an outgroup on a comparison dimension of value to the ingroup member which affect the social identity of that member. SIT proposes the axiom that there is a motive to evaluate group memberships positively so as to enhance social identity, and that this positive differentiation of ingroup from outgroup is achieved through comparison of the ingroup to an outgroup. An important difference between this approach to social comparison and that of Festinger is that Festinger articulated comparison processes at an

individual level, between individuals as individuals, where individual characteristics are evaluated and self-esteem and self-
knowledge are affected. SIT discusses social comparison processes at
a group level, where group memberships are evaluated and social
identities are shaped and valorized.

Intergroup differentiation

We can now return to the results from the minimal group
experiments, and see how the principles of SIT can be marshalled to
explain those results. Recall that in the minimal group experiments
subjects acted on the basis of a trivial or even explicitly random
classification by discriminating between an ingroup and an outgroup
member. This is an enigma from the point of view of realistic conflict
theory.

Subjects in a minimal group experiment are confronted with an
almost empty situation. They are allocated to one of two groups on
the basis of some trivial or random act, they are separated from
anyone other than the experimenter, and they are asked to allocate
points to other subjects who are identified only by a number and
their group membership. What meaning does – or even can – such
an empty situation have for subjects? According to SIT, the subjects
recognize their group membership. They are also motivated to
enhance their social identity. The situation is so minimal and empty
that there is only one avenue open to do this. Subjects can only
enhance their social identity by striving to differentiate their group
from the other group, and by elevating their group relative to the
other group. Doing so puts their group in a superior position relative
to the other group, and, hence, through social comparison, their
own group becomes positively valorized, which in turn, and through
their identification with that group, enhances their social identity.

SIT, formulated in such stark and minimal terms, does not claim to
be able to generalize its explanation of intergroup differentiation in a
minimal group experiment to situations of intergroup conflict and
hostility between 'real' groups. At the least, the history of intergroup
relations and the economic and social positions of the conflicting
groups must be considered. However, the principles of SIT are
claimed to undergird all intergroup contexts. One example of the
way in which minimal groups are not the same as real groups is
provided by Brown (1986), who notes that subjects in minimal
groups are free to enhance their social identity by discriminating in
their point allocations between ingroup and outgroup members.
There is nothing in the experimental setting to prevent them from
doing so. But members of real groups, with real status and power

differences between the groups, are not so free. It is not so easy, and often not possible at all, for members of minority groups in society to assert their group's superiority by inventing flattering comparison dimensions or comparison others. This brings us to a consideration of the consequences of threats to social identity.

Consequences of threats to social identity

If indeed people have a motive to evaluate their social category memberships positively and this is achieved through social comparisons between ingroup and outgroup, then it becomes theoretically important to consider what happens when individuals find themselves in groups which cannot be evaluated positively in relation to other groups. In such situations, the relative status inferiority of the ingroup constitutes a threat to the social identity of the individual group member. How does this person respond to such identity threats? SIT specifies two broad classes of behavioural response – exiting from the group, and remaining within the group but attempting to alter the status of the group. Whether an individual selects one or the other depends in large part on his or her beliefs regarding *social mobility* and *social change* (Ellemers, 1993). Social mobility refers to the belief that group boundaries are open rather than closed, that it is possible to leave one group and join another. Some groups are inherently closed – race and gender are prime examples.[1] Other groups are more open, but may not be perceived that way. Social change refers to the belief that the relative status of groups can be altered, that it is possible to change a negative valuation of an ingroup to a positive one. Again, the actual state of affairs may not be veridically represented in people's belief systems, but it is the belief in the possibility or impossibility of change which directs people's behaviour. As well as these two strategies, a third kind of response exists but has received little research attention within the framework of SIT, namely, to accept the validity of membership in the group and to accept the negative evaluation of that group.

Leaving the group   When individual members of a negatively valued group believe that group boundaries are permeable they may attempt to leave the group to join a more positively valued group. People who strive at upward social mobility, at attempting to improve their lot in life and the lot of their children, through hard work, self-education, and so on, are often attempting to leave one social position and attain another. The 'exit' option is only open, of course, for those groups where it is possible to leave. Many social groupings – race and gender, for example – are ascribed rather than achieved. They are groups from which there is no exit. Yet still members of such groups may attempt a *de facto* exit. Instances of members of minority groups 'passing' as members of the majority group are examples of one form of 'exit' from the membership group, even though the markers of the original group membership persist (Simpson and Yinger, 1985: 139–40). Even when exit from a group is logically possible, it is not always psychologically feasible. Many groups have well-developed norms against defection, as does our society generally. Ingroup loyalties, and the identity attachments to a group and its members, are often strong enough to prevent members attempting to exit.

Changing group status   According to SIT, the second form of 'positive' response to negatively valued group membership is to remain in the group and attempt to alter the valuation of that group. Tajfel and Turner (1986; see also Hogg and Abrams, 1988) specify two ways in which this sort of social change can be brought about: *social creativity* and *social competition*. The choice between the two depends largely on the perceived *security* of the relations between the two groups. Intergroup relations which are secure are those which are seen as stable and legitimate. These refer to the outcome of a social comparison between groups, as well as to the comparison itself, and are somewhat akin to the attributional dimensions specified in Kelley's attributional model (see Chapter 4). Unstable or illegitimate intergroup relations are *insecure* relations.

Any social comparison which leads to the ingroup faring worse than the comparison outgroup, and which occurs in the context of secure (stable and legitimate) intergroup relations, will threaten the ingroup's social identity, if that identity is not already negative. Being unable to deny the outcome of the comparison, and being unable to challenge the comparison itself since it is judged to be legitimate, the group members must find alternative ways of bolstering social identity. These strategies are grouped together in SIT and described as *social creativity*. The main defining quality of such strategies is that they represent attempts by ingroup members to 'seek positive distinctiveness for the ingroup by redefining or altering the elements of the comparative situation' (Tajfel and Turner, 1986: 19–20). There are three main such strategies.

First, members may attempt to introduce some new comparison dimension, on which the ingroup may fare more favourably. As an intergroup strategy, this will only succeed if, first, the ingroup members accept the new comparison dimension as valid, and, second, the outgroup can be swayed into accepting the new dimension. Ingroup acceptance is probably all that is needed for the strategy to be successful in bolstering social identity. One example of a group following this strategy comes from Lemaine (1966; Lemaine, Kastersztein and Personnaz, 1978), who provided groups of children with material to construct a hut. One group was given inferior materials, and naturally built a hut which was judged to be not as good as the other huts. Children in this group attempted to introduce new dimensions to be considered in the evaluation of the hut, such as the garden they had built around the hut, even though the criteria for judging the huts had been agreed on explicitly at the start of the competition.

A second social creativity strategy attempts to revalue the comparison dimension on which the group was evaluated negatively in the first place. As Hogg and Abrams (1988) note, this strategy is likely to be followed if the original dimension is one which is criterial to the group; that is, if giving up the negatively valued characteristic were to destroy the essence of the group. It is also likely when the negatively valued characteristic is immutable, as is the case with groups defined by colour or gender. The example cited in many textbooks is the revaluation of 'black' in the United States through the 1960s and afterwards. Prior to the rise of the civil rights movement in that decade, 'black' was a negatively valued character- istic. It defined individuals into a single category, and the category and its members were negatively valued by society. Anti-black prejudice in the United States was widespread and pernicious. It is not usually possible to change skin colour. Whereas the negative evaluation of 'black' was accepted by both white and black (as attested to by the Clarks' study of doll preference, described below), the rise of the civil rights movement was accompanied by a change among black people (and others) in their private and public acceptance of, and indeed pride in, 'black'; in their acceptance that 'black is beautiful'.

Finally, members of a group which is negatively valued through social comparison with a particular outgroup can search for a new comparison outgroup, or even replace the comparison outgroup with social comparisons at an individual level among members of the ingroup only. Just as Festinger's original, individual-level, formula- tion of social comparison theory got it wrong by emphasizing the self-evaluation motive rather than the self-enhancement motive, groups are likely to follow a 'self-enhancement' motive by seeking outgroups which will allow them to make downward, rather than upward, comparisons. Thus, many low status groups will often select as salient comparison referents groups of equal or lower status.

Alternatively, many members of low status groups turn inward to the group and make *intragroup* comparisons, rather than engage in *intergroup* social comparisons. Runciman (1966), for example, argued that one reason why the English working class has failed to develop any sense of class consciousness is that its members fail to evaluate their social conditions at a group or class level. Rather, the adequacy of pay and conditions and so on is evaluated through intragroup, interpersonal comparisons between individual workers. Not only does this mean that any political development of class consciousness is thwarted, but any invidious consequences of belonging to the working class, which are only assessable through social comparisons with other classes, are effectively ignored, and thus tolerated.

Social creativity follows from negative intergroup comparisons which are secure. When those comparisons are insecure, *social competition* is likely to follow. Social competition refers to direct challenges by the ingroup to the outgroup. These can take many forms, all of which are political; that is, they all involve attempts to change the social structure or the positions of groups within that social structure. One potent example of social competition as an intergroup strategy is direct confrontation (race riots in the United States, poll tax riots in Britain, civil strife in the former Yugoslavia, sectarian violence in Northern Ireland, civil war in Rwanda, and so on, but also including less extreme action such as industrial strikes, and organizing and signing petitions). Ingroup regrouping and reorganization is another strategy often followed by, for example, political parties after a heavy defeat in an election.

Perceptions of deprivation, injustice and discrimination are potent motives in social life. The perception of deprivation is a direct challenge to personal and/or social identity, and is likely to lead to engagement in social competition. The theory of relative deprivation (RD) formalizes the relationships between social comparisons leading to outcomes unfavourable to the individual or group and a variety of psychological and behavioural consequences. RD is a special case of SIT, but the theory of RD has been developed since 1949 (Stouffer, Suchman, De Vinney, Star and Williams, 1949) largely independently of SIT. However, both theories have much to contribute to each other (Kawakami and Dion, 1994; Walker and Pettigrew, 1984). The central notion in the RD construct is that perceptions of deprivation are *relative*, not absolute – they intrinsically depend on social comparison processes. A person who experiences RD believes that he or she is entitled to more or better outcomes than he or she currently has. A distinction is made between personal RD and group RD (Runciman, 1966): personal RD follows from social comparisons at an individual level (that is, between self and another individual, or between self and an ingroup); group RD stems from social comparisons at a group level (that is, between an ingroup and an outgroup). Several studies have documented that group RD leads to social outcomes such as strengthened group identity and participation in social protest (Abrams, 1990; Dion, 1986; Guimond and Dube-Simard, 1983; Kelly, 1993; Petta and Walker, 1992; Smith and Gaskell, 1990; Tougas and Veilleux, 1988, 1990; Walker and Mann, 1987), and occasional studies have shown that personal RD is related to individual-level outcomes such as psychosomatic symptoms and perceived stress (Abrams, 1990; Walker and Mann, 1987). The link between these two forms of RD and their particular consequent behaviours would appear to be identity. When outcomes are evaluated at an individual level, aspects of personal identity are salient, and it is likely that these would make more likely an explanation for the perceived deprivation couched in terms of attributes of the individual. However, when outcomes are evaluated at a group level, it is aspects of social identity which are salient and likely to colour explanations for the deprivation and to influence the choice of behaviours designed to remedy the problem. The link between comparisons and identity can run the other way too: when personal identity is salient, individual-level comparisons are more likely, and when social identity is salient, group-level comparisons are more likely.

To conclude this section, then, it can be seen that most, if not all, attempts by a negatively valued ingroup to revalue its status, by engaging in either social creativity or social competition, are likely to be met with resistance by the dominant outgroup. A group does not relinquish its favoured position easily or voluntarily – for political reasons as well as reasons of maintaining a favourable social identity. It is a fairly safe prediction that any intergroup strategy which attempts to alter the relative social status of different groups will increase intergroup tensions and hostilities. Indeed, such tensions and hostilities are only likely to diminish or disappear when the dimensions and outcomes of intergroup comparisons are judged, especially by the unfavoured group, to be legitimate. The processes of creating and maintaining perceived legitimacy at a reasonably consensual level are not addressed in SIT. However, social representations theory and, in particular, the construct of ideology are useful in examining such processes, and these are discussed in Chapters 6 and 11.

Accepting a negative social identity   The consequences of accepting a negatively valued group membership would appear to be profound. One of the most famous examples from the social psychological literature is provided by a study of young children in the United States conducted in the 1940s by the Clarks (Clark and Clark, 1947). In this study, black and white children were shown two dolls, one black and one white, and were then asked which doll they would like to play with, which is a nice doll, which doll looks bad, and which doll is a nice colour. The white children almost always chose the white doll to play with and as nice. A majority of the black children also chose the white doll to play with and as nice, and chose the black doll as the one that looks bad. Importantly, the black children were well aware that they themselves were black. The Clarks' doll preference study has been replicated several times in the United States, and also with New Zealand Maoris (Vaughan, 1978b), with French Canadians (Berry, Kalin and Taylor, 1977), and in Wales (Bourhis, Giles and Tajfel, 1973). What the black children in the Clarks' study, who were aged from 3 to 7, appear to be displaying is an internalized ingroup derogation. There is some evidence that the pattern of preferences of black children has shifted since the 1960s to display greater ingroup pride (for example, Hraba and Grant, 1970). The costs, both psychological and social, of internalized ingroup derogation have largely been ignored by social psychology, but it is likely that internalized ingroup derogation helps justify the social system responsible for producing the relative social positions of the ingroup and outgroup, and leads to a sense of fatalism which inhibits any form of social action which might lead to social change (Jost, 1995). It is also wise to be cautious in making the inferential leap from membership in a devalued group to self-deprecation, since doing so leads to the conclusion of psychological deficiency in members of such groups and is often not supported by studies of black self-esteem (Aboud, 1988; Simpson and Yinger, 1985: 127–31).

Consequences of a positive social identity

Social identity theory has only addressed the consequences of threats to social identity, and of a negative social identity. It has not considered the flip-side of the coin – the consequences of positive social identity. SIT explicitly assumes as a major premise that people (and groups) strive to achieve and maintain a positive social identity. This is achieved through positive differentiation of the ingroup from the outgroup. But is a positive social identity an unmitigated good thing? Nowhere is it considered that achieving a positive social identity may have deleterious, as well as beneficial, effects. There is no research on this question, so our treatment here is largely speculative.

We can consider the question as roughly analogous to the question of whether there are any negative consequences of positive self-esteem at a personal level. While the evidence of psychological research points to the benefits in terms of psychological health of having positive, or high, self-esteem, and while the massive weight of the pop psychology industry is heavily invested in promoting positive self-esteem, the picture is not uniformly rosy. Chapter 4 on attribution mentions some studies which document that people who 'suffer' positive self-esteem are more prone to attributional biases which unfairly allow them to claim the psychological credit for positive events and to be absolved of responsibility for negative events. Having a positive self-esteem, then, is not necessarily all positive. At a group level, it would appear reasonable to accept that people are motivated to achieve and maintain a positive social identity, and that they do this largely through positive intergroup differentiation. What, if any, might the costs be of doing this, though?

We can suggest that there may be two kinds of cost, one personal and the other social. The personal costs of positive social identity may come in the form of greater demands placed upon individual group members by the group to maintain ingroup cohesiveness and uniformity. Identifying strongly with a particular group may buy the individual positive social identity, but at the price of a degree of individual autonomy. Whether individual autonomy is good or bad depends on whether one views the question from the point of view of the individual or the group, and on whether one views the question from the point of view of a collectivistic culture or an individualistic culture. But it is probably undeniable that, in strongly individualistic cultures at least, loss of individual autonomy constitutes a cost.

At a social level, the major cost must be intergroup tensions and hostilities. Again, whether these are good or bad must be decided within a framework of values and morals, where empirical research is of little help or relevance. SIT recognizes that intergroup tensions are a likely consequence of striving for positive intergroup differentiation. We are not naïve enough to suggest that a warm, fuzzy, conflict-free society is either possible or even desirable, but social conflict is costly for society.

Another, and related, social cost is simply outgroup derogation, whether that leads to conflict or not. If there is a motive to achieve a positive social identity, and if that is (only) achieved through positive intergroup differentiation, then it follows that outgroup derogation is a necessary consequence of striving for positive social identity.

Roger Brown (1986) was the first to point out that in those minimal group experiments which measure variables other than just the points allocated to one person or another, intergroup differentiation is often achieved not by constructing a *negative* image of the outgroup, but rather by having a neutral image of the outgroup, neither positive nor negative, and by constructing a *positive* ingroup image. Thus, the relative positions of the two groups in the eyes of the ingroup members produce a net effect which enhances social identity. But these are minimal groups, after all. If only it were so in the real world. It is unfortunate that most real groups appear to achieve positive intergroup differentiation not by making the ingroup positive and the outgroup a bland, neutral nothing, but by actively and strongly derogating the outgroup and, usually, also enhancing the ingroup.

There is some evidence that subjects participating in a minimal group experiment in which they differentiate – discriminate – between members of the ingroup and members of the outgroup achieve an increase in self-esteem (Abrams and Hogg, 1988: Hogg and Abrams, 1990; Hunter, 1993). There is also evidence that self-esteem is positively related to prejudice (Bagley, Verma, Mallick and Young, 1979). In the absence of empirical evidence, we can complete the syllogism logically, and suggest that the drive to achieve and maintain a positive personal and social identity leads directly to a mental (and perhaps social) arrangement of ingroups and outgroups which fosters positive intergroup differentiation, and that one manifestation of this differentiation is prejudice and hostility directed toward negatively valued outgroups. From a different point of view, Simpson and Yinger (1985: 158–67) count the costs of prejudice borne by majority group members as including: the cost of ignorance, especially when the scapegoating of minority groups deflects attention away from real social and economic problems; the cost of moral ambivalence produced by the tension between the horns of the fundamental social dilemma involving societal and personal commitments to the tenets of freedom and equality of all people, on the one hand, and acknowledging and participating in the reduced freedom and inequality of minority group members, on the other; and economic costs produced by higher crime rates, higher unemployment rates, and worse health status usually associated with minority group status. While it may seem a long hop from randomly created, trivial 'groups' of people allocating points to fictitious individuals in a social psychological laboratory to the major social problems detailed by Simpson and Yinger, advocates of SIT implicitly argue that the fundamental processes operating in both arenas are the same.

RECENT DEVELOPMENTS

As mentioned earlier, SIT is as much a movement in European social psychology as it is a well-defined theory. In both senses, though, it is not static. Although Tajfel, the originator of the theory, died more than 10 years ago, SIT has continued to develop, both as a movement and as a theory. We here touch upon just a few of the recent developments in SIT.

A typology of groups

What is a group? Social psychology has wrestled with this problem on and off for much of this century. Definitions vary, and at times appear to contradict one another, or be almost unintelligible, or bear no resemblance at all to what we usually think of when we use the word 'group'. Consider these examples:

> We may define a social group as a unit consisting of a plural number of separate organisms (agents) who have a collective perception of their unity and who have the ability to act/or are acting in a unitary manner toward their environment. (Smith, 1945: 227)

> Conceiving of a group as a dynamic whole should include a definition of group which is based on interdependence of the members (or better, of the subparts of the group). It seems to be rather important to stress this point because many definitions of a group use the similarity of group members rather than their dynamic interdependence as the constituent factor. . . . One should realize that even a definition of group membership by equality of goal or equality of an enemy is still a definition by similarity. (Lewin, 1951: 146–7)

> A group is a social unit which consists of a number of individuals who stand in (more or less) definite status and role relationships to one another stabilized to some degree at the time and which possesses a set of values or norms of its own regulating the behaviour of individual members, at least in matters of consequence to the group. (Sherif and Sherif, 1956: 144)

> A group, in the social psychological sense, is a plurality of persons who interact with one another in a given context more than they interact with anyone else. (Sprott, 1958: 9)

> We define 'group' as a collection of individuals whose existence as a collection is rewarding to the individuals. (Bass, 1960: 39)

> [Non-social groups are groups] in which two or more people are in the same place at the same time but are not interacting with each other.

> [Social groups are] groups in which two or more people are interacting with each other and are interdependent, in the sense that to fulfil their needs and goals they must rely on each other. (Aronson, Wilson and Akert, 1994: 326–7)

> In a group, people are interdependent and have at least the potential for mutual interaction. In most groups, members have regular face-to-face contact. (Taylor, Peplau and Sears, 1994: 345)

These definitions show the array of conceptualizations of a group. Not untypically, they variously define a group using interaction among members, interdependence among members, rewarding relationships among members, a sense of 'we-feeling', goal or need fulfilment, or an ingroup structure as the criterial property (Shaw, 1971). None of them fits the intergroup phenomena observed in minimal group experiments. In these experiments there is no interaction among group members, there is no interdependence, there is no structure. But there is intergroup differentiation. Obviously, none of the above definitions, or any similar definitions, can account for this. The minimal group results change the conceptualization of a group. How, then, are groups to be conceptualized?

Tajfel and Turner write: 'We can conceptualize a group . . . as a collection of individuals who perceive themselves to be members of the same social category, share some emotional involvement in this common definition of themselves, and achieve some degree of social consensus about the evaluation of their group and of their membership in it' (1986: 15). Even more basically, Brown offers this: 'A group exists when two or more people define themselves as members of it and when its existence is recognized by at least one other' (1988: 2–3). This is about as simple, as minimal, as it can get; and it fits the results of the minimal group experiments. Such a definition is cognitive; all that is necessary to generate intergroup behaviour is a cognitive recognition by two or more people that they share membership in a social category, and that someone else also recognizes that category.

With a cognitive conceptualization of a group, SIT then tends to assume that all groups are alike, that group members are motivated to achieve and maintain a positive social identity through intergroup differentiation, that all groups are essentially equivalent in allowing group members to achieve positive social identity. But it is unlikely that group life is that simple. There are groups and there are groups. Some groups are constitutionally more important to their members' identity than are others, and some groups depend more on their relationship with other groups to establish their identity than do other groups.

These points were recognized by Hinkle and Brown (1990), who proposed an initial taxonomy of groups. SIT predicts that the more group members identify with a particular group the more they will demonstrate ingroup bias based on comparisons between the ingroup and the outgroup. In examining the pertinent empirical literature Hinkle and Brown found that the results were, at best, only mildly supportive. To resolve the discrepancy between the theoretical prediction and the data, Hinkle and Brown suggested the obvious, but theoretically overlooked, point that not all groups are the same, and that perhaps predictions derived from SIT, or from other group theoretical perspectives, apply only to some sorts of groups. How should a taxonomy of groups be constructed? Hinkle and Brown suggest groups can vary on two important dimensions – individualism–collectivism and relational ideology. The first dimension refers to the extent to which a culture emphasizes individual autonomy from groups or individual relatedness and cooperation within groups (Hofstede, 1980, 1983; Triandis, Bontempo, Villareal, Asai and Lucca, 1988). Cultures are said to vary from individualistic to collectivistic. Australia, the United Kingdom and the United States are examples of the former; China, Indonesia and Greece are examples of the latter. The individualistic–collectivistic dimension is a cultural variable. Its individual analogue is referred to as idiocentric–allocentric.

The second dimension refers to the extent to which a group is constitutionally competitive, or concerned with its status relative to other groups. Hinkle and Brown suggest that juries, writers' circles and therapy groups are unlikely to be concerned with their status relative to other juries, writers' circles or therapy groups, and are constitutionally never likely to be concerned with anything much other than intragroup processes. On the other hand, sporting teams are a good example of a group for which relational, or comparative, qualities are essential.

Crossing the two dimensions of individualism–collectivism and relational ideology creates a fourfold classification. Hinkle and Brown suggest that SIT's predictions most strongly apply to groups which are collectivistic rather than individualistic and which are relational rather than independent. In collectivistic groups, individuals are strongly related to the group; their identity is much more strongly rooted in the group than is the case with members of individualistic groups. The relative position of the ingroup is therefore more important to group members' social identity in collectivistic groups than in individualistic groups. Similarly, relational groups are more likely to evaluate their merit through social comparison with other groups than are non-relational groups.[2]

Brown, Hinkle, Ely, Fox-Cardamone, Maras and Taylor (1992) report three separate studies examining the two dimensional taxonomy. In all three studies, the two dimensions were more or less orthogonal. When subjects were sorted into one of the four groups formed by splitting each of the two dimensions at its median, only those subjects in the collectivistic–relational cell showed a strong correlation between strength of ingroup identification and ingroup favouritism. Subjects in the other cells showed effectively no association between identification and favouritism. Thus, these three studies provide some initial evidence in support of the premise that not all groups function the same way in providing group members with positive social identifications. Further work is no doubt needed to examine more fully the dimensions proposed by Hinkle and Brown, and to consider the possibility of other dimensions. A full taxonomy of groups, and a detailed consideration of how and why theories such as SIT may only apply to some groups and not to others, would be invaluable in the further development of theories on intergroup behaviour.

Multiple group memberships

SIT, and most other group theories, consider only two groups at one time. To be sure, third groups do lurk somewhere in the implicit theoretical background, but only ever as vague 'possible comparison alternatives' or something similar. The social world is obviously made up of more than two groups at once, individuals belong to more than one social group at one time and intergroup relations often reflect multiple group settings. Several researchers (Brown and Turner, 1979; Commins and Lockwood, 1978; Deschamps, 1977; Deschamps and Doise, 1978; Diehl, 1989; Vanbeselaere, 1987) have investigated the area of cross-categorization effects. Such studies create four groups, rather than two, by crossing two dichotomous categories (A/B and X/Y). In an early cross-categorization study, Commins and Lockwood (1978) crossed membership in groups of underestimators and overestimators with membership in religious groups. The study took place in Northern Ireland, and, of course, the religious groups were Catholics and Protestants. There was less evidence of ingroup bias in the mixed conditions than in the single conditions. Although the differences fell just short of the tradition-ally accepted statistical criterion of significance, any technique which can cross religious affiliation in Northern Ireland with another trivial classification and produce a decrease in ingroup bias must be counted as theoretically and socially significant.

In a more controlled laboratory setting, Deschamps and Doise (1978) concluded that cross-categorization eliminates ingroup bias. Brown and Turner (1979) argued that this effect was due to the different strength of the two categorization dimensions, and subsequently conducted a study using more equivalent categorization dimensions. They reported some evidence of ingroup bias, but it was markedly weaker than that typically found in two-group experiments. Ingroup bias was strongest in comparisons with the group that was opposite on both categorization dimensions (for example, AX vs BY; this is known as the double-outgroup effect). Vanbeselaere (1987) also found strongly reduced ingroup favouritism in a cross-categorization condition, and only qualified support for the double-outgroup effect. Deschamps (1984) speculated that the reduced, but still apparent, ingroup bias could be a product of the increased number of categories that subjects must consider.

Recently, Hartstone and Augoustinos (in press) conducted a minimal group experiment involving three independent groups, rather than the usual two, to assess whether ingroup bias is restricted to dichotomous categorization or also extends to multiple-group settings under minimal conditions. Some subjects were placed in a two-group setting, and produced the normal ingroup bias. However, subjects placed in a setting with three minimal groups did not produce any significant ingroup bias, suggesting that there may be something particular about dichotomous categorization which elicits ingroup favouritism and outgroup discrimination. It is certainly conceivable from a social identity perspective that a three-group context would elicit ingroup favouritism in the same way a two-group context does, as group members strive to differentiate their respective group positively from the other two. It appears, however, that in a three-group situation mechanisms other than, or in addition to, those cognitive and motivational factors that operate in a two-group setting must be considered.

Oakes (1987) emphasized that category salience is a significant determinant of how subjects generally construe intergroup situations, and of how they behave within specific intergroup experimental contexts. When awareness of group membership is increased, self-categorization as a group member is enhanced, making intergroup differentiation more likely. She argues that 'the sharper the contrast afforded by an intergroup comparison, the more salient intergroup differentiation tends to become' (1987: 120). Hartstone and Augoustinos (in press) suggest that a two-group context provides a clearer and more distinctive differentiation between categories than does a three-group context, at least in artificially created minimal group situations. A three-group structure appears to hinder ingroup–outgroup identification, or an 'us vs them' comparative contrast.

Recent intergroup relations research has emphasized .'real life' social groups rather than the artificially created minimal groups in laboratory settings. In the real world, intergroup discrimination between three distinct social groups undoubtedly occurs. The current war in the Balkans between Serbs, Croats and Muslims is testimony to this. Despite the complexity of multiple group contexts and multiple group identifications which cut across categories, it appears that where real social groups are concerned, intergroup discrimination does occur. While Vanbeselaere (1987) failed to find a strong double-outgroup effect in his minimal cross-categorization study, more recently Hagendoorn and Henke (1991) found a clear double-outgroup effect in their study of intergroup relations in north India: high-caste Hindus discriminated more against lower-class Muslims compared to low-caste Hindus and upper-class Muslims.

In a study most comparable to the three-group study, Wilder and Thompson (1988) found contextual variations in how a moderately different outgroup was evaluated when an extremely different outgroup was present. Wilder and Thompson found that the presence of an extreme outgroup led to a more positive evaluation of a moderately acceptable but unpreferred outgroup, but a more negative evaluation of a moderately rejected outgroup. In the former condition, the moderately acceptable outgroup was assimilated to the ingroup, but in the latter condition differences between the ingroup and the moderately rejected outgroup were accentuated. 'Thus a more distant outgroup can make a closer one more palatable, but only when the latter is not judged to be too different in the first place' (Wilder and Thompson, 1988: 66). Indeed, in the presence of the extreme outgroup, subjects did not demonstrate any ingroup favouritism over the 'acceptable' outgroup. This study strongly suggests that the way in which a specific outgroup is evaluated depends on the presence of other outgroups and the nature of the social comparisons made with each respective group. Perhaps sharper intergroup contrasts are afforded by 'lumping' several outgroups together as 'them' in the 'us vs them' dichotomy, or perhaps one outgroup appears more prototypical or challenging and hence becomes the target, while the other outgroup becomes more acceptable to the ingroup and is assimilated within the ingroup, or perhaps the very nature of what is defined as 'ingroup' and 'outgroup' shifts depending on the comparative context. This last possibility is considered in more detail by self-categorization theory, which is discussed below.

While the results of Hartstone and Augoustinos's three-group study can be accommodated by the principles of SIT and self-categorization theory, they also raise a recurring problem with the minimal group studies. Consistent with Lakoff's (1987) basic oppositional model, if the presence of two groups can more readily 'prime' or access a contrastive and competitive intergroup orientation, then the robust findings of the minimal group paradigm may reflect a culturally and linguistically based predisposition to respond competitively in such situations – a predisposition which disappears when a third group is included. This resurrects the 'demand characteristics' explanation of the minimal group findings.

Self-categorization theory

Tajfel and Turner (1986) based SIT upon the interpersonal–intergroup dimension. But how and why is a situation construed by an individual as 'interpersonal' or 'intergroup' or in between? Partly in response to this, and other, problems Turner (1985; Turner and Oakes, 1989; Turner et al., 1987) developed self-categorization theory (SCT).

In SCT, social identity and personal identity are not qualitatively different forms of identity, but rather represent different forms of self-categorization. Self-categorization can occur on three broad levels: the *superordinate* level (for example, defining self as part of humanity), the *intermediate* level (for example, defining self by particular group memberships) and the *subordinate* level (for example, defining self in individual, personal terms). In some ways, these levels of categorial abstraction of the self resemble the ways in which responses to the Twenty Statements Test are classified (for example, Zurcher, 1977). Naming these levels superordinate, intermediate and subordinate is not intended to convey any greater value in one than the other. They are so-called because of their relative inclusiveness. Higher-order categories include within them all lower-order categories. The ordered structure of categories used by SCT comes from influential work on the categories used by people in the cognitive representation of the physical world (Rosch, 1978).

Self-categorization at one level or another follows the principle of meta-contrast. Categorization always occurs within a social context; it can never be acontextual. Within any one context there always exist several classificatory possibilities. The choice of one possibility rather than another is determined by the *meta-contrast ratio*. The meta-contrast ratio is the ratio of the perceived intercategory differences and the perceived intracategory differences. When the social categories in a situation have meaning for the individuals in that situation, then personal self-categorizations become more salient when the meta-contrast ratio is small (that is, perceived intercategory differences do not greatly exceed perceived intracategory differences) and social self-categorizations become more salient when the meta-contrast ratio is large (that is, perceived intercategory differences greatly exceed perceived intracategory similarities).

Identity, either personal or social, is thus a fluid and contextualized phenomenon. The same relations between people can be perceived either as differences forcing them into different social categories or as similarities binding them within the same social category, depending on the comparative context. For example, a social psychologist at a meeting of the Psychology Department in which he or she works will likely perceive few commonalities and many differences between self and the others in the room, unless of course it is a department fortunate enough to be blessed with several social psychologists. However, the same social psychologist attending a meeting of a university-wide committee is now likely to perceive more commonalities between self and the other psychologists, because of the presence of others providing a greater array of differences. On the other hand, when that social psychologist attends an annual national meeting of social psychologists, differences among all those social psychologists are likely to loom large on the psychological horizon. How one self-categorizes depends entirely on the social context; what is a difference in one context becomes a commonality on another.

Individual ingroup members are more or less *prototypical* of the ingroup, but prototypicality is relative, shifting with differing comparative contexts. An individual's prototypicality is defined by the ratio of the perceived difference between that individual and the other individual members of the ingroup and the perceived difference between that individual and outgroup members. The more an individual resembles other ingroup members (that is, the distance between that individual and the other ingroup members is small) and the more that individual is unlike outgroup members, the more that person is prototypical of the ingroup. The popularity and social attractiveness of specific individual ingroup members is predicted to be directly a function of individual prototypicality (for example, Hogg and Hardie, 1991).

Because self-categorization is context-specific, and self can be variously categorized in individual or group terms, the distinction between personal and social identity originally made in SIT is no longer justified. Rather, personal and social identities represent different levels of self-categorization. The personal is social, and the social personal. As self-categorizations become more social, self is said to become depersonalized. This is not meant in a pejorative sense, but rather just in the sense that the self-categorization is relatively less imbued with personalistic connotations. When self is categorized it is also stereotyped. As will be discussed later in Chapter 9, stereotyping is usually thought of as a process applied to outgroups in which outgroup members are ascribed the same traits or qualities because of their group membership. SCT suggests that self-perception operates in the same way, that self is judged stereotypically on the basis of self-categorizations; to self-stereotype is to perceive identity between self and the ingroup.

Self-categorization theorists insist that SCT is not intended to supersede SIT. It is an extension of it, developing the construct of identity and the process of categorization, reconceptualizing the distinction between personal and social identity, and providing a mechanism for predicting when and how people will self-categorize in one way or another. Whereas SIT is primarily a motivational theory, SCT is primarily cognitive. SCT has been applied to several traditional problems in social psychology, being successful at least in reconceptualizing the fundamental nature of problems such as stereotyping (for example, Oakes et al., 1994) and group polarization and crowd behaviour (for example, McGarty, Turner, Hogg, David and Wetherell, 1992; Turner et al., 1987).

CRITICISMS OF SOCIAL IDENTITY THEORY

Despite the fact that SIT has achieved a position of almost overwhelming prominence in European social psychology, and has been strongly influential outside Europe, it has not been without its critics.

The minimal group paradigm was intended to represent only the classification of individuals into categories on a random or trivial basis. This view has been criticized, on the grounds both that the categories created are not minimal and that such categories are so minimal that they are irrelevant to real groups. Rabbie and Horwitz (1988) suggested that even when minimal groups are created in a random manner this does not necessarily mean that individual subjects do not see an interdependence among themselves. Inter-dependence can arise in one of two ways. First, subjects may believe that the experimenter *must* have some investment in imposing classifications upon them, thereby imputing some meaning to those classifications. Second, and more convincing, subjects' allocation decisions may be influenced by their knowledge that they will receive at the end of the experiment the amount of money that others had allocated to them. Rabbie, Schot and Visser (reported in Rabbie and Horowitz, 1988) instructed subjects that the amount of money they would receive depended only on the allocations made by members of the outgroup. In this case, subjects favoured the outgroup rather than the ingroup; that is, subjects' allocation decisions were strategically influenced by their knowledge of the structure of interdependence in the situation. The implication of this must be that ingroup bias is *not* an automatic consequence of classification. The most basic of minimal situations would be one in which the amount of money a subject receives is independent of the allocation decisions of either ingroup or outgroup members. If ingroup bias occurs when there is no interdependence then that would constitute stronger evidence of an automatic classification effect. To our knowledge, such an experiment has not been carried out, though minimal group studies have been conducted where point allocations do not represent monetary rewards. Rabbie and Horowitz (1988) continued their analysis to the conclusion that a distinction must be made between categories and groups, the latter being different from the former because a group is a 'locomoting entity', it displays social movement toward benefits and away from harm. Any analysis of intergroup relations resting on the operations of categorizations must be, according to Rabbie and Horowitz, incomplete.

In contrast to the view that minimal groups are not minimal, some have argued that they are so minimal that they render any social psychology built upon them likewise minimal. In one of the most vehement criticisms of SIT ever published, Schiffman and Wicklund (1992) argue that the minimal group paradigm struggles to establish a phenomenon worth bothering about (because of the lack of convincing evidence supporting the putative mechanisms driving SIT, namely self-esteem enhancement, and because it has not been convincingly demonstrated that the ingroup bias in minimal group studies is not due to demand characteristics), and even if the ingroup bias effects produced in minimal group studies do merit theoretical attention they do not justify the development of a whole theory. Any and all minimal group effects can be subsumed within extant theories, such as the theories of self-evaluation maintenance (Tesser, 1986) and symbolic self-completion (Wicklund and Gollwitzer, 1982). SIT does not properly constitute a psychological theory, since it posits no prior psychological mechanisms to account for what the individual brings to the group setting, it implies that an individual will adopt any social identity, and that the notion of 'group' in SIT is physicalistic rather than psychological.

While it is encouraging to see a more critical view of SIT being canvassed than has been the case over the last two decades, we believe that Schiffman and Wicklund are misled in some of their criticisms. They appear to ignore the dates on publications when they charge that SIT can be subsumed within extant theories, that given self-evaluation maintenance and symbolic self-completion theories there is no need for SIT. SIT was developed prior to, or coterminously with, these theories. To the extent that these different theories purport to account for the same phenomena (a point we would dispute) there is no historical reason to favour one over the others. Theoretical primacy should be resolved by recourse to theoretical adequacy and inclusivity, not by historical precedent. Criticism that SIT does not account for individual differences (in self-esteem, need for group membership, etc.) must be acknowledged as an area in need of research attention, not as a cause of theoretical despair. There is no inherent reason why SIT cannot account for such individual differences, and SIT is far from alone among social psychological theories in failing to consider individual differences. Indeed, it is almost a hallmark of social psychological theories that they do not consider differences among individuals, otherwise they would be theories of personality. But that is not an adequate defence, since theories should be driven by, and constrained to, the phenomena they attempt to describe and explain, not by disciplinary boundaries and rivalries.

The remaining two criticisms – that SIT assumes that people will adopt any social identity, and that group membership is physicalistic, not psychological – are related. The first of these two points is, we believe, a valid criticism of SIT, but as with the point about individual differences, it is not a necessary or inherent limitation of the theory. Undoubtedly people do not accept any social identity thrust upon them; they actively seek, avoid, resist, dispute and negotiate social identities. But recognizing that does not undercut SIT; it only points to a limitation of the theory's present understanding of the construction of social identity. The charge that classification into ingroup and outgroup in a minimal group setting relies on physicalistic rather than psychological criteria says little. To be sure, the experimental paradigm imposes a 'physicalistic' classification on subjects, and examines the effects of doing so on those subjects' behaviour. But the very point of the minimal group paradigm is that such minimal physicalistic classifications come to have meaning, come to be psychological classifications, for many subjects. This criticism is a restatement of the aims of SIT in its use of the minimal group paradigm, not a criticism.

Two other points are germane to a consideration of the minimal group paradigm. The first is that, by emphasizing the processes of group identification and formation, SIT tends to ignore the system-justificatory functions of particular group identities (Jost and Banaji, 1994). We deal with this point in more detail in Chapter 11. The second is that the minimal group paradigm was developed to provide a baseline on to which would be layered different aspects of groups, such as different relations of interdependence, different size, different status, and so on. Minimal groups were not expected to display any group bias, and the fact that they did disrupted the original research programme and led to the development of SIT. Some research has been conducted within the context of SIT with real groups and occasionally studies have examined the effects of interdependence, size, status and power on artificial intergroup relations in the laboratory. More research in this vein would be a welcome development and return to the original aims of the research programme.

Another major criticism of SIT centres on its claim that intergroup differentiation between ingroup and outgroup ought to increase self-esteem. This is a fundamental postulate of SIT. Despite the basic nature of this hypothesis, there are remarkably few studies testing it, and the evidence from those few is remarkably mixed (see Abrams and Hogg, 1988; Hogg and Abrams, 1990; and Hunter, 1993, for reviews). Extracted fully, the self-esteem hypothesis in SIT contains two parts: that self-esteem of people who display ingroup bias ought to increase as a causal consequence, and that those people with low self-esteem ought to engage in greater ingroup biasing behaviour than those with higher self-esteem. There is no firm evidence supporting either of these two hypotheses. The most likely conclusion to be drawn is that the theory has not fully articulated the role of self-esteem in intergroup differentiation. It is plausible to argue that self-esteem should not be the construct of interest anyway. SIT is concerned more with social identity than with personal identity, and the evaluation of social identities does not constitute self-esteem, which is the evaluation of personal identities. The proper focus of investigation should therefore be group-esteem. This tack has been followed empirically and theoretically by, among others, Crocker and Luhtanen (1990; Luhtanen and Crocker, 1991, 1992). One recent example of research which shows that group-esteem and self-esteem can operate in opposite directions is provided by Long, Spears and Manstead (1994). In a somewhat different vein, Hunter (1993) has argued, first, that the measures of self and group-esteem which are usually used are inadequate because of their simplifying assumptions of unidimensionality, and, second, that individuals' self- and group-esteem are not likely to be influenced by randomly created trivial groups in a minimal group setting. Following the first point, Hunter has demonstrated that psychometrically more astute multidimensional measures of self-concept and self-esteem do detect group influences, but only on some dimensions. And following his second point, these effects are detectable with real, rather than contrived, groups. The general conclusion regarding the relationship between category member-ships, intergroup differentiation and personal and social identities and esteems must be that the whole area, which is central to SIT, has been underexamined, and that if future theoretical and empirical examination fails to articulate and support these relationships then perhaps SIT itself ought to be re-examined.

SUMMARY

This chapter has outlined the minimal group paradigm and the prevalent tendency toward ingroup bias. Social identity theory was described as an explanation developed to account for ingroup bias in the minimal group setting. It was argued that SIT may not be as widely generalizable as is often assumed, being limited to groups displaying a relational ideology in a collectivistic context, and that the ingroup bias effect may be partially a product of the dichotomous nature of the minimal group situation. Criticisms of SIT were also discussed.

NOTES

1   Here and elsewhere we describe race and gender as closed groups. Strictly speaking, though, neither is completely closed. It is possible to alter the phenotypic markers of race and gender, by using medication to alter skin complexion or surgery to alter sex characteristics. These are drastic and rare behaviours, though. For most intents and purposes, and certainly for ours in this chapter, race and gender are closed groups.

2   It is interesting to note that a theoretical argument can be made supporting predictions in the opposite direction. Individualistic cultures promote competition more than do collectivistic cultures, and therefore might be expected to produce stronger tendencies toward intergroup differentiation, and toward evaluating individual and group characteristics relatively. Such an argument would fit results from some minimal group studies suggesting that females are less likely to engage in competitive strategies than are males (for example, Williams, 1984), although the gender difference is not always found. It is also consistent with some cross-cultural evidence that the ingroup bias typically found in minimal group studies is weaker, though still present, in more communally oriented cultures.

6

SOCIAL
REPRESENTATIONS

The central and exclusive object of social psychology should be the study of all that pertains to *ideology* and to *communication* from the point of view of their structure, their genesis and their function. The proper domain of our discipline is the study of cultural processes which are responsible for the organization of knowledge in a society, for the establishment of inter-individual relationships in the context of social and physical environment, for the formation of social movements (groups, parties, institutions) through which men [and women] act and interact, for the codification of inter-individual and intergroup conduct which creates a common social reality with its norms and values, the origin of which is to be sought again in the social context. (Moscovici, 1972: 55–6; original emphasis)

Moscovici's theory of social representations emerged largely as a result of such concerns, and began to develop and flourish amidst calls for a more *social* social psychology. The theory of social representations has as its imperative to reintroduce a social focus to the study of social psychology by reinstating the primacy of collective concepts such as culture and ideology. It seeks to understand individual psychological functioning by placing the individual in his or her social, cultural and collective milieu. The theory views psychological experience as being mediated and determined by the individual's belongingness to a collectivity of others who share similar views, experiences and a common environment and language. Unlike the atomistic notion of the individual which characterizes many theories of social psychology, social representations theory begins with the premise that the individual is primarily a social being whose own existence and identity is rooted in a collectivity. It therefore attempts to understand how social processes impinge upon and influence the social psychological functioning of individuals and groups. Social representations theory, however, does not juxtapose the individual and society, but rather sees the former in a dialectical relationship with society, both as a product of society (its conventions, norms and values) and as an active participant who can effect change in society.

SOCIAL REPRESENTATIONS THEORY

Definition of social representations

The concept of 'representation' has had a long history and spreads across a number of interrelated disciplines in the social sciences. Moscovici draws on diverse sources when explicating the theory of social representations. This ranges from the anthropological work of Lévy-Bruhl, which is concerned with the belief systems (collective representations) of small-scale traditional societies, to Piaget's work in child psychology, which focuses upon the child's understanding and representation of the world (Moscovici, 1989). The most important influence on Moscovici's theory, however, is Durkheim.

Moscovici initially based the concept of social representations on Durkheim's (1898) notion of 'collective representations'. Durkheim used this concept to differentiate collective thought from individual thought. Collective representations were seen by Durkheim to be widely shared by members of a society, to be social in origin and generation, and to be about society. Although he regarded representations as emerging from a 'substratum' of individuals, he strongly maintained that they could not be explained at the individual level. Instead, collective representations such as myths, legends and traditions were phenomena with their own distinctive characteristics, independent from the individuals who expounded them, which required explanation at the sociological or societal level (Lukes, 1975).

For Moscovici, social representations are the ideas, thoughts, images and knowledge which members of a collectivity share: consensual universes of thought which are socially created and socially communicated to form part of a 'common consciousness'. Social representations refer to the stock of common knowledge and information which people share in the form of common-sense theories about the social world. They are comprised of both conceptual and pictorial elements. Through these, members of a society are able to construct social reality. Moscovici has defined social representations thus:

> . . . social representations are cognitive systems with a logic and language of their own. . . . They do not represent simply 'opinions

about', 'images of' or 'attitudes towards' but 'theories' or 'branches of knowledge' in their own right, for the discovery and organisation of reality. (Moscovici, 1973: xii)

Social representations . . . concern the contents of everyday thinking and the stock of ideas that gives coherence to our religious beliefs, political ideas and the connections we create as spontaneously as we breathe. They make it possible for us to classify persons and objects, to compare and explain behaviours and to objectify them as parts of our social setting. While representations are often to be located in the minds of men and women, they can just as often be found 'in the world', and as such examined separately. (Moscovici, 1988: 214)

As evidenced by the above quotes, the primacy of the cognitive is an important defining feature of the theory. Human thought is regarded as an *environment* – always present and enveloping. Representations are hypothesized to mediate and determine cognitive activity, giving this activity its form and meaning.

Social representations range from hegemonic structures that are shared by a society or nation to differentiated knowledge structures that are shared by subgroups within a collectivity (Moscovici, 1988). The former are highly coercive and prescriptive through their continual historical reproduction and are akin to Durkheim's original notion of *collective* representations. Collective representations are more characteristic of small traditional societies, such as the witchcraft belief system among the Azande (Evans-Pritchard, 1976). Hegemonic representations are more difficult to locate within contemporary industrial societies. The individualist conception of the person as the centre of cognition, action and process could be said to be such a collectively shared representation which permeates most aspects of thinking within western industrialized societies (Lukes, 1973), a theme to which we will return in subsequent chapters of the book.

Moscovici's concept of *social* representations is differentiated from Durkheim's *collective* representations in that the former emphasizes the dynamic and changing nature of representations ('social life in the making') and also takes into account the array of differentiated knowledge shared by subgroups within contemporary western societies (Moscovici, 1988: 219). It is through shared representations that social groups establish their identities and come to differentiate themselves from other groups within society. Like Durkheim, Moscovici argues that social psychology's primary task is to study the origins, structure and inner dynamics of social representations and their impact on society; that is, to study the nature of a 'thinking society' (Moscovici, 1984a). Just as society can be considered to be an economic and political system, so also should it be viewed as a thinking system (Moscovici, 1988). Social psychology should therefore concern itself with the nature of a thinking society and become an 'anthropology of the modern culture' (Moscovici, 1989: 34).

The role of representations is to conventionalize objects, persons and events, to locate them within a familiar categorial context. Representations are also prescriptive in nature: determined by tradition and convention, representations impose themselves on our cognitive activity. Often we are unaware of these conventions, so that we remain unaware of the prejudices and social determination of our thought, preferring to view our thoughts as 'common sense'. Indeed, Moscovici has likened the study of social representations to the study of common sense, making this approach very similar to that of Berger and Luckmann's (1967) on the social construction of reality.[1]

> By social representations we mean a set of concepts, statements and explanations originating in daily life in the course of inter-individual communications. They are the equivalent, in our society, of the myths and belief systems in traditional societies; they might even be said to be the contemporary version of common sense. (Moscovici, 1981: 181)

In addition to their consensual nature, what makes representations social is their creation and generation, through social interaction and communication by individuals and groups. Social representations originate from social communication and construct the understanding of the social world, enabling interaction within groups sharing the representation. The theory's clear imperative is the need to study social communication and interaction as the *sine qua non* of social cognition.

Unlike Durkheim, whom Moscovici argues has a rather static conception of representations, Moscovici emphasizes the plasticity of representations, characterizing them as dynamic structures: '. . . there is a continual need to reconstitute "common sense" or the form of understanding that creates the substratum of images and meanings, without which no collectivity can operate' (Moscovici, 1984a: 19). Once created, representations behave like 'autonomous entities' or 'material forces':

> . . . they lead a life of their own, circulate, merge, attract and repel each other, and give birth to new representations, while old ones die out . . . being shared by all and strengthened by tradition, it constitutes a social reality sui generis. The more its origin is forgotten, and its conventional

nature ignored, the more fossilised it becomes. That which is ideal gradually becomes materialised. (Moscovici, 1984a: 13)

Central to Moscovici's concept of social representations are the two processes that generate these representations: anchoring and objectification. These are the processes by which unfamiliar objects, events or stimuli are rendered familiar. The purpose of all representations is to give the unfamiliar a familiar substance. Moscovici accords primary importance to the need for individuals to make sense of and grasp the nature of an unfamiliar object, because that which is foreign and alien is threatening and frightening. People make sense of that which is unfamiliar by giving it meaning, and the role of representations is to guide this process of attributing meaning. People search for meaning among what they already know and with which they are familiar.

> . . . the images, ideas and language shared by a given group always seem to dictate the initial direction and expedient by which the group tries to come to terms with the unfamiliar. Social thinking owes more to convention and memory than to reason; to traditional structures rather than to current intellectual or perceptual structures. (Moscovici, 1984: 26)

Anchoring

Anchoring refers to the classification and naming of unfamiliar objects or social stimuli by comparing them with the existing stock of familiar and culturally accessible categories. In classifying, we compare with a prototype or model, and thus derive a perspective on the novel stimulus by determining its relationship to the model or prototype. When we compare, we either decide that something is similar to a prototype, that is, we generalize certain salient features of the prototype to the unfamiliar stimulus, or we decide that something is different, that is, we particularize and differentiate between the object and the prototype. If we decide in favour of similarity, the unfamiliar acquires the characteristics of the model. In some cases when discrepancy exists, the object is readjusted so as to fit the defining features of the prototype. Thus classifying and naming always involve comparisons with a prototype.

> The ascendancy of the test case is due . . . to its concreteness, to a kind of vividness which leaves such a deep imprint in our memory that we are able to use it thereafter as a 'model' against which we measure

individual cases and any image that even remotely resembles it. (Moscovici, 1984a: 32)

Moscovici refers to the assignment of names and labels in our culture as a 'nominalistic tendency'. The process of naming something takes on a solemn significance. It imbues that which is named with meaning, and thus locates it within a society's 'identity matrix'. Only then can the object be represented. 'Indeed representation is, basically, a system of classification and denotation, of allotting categories and names'. Thus, representations are reflected in the way we classify and allot categories and names to stimuli because, by classifying or categorizing, we are, in essence, revealing our conceptual frameworks, 'our theory of society and of human nature' (Moscovici, 1984a: 30). By classifying and naming an object, we are able not only to recognize and understand it but also to evaluate it, either positively or negatively, or view it as normal or abnormal. Thus 'naming is not a purely intellectual operation aiming at a clarity or logical coherence. It is an operation related to a social attitude' (Moscovici, 1984a: 35).

Objectification

Objectification is the process by which unfamiliar and abstract notions, ideas and images are transformed into concrete and objective common-sense realities. 'To objectify is to discover the iconic quality of an imprecise idea or being, to reproduce a concept in an image' (Moscovici, 1984a: 38). Eventually, 'the image is wholly assimilated and what is *perceived* replaces what is *conceived*. . . . Thus by a sort of logical imperative, images become elements of reality rather than elements of thought' (Moscovici, 1984a: 40).

The proposition that ideas or images are transformed into material forces which shape and constitute reality is, again, very similar to Berger and Luckmann's (1967) views on the social construction of reality. Many scientific and technological concepts undergo such a transformation as they disseminate into everyday lay usage and discourse. Moscovici's (1961) own research on the diffusion of psychoanalytic concepts throughout sections of French society is essentially a study of the objectification process. Moscovici was able to show how laypeople adopted Freudian notions such as 'complexes' and 'neuroses' and used them to explain their own behaviour and the behaviour of others. In the process of this usage, these conceptual and analytic categories were transformed into objective entities with physical properties rendering them with an independent existence. So, abstract constructs such as 'mind' or 'ego' are perceived as physical entities, and 'complexes' and 'neuroses' are construed as objective conditions that afflict people. This process of objectification is akin to that of the metaphor, whereby any new phenomenon may be accommodated in terms of its similarity to the already known (Lakoff and Johnson, 1980). The process of objectification primarily refers to the human tendency to simplify or distil complex information into a core or 'figurative nucleus' of pictorial and cognitive elements which are stored in memory and accessed when required.

As Moscovici and Hewstone (1983) point out, the diffusion and popularization of scientific concepts throughout society is occurring at a rapid rate through the mass media. The increasing proliferation of scientific 'knowledge' throughout all sectors of society has made the lay public 'amateur' scientists, 'amateur' economists, 'amateur' psychologists, 'amateur' doctors, etc. Ordinary people with little expert training discuss issues such as the greenhouse effect, damage to the ozone layer, inflation and the current accounts deficit, stress-related ailments, familial and relationship problems, cancer prevention diets, etc. Most of this knowledge becomes an integral part of mass culture and, ultimately, what will come to be regarded as common sense.

Furthermore, Moscovici and Hewstone (1983) describe the three external processes by which knowledge is transformed into common sense or a social representation: the personification of knowledge, figuration and ontologizing. First, the personification of knowledge links the idea, theory or concept to a person or group – for example, Freud and psychoanalysis, or Friedman and monetarism. The association of an idea to a person gives the idea a concrete existence. Second, figuration is the process by which an abstract notion is embodied or dominated by a metaphorical image so that, again, what is conceptual is made more accessible or concrete. For example, Hewstone's (1986) study on social representations of the European Community found that people used metaphorical language and images which had originated in the media, such as milk 'lakes' and butter 'mountains' when referring to food surpluses of the community. More recently, the 'Gulf War' (1990–1) engendered many graphic metaphors which originated in the media. A prime example was the description of hostages in Iraq before the onset of the war as Hussein's 'human shields'. Third, ontologizing is the process by which a verbal or conceptual construct is imbued with physical properties as in the above examples of abstract concepts such as 'mind' or 'neurosis' being construed as material phenomena. These three processes all contribute to making highly specialized and technical knowledge more accessible to the lay community so that communication about this knowledge is able to take place.

The consensual and reified universes

There are two distinguishable theories contained within Moscovici's writings: the phenomenal theory and the meta-theory (Wells, 1987). Thus far, only the phenomenal theory has been detailed, which describes the phenomena of social representations as socially and culturally conditioned ways of understanding everyday reality and the processes by which they are generated: anchoring and objectification. The meta-theory refers to the assertion by Moscovici that there are two distinct and different types of reality: the reified and the consensual universes; the world of science and the world of common sense. The transformation of expert knowledge into common sense marks the distinction between the reified and consensual universes. The consensual universe is comprised of social representations which are created, used and reconstituted by people to make sense of everyday life. The reified universe is one which the expert scientist inhabits – one in which the scientist subjects reality to rigorous scrutiny and experimentation. The laws of science govern the reified universe in which human thinking takes a logical and rational form. Moscovici argues that it is the consensual universe with which social psychologists should be interested: how ordinary people create and use meaning to make sense of their world. Moscovici writes,

> It is readily apparent that the sciences are the means by which we understand the reified universe, while social representations deal with the consensual. The purpose of the first is to establish a chart of the forces, objects and events which are independent of our desires and outside of our awareness and to which we must react impartially and submissively. By concealing values and advantages they aim at encouraging intellectual precision and empirical evidence. Representations, on the other hand, restore collective awareness and give it shape, explaining objects and events so that they become accessible to everyone and coincide with our immediate interests. (1984a: 22)

This is, however, a particularly traditional but naïve view of the scientific production of knowledge, a view which is increasingly being criticized by those interested in the sociology of scientific knowledge.[2]

The increasing proliferation of science and expert knowledge endows the reified universe with considerable significance in the modern world. This expert knowledge is transformed or re-presented and appropriated in the consensual universe so that it is made more accessible and intelligible. This re-presented version eventually takes form and contributes to the stock of common-sense knowledge which people draw upon to understand social reality. Laypeople reduce complex ideas and theories to a 'figurative nucleus' of images and concepts to re-present this knowledge in a more simplified and culturally accessible form.

The case of psychoanalysis has already been discussed. Moscovici and Hewstone (1983) also discuss the transformation which the theory of hemispheric specialization underwent when popularized in the consensual universe. Most laypeople, through the popular press and media, have been introduced to the notion that the left hemisphere specializes in logical, rational and analytic thinking, while the right hemisphere is said to engage in more intuitive, emotional and subjective functions. This cerebral dualism, which originated in the reified universe of neuroscience, was used by people and the popular press to explain a wide range of opposing cultural tendencies in human behaviour, such as femininity vs masculinity, rational vs intuitive thought. The split brain view has proliferated so widely that it is now endowed with an objective reality and has become part of common-sense knowledge: a social representation.

> Once a society has adopted such a paradigm or figurative nucleus it finds it easier to talk about whatever the paradigm stands for, and because of this facility the words referring to it are used more often. Then formulae and clichés emerge that sum it up and join together images that were formerly distinct. It is not simply talked about but exploited in various social situations as a means of understanding others and oneself, of choosing and deciding. (Moscovici, 1984a: 39)

EMPIRICAL RESEARCH IN THE SOCIAL REPRESENTATIONS TRADITION

Several criticisms have been levelled at Moscovici's concept, including debate as to whether social representations indeed constitutes a 'theory' (see Potter and Litton, 1985, and replies by Hewstone, 1985; Moscovici, 1985; Semin, 1985). Jahoda's (1988) reservations about the status of the theory of social representations rest on the question of its distinctiveness from other allied concepts such as attitude, ideology, culture or belief system. There is little doubt that the concept of social representations has a strong affinity with these concepts. What Moscovici's theory has done, however, is to reintroduce the neglected collective and social nature of these concepts into the domain of social psychology.

More recently, attempts have been made to delineate the relationship between the concept of social representations and other allied concepts such as belief systems, values and ideology (Fraser and Gaskell, 1990). Indeed, Chapters 7 and 8 will explore points of convergence between social representations theory and concepts which are currently having a large impact on social cognition research, particularly the concepts of schema and attribution. What distinguishes the concept of social representations from the traditional treatment of concepts such as values, belief system and ideology is that it has been presented within a theoretical social psychological framework. These concepts, while frequently referred to within the social psychological literature, have not been contextualized within any over-arching social theory. What empirical research has been conducted on ideology, values and beliefs has focused on measuring variability in these domains, treating them more as personality constructs and, therefore, essentially as individual phenomena (for example, Eysenck and Wilson, 1978, Rokeach, 1960).[3] Notable is the very different epistemological status these concepts have within other disciplines, such as sociology and anthropology. The same can be said about the concept of attitude in traditional social psychological theory. This is made clear in Chapter 2, where we document the psychological research pertaining to this construct. Thus social representations theory attempts to deindividualize these concepts and reinstate their collective character within an integrated *social psychological* theory (Jaspars and Fraser, 1984).

Specific criticisms of the theory will be detailed in the next section, but it needs to be emphasized at this point that many critics have argued that the concept is vague and loosely defined, and that the theory is too abstract in nature and therefore difficult to translate empirically. The vagueness of the concept and its associated corollaries, in fact, is what Moscovici sees as a welcome strength, having a positive role to play in the conduct of research. Moscovici argues that prescriptive definitions and formulae for conducting research stifle the creative generation of ideas. Social representations theory is not at the stage of development where predictive experimental hypotheses can be formulated but, far from viewing this as a problem, Moscovici (1985) prefers to see the generation of data and theories via descriptive and exploratory research.

As Semin (1985) points out, the elusiveness surrounding Moscovici's concept is, to some extent, unavoidable, given the inherent difficulties of studying social psychological phenomena at the collective level as compared to the traditional individual level of analysis. Critics' objections to social representations research are related not only to the notion itself but also to Moscovici's perhaps *laisser-faire* approach to the methodology that is to be utilized for such research. The use of a wide range of methodologies is needed to translate empirically Moscovici's notion of a 'thinking society'. To date, empirical investigations have ranged from the experimental (Abric, 1984; Codol, 1984) and quantitative (Doise, Clemence and Lorenzi-Cioldi, 1993), to the ethnographic (Jodelet, 1991). Indeed methods other than the conventional positivist experiments are encouraged and favoured, since the very nature of collective phenomena makes them difficult to research adequately in a laboratory setting alone (Farr, 1989).

The next section surveys empirical studies which are representative of the social representations tradition. It does not intend to document definitively the empirical research to date, for this is quite extensive and covers many content areas (see Breakwell and Canter, 1993; Farr, 1987; Jodelet, 1989). Rather, this section is designed to give a flavour of the kinds of representations studied thus far, and to illustrate the range of methodologies which have been used to research this elusive concept. Further empirical studies will be referred to and documented throughout subsequent chapters when illustrating specific theoretical and conceptual issues.

Herzlich (1973) on representations of health and illness

One of the most widely cited studies in the social representations literature is Herzlich's (1973) study on the representations of health and illness in France in the 1960s. An open interview method was used, structured around themes which were found to be important in a pilot interview study of 20 subjects. Eighty subjects were interviewed, half of whom were classified as professional people, the other half as middle class. Most of the respondents lived in Paris, and 12 lived in a small village in Normandy.

One of the most dominant and recurring themes that Herzlich found was the view that the urban way of life is a primary determinant in the genesis of illness. Many respondents described how city life resulted in fatigue and nervous tension. This state, in turn, made the individual less resistant and more vulnerable to disease and illness. Mental disorders, heart disease and cancer were illnesses most frequently referred to by respondents as being generated by the way of life. While the external environment, that is, urban life, was the most important causative agent in illness, internal factors such as the individual's predisposition, constitution and temperament were thought to determine whether individuals are able to resist or defend themselves from the onset of illness.

Illness was seen to be generated by the external environment; the individual was seen as representing the source of health. Illness was not viewed as an inherent part of the individual, but as something external to him or her. Thus health and illness were seen to be the outcome of struggle and opposition between the passive individual and an active factor, the way of life.

Respondents described urban life as being both unhealthy and constraining. The quality of food in the cities was viewed with suspicion, the air and water viewed as being contaminated with pollutants. Two-thirds of the sample referred to the notion of toxicity. Surprisingly, only half of the sample referred to the more popularized notion of germs. Toxicity referred to the ingestion and retention of harmful substances in the food, air and water. It was regarded as a cumulative process which was dangerous in the long run. Noise and the rhythm of life in cities were seen as constraining. These negative aspects of urban life were seen as being imposed upon the individual, who is powerless and helpless to change the situation. Frequent references were made to healthier ways of life, such as life in the country where food, water and air are cleaner and the pace and rhythm of life are slower and calmer. Technology and the products of human activity were equated with all that was regarded as unhealthy and artificial.

> If illness arises from a conflict between the individual and society, the unhealthy arises in the last resort from the antagonism perceived to exist between what is felt to be the nature of man [sic] and the form and product of his activities. (Herzlich, 1973: 38)

Herzlich concludes that the representation of health and illness seems to be structured around a number of opposing concepts: internal vs external, healthy vs unhealthy, natural vs unnatural, the individual vs society.

Respondents used many categorizations and classifications to differentiate illnesses, but these were applied in a haphazard way. Indices of classification included severity, whether or not it was painful, duration and nature of onset. The interesting feature about the indices is their non-medical character. Illnesses were not categorized along organic, anatomical or physiological attributes, as they are usually by the medical profession. Instead, respondents used attributes which conveyed information about the degree and ways in which the illness affects the life of the individual. People used predominantly a personal frame of reference when classifying illnesses. This was how various illnesses acquired their meaning and shape. People spoke of illness in terms of the extent of interruption in the daily activities and role responsibilities of the individual. The real criterion of illness was not its inherent anatomical or physiological character, but the level of inactivity and disruption it held for the individual. For many, inactivity was regarded as the most important feature of illness, even more important than pain. Mood and personality changes were thought to be associated with disruption to normal life. Thus, as with health, behavioural criteria are important in defining illness. The experience of illness, therefore, acquires meaning through its effects on the individual's daily life, role obligations and relations with others.

Herzlich concludes that the stable conceptual framework of the representation of health and illness in her study was structured around the dichotomy between individual and society. Health is seen as a subjective experience which allows individuals to be integrated in their society and to participate and fulfil their role obligations. On the other hand, illness, through inactivity and disruption, results in exclusion from society. Thus the subjective states of health and illness acquire meaning through the social behaviour of the healthy and the sick person.

Herzlich's research has been treated as a milestone in social representations research, not merely for its findings but also for the use of a qualitative methodology advocated by critics of mainstream experimental research. Farr (1977) approvingly cites Herzlich's research as an example of the collection of 'naïve unnegotiated accounts' advocated by Harré and Secord (1972). However, Farr also emphasizes the problems associated with eliciting lay accounts from respondents and accepting the accounts at 'face value'. Farr argues that the result obtained by Herzlich, mainly that illness was equated with society and health with the individual, is an 'attribution artefact' and is common when people are asked to discuss favourable outcomes (health) as compared to unfavourable outcomes (illness). This is because the former are usually attributed to the self and the latter to the environment. Thus the individual (health) and society (illness) dichotomy found in Herzlich's research is an artefact of the 'self-serving' bias that attribution theorists have found in more mainstream research contexts (see Chapter 4). Farr suggests that, whenever a research procedure is adopted to elicit accounts of favourable as opposed to unfavourable events, one can predict a priori that respondents' accounts will reflect such an attributional structure.

Of course, medical anthropology has traditionally concerned itself with how the experience of health and illness is understood and communicated within cultural collectivities (Evans-Pritchard, 1976; Kleinman, 1980). Similarly, there is growing interest in lay conceptions of health and illness within the mainstream of social and health psychology (for example, Lau and Hartman, 1983; Lau, Bernard and Hartman, 1989; Meyer, Leventhal and Guttman, 1985). Some of this research will be described in Chapter 8 when we consider the relationship between explanations for everyday experiences and events and social knowledge. While most of this research is referred to as 'common-sense representations' of illness, it does not adopt a social representations theoretical perspective but, rather, uses theoretical models predominant within social cognition research to understand the way in which people cognitively organize, structure and understand information about illnesses in general and specific disease processes. This research has involved a combination of methods to explore representations of illness including open-ended and fixed questionnaire responses. What distinguishes this research from Herzlich's is the application of sophisticated quantitative analyses to the obtained data.

Representations of mental disorder

Another research study in the social representations tradition in the health area is de Rosa's (1987) research on the representations of mental illness by Italian children and adults. de Rosa argues that the social images of madness throughout history yield multifaceted or 'polymorphic' representations of madness. These have been produced by the dialectical relationship between representations originating and emerging from the scientific and legal worlds (the reified universe) and the everyday consensual world which is filled with lay images, beliefs and common understandings of madness. de Rosa argues against the orthodox historical view of madness which sees it as a linear progression from the conception of mental illness as supernatural possession, dominant in the Middle Ages, to the medicalized and psychotherapeutic conceptions of the present day. Rather, she argues that from the time of Hippocrates and Plato there have existed multiple images and conceptions of madness, most of which still remain in our collective awareness.

In a number of studies, de Rosa traces the developmental path, from childhood to maturity, of the social representations of madness. As well as using verbal questionnaire techniques in the form of social distance scales and semantic differentials to elicit these representations, she asked her respondents to produce pictorial representations of madness which were content analysed. We will only be detailing her research results utilizing the latter (non-conventional) method, not only because of the richness of the data it produced but also to illustrate the range of methodologies which have been utilized in the empirical work on social representations.

Seven hundred and twenty subjects (children aged between 5 and 16 years and adults of different sex, social class, urban and rural residence) produced 2160 drawings for analysis. Each subject was asked to produce three drawings: one of a human figure, a drawing of a 'madman' (test B) and a drawing 'as' a madman (test C), all of which were coded on various dimensions. It was hoped that test C drawings would stimulate the expression of projective elements which may be inhibited in the drawings of test B. de Rosa compared these drawings with iconographic material such as popular and artistic prints, anthropological and mythological references from various historical periods, in order to investigate core figurative representations which appeared in the subjects' drawings.

In analysing the drawings, de Rosa found that for both children and adults the madman was represented as a social deviant, whereas the drawings 'as' a madman (test C) contained magic-fantastic elements. Test C drawings ranged from positive connotations of the madman to negative connotations. The former consisted of drawings of clowns, jesters, buffoons and fairies. In some drawings the madman was represented as an 'artist' (for example, a painter) or 'egghead' (a genius). All of these figures represent an element of expressive freedom. At the negative pole, drawings of devils and monsters predominated. de Rosa points out that it is not difficult to find such representations in historical iconographic material, particularly that which expresses the 'positive' side of madness. These likeable 'madmen' are viewed as escaping from the routine of everyday roles, behaviour and 'normal' parameters of thought (for example, the Fool in the tarot cards).

Demonic representations of madness, explicit in some of the drawings, were a common representation in medieval times. Also prototypical were representations of the madman as a monster. The monstrous features varied, but dominant was the theme of human–animal contamination (for example, cock-man, monkey-man, toad-woman). Mythological as well as misshapen figures were also common (for example, centaur, cyclops, androgynous figures).

Test B drawings, as mentioned earlier, depicted elements of deviation rather than the monstrous. These represented the mad-man as a social outsider. Stereotypic nuclei included individuals breaking social norms by behaving incongruously and inappropriately (for example, undressing in the street, cursing and raving). Other drawings contained deviation in the form of violent and criminalized elements, expressing the stereotype of the mad murderer. Western history attests to the dominance of the criminalized representation of madness.

Interestingly, madness as a social deviation was also represented by more contemporary versions of deviant behaviour such as drawings of drug addicts and drunkards. The social dropout was a common representation in the drawings of adolescents. Common also was the depiction of the madman as a tramp, ragamuffin, dirty and dressed in ragged clothes.

While the representation of madness as deviation was common and recurrent, the medicalized representation was not common in the drawings of children or adults. While research using verbal methods finds that, from the age of 8–9 years, the medicalized representation begins to replace the criminalized representation, this linear progression was not evident in the drawings. de Rosa speculates that this may reflect the difficulty of expressing such a representation pictorially. Drawings which contained medicalized elements included drawings of institutionalized people, the organically sick, the physically handicapped and the cognitively deranged who were subject to delirium or hallucinations. Some drawings also represented madmen as neurotic individuals, obsessed by their own problems, and as depressed people with suicidal and self-injuring tendencies.

de Rosa shows how the range of stereotypic nuclei produced in the drawings by children and adults corresponds to the variety of conceptions of madness found throughout history and within contemporary society. The cognitive formation of stereotypes of madness seems to revolve around the bipolar themes of normal–abnormal, healthy–sick, beautiful–ugly. Psychosocially, these bipolar themes, with their evaluative connotations, are fundamental in the establishment and development of ingroup and outgroup relations within any society.

Outside the social representations tradition there has been a long history of attitudinal research in the mental health area. This has comprised research on public attitudes toward the mentally ill and mental illness in general (Rabkin, 1972; Sarbin and Mancuso, 1970), attitudes of mental health personnel toward conflicting models of mental illness (Cohen and Struening, 1962; Gilbert and Levinson, 1956; Nevid and Morrison, 1980), and psychiatric patients' attitudes to their disorders (Rabkin, 1972).

Within this latter line of research, mental health representations have been shown to have important behavioural implications for patients. Farina, Fisher, Getter and Fisher (1978) found that subjects who received a disease representation of mental disorder were more likely to adopt a helpless orientation toward therapy than subjects who were exposed to a social learning representation. In a similar vein, Augoustinos (1986) found that psychiatric inpatients who conceptualized their problems as an 'illness' were significantly more likely to adopt a sick role than patients who defined such problems in non-medical (psychosocial) terms. Thus, research outside the social representations tradition has investigated the way in which models, and knowledge about mental disorder which originate in the scientific universe, are adopted by patients to make sense of their situation. The 'theories', 'models' or 'representations' that they adopt can have important behavioural consequences.

de Rosa's research can be contrasted with attitudinal studies of mental illness by her efforts to elicit, non-verbally, figurative images of mental illness. By comparing and evaluating these with historiographic material, connections are made between her respondents' representations and western society's cultural or collective representations of madness.

Intergroup representations

Empirical research has also investigated Moscovici's claim that different categories of people hold different representations of their social world, and that such shared representations are fundamental in establishing group identities (Moscovici and Hewstone, 1983). Hewstone, Jaspars and Lalljee's (1982) study on the different intergroup representational structures held by public and comprehensive schoolboys in England and Di Giacomo's (1980) research on the different lexicons used by university students and the student leaders of a protest movement will be discussed as studies designed to investigate this claim.

Hewstone et al.'s (1982) research attempts to demonstrate the dialectical nature of the relationship between social representations, social identity processes and intergroup attributions. The research was conducted on two groups which have had a history of intergroup conflict in England: schoolboys from a private fee-paying school (referred to as a 'public school' in England) and schoolboys from a state school (referred to as a 'comprehensive school' in
· England). Given the clear difference in status and the traditional rivalry between the two education systems, the schoolboys were expected to have well-defined and extensively shared representations of themselves and of each other. These representations were

hypothesized to contribute to the establishment of a positive social identity for each group, via the process of intergroup social comparisons.

Twenty public school (PS) boys and 20 comprehensive school (CS) boys with an average age of 16 years were asked to write a 20-minute essay on the similarities and differences between PS boys and CS boys. The 40 essays were content analysed by eight independent judges. The intergroup similarities and differences were coded by a word or phrase on a separate index card. Judges then placed all cards with similar phrases, words and meanings into the same pile and assigned a name to each category.

Interestingly, very few intergroup similarities were mentioned. The overwhelming number of contrasts made by the schoolboys noted differences between the respective groups. There was considerable agreement between the groups on the following differences: the better future prospects and superior social background of the PS boys; academic values, for example PS boys saw themselves and were seen by CS boys to be more hard-working and disciplined; and academic structure, for example PS boys referred to streaming, small classes and the extensive choice of subjects which led to better academic standards, and CS boys also mentioned better structures in PS schools such as small classes and well-paid teachers.

Despite this agreement the respective schoolboys appeared to attach different evaluative connotations to these categories. Whereas the PS boys described themselves as 'hard-working', the CS boys were more likely to describe them as 'swots'. PS boys saw their school as providing a 'training for life', whereas CS boys saw public schools as an environment in which to meet 'string-pullers'. The authors argue that these evaluative elements may contribute to the establishment of a positive ingroup identity.

Each school group also mentioned their own unique differences between the groups which were not shared by the other. PS boys were more likely to refer to their own superior intellectual ability and to the discipline problems and anti-social behaviour of CS boys. They were also more likely to refer to the coeducational nature of comprehensive schools, which led to better relations between boys and girls, and to the different political and social attitudes of CS and PS boys. In contrast, CS boys were more likely to mention the 'snobbishness' of PS boys and their socially superior language. They also characterized PS boys as being polite, boring and hard-working. As the authors point out, it is interesting that the PS boys' essays contained both positive (for example, intellectual ability) and negative characteristics (for example, poor social relations with girls) of their own group, whereas the CS boys did not define themselves in respect of their own positive features, but as a contrast to the negative characteristics they ascribed to the PS boys. This, of course, may reflect the differences in social status between the two groups, the PS boys' higher status allowing room for negative descriptions of their own group, which would not seriously endanger their overall positive social identity.

The authors conclude that, although there were some categories shared by both groups, overall, the two groups of schoolboys possessed very different representations of themselves and of each other which were shared extensively within their own respective group. Such representations may be important in establishing positive ingroup identities by which groups define themselves and their relative place in society.

Di Giacomo's (1980) research investigated the social representations of a protest movement held by students at the Catholic University of Louvain. The aim of the protest was to challenge the Belgian government's policy to increase annual enrolment fees at universities, along with proposed reductions in student grants and university budgets. He compared the students' representations with the stated aims and objectives of the local protest committee, to understand why the student population as a whole, despite its strong opposition to the government decisions, failed to ally itself with the local leaders of the protest movement.

Di Giacomo used an unstructured, descriptive method to investigate these representations. Nine 'target words' (TW) were chosen which appeared central in the conflict, and a method of free association in response to these words was used as a way of eliciting representations about the committee, its political position and strategy, representations of the students themselves and representations of power. Eight interviewers collected data from 281 students. Each subject was asked to free associate in response to one of the target words. In this way, adjectives evoked by each stimulus word were collated in the form of a dictionary. These initial responses were content analysed for similarity in meaning, thereby reducing the number of different words elicited for each target stimulus. The similarity in the number of common words was then calculated between all possible pairs of the target words. This produced a similarity matrix which was then analysed by hierarchical clustering and multidimensional scaling methods.

The analysis primarily differentiated between target words associated with the political sphere (TW: power, extreme right, extreme left) and those associated with the student protest movement (TW: students, executives, Students' General Assembly [AGL], strike, committee, workers). Di Giacomo concludes from this that the students (TW: students), their protest (TW: strike) and the groups formed to organize the protest (TW: committee, AGL) were not viewed within the traditional right–left ideological continuum, within which political issues are usually embedded. This was quite contrary to the position taken by the protest committee, which did represent the issue within the above political framework. The students' dictionaries also clearly separated themselves (TW: students) from 'workers', which was also contrary to the committee's position, which advocated an alliance between students and workers for the protest.

The multidimensional scaling analysis yielded results which pointed further to different representational structures between the students and the protest committee. Most interesting was the second dimension which separated 'students' and the 'committee'. Within this dimension, students placed themselves closest to 'executives'. Di Giacomo argues that the students identify with this group more than with the workers because they see themselves as future executives. While they may be powerless now, their upwardly mobile future ensures that they will move closer to power, having more in common with 'executives' and less in common with 'workers'.

Overall, Di Giacomo concludes that, given the representational structures produced by the student dictionaries, it is not surprising that the students refused to ally themselves with the political goals and strategies of the protest committee. The students did not identify with the committee's construction of the issue in political terms, nor did they identify with the committee's call for student–worker solidarity. Basically, the committee failed to organize a popular student protest movement against the government's decisions, because the students did not represent themselves or the issue in the same way as the protest committee.

Social representations in the laboratory

Social representations research has also been carried out in traditional laboratory settings. The experimental studies of Abric (1984) have demonstrated neatly the way in which representations determine social action and behaviour. Abric's studies involve the use of the Prisoner's Dilemma Game, which has been a popular method in experimental psychology for the study of factors which influence human interaction in situations of competition and cooperation. Abric proposes that studies to date have only focused upon the objective conditions of the experimental situation, without investigating the way in which the player or subject construes or represents the situation itself – of the significance and meaning it holds for the subject.

In Abric's study, 40 subjects are given non-competitive instructions in the context of a Prisoner's Dilemma Game. Half are told their opponent is another student and the other half are told they are playing against a machine. However, in both cases, unknown to the subjects, the opponent is the experimenter who uses the same tit-for-tat strategy. After 50 trials, subjects are told that they are now playing against another opponent, again either a student or a machine. For two of the groups (experimental groups), the type of opponent changes (student to machine, or machine to student). For the two control groups, the type of opponent remains the same (student to student, or machine to machine). As with the first part of the experiment, in reality the opponent remains the experimenter, who continues to use the same strategy. Abric hypothesizes that the image of the opponent as either human or machine, rather than the actual strategy adopted by the opponent, will determine what strategy the player adopts. Knowledge of a human opponent is likely to encourage the use of a cooperative strategy by the subject, compared to the image of a machine opponent. Indeed, Abric found this to be the case.

Furthermore, the change of opponent from machine to human halfway through the game led to an increase in the level of cooperation adopted by the student, and a change halfway from student to machine led to a reduction in the level of cooperation. Thus, the 'representation' players had of their opponent led to the adoption of different strategies by the players: a reactive strategy for the human opponent and a defensive or non-reactive approach for the machine opponent.

Similarly, within the mainstream of the social perception literature, it has been found that manipulating a player's expectations (representations) of an opponent's dispositional nature and game-playing strategies in competitive situations can lead to the adoption of game-playing tactics by the player which elicit behavioural confirmation of those expectations (Kelley and Stahelski, 1970; Snyder and Swann, 1978). Thus labelling an opponent as 'hostile' or 'competitive' leads to the adoption of hostile or competitive behavioural strategies by a player; strategies which are, in turn, reciprocated by the opponent. Thus expectations and stereotypes (representations) about others 'can and do exert powerful channelling effects on subsequent social interaction such that actual behavioural confirmation of these beliefs is produced' (Snyder and Swann, 1978: 157). Such experimental effects have significant implications for social interaction and communication processes in general, as various theorists and researchers have shown (Becker, 1963; Goffman, 1963; Rosenthal, 1974). The operation of behavioural confirmation effects are discussed in the context of intergroup relations in Chapter 9.

Overview of social representations research

It is evident from the above small-scale, but representative, review of social representations research that research in this tradition has varied both in content and in method. There is no one integrative approach which characterizes the research, other than the adoption of social representations theory as a guiding framework. Further, it is also apparent that most of this research can be linked to research in more mainstream approaches in social psychology. More will be said about exploring the usefulness of such links in subsequent chapters but, thus far, it is evident that the issues and topics which have characterized social representations empirical efforts are ones that have been explored by more 'traditional' approaches. A strong feature of the empirical work in the social representations tradition is its emphasis on the *content* of social knowledge domains. Thus much of the research on social representations explores and describes the content of people's beliefs, values and knowledge rather than cognitive processes linked to this knowledge.

Farr (1990) also points out that many topics studied under the rubric of social representations tend to be social issues which have attracted extensive media coverage. For example, recently there have been several efforts at delineating the social representations of AIDS (Apostilidis, 1992; Joffe, 1992; Markova and Wilkie, 1987; Páez, Echebarria, Valencia, Romo, San Juan and Vergara, 1991).

CRITICISMS OF SOCIAL REPRESENTATIONS THEORY AND RESEARCH

Wells (1987) has identified two distinguishable theories within Moscovici's formulation of social representations: the phenomenal theory and the meta-theory. It is useful to make this distinction since one can agree with one without necessarily embracing the other. The criticisms we present here are of the phenomenal theory, pertaining to Moscovici's definition of social representations as systems of thought, values and beliefs which are socially created and communicated.

How social is social representations theory?

Before considering particular elements of social representations theory it is perhaps worthwhile considering the question of how *social* social representations theory really is. In an interesting paper entitled 'Social Representations: Social Psychology's (Mis)use of Sociology', Parker (1987) challenges whether indeed the theory of social representations is more social than mainstream social psychological theories. He is critical of the tendency for social psychologists to use sociological theory as a means of overriding the problems of positivism and individualism which have plagued the discipline since its beginnings as an experimental science. Parker argues that the Durkheimian tradition, to which Moscovici refers as a forerunner to the theory of social representations, does not solve these dual problems; it simply gives the impression of doing so. Durkheim's sociology is itself plagued by positivist and individualist elements. Moscovici uses the dualism which Durkheim establishes between collective and individual representations to argue that research into the latter is necessary and complementary to an understanding of the social and symbolic nature of collective representations. By arguing that social representations are not only symbolic but also cognitive, Parker argues that Moscovici individualizes the concept. Social representations are thereby defined as cognitive structures residing in the mind of each individual, making subjective meaning more important than the socially shared and symbolic nature of these contents. Far from breaking with traditional approaches in social psychology, Parker argues that the theory of social representations can easily be accommodated and absorbed by the mainstream. In a similar vein, Allansdottir, Jovchelovitch and Stathopoulou (1993) argue that the inherent versatility and openness in the concept of social representations makes it vulnerable to (mis)appropriation by individualistic mainstream approaches within social psychology.

Harré (1984) expresses similar concerns, arguing that the theory implies a distributive model of representations. Rather than viewing representations as cultural products arising from collective activities, they are seen as cognitive contents which are present 'in the heads' of every individual in a defined collectivity. According to critics like Harré and Parker, the cognitivist focus on the internal contents of the mind has the net effect of individualizing the concept of representation and stripping it of its social and collective character. Moscovici's (1984b) defence against these criticisms is that it is just as legitimate to study the way in which concepts and images become a part of individual consciousness as it is to study collective phenomena such as the literature and publications of a particular group. The study of social representations should include both kinds of phenomena as, indeed, it has. Clearly, while some social representations may be independent of individual cognition, many representations which circulate within a culture or group are undeniably apprehended at the individual level. As Hewstone et al. argue, 'these shared systems of belief constitute "bridges" between individual and social reality, and make the study of such representations social psychological rather than sociological' (1982: 242–3). Cognitively oriented sociologists (Morgan and Schwalbe, 1990) and anthropologists (Sperber, 1984, 1990) have also advocated the study of the cognitive contents of people's minds, believing that this content reflects the collective knowledge and consciousness of the social groups to which people belong.

What constitutes a group?

What is a group and how can it be identified? In Chapter 5 we presented a number of definitions of a 'group' which social psychologists have furnished over the years. What is clear is that there are no agreed upon criteria as to what constitutes a group. Central to social representations theory is the group-defining nature of representations. However, Potter and Litton (1985) express concern at the way in which groups have been defined and delineated within social representations research. Naturally occurring groups are usually chosen as units of analysis in the empirical studies thus far, without solving the problem of whether the 'group', as defined by the researchers, has any psychological salience to the individuals who are said to occupy it. Potter and Litton argue that the definition of a group is problematic, given that the constitution of a group is itself determined by members' representations of the 'group'. Thus,

> group categories can themselves be understood as social representations constructed by participants to make sense of their social worlds. The potential inconsistency arises because the object which is the topic for analysis is also an analytic resource. (Potter and Litton, 1985: 83)

Group membership should therefore not be taken as a given when reaching conclusions in social representations research, but should itself be the target of such research. It is therefore important that participants actually identify with the social categories they are assigned. Harré (1984) expresses a similar concern in his reflections on the theory.[4]

What constitutes consensus?

Another notable concern is the ambiguity surrounding the notion of consensus which is supposed to characterize a social representation (Litton and Potter, 1985; Potter and Litton, 1985). One of the central and, indeed, defining features of a representation is its shared or consensual nature, which contributes to the establishment of a group's identity (Moscovici and Hewstone, 1983). Potter and Litton (1985) and Potter and Wetherell (1987) argue that the theory of social representations implies a well-defined notion of consensus but, in reality, says little about the degree or level of consensus necessary before a representation can be said to be shared by a group. This is of particular importance, since individual variation will always exist within a group's shared perspective. These critics argue that in empirical studies to date (for example, Di Giacomo, 1980; Herzlich, 1973; Hewstone et al., 1982) there is often a presupposition of consensus and the use of analyses which ignore diversity. They have criticized Hewstone et al.'s (1982) study and Di Giacomo's (1980) research for employing analyses which utilize aggregate or mean scores which have the net effect of homogenizing possible intra-group differences or variations.

> . . . in the empirical studies undertaken so far consensus tends to be presupposed and internal diversity disguised by the use of certain analytic procedures. Distinct social groups and populations are assumed to have specific, shared, social representations. This leads to an emphasis on similarity at the expense of variation and difference. (Potter and Litton, 1985: 84)

Similar reservations are directed at Herzlich's (1973) work on the representations of health and illness in French society. As argued earlier, it is difficult to discern, independently from the interview data she presents, the degree of consensus evident in her respondents' accounts.

Potter and Litton (1985) argue that it is essential to differentiate between different levels of consensus and that, in their discourse studies at least, levels of consensus differ with different contexts of language use (Litton and Potter, 1985). In their analysis of the range of explanations or social representations yielded by the media and respondents to the St Paul's street riot of 1980 in Bristol, England, these authors demonstrate that, while at a general level there was considerable consensus as to the available range of explanations to account for the riot, at more specific explanatory levels there was considerable variation as to whether people fully or partially accepted or rejected these available accounts as having any legitimate explanatory power.

Litton and Potter distinguish between the 'use' and 'mention' of an explanation. The former refers to an explanation that is actually utilized to make sense of an event, whereas 'mention' refers to a representation or explanation that is not actively used but is referred to as an available explanation. The authors found that, while many subjects revealed their preferred explanations for the street disturbances, they also 'mentioned' other available or competing explanations whose relevance they rejected. Furthermore, they make a distinction between the 'use' of an explanation in theory or in practice. Far from creating a consensual universe, the authors present their empirical study as evidence for the existence of conflicting and contradictory social representations.

While there is some validity regarding the essential point that the existence of consensus has not been demonstrated sufficiently in empirical studies of social representations thus far, Potter and Litton's contrary analysis remains problematic. Explanations for a highly controversial and dramatic event, such as a riot, by definition will inevitably yield a range of conflicting explanations. A riot's political nature and deviational salience guarantees such a response. When Moscovici argues that there is a consensual universe, it is unlikely that he has in mind highly controversial and political issues which form an arena for considerable debate and conflict within and between social groups in any society. Nor does he deny that diversity exists within a consensual framework. 'We can be sure that this consensus does not reduce to uniformity; nor, on the other hand, does it preclude diversity. . . . There is a consensual universe, but there is not a precise consensus on every element at each level' (Moscovici, 1985: 92). It is diversity at different levels that gives a representation its dynamic nature and leads to its continual renegotiation in social interaction and communication. Indeed more recent social representations empirical research recognizes that individuals position or orient themselves differently in relation to consensual meaning systems (Augoustinos, 1991a; Doise, Clemence and Lorenzi-Cioldi, 1993; Hraba, Hagendoorn and Hagendoorn, 1989). Thus, while at the collective level social representations function as shared objectified structures, at an individual level there is considerable variety as to how the elements of the representation are framed and articulated.

In presenting the diversity which existed in the practical use of explanations to account for the riot, Litton and Potter also avoid the obvious problem of 'who' was making the statements. Moscovici's theory would predict overall group differences in responses, depending on respondents' respective social identifications and affiliations. While Litton and Potter raise this possibility, they do not deal directly with this issue but prefer to treat it as a further problematic, given the difficulties in defining the constitution of a social group without reference to respondents' subjective categorizations or social representations of group entities.

To conclude their critical evaluation of Moscovici's concept, Potter and Litton suggest that the study of social representations might prove to be more fruitful by studying 'linguistic repertoires'. It is argued that a study of discourse will reveal the types of grammatical and stylistic constructions and metaphors (linguistic repertoires) people draw on in different contexts. These changes in language style in different functional contexts in effect reveal the individual's social representations. Neither Moscovici (1985), Semin (1985), nor Hewstone (1985) agrees with this reconceptualization of social representations as linguistic repertoires. Although language should form an essential component of the study of social representations, research should not be limited to aspects of language. Images and preverbalized concepts are also central to the study of social representations. de Rosa's (1987) research on pictorial representations of madness well illustrates this latter point.

What Potter and Litton are suggesting, however, is more substantial than simply a study of linguistic repertoires which reflect underlying representations. Their critique of social representations theory is part of a larger critique that Potter and his colleagues have waged on cognitivism as a dominant paradigm within psychology (Edwards and Potter, 1992; Potter and Wetherell, 1987; Wetherell and Potter, 1992). Potter et al. want to move away from the study of cognitive contents and associated assumptions pertaining to internal mental processes to a study of everyday discourse – something which is immediately accessible and does not require assumptions about underlying cognitive entities and processes. This radical perspective questions the very notion of *representation* and is perhaps best reflected in Ibañez's view that we 'do not live in a world of representations but in a world of discursive productions' (1994: 363). We will be discussing this challenging critique in more detail in Chapter 10.

SUMMARY

Social representations refer to the ideas, thoughts, images and knowledge structures which members of a society or collectivity share. These consensual structures are seen to be socially created via social communication and interaction by individuals and groups. The role of representations is to conventionalize or anchor social objects, persons and events within a familiar categorial context – to give the unfamiliar meaning. Representations are reduced or objectified into both cognitive and pictorial elements which together form a core or figurative nucleus stored in memory and accessed during communication and interaction. Many of our social representations come from the world of science communicated to us through the mass media and elaborated upon by ordinary people to help make sense of everyday life.

While there are many problems which plague the precision with which social representations theory has been presented, and with the extent to which there are empirical demonstrations of the utility of the concept, there is a sufficient amount of theory and data at present to suggest that the study of social representations contributes to an understanding of shared social knowledge. While social representation theory and research have been branded as distinctly 'European' (Jaspars, 1986; McGuire, 1986), they do have more than just passing similarities to areas of mainstream research in social psychology. Some of these areas were outlined earlier when presenting examples of social representations research. Conceptual connections can also be made between Moscovici's theory and the currently dominant social cognitive concepts of schema and attributions. Chapter 7 explores the links between social representations theory and social schema theory, itself a theory based on the concept of internalized social knowledge, and Chapter 8 deals with links between social representations and attributions as consensual causal explanations for societal events.

NOTES

1 Some elements of social representations theory sit comfortably with Gergen's (1985) social constructionist approach within social psychology. The more relativist and anti-cognitive variants of social constructionism however, do not so readily accommodate all aspects of Moscovici's theory. See Chapter 10 for a discussion of these.
2 Wells (1987) and McKinlay and Potter (1987) express doubts over Moscovici's fundamental distinction between scientific and consensual knowledge, a distinction which is consistent with the orthodox view in the sociology of scientific knowledge. Indeed, scientific knowledge has traditionally been given this revered status (Mulkay, 1979). While Moscovici maintains that the scientific universe is a world of facts and objective scientific endeavours, independent of representations, at the same time he argues that everyone is subject to the influence of social representations. This implies that scientists too must rely on social representations to construct reality and to imbue their activities with meaning. They, therefore, must inevitably draw upon social representations when engaged in scientific work. Scientific knowledge is not immune from social representations, as is claimed by Moscovici. Recent work in the sociology of scientific knowledge argues this precise point (Gilbert and Mulkay, 1984; Latour, 1991).

3 Not all social psychological approaches to the study of values, belief systems and ideology have been individualistic in nature. Most notable of the exceptions is Billig's (1982) treatise on ideology and social psychology. Chapter 11 of this book deals with the social psychological study of ideology in some detail.

4 The definitional tension between 'objective' and 'subjective' categories is a recurring problem within social science research (Chamberlain, 1983). The controversy over how group categories are defined and constructed will be discussed in Chapter 10.

PART II

INTEGRATIONS, APPLICATIONS AND CHALLENGES

7

SOCIAL SCHEMAS AND SOCIAL REPRESENTATIONS

The relationship between the theory of social representations and research in mainstream social cognition has often been alluded to. Indeed, Moscovici's theory has gained momentum outside Europe with the increasing realization that social representations can add a wider social dimension to social cognition approaches. The present chapter is an attempt to forge links between Moscovici's concept and that of mainstream social schema models, and the next chapter explores the contribution social representations theory can make to attribution theory. We should make clear at the outset, however, our reservations in attempting conceptual 'integrations' of this nature. It has been legitimately argued by various commentators that efforts of this kind run the risk of individualizing the concept of social representations, thereby making it vulnerable to appropriation by mainstream cognitive approaches (Allansdottir et al., 1993; Parker, 1987; Potter and Billig, 1992). We acknowledge these risks but at the same time feel that efforts at conceptual integration are essential reflexive exercises or practices which may further our understanding of the nature of human thinking. We are certainly not prescriptive about the integration we present. We leave it up to the reader to decide on whether the two approaches can be (or should be) integrated. We will return to this issue at the end of the chapter.

Despite the qualitatively different 'feel' social representations theory and research has to social schema theory and research, there are points of convergence and parallels between the two perspectives which are difficult to ignore. Essentially, both theories are 'knowledge structure' approaches to social cognition. Like social representations, social schemas have been construed as internalized social knowledge which guides and facilitates the processing of social information. Both are conceptualized as memory traces with an internal organizational structure (Fiske and Taylor, 1984, 1991; Moscovici, 1981, 1984a; Taylor and Crocker, 1981). Schema research and social representations also emphasize the use of cognitive short-cuts, or heuristics, in the processing of social information (Moscovici, 1981, 1984a; Nisbett and Ross, 1980). Furthermore, both schemas and representations are conceptualized as affective structures with inherent normative and evaluative dimensions (Fiske, 1982; Moscovici, 1981, 1984a). Thus social representations and social schemas as internalized social knowledge have similar processing functions; they are organized and stored in memory and guide the selection, meaning and evaluation of social knowledge and information.

However, while the processing functions of social representations can be incorporated into the information processing models of mainstream schema research, there are important divergences between the two theories (Semin, 1985). Schema theory is essentially an information processing model predominantly studied within an individualistic perspective; the theory of social representations purports to be much more than this. It is a theory which attempts to understand individual social psychological functioning by making links with societal and collective processes (Forgas, 1983). The two theories are therefore articulated at different levels of explanation (Doise, 1986).

Social schema theory may benefit from a social representations perspective. The latter can provide a social (societal) context that is missing from most schema approaches. To date, Moscovici's theory has attracted little recognition within mainstream social psychology (Zajonc, 1989).[1] Moscovici, on the other hand, has, at times, acknowledged the relevance of social cognition research, and has borrowed from its findings, but, on most occasions, has dismissed the work as inadequate because of its asocial and decontextualized nature. In 'The Coming Era of Representations' (1982) Moscovici has little confidence of a rapprochement between the two research traditions but, more recently (Moscovici, 1988), he acknowledges that there are points of convergence.

Given the psychological processes inherent in the concept, Jahoda (1988) has suggested that social representations research be incorporated within mainstream work on social cognition. Parker (1987) has predicted pessimistically that the theory of social representations, far from breaking with mainstream work, will inevitably become absorbed by it because of the concept's inherent notions of individual cognition, action and representation; that is, the concept is plagued with an inherent individualism.

As will be argued in this chapter, and as has been argued by Moscovici (1988), though there are similarities between social representations and social cognition research, they remain at present distinct and different approaches. Social cognition research in general, and schema theory in particular, fails to take into account the social interactive and cultural context within which human cognition takes place. Schema theory has been characterized by a focus on delineating the *processing* functions of schemas without due consideration to context or content. For Moscovici, the information processing functions central to schema theory are viewed as being determined by content itself. Social representations act as reference points for the selection, categorization and organization of social information (Semin, 1989). Lamenting the direction which social cognition research had taken, Forgas argued,

> Social psychology is not primarily the study of how isolated, individual information processors manage to make sense of the social stimuli presented to them. Far more, it is a field devoted to understanding motivated, normative social behaviour. It is remarkable that even though much of the critical impetus for a reformed social psychology over the past decade came from an intellectual tradition which objected to the extreme individualism of the discipline . . . the recent social cognition paradigm turned out to be even more individualistic than its predecessors. Its models and theories come nearly exclusively from cognitive psychology: a single individual gazing into a tachistoscope, reading scenarios or pressing buttons in a reaction-time experiment is the most typical target for research. (1983: 130–1)

Schema theory views social knowledge as a 'fixed given' with little reference to the way individuals construct social reality through social interaction and communication. Indeed, this deficit has been recognized by researchers within the mainstream. Zajonc has argued repeatedly that the study of cognition should take place within its natural context of interaction and communication (Zajonc, 1960; Zajonc and Adelman, 1987). Most cognitions emerge and develop from communication with others. Communication is the process by which cognitive contents are received and transmitted from one person to another. Zajonc states,

> Yet it is a strange paradox that cognition is studied in isolation of a very essential social process that is its immediate antecedent and conse-quence – communication. . . . Cognition is the currency of communica-tion. The constraints on communication and the transmission of mental content between minds, the transformations of these contents, and the resulting change in the participants, are rarely studied in the

mainstream social psychology. Yet soon we will need to know about these processes if we are to understand even the contents of individual minds. For they are under serious collective influences. (1989: 357)

To communicate, individuals must anticipate the sharedness of cognitive contents and their structure. Some degree of consensual knowledge must be assumed between participants for social inter-action and communication to take place (see Guerin and Innes, 1989; Morgan and Schwalbe, 1990; Sedikides, 1990).

There has also been little work on specifying the *content* of various schema domains, the underlying assumption being that the process-ing functions of schemas are universal, not only to individuals and groups but also across content domains. Although there has been some theoretical and empirical work recognizing that the content of a knowledge structure, representation or schema may have some bearing on the way it is processed, generally this has been limited to *individual factors* influencing schema acquisition and processing, such as the degree of personal relevance the schema has to the individual (Higgins et al., 1981) or individual differences in expertise with the knowledge structure (Fiske et al., 1983).

The shortcomings of schema theory will be demonstrated through-out this chapter by emphasizing the added social and contextual perspective social representations theory can provide. So long as schema theory remains at the individual level of analysis, it can never explain adequately the totality of social cognitive processes. It will also be argued, however, that the theory of social represen-tations needs a clearer cognitivist perspective in order to understand how social representations are acquired, processed, developed, structured and used by individuals in the course of everyday social interaction. Codol has stated,

> As far as the mechanisms and the processes whereby representations are elaborated and communicated are concerned, they can only be understood in a dual and doubtless highly complex way which involves, on the one hand, both intergroup and interpersonal relationships and, on the other hand, the more specific cognitive mechanisms whereby individuals first perceive and then reinspect reality. (1984: 241)

The aim of this chapter is not to fulfil Parker's prophecy and reduce the concept of social representations to a purely cognitive, individual phenomenon. The present chapter is a preliminary effort to forge links between what are both knowledge structure approaches to social cognition, the one collective, the other individual, by demonstrating how both can mutually benefit from recognition of each other. Doise (1986) has demonstrated how unification of different analyses may lead to better future research. We believe that an attempt at articulation between these different levels of explanation may lead to a more thorough understanding of social, cognitive processes (Doise, 1986; van Dijk, 1988). While this chapter advocates links between these different social psychological approaches, it is interesting to note that Morgan and Schwalbe (1990) have put forward similar arguments for an interdisciplinary merger between these two social psychological traditions and certain sociological theories.

COMPARISON OF SOCIAL SCHEMAS WITH SOCIAL REPRESENTATIONS

While most schema theorists cite Bartlett's work on remembering (1932b) as the intellectual tradition upon which schema models are based, Edwards and Middleton (1986) emphasize the misleading way in which Bartlett's concept has been borrowed and applied in contemporary cognitive theory. Bartlett emphasized the affective, cultural and contextual nature and functions of schemas.

> For Bartlett, schemata were not static knowledge structures stored in the brains or minds of individuals for the interpretation of experience, but rather, functional properties of adaptation between persons and their physical and social environments. Their essential properties therefore were social, affective and purposive, the basis of actions and reactions in the contexts of living one's life. (Edwards and Middleton, 1986: 80)

Indeed, it has been argued that Bartlett's concept of schema has more in common with the concept of social representation than with the present-day cognitivist version of schema (Semin, 1989).

Social psychologists have been quick to utilize the schema concept in social knowledge domains, because of its potential to handle the complexity that such information entails (Fiske and Linville, 1980). Whether, indeed, the concept has fulfilled this potential is problematic. While critics have been quick to criticize Moscovici for his refusal to lay down a prescriptive definition and methodology for the study of social representations, his concept is perhaps no more ill defined and problematic than most other concepts in the social cognition mainstream (Moscovici, 1988). The ecological validity of the schema concept has been seriously questioned (Baron and Boudreau, 1987), and, as was made clear in Chapter 3, the concept has been criticized for its circularity and potential to explain almost anything.

We may now consider, in turn, a number of points on which social schemas and social representations may be compared and contrasted, and show where each of the two concepts may be able to benefit from an analysis of the other.

Schemas and representations as theory-driven structures

Schemas have been construed as lending organization to experience. As we saw in Chapter 3, within this theoretical framework information processing is conceptualized predominantly as theory- rather than data-driven; that is, it relies on people's prior expectations, preconceptions and knowledge about the social world in order to make sense of new situations and encounters.

So, too, social representations have been conceptualized as 'theories' which individuals have about the nature of events, objects and situations within their social world. Both concepts are concerned with the way in which existing knowledge structures are used to familiarize and contextualize social stimuli.

In social representations theory, anchoring is the process by which the novel or strange is rendered familiar, by comparisons with ordinary categories and classifications. As Billig (1988) points out, the process of anchoring bears strong similarities to information processing mechanisms associated with schema models. The comparison and categorization of unfamiliar or novel social stimuli to similar categories is therefore an essential processing function of both schemas and representations. As with schemas, representations allow 'something unfamiliar and troubling, which incites our curiosity to be incorporated into our own network of categories and allows us to compare it with what we consider a *typical* member of this category' (Moscovici, 1981: 193; emphasis added). What is more, both theories regard the mechanisms of comparison, categorization and classification as universal processes; as inherent and central features of human cognition (Billig, 1988).

Both schema models and social representations theory emphasize how the activation and use of existing knowledge and preconceptions can bias social judgements. Schema models in particular stress how people use schemas to fill in missing information, direct a search for more information or provide the basis for applying short-cuts for problem-solving. People are viewed as 'cognitive misers' who simplify reality. Similarly for Moscovici, the prototype, which is the basis upon which classifications are made, 'fosters ready-made opinions and usually leads to over-hasty decisions' (1984a: 32).

Despite these similarities, there are important differences between the two approaches. First, as Billig (1988) has indicated, schema models have treated the processes of classification and categorization as elements of individual cognitive functioning. Social representations theory, on the other hand, regards anchoring as a social process. Where do the categories of comparison come from if not from the social and cultural life of the individual, whose own experience is embedded in the traditions of a collectivity? Schema models have little to say about where these categories come from. They are simply seen as cognitive structures originating and existing inside individuals' heads, not as structures which may reflect an historical and cultural reality.

The process of anchoring, as defined by Moscovici, implies something stronger than merely contextualizing social stimuli in a familiar categorial context. Moscovici seems to imply that objects and ideas are epistemologically located by the process of anchoring. Anchoring actually defines the nature of the stimulus by the process of allocating names and labels.

Second, schema theory presupposes a rational view of people as information processors. The errors or biased judgements so typically found in social cognition research are argued to be a result of people applying incorrect laws of judgement or making hasty decisions in the face of little data. Moscovici (1982) has argued that errors or bias are not purely a matter of bad information processing but reflect underlying preconceptions or social representations which lead to these distortions. For example, the so called 'fundamental attribution error' (Ross, 1977), the tendency to attribute causality to the disposition of the person rather than to situational factors, may not simply be an error of judgement. As we noted in Chapter 4 its pervasiveness suggests that it is motivated by a strong individualist ideological tradition in western societies, or social representation which views the person as being the centre of all cognition, action and process (Lukes, 1973).[2] Thus, Moscovici does not view these errors in simple rationalist cognitivist terms, but as grounded in dominant preconceptions shared by collectivities.

While both theories conceptualize social cognition as predominantly theory-driven, as we detailed in Chapter 3, this view of information processing has begun increasingly to be challenged (Higgins and Bargh, 1987). Considerable research has demonstrated that people *are* influenced by the nature of the stimulus information (for example, Hastie and Kumar, 1979) and that data-driven rather than theory-driven processing is more likely to occur in certain situations and conditions. There is an obvious interaction between schema and data and this interaction is further influenced by the motivating needs and requirements of the individual.

What may be important is the degree to which a schema, or representation, may be activated by environmental data. In Chapter 3 we made reference to Forgas's (1985) research which found different processing strategies being adopted depending on the nature of the stimulus information. The more culturally salient and consensual the stimulus, the more likely schematic processing is to be activated, whereas information with low cultural salience because of its novelty and distinctiveness is more likely to be data-driven. Social representations, if they are pervasive, collective and akin to 'common sense', may be particularly easily activated by data, and such activation may be more automatic and uncontrolled and, hence, have an effect upon judgement of which the person is essentially unaware. It follows, then, that social representations, as culturally salient and consensual phenomena, are more likely to be activated in this way.

The tension between theory- and data-driven processing sits easily with Billig's (1988) proposal to look for countervailing cognitive mechanisms in human thought. In particular, the process of anchoring information should be juxtaposed with that of *particularizing* information, where data are treated as different and set apart because they fail to fit familiar categories of use. Billig emphasizes that, while particularization is not ignored by Moscovici (1982), he views it as a process which results from the initial anchoring or categorization of information, not as a process contradictory to anchoring. This is an interesting idea, for it leaves open the possibility of change in representations and may provide the mechanism by which to research the dynamic and changing nature of representations about which Moscovici speaks. To what extent are schematic structures or representations challenged by the introduction of information which does not fit easily with the usual categories of comparison and classification? The issue of change in representations will be discussed more fully later.

Schemas and representations as memory traces

In Chapter 3 we described schemas as memory structures which facilitated the recognition and recall of information. We also demonstrated how schemas can influence processing time, with the research literature predominantly indicating faster processing times for schema-relevant as opposed to schema-irrelevant information (for example, Rothbart et al., 1979). However, there is some research contradicting this general rule; that is, inconsistent information or schema-incongruent material, because it is novel and distinctive, may be better recalled than consistent information (for example, Hastie and Kumar, 1979). Again, this highlights that some information is data-driven or particularized.

Certainly, social representations have been conceptualized as memory traces which facilitate the structuring and recall of complex social information (Moscovici, 1981, 1984a). However, little experimental research has been carried out in the representations literature on the recall and processing time of material related to representational structures. Indeed, Moscovici would probably eschew such efforts. While we share some of Moscovici's reservations about the usefulness of such mainstream information processing approaches, research of this nature may ultimately prove to be very valuable. Experiments on the recognition and processing time of representations may be a useful way to identify the pervasiveness of certain representations. Images, values, ideas, categories, that are easily recognized and quickly responded to by many people within a group may be a defining characteristic of a social representation. As argued earlier, social representations are more likely to be characterized by a certain degree of uncontrolled or automatic processing which would suggest faster processing time and recognition. Within the schema literature, well-learned and consensual structures, such as highly organized and stereotyped event schemas or scripts (Schank and Abelson, 1977), usually do not evoke exhaustive cognitive processing because people come to expect the sequence of events that follows. People's prior expectations and knowledge structures will determine what incoming social information they will need to engage in greater cognitive activity. Schema- or representation-consistent information will not require in-depth processing, given that the information is expected and, therefore, automatically processed. However, schema- or representation-inconsistent information may depend upon memory-based cognitive processing (Devine and Ostrom, 1988; Hastie and Park, 1986).

Indeed, it would not require much to reconceptualize cognitive scripts or event schemas as social representations in Moscovici's sense. Many of the cognitive scripts used in experimental settings are highly consensual in nature, such as the oft-quoted restaurant script. Event schemas are reliable knowledge structures from which to set goals and anticipate the future precisely because they are consensually based and socially prescriptive. The same could be said for social stereotypes. Recent research on the activation of stereotypes, within the social schema tradition, shows that American whites may have easily primed negative schemas about American blacks (Dovidio, Evans and Tyler, 1986). The actual content of these stereotypes seems to be widely shared, consensual in form, and may even be automatically activated. Devine (1989a) has shown that even non-prejudiced whites know and recognize, and therefore share with highly prejudiced people, the negative cultural stereotype of blacks. Furthermore, both prejudiced and non-prejudiced people show the same speed of activation of the stereotype by primes presented outside awareness. We will discuss this research in more detail in Chapter 9, but for now the point we emphasize is that the mainstream cognitive research on stereotypes suggests that they have certain defining properties of what Moscovici would call 'social representations'.

Schemas and representations as evaluative and affective structures

We have defined schemas as evaluative and affective structures which, when activated, can access schema-associated feelings and judgements. Similarly, the process of classifying and naming (anchoring) in social representations theory is conceptualized as not only a cognitive process but also an evaluative one. Social categories for Moscovici are inherently value-laden.

> Neutrality is forbidden by the very logic of the system where each object and being must have a positive or negative value and assume a given place in a clearly graded hierarchy. When we classify a person among the neurotics, the Jews or the poor, we are obviously not simply stating a fact but assessing and labelling him [or her], and in so doing, we reveal our 'theory' of society and of human nature. (Moscovici, 1984a: 30)

The unity of evaluation and cognition, as presented by Moscovici in the quote above, is, however, challenged by recent research in the schema literature. Devine's (1989a) recent research separates the cognitive component of stereotypes from its evaluative, prejudicial component. Devine argues that, while most people know and recognize the cognitive content of stereotypes of social groups within their culture, this knowledge should not be equated with prejudice toward particular groups. Prejudice toward a group is determined by the degree to which a person accepts or endorses the stereotype. Stereotypes and personal beliefs should be conceptualized as distinct components within people's knowledge structures of particular social groups. As such, there may be varying levels of consensual representations. For example, at the collective level the content of stereotypes about men and women may be extensively shared within a society, but at the intergroup and individual levels these stereotypes are evaluated and accepted differentially by different groups and individuals in the society. We discuss this research more fully in Chapter 9.

While an evaluative attitude may be based upon beliefs with little associated affect, many important attitudes are primarily determined by the affective reaction elicited by an object (Abelson, Kinder, Peters and Fiske, 1982; Innes and Ahrens, 1991). An important issue is the degree to which affective reactions may be acquired and may be communicated to others so as to be shared reactions and not only idiosyncratic responses to social events. Nationalism and collectivist racism are cases in point.

There is no doubt that more work needs to be done to understand the complex relationship between cognition, evaluation and affect in knowledge structure approaches, or what Moscovici refers to as the symbolic functions of social representations.

Internal organization of schemas and representations

A further similarity between schemas and representations is their theorized internal organizational structure. Empirical research in the schema tradition has demonstrated that people classify and order closely related content in ways which facilitate economic and efficient access to this information. Consistent with Rosch's work on the organization of linguistic categories, schemas are found to be hierarchically structured with abstract categories at the top of the structure subsuming more concrete and specific categories at the bottom. As with schemas, Abric (1984) has proposed that a representation is composed of a number of interdependent and hierarchical elements. These elements are organized and structured around a nucleus or core. The structural core is said to have two essential functions: an organizing function which unifies and stabilizes the links in the representation, and a creative function in which the core determines the meaning and value of the elements in the representation. For example, some nuclei are characterized by a strong affective component which determines the resultant evaluative links in the representation.

It is fair to say that a lot more research could be conducted on identifying the structure of various representations and schemas. As schema theorists have argued (Fiske and Taylor, 1991), the internal organization of schemas would differ on the basis of their content, complexity and salience to the individual. In contrast, social representations theory would emphasize the need to investigate

social group differences in the structural organization of representations and to look for the underlying social and ideological functions
which such structures may reinforce. For example, in a series of
multidimensional scaling studies in which students of three different
age cohorts made similarity judgements between 12 social groups
characterizing Australian society, Augoustinos (1991a, 1991b) found
that all the resultant representations reflected a hierarchical socio-
economic separation of the groups. These representations reflected
Australian intergroup differences with respect to power, wealth and
status. So dominant and pervasive is this hierarchical representation
of social groups that it may generalize to 'non-economic' areas such
as in our everyday social relations (Moscovici, 1988). Herzlich's
(1973) work on health and illness in French society found the
contents of such representations to be structured around an
individual–society dichotomy. These studies come close to locating
the core of their respective representations, in that the central
theme(s), around which other elements are organized, have been
identified. More generally, Billig (1988) has proposed that the major
task of social representations research is to look for countervailing
themes implying that representations are characterized by a contradictory structure.

The study of structure, in addition to content, is therefore an
important task for social representations research. The nature of the
acquisition of the representation plays a role in determining the
internal structure, just as is likely to be the case with schemas. At
issue may be the nature of the experience that produces individual
cognitive schemas, as against shared social schemas or representations. Since some schemas, such as social stereotypes, are assumed
to be highly consensual (Andersen and Klatzky, 1987), it may be
possible to investigate the organizational structure of social representations with the methodology utilized by researchers in the schema
literature. However, unlike schema research, the social and ideological functions of the way in which representations are organized
should be a central feature. For example, schema research has had
little to say about why schemas characterized by dominance relations
are linearly organized. How is this reflected in the wider society, and
what ideological or group motivations and interests maintain and
perpetuate such a structure?

The origins and development of representations and schemas

Social schema theory says very little about the social origins of
schemas or 'where they come from' (Eiser, 1986). As we have argued

throughout, schemas have been conceptualized within an individualistic perspective; that is, schemas are seen as cognitive structures
which exist inside individuals' heads. Apart from research on
prototypes and highly consensual and unambiguous event and role
schemas, little theoretical or empirical work has been carried out to
ascertain the degree to which various schematic structures may be
shared, or how they may arise from social interaction and communication. For example, a great deal of research has been carried out into
the way in which self schemas may guide behavioural interaction,
but there has been little research into the effect of the experience of
interactions upon self-relevant structures (Markus and Wurf, 1987).

Some of the acquisition processes studied by schema researchers
were detailed in Chapter 3. What is most striking about this work is
the highly cognitive and asocial nature of these processes. For
example, in their discussion of accretion, tuning and restructuring as
processes of schema acquisition, Rumelhart and Norman (1978)
make few references to the social interactive context, and Fiske and
Dyer's (1985) non-monotonic schema learning model is a highly
cognitive account of how schemas develop over time. Notwithstanding the importance of these processes in the acquisition and learning
of schemas, they do not convey the social essence of such knowledge
structures. Are any of these knowledge structures shared and, if so,
by whom and by how many? What is the nature of the social
distribution of such structures; that is, are there group variations in
the content of such structures? Although we are told they are
derived from experience, we are not told if particular schemas are
more prevalent than others, because they are created and permeated
by social institutions or particular social groups for particular
purposes – whether it be for ideological motivations or for general
socio-cultural system-support. Furthermore, content is not seen as
influencing schema acquisition in a significant way. Rather, the
processes of schema development are assumed to be universal across
different content domains and across different groups of people.
Cognitive developmental theory has assumed that the acquisition of
social knowledge proceeds in logical, sequential and universal
developmental stages, which are internally controlled by the
cognitive capacities of the individual. Group differences, which have
been found in the content of social cognition, have not been
interpreted as reflecting genuine variations in the social distribution
of knowledge, but as differences in stages of cognitive development
(Emler, 1987).

Although the theory of social representations does not say very
much about the processes involved in the acquisition and development of representations, it does contrast with schema theory by

categorically placing the study of cognitive structures within a societal and social interactional context. Social representations originate from social interaction and construct the understanding of the social world, enabling interaction between groups sharing the representation (Duveen and de Rosa, 1992; Moscovici, 1985). The theory's clear imperative is to look for group differences in the content and structure of social knowledge. There is an obvious need for the introduction of a developmental perspective, in both social schema and social representations research, to delineate more clearly the processes of acquisition and the development of social knowledge.

Given the unresolved nature of the consensus issue in empirical studies of social representations, one possible avenue for studying the development of consensual knowledge is from within a developmental perspective. Notwithstanding diversity, Moscovici's theory would predict that with increased age, and therefore increased social communication and interaction, representations of the social world become more consensual in nature. Several multidimensional scaling studies by Augoustinos (1991a, 1991b) investigating the development of young people's representations of Australian society confirmed that with increased age individual variation in these representations decreased considerably. Thus although there was not complete consensus, as socialization proceeded from early adolescence to adulthood, societal representations became more consensual and shared. Unlike most studies in social representations, consensus was not assumed but was measured and confirmed by analyses sensitive to individual differences. In a similar vein, Hraba et al. (1989) found that, while there was considerable agreement among respondents regarding the content of the ethnic hierarchy in the Netherlands, suggesting the existence of a consensual representation, the form of the hierarchy varied across domains and different contexts of use. Both these studies suggest that consensual representations are not necessarily static structures, but are used in dynamic and flexible ways by different people across different situations. This interpretation sits equally well with Moscovici's formulation and Litton and Potter's (1985) criticisms of the consensus issue.

The development of consensual knowledge demonstrates the inherently social nature of cognition – the societal context within which cognitive and affective processes take place interacts with and determines individual processes. The greater the degree of social consensus about the nature of a phenomenon in society, the more likely it is that an individual will select and organize information about the object in accordance with societal expectations (Tajfel, 1978b). What is often viewed as an individual cognitive process is really a product of wider social psychological processes and influences.

The stability of schemas and representations

In Chapter 3 we documented the empirical research related to schema change. While certain conditions may instigate and facilitate schema change, generally it has been assumed that social schemas, once developed and strengthened through use, are stable and static structures (Weber and Crocker, 1983). Moreover, as unified structures, schemas are activated in their entirety, even when only one of their components is accessed (Fiske and Dyer, 1985). In contrast, representations are regarded by Moscovici to be dynamic and changing structures. He refers to the continual renegotiation of social representations during the course of social interaction and communication by individuals and groups. This suggests that such cognitive structures may be context-dependent – changing or being modified by situational constraints and disconfirming experiences. An historical perspective here is important (Gergen, 1973). Certainly, social schematic research has proceeded in an ahistorical direction. Contrast this to the work by Jodelet (1984) in the social representations tradition, which focuses on the changing and historically dependent representations of the body (compare also Ostrom, 1989).

Moscovici refers to representations as being imbued with a life force of their own: merging, repelling and interacting with other such structures and, indeed, with individuals and groups, suggesting a certain dynamism and changing quality that is absent from the social schema literature. However, once these structures are transformed into material and objective entities, they are said to become fossilized or static – their origins forgotten, coming to be regarded as common sense. This, of course, bears some similarity to the notion of schematic structures being unified and activated almost automatically through the associative links in the structure. Thus, while both theories suggest that, once developed, these cognitive structures may become resistant to change, they differ in the emphasis they place on the degree to which representations and schemas are flexible and dynamic during the course of their development and contextual use. Furthermore, the social representations literature suggests that, after a period of unquestioning acceptance or fossilization, subsequent sociological or historical forces may act to renegotiate and/or totally transform these structures.

McKinlay and Potter (1987) see the historically prescriptive nature of representations, on the one hand, and the dynamic and changing nature of representations, on the other, as a contradiction in Moscovici's theory. They argue that the strength of the former thesis negates the possibility of change. On the contrary, one may ask what is history if not the resolution of the contradictory forces of tradition and change. Billig (1988) argues quite clearly that social cognition research should be about the study of contradictory cognitive processes and countervailing themes in human thought. The study of social representations presents a vehicle for studying such contradictory processes: how tradition is preserved and protected at certain historical times, and challenged or overhauled at others.

Abric (1984) has proposed that a representation may change if there is a radical threat to the central organizing structure of the representation – the nucleus. Change in the meaning and values attached to the peripheral elements will only lead to superficial change, but a transformation in the nucleus will change the whole nature and structure of the representation itself. The study of structure and the stabilizing core of representations may, therefore, be the vehicle by which to study the dynamic processes of evolution and change in representations.

THE SOCIO-GENESIS OF SOCIAL KNOWLEDGE

As with theory and research in social cognition, social representations researchers have been interested in linking the theory to developmental psychology (Duveen and de Rosa, 1992; Duveen and Lloyd, 1990). This is not surprising, given the acknowledged influence of Piaget on Moscovici's theoretical formulations (Moscovici, 1989). Piagetian theory's focus on the manner in which the child gradually and actively learns to understand and represent both the physical and social worlds can be accommodated by the constructivist position taken by both social schema and social representations theory. If representations and schemas exist as knowledge structures which are socially constructed and communicated to understand everyday life, then the child is born not only into a physical world but also into a world of representations, a 'thinking society'. How does the child come to be psychologically influenced by social knowledge not as a passive object but as an active participant in his or her everyday lived social experience? How does this knowledge ultimately contribute to and constitute the individual's social identity? These are some of the questions which have been posed by developmentalists who have embraced Moscovici's theory of social representations (Duveen and de Rosa, 1992).

Duveen and Lloyd (1990) have proposed that, as with Piagetian theory, social representations should be viewed as a genetic theory in which the structure of any social representation at a point in time is a result of a developmental process. The authors differentiate between three types of processes by which social representations exert a psychological influence on development: socio-genesis, onto-genesis and micro-genesis.

Socio-genesis describes the processes of generation and diffusion of social representations which are adopted and reconstructed by different social groups throughout society. Of course, much of this social knowledge originates from the reified scientific world, but such knowledge is also generated within everyday social discourse and interaction. Onto-genesis refers to the process by which children learn and adopt the social representations of their community. As mentioned previously, this is not a passive process but one in which the child actively reconstructs and elaborates existing representations. At any one moment some representations are more psychologically active than others, particularly if they are bound to a person's sense of social identity (Duveen and Lloyd, 1990). The micro-genesis of social representations refers to the ways in which social representations and their associated social identities are activated in everyday interaction and communication. Representations which are evoked in social interaction help to establish a shared frame of reference so that communication can take place between individuals. They also define the social identities of the participants, and therefore help prescribe appropriate social relations in any social encounter. This is not to say that the representations and their associated social identities are static and unchanging. Any interaction can lead to their structural renegotiation. Since the three processes are interrelated and mutually influential, micro-genetic processes can lead to onto-genetic transformations in representations, while socio-genetic changes will ultimately filter downwards, leading to changes at the onto-genetic and micro-genetic levels.

Duveen and Lloyd (1990) apply the above developmental perspective to a number of their studies which have dealt with the social representations of gender among young children. These studies have investigated the developmental process by which preschool children internalize the dominant and consensual representations of gender. In a series of studies these authors have examined how children respond to external gender signals and use internalized gender signs in their play activity (Lloyd and Smith, 1985; Lloyd, Duveen and Smith, 1988). Their studies have shown that an internalized gender (social) identity does not occur until the age of about 2 years. The child is only then able to represent internally the meaning of this identity, and is therefore able to enact it autonomously in everyday interaction.

Other developmental studies embracing the social representations perspective include Corsaro's (1990) research in both American and Italian nursery schools studying preschoolers' representations of adult rules, and Emler, Ohana and Dickinson's (1990) review of several studies researching children's representations of authority and income inequalities. While within this developmental perspective interest has predominantly focused on children's representations of social objects, there has also been a related interest in the representations adults have of the child and the status of 'childhood' (Chombart de Lauwe, 1984; D'Alessio, 1990; Molinari and Emiliani, 1990).

While there have been empirical studies linking social representations concepts with aspects of developmental theory, social representations theory lends a unique and distinctive contribution in understanding the development of social knowledge. While both theories stress the constructivist and active role of the child in grasping and understanding the social objects he or she encounters, the two theories have different views about the nature and status of social knowledge which surrounds the child and the processes by which the child acquires this knowledge. It is worthwhile following this argument in some detail, for it raises some crucial criticisms with respect to traditional developmental approaches (Duveen and de Rosa, 1992; Emler, 1987; Emler et al., 1990).

Emler and his co-workers (Emler and Dickinson, 1985; Emler et al., 1990) have argued that developmental theory has been imbued with two major assumptions. First, socio-cognitive development is construed as a process by which the world presents physical and social objects and experiences to the child, which are then to be interpreted and understood correctly. Socio-cognitive development is seen as the sequential progress the child makes toward reaching adult levels of comprehension. Linked to this is the proposed cultural universality of the socio-cognitive sequence. While some developmentalists concede that cultural and social influences are of psychological importance, this is seen to influence only the content of social knowledge, not its structure. All social knowledge, it is argued, proceeds in the same sequential manner. Second, it is assumed that this process is internal, individual and self-generated by the child's increasing capacities to solve problems.

The theory of social representations challenges these central assumptions. First, it stresses that all knowledge is socially constructed by a given collectivity and, second, it insists that the attainment of knowledge is not an individual, internal process but a social one. The child is born into a community which has generated its own ways of understanding and interpreting. In the process of socialization the child attains not only the content of this social knowledge, but also the dominant methods of thinking within the community. These are central features of a community's collective memory so that each child does not solely and individually have to solve each problem encountered: solutions and methods are already provided for the child by his or her cultural collectivity.

> . . . if the social environment presents children with problems to be solved, it also presents them with solutions and arguments for solutions. Different social environments can present different solutions or different arguments, or both. . . . Thus the development of social knowledge is the development of knowledge about one's social group's stock of solutions and arguments about solutions. This does not mean that the child is simply the passive inheritor of these cognitive entities as a static body of cultural knowledge. On the contrary, these solutions are open to almost endless argument, . . . and the child is a potential participant in that argument. (Emler et al., 1990: 52)

In addition, these authors point out that developmentalists have concerned themselves with the study of the application of mental principles which are assumed to be knowledge-free. Principles of moral judgement have been traditionally treated in this way, assuming that they reflect abstract cognitive operations which are independent of the social beliefs and values of individuals. Furthermore, while developmental psychology emphasizes the active and constructivist role of the individual in social knowledge development, as an agent of action upon the environment, Emler et al. (1990) also point out that virtually nothing is said about the effects of the environment upon the individual – that is, individuals are also the recipients of environmental action, over which they may have little control. Thus social knowledge is not only about what and how one can do things in the environment, but also about what and how the environment impinges upon the individual.

PROBLEMS WITH INTEGRATION

As we mentioned at the outset of this chapter, there are conflicting positions regarding the conceptual utility and epistemological desirability of integrating the theories of social schema and social representations. Allansdottir et al. (1993) refer to attempts to integrate social representations theory with traditional and mainstream approaches as 'gluing practices' which threaten to individualize and decontextualize the theory. They argue that many researchers have treated social representations as a 'convenient social package' which can be simply added to traditional notions. Of considerable concern to these authors is the 'statisticalization' of the concept by the use of traditional empirical methods to measure sharedness in representations and in the identification of a 'social representation' – methods such as multidimensional scaling and cluster analysis. As such, 'The theoretical integrity of the concept is compromised . . . it is nominally there, but it cannot speak with its own voice' (Allansdottir et al., 1993: 11).

The concerns raised by Allansdottir and her colleagues are perhaps not overstated given the predominance of individualistic conceptual and methodological frameworks within social psychology. There is also little doubt that the use of quantitative techniques does run the risk of objectifying the concept of social representation so that a social representation is merely defined by its consensual nature or clustering structure. However, the notion of sharedness in social representations is central to the theory, and quantitative techniques to measure this, albeit limited, are nevertheless useful. Sharedness is not the sole defining feature of a social representation, but it is an *essential* feature which ought to be detectable using quantitative methods. Other important features need to be considered such as the centrality of the phenomenon or object in social life, the extent to which it is objectified and the social functions it serves. A social representation is not based on sharedness alone – not every social object is a social representation. This can be contrasted to schema theory, where a defining feature of a social schema is that it refers to a 'social' object, so that any social object can have its own organizational schema. Likewise, multi-dimensional and clustering techniques may be useful methodological tools but a social representation should not be equated with an identified cluster or structure alone (Augoustinos, 1993).

It is clear that quantitative methods are limited in their usefulness to study the more interactive and dynamic aspects of social representations: how they emerge in the course of everyday conversation, how they are constituted and transformed through discourse and socio-historical circumstances. Any methodology, quantitative or qualitative, should be used to demonstrate the social and historically specific context of psychological life. Method should not be the driving force behind social representations research or traditional social cognitive research.

Criticisms that social representations theory 'will drift towards cognitive reductionism' (Potter and Billig, 1992: 15) because of the cognitivist elements contained within it have more challenging implications for the theory. Ridding social representations theory of the cognitivist traces inherent within it necessitates denying the role of cognition in the construction of social reality, or, at the every least, remaining agnostic about this. This, of course, raises the spectre of reconceptualizing social representations in non-cognitive terms, such as linguistic repertoires (Potter and Litton, 1985) or discursive practices (Potter and Wetherell, 1987). This issue forms the cornerstone of Chapter 10, which deals with recent anti-cognitivist approaches to the study of social life.

SUMMARY

The major difference between the study of social representations and social schemas is that social representations are much more than an information processing model articulated at the intra-personal level of explanation. Unlike social schema research, social representations research does not limit itself to the study of simple cognitive structures, but is predominantly concerned with complex cognitive structures such as belief systems and cultural value patterns. As such, it is a much more ambitious theory necessitating multi-disciplinary endeavours. Furthermore, Moscovici's concept of objectification, which has important implications for the sociology of knowledge, has no parallel in the social schema literature. As in schema theory, the theory of social representations attempts to understand individual psychological functioning, but by taking into consideration wider societal and social psychological processes. The two theories are therefore articulated at different levels of explanation. Certainly, the theory of social representations can provide schema theory with a much needed societal context but, at the same time, 'social representations incontrovertibly partake of the nature of cognitive phenomena – even if certain of their characteristics partially escape being included within their framework' (Codol, 1984: 240). While it may not be possible or desirable to integrate the two theories fully, this chapter emphasizes how different levels of explanation have been invoked to account for the way existing social knowledge is used in social cognitive processes.

NOTES

1 While Fiske and Taylor (1991) cite a paper by Moscovici in their recent second edition of *Social Cognition*, there is no mention of Moscovici in the Name Index. Fiske and Taylor cite Hewstone et al.'s (1982) research, but only refer to the intergroup attributional findings, making no reference to social representations theory.

2 We will have more to say about individualism as a pervasive representation influencing the content of cognition in the following chapter.

8

ATTRIBUTIONS AND SOCIAL REPRESENTATIONS

In this chapter we will be continuing the theme of conceptual and theoretical integration by making links between attribution theory and social representations theory. Just as attribution theory seeks to understand the processes by which people attribute causes to their own behaviour and to the behaviour of others, social representations theory emphasizes the explanatory function of the knowledge and meaning systems embodied by social representations. Both theories refer to a fundamental human need to understand and explain events, and in so doing offer a psychological perspective to the role of social explanation in everyday life. While both theories emphasize the importance of explanation in social life, the two theories are articulated at different levels of analysis (Doise, 1986). Attribution theory focuses primarily on the individual cognitive processes involved in making causal explanations, while social representations theory emphasizes the social and collective nature of explanations. We will argue that the study of social representations is crucial for understanding what kinds of attributions people make and in what contexts they are made. More specifically, this chapter will focus on the social origins of attributions: on the wider societal beliefs and knowledge which form the basis for the construction of explanations.

ATTRIBUTIONS, SOCIAL KNOWLEDGE AND REPRESENTATIONS

As we made clear in Chapter 4, during the 1980s, attribution theory was the dominant force in American social psychology. Since Heider's (1958) pioneering formulations about common-sense causal explanations, attribution theory underwent several extensions, the most notable being Jones and Davis's (1965) correspondent inference theory and Kelley's (1967) theory of covariation. More recent extensions to the large body of work on attributional processes have been critical evaluations of the conceptual assumptions and limited empirical applications of this research. What has been most evident in this research is that the attribution process has been conceptualized primarily as an intra-individual phenomenon. Individuals are construed as information processors who attend to and select information from the environment, process the information cognitively, and then arrive at a causal analysis of the behaviour in question. There is little discussion in most attribution research of the social interactive and cultural context within which causal attributions are made. Attribution theory has therefore been criticized for being predominantly an individualistic theory requiring a greater social perspective (see Hewstone, 1983).

As well as being very individualistic and cognitive in nature, critics have argued that attribution theory exaggerates the tendency for people to seek causal explanations for everyday occurrences and events. It has been suggested that people do not engage in such exhaustive cognitive activity as, for example, Kelley's covariation model would suggest, but rather that they use heuristics as short-cuts for making judgements and inferences generally and, more specifically, for attributing causality (Fiske and Taylor, 1991). Weiner (1985) has addressed this issue by examining whether people engage in spontaneous causal thinking or whether, in fact, the extent and nature of attributional activity that the research suggests is an artefact of the reactive methodologies used in attribution research. Most mainstream research in causal attributions requires respondents to indicate their agreement or disagreement with attributional statements specified by the researchers. There is a dearth of studies which investigate attributions and explanations in natural contexts such as in conversation and in the print media. In reviewing the small number of attributional studies which utilize non-reactive methodologies, Weiner (1985) concludes that people do indeed engage in 'spontaneous' causal thinking, but mostly for unexpected events and especially when confronted with failure. This conclusion is consistent with that of others who have argued that people look actively for causal explanations for the unexpected or different (Hewstone, 1989b) and that in such situations the complexity of attributions increases (Lalljee, Watson and White, 1982).

While there is agreement that expectations determine the extent to which people actively think about causes, there has been little research to date concerning where these expectations and explanations come from. Do they simply emerge autonomously within each individual's head as a consequence of some cognitive process or are these expectations and explanations shaped by and drawn from socio-cultural knowledge and beliefs that people share? If we accept that explanations for everyday events and experiences are social phenomena which are negotiated and communicated during social interaction, then we require an approach which emphasizes the contents of social knowledge; an approach which is central to social representations theory. Indeed, Moscovici and Hewstone have proposed that social representations should be viewed as the foundations upon which attributions are built (Moscovici, 1981, 1984a; Moscovici and Hewstone, 1983).

> A theory of social causality is a theory of our imputations and attributions, associated with a representation . . . any causal explanation must be viewed within the context of social representations and is determined thereby. (Moscovici, 1981: 207)

Social representations form the foundations of people's expectations and normative prescriptions, and thus act as mediators in the attributional process (Hewstone 1989a, 1989b). In a similar vein, Lalljee and Abelson (1983) advocate a 'knowledge structure' approach to attribution. Well-learned and consensual structures, such as highly organized event schemas or scripts (Schank and Abelson, 1977), do not usually evoke causal explanations because people come to expect the sequence of events that follow. People's prior expectations, beliefs, knowledge or schemas will determine what incoming social information they will need to engage in causal attributions. Following the principles of schema functioning we detailed in Chapter 3, information which is consistent with a person's schema or representation will not require an in-depth search for causality, given that the information is expected and therefore automatically processed. However, information which is inconsistent with expectations or existing knowledge will require a more detailed search for an explanation.

> Thus social representations impose a kind of automatic explanation. Causes are singled out and proposed prior to a detailed search for and analysis of information. Without much active thinking, people's explanations are determined by their social representations. (Hewstone, 1989b: 261) (Please note, the original is in French; the above is Hewstone's translation in English.)

The social foundation of such automatic explanations is that they are learned and thus socially communicated through language. Hewstone (1983, 1989a, 1989b) suggests that the use of cultural hypotheses to explain behaviour and events can be regarded as a kind of 'socialized processing'. Culturally agreed upon explanations eventually come to be regarded as common-sense explanations. Each society has its own culturally and socially sanctioned explanation or range of explanations for phenomena such as illness, poverty, failure, success and violence. We will be looking at the range of explanations people make for such social issues within western industrialized societies later in this chapter and also in Chapter 11, but for now the point we wish to emphasize is that people do not always need to engage in an active cognitive search for explanations for all forms of behaviour and events. Instead, people evoke their socialized processing or social representations.

Such a knowledge- or representation-based approach to attribution will necessitate the study of social knowledge itself. Research into the information base which people possess regarding particular social domains will reveal pre-existing knowledge structures and expectations which people use to filter and process incoming information. Instead of focusing exclusively on processes by which causal statements are generated, a knowledge-based approach to attribution would extend attribution research by studying the actual language people use when making attributional statements in naturalistic conversations and environments. Furthermore, such an approach may contribute to our understanding of the social origins of causal attributions and thus answer the often neglected question of where attributions come from (Pepitone, 1981).

THE SOCIAL ORIGINS OF THE FUNDAMENTAL ATTRIBUTION ERROR

The study of perceived causation embodied in attribution theory concerns itself essentially with what passes as everyday social explanation. Central to the theory is that two main kinds of attributions are made by people to account for causality: dispositional or personal attributions and situational or contextual attributions. These two modes of explanation correspond to what Billig (1982) refers to as the 'individual' and 'social' principles. In Chapter 4 we discussed one of the most consistent findings in attribution research – the fundamental attribution error: the tendency to over-attribute another person's behaviour to dispositional characteristics of the person, rather than to situational or contextual factors (Ross, 1977). Considerable debate and discussion has centred on the reason for this error or, perhaps more accurately, 'bias' (Harvey, Town and Yarkin, 1981; Kruglanski and Ajzen, 1983). Heider (1958) himself was the first to advance a cognitive explanation, arguing that behaviour has such salient features that it tends to engulf the field. Fiske and Taylor, in support of this cognitive explanation, describe how situational factors which give rise to behaviour, such as the social context, roles or situational pressures, are 'relatively pallid and dull and unlikely to be noticed when compared with the dynamic behavior of the actor' (1991: 67). The fundamental attribution bias has therefore primarily been explained by dominance of the actor in the perceptual field.

More recently, it has been suggested that this dispositionalist bias is not a universal law of human cognitive functioning, but rather it is deeply rooted in the dominant ideology of individualism within European and American culture (Bond, 1983; Farr and Anderson, 1983; Moscovici and Hewstone, 1983). The tendency to favour personal over situational causation was first noted by Ichheiser (1949), but, instead of viewing this phenomenon as an individual 'error' in cognitive judgement, he viewed it as an explanation grounded in American society's collective and cultural consciousness (Farr and Anderson, 1983). The dominant representation of the person in western liberal democracies is that of an important causative agent, over and above situational and contextual consider-ations. Political philosophers (for example, Lukes, 1973; Macpher-son, 1962) have posited the importance of individualism as an ideological doctrine specific to liberal democratic societies and, most particularly, within American social, cultural and political life. Lukes (1973) documents how political, economic, religious, ethical, episte-mological and methodological domains have been imbued with individualist tenets. Emerging as a philosophical doctrine in the nineteenth century with the advent of the capitalist mode of pro-duction, liberal individualism's central tenets emphasize the import-ance of the individual over and above society, and view the individual as the centre of all action and process. While this representation of the person may seem self-evident and not particularly controversial, the anthropologist Geertz has said the following about the individualistic representation of the person:

> The western conceptions of the person as a bounded, unique, more or less integrated motivational and cognitive universe, a dynamic centre of awareness, emotion, judgement, and action organized into a distinctive whole and set contrastively both against a social and natural background is, however incorrigible it may seem to us, a rather peculiar idea within the context of the world's cultures. (1975: 48)

If, indeed, attributions and explanations are grounded in social knowledge, then cultural variations in the representation of the person should yield cross-cultural differences in the prevalence of person attributions. We now turn to a small number of studies which may help us to understand the impact of cultural representations on attributions.

Culture and attributions

Before any research was undertaken specifically to investigate the role of cultural influences on attributions, developmental research had documented a significant tendency for dispositional attributions to increase with age in western cultures. Whereas young western children predominantly make reference to contextual factors to explain social behaviour, western adults are more likely to stress dispositional characteristics of the agent (Peevers and Secord, 1973; Ruble, Feldman, Higgins and Karlovac, 1979). Anthropologists such as Shweder and Bourne (1982) have also noted that non-western adults place less emphasis on the dispositional characteristics of the agent and more emphasis on contextual or situational factors compared to western adults. Of particular interest is that social psychologists in general are loath to explain these developmental and cross-cultural differences from within a social constructivist framework. Rather, these effects were initially explained within cognitive and experiential terms. For example, the relative infrequency of person attributions made by younger children was explained by reasoning that young children are limited in their cognitive capacity to make dispositional attributions because this requires the cognitive competence to generalize behavioural regularities over time. It was argued that children did not acquire the cognitive capacity to do this until they were older. Similarly, it was argued that non-western adults are less likely to make dispositional categorizations because the cognitive capacity to do so is more likely to be associated with the experiential conditions of complex modernized societies (Miller, 1984).

Joan Miller was among the first social psychologists to point out that such explanations disregard the possibility that developmental and cultural differences may 'result from divergent cultural conceptions of the person acquired over development in the two cultures rather than from cognitive or objective experiential differences between attributors' (1984: 961). Western notions of the person are essentially individualistic – emphasizing the centrality and autonomy of the individual actor in all action – whereas non-western notions of the person tend to be holistic, stressing the interdependence between the individual and her or his surroundings. The developmental or age differences in attribution merely reflect the enculturation process – the gradual process by which children adopt the dominant conception of the person within their culture.

Indeed, Miller's (1984) research confirms this cultural hypothesis. A cross-cultural study was undertaken to compare the attributions made for prosocial and deviant behaviours by a sample of Americans and Indian Hindus of three different age groups (8, 11 and 15 years), together with an adult group (mean age = 40.5 yrs). Miller found that at older ages Americans made significantly more references to general dispositions ($M = 40$ per cent) than did Hindus ($M < 20$ per cent), most of these dispositions referring to personality character-istics of the agent. However, there were no significant differences which distinguished the responses of the 8- and 11-year-old American children from those of their Hindu counterparts (the difference was an average of 2 per cent). While children displayed few cross-cultural differences in the number of contextual attri-butions they made, these were referred to frequently at younger ages in both Hindu and American children.

Within culture developmental trends indicated a significant linear age increase in reference to general dispositions among Americans. In contrast, a significant linear age increase in references to the context was evident amongst the Hindus, which emphasized social roles and patterns of interpersonal relationships. As Miller points out, 'such modes of attribution may be seen to be reflective of Indian cultural conceptions in their emphasis in locating a person, object, or event in relation to someone or something else' (1984: 968). For example, the following explanations were given by an American and Hindu subject in a story about an attorney who, after a motor cycle accident, left his injured pillion passenger in hospital without consulting with the doctor while he went on to work:

> *American*: The driver is obviously irresponsible (agent-general dispo-sition). The driver is aggressive in pursuing career success (agent-general disposition).
> *Hindu*: It was the driver's duty to be in court for the client whom he's representing (context-social/spatial/temporal location). The passenger might not have looked as serious as he was (context-aspects of persons).(Miller, 1984: 972)

Moreover, Miller found that these results could not be explained by the competing cognitive and experiential interpretations. No significant age or culture effects were observed in a classificatory task designed to assess a subject's ability to classify on the basis of conceptual similarity. All age and cultural subgroups were able to identify correctly word pair relationships in their abstract mode on an average of at least 82 per cent of the time. Although this does not eliminate the possibility that age and/or cultural differences in classificatory abilities exist, it at least demonstrates that subjects of all ages in both cultures demonstrated at least some ability to classify on the basis of conceptual similarity.

To test the experiential hypothesis against the cultural hypothesis, Miller compared subgroups of Indian adults who varied in their exposure to modernization, and subgroups who varied in their subcultural orientation. These subgroups included: (1) a Hindu middle-class sample; (2) a lower middle-class Hindu sample; and (3) a lower middle-class Anglo-Indian sample of mixed Euro-Indian descent. If the experiential hypothesis was to be confirmed, references to general dispositions of the agent would be related significantly to exposure to modernizing conditions, which, in turn, would reflect socio-economic class differentials: the middle-class Hindus making the greater reference to dispositions; the lower middle-class Anglo-Indians making slightly less reference to dispositions; and the lower middle-class Hindus making the least reference to dispositional factors. Instead, it was found that the lower middle-class Anglo-Indians made the greatest reference to dispositional factors, differing significantly from both middle-class and lower middle-class Hindus, who, in turn, did not differ significantly from each other, despite the marked difference in their socio-economic status. This finding is accounted for by the maintenance of a semi-westernized cultural meaning system among the Anglo-Indian group, which is consonant with the cultural interpretation of attributional variance. Thus, not only did the prevalence of dispositional attributions vary across cultures, it also varied with subcultural orientation within India.

It appears, therefore, that the tendency to over-rate personal/ dispositional factors of the agent in western adults cannot be explained adequately by cognitive and experiential interpretations alone. The attribution 'bias' may not simply be a cognitive property or universal law of psychological functioning – it may be culture-specific. Though the agent of action tends to dominate the perceptual field for Anglo-Americans, the 'person' does not seem to enjoy the same degree of perceptual dominance amongst non-western people.

LAY EXPLANATIONS FOR SOCIAL ISSUES

It is clear that attributions or lay explanations for behaviour, occurrences and events are not only the outcome of internal, individual cognitive processes, but that, rather, attributions are social phenomena in that they are based on widely held and shared beliefs in the form of social and collective representations (Fraser and Gaskell, 1990). Just as Moscovici has referred to a 'thinking society', Hewstone (1989a) refers to an 'attributing society' – the propensity of people to seek explanations within the predominant cultural framework, especially for societal problems and issues. Our explanations for social phenomena are shaped not only by culture but also by scientific and expert knowledge. The diffusion and popularization of scientific concepts throughout society is occurring at a rapid rate through the mass media so that, increasingly, expert knowledge contributes to the stock of common sense which people draw upon to understand social reality. Thus, people can be regarded as 'amateur' scientists, 'amateur' economists, 'amateur' psychologists, etc., as they draw upon this information to explain a range of phenomena such as the greenhouse effect, a depressed economy or problems in their interpersonal relationships. Some of this knowledge becomes an integral part of mass culture and, ultimately, what will come to be regarded as 'common sense' (Moscovici and Hewstone, 1983).

The attributions that people make for societal events and issues provide social psychologists with insight into a society's prevailing explanations or meaning systems. Research into lay explanations and attributions has focused on a number of social issues, some of which we discuss below. This review is not intended to be exhaustive but it does identify the social base from which explanations emerge and the manner in which explanations are linked to particular social and political identifications. Explanations are therefore not purely cognitive phenomena, but are social in origin, sometimes widely shared, and ultimately shaped by socio-historical forces.

Explanations for success and failure

Thus far we have discussed the pervasiveness of individualism as an ideological orientation within western industrialized societies and the way this influences and shapes causal explanations people give for behaviour and events. The prevalence of such explanations in western societies has also been found in sociological research pertaining to beliefs about social mobility (Mann, 1970; Schlozman and Verba, 1979) and in psychological studies of causal explanations for academic achievement, an area in which attribution research has been prolific (Weiner, 1986).

While there has been considerable debate within social theory concerning the extent to which contemporary liberal democratic societies are characterized by hegemonic beliefs and values,[1] an exhaustive review of the sociological research by Mann in 1970 found that one of the few value orientations in which studies indicated a dominant consensus was in relation to individualist values of achievement. His review found that a significant degree of 'dominant consensus' existed within and between different socio-economic groups in both England and the United States regarding statements such as 'it is important to get ahead', and that hard work and ability rather than luck are instrumental for success. Likewise, Connell (1971) found that among Australian adolescents these beliefs were particularly strong for highly valued pursuits such as materialistic and occupational goals. Schlozman and Verba (1979) found that among their American workforce sample 68 per cent regarded hard work as the most important factor in determining who gets ahead, only 8 per cent regarded luck as important and 24 per cent posited family background as instrumental. Overall, Schlozman and Verba found few occupational differences in attitudes toward success and the availability of opportunities for social mobility within the United States. Furthermore, they found little difference in strength of commitment to individualistic notions of success between employed and unemployed members of the same occupational level. At least 60 per cent of people in each unemployed category believed that hard work is instrumental to success.

Most psychological research on achievement attributions has drawn from the work of Weiner (1986), who has used four major causal categories to study success and failure attributions, these being ability, effort, luck and task difficulty. A recent review of the research literature on academic success by Dandy (1994) suggests that students are more likely to endorse internal attributions for success than external attributions. For example, Australian research has found an overwhelming preference among secondary school students for personal over situational attributions when accounting for academic success and failure (Augoustinos, 1989, 1990). Students were more likely to endorse causal statements reflecting a candidate's intellectual abilities and effort in achievement attributions than causal references to external factors such as luck and task difficulty. Ability and hard work were regarded as necessary for academic success and their absence as instrumental in academic failure. This preference for personal attributions was evident for students from both ends of the socio-economic spectrum and was significantly more pronounced among the older students (16- to 17-year-olds) compared to the younger students (13- to 14-year-olds). In a similar vein to Miller's cross-sectional research, but lacking a cross-cultural focus, this lends further support to Miller's developmental finding that internal personal attributions increase with age in western cultures.

Poverty

An area which has attracted considerable research interest by social psychologists is lay explanations for poverty. As will become clear, explanations for a socio-economic outcome like poverty are not unrelated to explanations for social mobility and success and failure. One of the earliest studies focusing on this theme was Feagin's (1972) American survey of around 1000 randomly selected subjects. Feagin found that individualistic explanations for poverty, such as lack of thrift and proper money management, lack of effort and loose morals, were favoured over societal and fatalistic explanations like bad luck. Feagin was struck by the extent to which his respondents primarily held the poor responsible for their situation and entitled his study 'Poverty: We Still Believe That God Helps Those Who Help Themselves'.

In an Australian study, Feather (1974) found a similar preference for individualistic explanations, though Australians were less likely to endorse individualistic explanations compared to Feagin's American sample. As well as an overall prevalence of individualistic explanations, both studies found demographic differences in preferences for explanations. Feagin found that respondents who were most likely to endorse individualistic explanations were white Protestants and Catholics, respondents over 50 years of age, those of middle socio-economic status and respondents with middle levels of education. People most likely to endorse societal-structural reasons for poverty were black Protestants and Jews, respondents under 30 years of age and those of lower socio-economic status and education. The most striking group difference in Feather's study was that older respondents were more likely to support individualistic explanations than younger respondents. Other studies which have found a predominance of individualistic explanations for poverty and for these to be related to demographic characteristics include Caplan and Nelson (1973), Singh and Vasudeva (1977) and Townsend (1979). Feagin (1975) emphasizes the functional purposes and political implications emanating from different explanations for poverty. By blaming the victim, individualistic explanations undermine structural efforts at redistributive justice. Such explanations 'mesh well with establishment attempts to maintain the status quo, whereas structural interpretations lend themselves to attempts at counter-ideologies and at structural reforms in this society' (Feagin, 1975: 126).

Given the political and ideological overtones with which different explanations are imbued, it is not surprising that explanations for poverty have also been found to be related to political identifications and voting behaviour. In a British middle-class sample, Furnham (1982a) found that Conservatives rated individualistic explanations as significantly more important than did Labour voters. In turn, Labour voters differed significantly from Conservatives in that they placed more importance on societal-structural reasons (see Table 8.1).

All the above studies have focused primarily on the views of adult respondents. The first study to investigate adolescent explanations for poverty was conducted by Furnham (1982b), who found that public schoolboys (from middle- to upper-class backgrounds) were more likely to endorse individualistic explanations than comprehensive schoolboys (from lower socio-economic backgrounds). The latter rated societal factors as significantly more important. There were no school differences for fatalistic explanations. More recently, Stacey and his colleagues have investigated attributions for poverty in New Zealand adolescents. Stacey and Singer (1985) found that secondary school students rated familial factors as most important in explaining poverty, followed by societal, individualistic and luck attributions. This pattern of attributional preferences was also found in a sample of teenage university students (Stacey, Singer and Ritchie, 1989). Consistent with Feather's (1974) earlier study, it seems that younger people are less likely to endorse individualistic explanations for poverty.

The relationship between age and explanations for poverty is consistent with the cross-sectional studies on causal attributions for socially desirable and undesirable behaviour (Miller, 1984) and for success and failure (Augoustinos, 1989, 1990) which, together, suggest that, with increased age, attributions within western society become more internal and individualistic in nature. There are two possible explanations for this finding. First, consistent with Miller's research, there is the developmental explanation which suggests that, with age, the dominant political, social and economic values of individualism influence the nature of explanations people make for social issues such as poverty. Alternatively, an historical explanation would suggest that people in general are placing less emphasis on individualistic causes for poverty. Feagin's study took place some 20 years ago. Even though he was dismayed by the prevalence of victim blaming in his sample, he concluded that his subjects in 1969 were

Table 8.1 Comparisons between British Conservative and Labour voters' explanations for poverty

Explanations	Conservative	Labour
Individualistic		
1 Lack of thrift and proper money management by poor people	3.07	5.17*
2 Lack of effort and laziness by the poor themselves	3.57	5.02*
3 Loose morals and drunkenness among the poor	4.62	5.82*
4 No attempts at self-improvement among the poor	3.42	4.65*
Societal		
1 Low wages in some businesses and industry	3.27	1.95*
2 Failure of society to provide good schools	5.52	3.72*
3 Prejudice and discrimination against poor people	4.93	3.95*
4 Failure of industry to provide enough jobs for poor people	4.30	3.07*
5 Being taken advantage of by the rich	4.70	3.50*
6 Inefficient trade unions	5.21	4.10*
7 High taxes and no incentives in this country	4.93	3.95*
Fatalistic		
1 Lack of ability and talent among poor people	3.92	4.80
2 Sickness and physical handicap	3.82	3.20
3 Just bad luck	5.67	5.25
4 Lack of intelligence among poor people	4.25	4.67

* Significant at or below $p < 0.05$
Numbers are means on a seven-point scale where a low mean indicates stronger agreement with the statement.

Source: Adapted from Furnham, 1982a: 315

more likely to support structural causes compared to subjects in an earlier study in 1945. Thus beliefs and explanations for poverty may be changing over time. Of course, the only way to disentangle the developmental hypothesis from the historical one is to conduct longitudinal studies using different age cohorts; something which has not been done in this area to date.

Unemployment

Psychological studies on explanations for unemployment have not found such a pervasive influence of individualist explanations. Using Feagin's (1972) three categories of explanations (individualistic, societal and fatalistic), which have characterized the work on explanations for poverty, Furnham (1982c) found that individualistic explanations for unemployment were least important, and societal explanations most important, in a sample of 284 predominantly middle-class, well-educated Britons. His sample also included 100 unemployed subjects who had been unemployed for between three and five months. While significant differences were found between the employed and unemployed in their endorsement of various explanations, all subjects preferred societal over individualistic explanations. Both employed and unemployed subjects rated world-wide recession and inflation, together with the policies and strategies of British governments, as the most important causes for unemployment. Similarly, Gaskell and Smith (1985) asked a randomly selected sample of British male school leavers to respond to an open-ended question on the main causes of unemployment among young people, and on attributing responsibility for reducing unemployment to either the unemployed themselves (internal) or the government (external). External (societal) attributions of unemployment were considered more important than internal or individualistic attributions.

In an Australian study, Feather (1985) found a similar preference for external/societal explanations of unemployment among a sample of psychology students. Factors such as defective government, social change and economic recession were rated as more important than lack of motivation or personal handicap on the part of the unemployed. However, it was also significant that one individualistic factor, which referred to the lack of skills and competence in the unemployed, was rated as the most important factor of all.

As with the research on poverty, the relationship between explanations for unemployment and demographic variables, political and value orientations have also been explored. For example, Furnham (1982c) found that Conservatives rated individualistic factors as more important than did Labour voters, whereas Labour voters rated societal-structural reasons as more important. Likewise, Feather (1985) found conservative attitudes to be significantly related

to the endorsement of individualistic explanations for unemployment, and Furnham (1982d) found a link between such explanations
and a strong endorsement of Protestant work ethic beliefs (Furnham,
1984).

Overall, it seems that for unemployment societal and structural
factors are rated as most important, suggesting the existence of a
shared representation which attributes this problem primarily to
social, political and economic forces. It should be stressed, however,
that, while external and structural factors dominate the explanations
for unemployment in the studies reviewed, specific individual factors, such as skill and motivation deficiencies, have also been rated
highly as reasons for unemployment. Kelvin (1984) argues that as
unemployment increases and becomes a major economic problem,
individualist explanations for its occurrence are likely to become
less important, as most people, particularly the media, focus on
structural and socio-economic explanations. Furnham and Hesketh
(1988) found some support for this when comparing explanations for
unemployment given by New Zealanders and Britons. The British,
who were experiencing a higher rate of unemployment in their
country at the time of the research than New Zealanders (12 per cent
and 4 per cent respectively), endorsed more societal than individualistic explanations. As with research on lay explanations for poverty,
studies which examine historical trends in explanations for unemployment, with a specific emphasis on cohort effects, would be of
considerable advantage (see Jennings and Markus, 1984).

Riots

As extreme and negative events, riots arouse interest and spontaneous efforts at explanation both by the media and by the general
public. The recent May 1992 riots in Los Angeles were no exception,
as social commentators and ordinary people around the world
offered a variety of explanations for the civil disorder that ensued
following the acquittal of the four police officers charged with
assaulting black motorist Rodney King. Two psychological studies
which have systematically investigated the causes attributed to riots
will be examined in order to understand the underlying psychological
nature of such explanations.

An early study by Schmidt (1972) investigated the nature of
explanations which had been advanced for the civil disturbances
experienced all over the United States in the summer of 1967.
Schmidt analysed the content of the print media's explanations for
the riots and arrived at 76 different kinds of explanations. To
determine the underlying structure of these explanations, he asked

40 male judges to sort the explanations in terms of their similarity to each other. A multidimensional scaling analysis of the data found that the explanations could be differentiated along two major dimensions. The first dimension included explanations which referred to the criminal nature of the riots and the rioters. This included explanations which referred to the rioters as political extremists who were engaged in revolutionary behaviour. All these explanations emphasized the role of the rioters themselves. In contrast, the second dimension included explanations which referred to the social, physical and economic conditions surrounding the rioting such as unemployment and poverty. Associated with these were explanations which stressed the government's failure to improve living conditions, which, in turn, led to the psychological characteristics of hopelessness, despair and frustration amongst the rioters.

Schmidt also asked independent judges to rate the 76 explanations in terms of the following properties: legitimate–illegitimate cause, internal–external cause, and social-institutional–physical-environmental cause. The two dimensions yielded by the multidimensional scaling analysis were significantly consistent with the way in which the judges rated the explanations as internal vs external. Explanations emphasizing the behaviour and role of the rioters themselves were more likely to be rated as internal causes, whereas explanations which emphasized the causal role of social and economic conditions were rated as external. This dimension also correlated significantly with the legitimate–illegitimate ratings of the explanations. Internal causes were more likely to be rated as illegitimate, whereas external causes were more likely to be viewed as legitimate. Explanations regarded as social-institutional in nature included references to the failure of government policies and agencies, whereas physical-environmental causes made references to unemployment and slum living conditions.

Litton and Potter (1985) found a similar internal–external distinction in explanatory accounts of the St Paul's riots in Bristol, England, in 1980. Litton and Potter analysed the numerous causal explanations which appeared in the print, radio and television media and interviewed six people who were present at or involved in the riot. Again, explanations could be distinguished as internal, which located the cause of the riot in the people who took part in the dramatic event, or external, in that the social and economic circumstances of the rioters were emphasized. Litton and Potter argued that while at a general level there was considerable consensus about the available range of explanations to account for the riots, at more specific explanatory levels there was considerable variation as to whether people fully or partially accepted or rejected these available accounts as having any legitimate explanatory power.

Litton and Potter demonstrate this with reference to two particular explanations for the riot: the role of race and the effects of government spending cuts on amenities. These authors demonstrated how these explanatory accounts were in some contexts actively 'used' to make sense of the riot, whereas in other contexts they were simply 'mentioned' as available explanations. Thus, despite the consensual range of available explanations for the riot, at more concrete levels there existed conflicting and contradictory accounts. In Chapter 6 we discussed how Litton and Potter presented this work as a critique on the notion of consensus in social representations theory. In contrast, we would argue that conflicting and contradictory explanations are not surprising for a highly controversial and dramatic event such as a riot. A riot's very political nature and deviational salience ensures the generation of competing explanations which are no doubt linked to particular social and political identifications. Indeed, Schmidt found in his study that the print media which identified with the political right and extreme left tended to advance internal explanations for the riots, whereas the centre left media preferred external causal explanations. Furthermore, Schmidt found an interesting time difference in the nature of explanations for the riots. During and shortly after the riots, internal explanations emphasizing the nature of the rioters and their illegitimate actions were significantly more prevalent than external explanations. With time, the latter increased with frequency as did references to the perceived legitimacy of the riots. As we made clear in Chapter 6, the problem with Litton and Potter's critique on the existence of consensual explanations is that they do not address the issue of the social and political identifications of the people providing the explanations. Social representations theory would predict significant group differences in preferred explanatory accounts.

Explanations for health and illness

Each culture provides a specific set of meanings which people use to understand the experience of illness and its treatment. Medical anthropology has traditionally concerned itself with how the experience of health and illness is understood and communicated within cultural collectivities. Kleinman (1980) refers to these meaning systems as explanatory models, in which identifying the aetiology or cause of an illness is a central component. For example, Evans-Pritchard (1976) found that among the Azande all misfortune, including illness and death, was believed to be caused by witchcraft.

While this may seem bizarre from a western scientific perspective, Pritchard discovered that this particular explanatory model was able to answer a crucial question which western scientific medicine cannot satisfactorily answer: the 'why me?' question. While western medicine advances biological explanations for illness, it cannot explain why a particular person becomes ill at a particular point in time. While references to chance, luck or the will of God are commonplace (Bulman and Wortman, 1977), the Azande have a ready-made explanation in that a witch targets a particular person at a specific time. In this way, illness explanations among the Azande also have a strong moral component.

With the increasing emphasis on preventive medicine, health and social psychologists have recently begun to explore the finer details of lay representations of physical illness in western societies, the assumption being that such representations have important health implications, both attitudinally and behaviourally. Lau and his colleagues (Lau and Hartman, 1983; Lau, Bernard and Hartman, 1989) have identified five themes or components of illness representations. These components are: *identity* – a label for the disease and its associated symptoms; *time line* – the course of the illness, whether it is acute or chronic; *consequences* – the short- and long-term effects of the disease; *cause* – factors which led to the onset of illness; and *cure* – prescriptions for recovery.

A predominant theme within this research has been the external/ internal dichotomy in illness causation. We documented in Chapter 6 how Herzlich's (1973) study on the representations of health and illness in France found that a prevalent view among her sample was that the urban 'way of life' is a primary determinant in the genesis of illness. Health and illness were seen to be the outcome of struggle and opposition between the passive individual and the 'way of life'. Herzlich concludes that the representation of health and illness was structured around a number of opposing concepts: internal vs external, healthy vs unhealthy, natural vs unnatural, the individual vs society.

Pill and Stott (1982, 1985) extended Herzlich's work by investigating concepts of illness causation and responsibility among working-class women in Wales. Their primary motivation for exploring lay explanations of health and illness was the shift in public health policy in Britain from curative to preventive medicine. Herzlich's research already suggested that illness was not directly attributed to the behaviour of the individual, but was seen to be brought about through stress and the role obligations associated with everyday urban life. Pill and Stott explored whether people accepted the notion of individual responsibility in the maintenance of health, which is explicit in preventive health philosophy. Both studies concluded that individual responsibility in the genesis of illness was given lower priority than external factors. The women they studied were more likely to emphasize factors outside the individual's control in the genesis of illness, such as the environment, weather, pollution, heredity, germs and infection. There were, however, some differences within this group of women. Women who had higher levels of education were more likely to mention lifestyle factors such as diet, hygiene, exercise and rest as causative agents in illness. These women were also more likely to emphasize preventive health practices and were more willing to attribute moral blame to the individual for illness.

Pill and Stott's research suggests that people may be resistant to public health experts' emphasis on individual responsibility for health care and the implementation of preventive health practices. It is unclear, however, to what extent such resistance is prevalent in groups other than working-class Welsh women. We have already emphasized the way in which cultural belief systems shape explanations. Furthermore, it is possible that with the increasing exposure of the public to the notion of preventive health practices, health-related attitudes and behaviour may change over time in accordance with this philosophy. It is perhaps ironic that for decades public health authorities in western countries have attempted to 'destigmatize' mental illness by encouraging people to view it in the same way they viewed physical illness as an amoral affliction over which an individual had little control. It was strongly believed that by educating the public to treat mental illness as an 'illness like any other' the tendency of blaming the mentally ill for their plight would wane. Now we are being encouraged to view all 'illness' (physical and mental) as being within the domain of individual control and responsibility, and thus moral accountability.

Beliefs in a just world

When we consider the general tendency for people within western cultures to make dispositional attributions for other people's behaviour (the fundamental attribution bias) and the preference among some social groups for individualistic explanations for success, poverty, unemployment, rioting and illness, we can see that such explanations emphasize and promote a belief that individuals determine their own 'fate'. This is linked to the phenomenon which Lerner (1980) has described as the *just world hypothesis*: the general belief that the world is a just place where good things happen to 'good' people and bad things happen to 'bad' people. 'Individuals have a need to believe that they live in a world where people generally get what they deserve. The belief that the world is just enables the individual to confront his physical and social environment as though they were stable and orderly' (Lerner and Miller, 1978: 1030). The belief in a just world is thus motivated by a functional and defensive need to view the misfortune of others as being, to some extent, 'deserved'. By viewing the world as stable and orderly and one in which we are not subject to random happenings, we protect ourselves from the possibility that misfortunes may strike us also at some time.

Many of the studies we have reviewed thus far suggest that individualist explanations for unemployment, poverty, rioting, etc., are linked to conservative values and attitudes. Likewise, beliefs in a just world have been found to be related to authoritarianism, the Protestant work ethic and unfavourable attitudes toward the poor and victims of social injustice (Rubin and Peplau, 1975). Just world beliefs often lead to victim-blaming. The poor are blamed for being lazy and careless with money, the mentally ill for not having the strength of character to pull themselves together, women for being raped, etc. Thus such beliefs may provide the justification for the further and continual oppression of individual victims and marginalized groups in society.

It should, however, be made clear that victim-blaming is not only a feature of lay thought but also a pervasive feature of many theories within psychology. We have already emphasized the strong individualist elements and assumptions contained in many social psychological approaches, but what perhaps we have not made as clear are the victim-blaming tendencies which are often associated with such theoretical and conceptual approaches. To take just one notable social issue as an example, in reviewing all of the articles which appeared over a six month period on the life experiences of black Americans, Caplan and Nelson (1973) noted that 82 per cent of these articles attributed black Americans' social problems to the 'personal shortcomings' of this group of people. Such person-centred explanations serve an important legitimating political function in that the site of change and 'therapy' becomes that of the individual or group rather than the social, economic and political structures and institutions of society. It is politically more expedient to change individuals than it is to change society.

THE INTERNAL/EXTERNAL DICHOTOMY

While the distinction between personal (internal) and situational (external) attributions is a central theme of both attribution research and of studies which have examined the content of lay knowledge and beliefs, there are conceptual and empirical problems associated with this dichotomy. The tendency is to conceptualize these attributions as being negatively related, whereas in reality people embrace and integrate both types of explanations. It is important to stress that in most cases people make both kinds of attributions. Thus personal and situational attributions co-exist and should not necessarily be viewed as contradictory (Billig, 1982). Furthermore, much of the research which has used taxonomies of perceived causation has failed to examine more complex structures of explanations. In a qualitative analysis of the structure of explanations in political conversation, Antaki (1985) found that single-cause explanations are rare, and that people make references to a number of attributions at different levels of explanation. Using a quantitative network analysis, Heaven (1994) found that explanations for poverty were interconnected with each other in complex chains. While a fairly consistent spatial representation of causes was obtained across different groups (societal explanations were generally positioned at the outer regions of the structure, within which the individualistic causes were positioned), interesting group differences in the causal chains were observed. In a sample of the Australian population it was found that those on the political left were more likely to perceive societal factors as core and proximal explanations for poverty, whereas those on the political right included both societal and individualistic causes.

SUMMARY

This chapter has tried to make clear that attributions or lay explanations are not only the outcome of individual cognitive processes but are also linked to social and cultural representations. Our belief systems, values, knowledge and expectations form a background from which explanations are constructed and elaborated. In turn, social representations are shaped and influenced by socio-historical and cultural forces and by the ever increasing contributions of scientific and expert knowledge to which we are exposed. We demonstrated this particularly in relation to the fundamental attribution bias. The resilience of the cognitive account for this bias in the face of a cultural explanation which is just as plausible (if not more so) suggests that the fundamental attribution bias is not only a pervasive feature of causal explanations offered by the 'amateur' scientist but also a dominant theme within psychological theory itself.

By bringing together attribution theory, a theory which is predominantly concerned with the cognitive processes involved in making causal analyses, and social representations theory, a theory which emphasizes the social and cultural context within which thinking is embedded, we have demonstrated the social psychological nature of everyday explanations for a range of social issues such as riots, unemployment, poverty, success and failure, and health and illness.

NOTE

1 The concept of ideological hegemony will be discussed in considerable detail in Chapter 11.

9

STEREOTYPES, PREJUDICE AND INTERGROUP ATTRIBUTIONS

A few years ago, when my (IW's) youngest child, Joel, was in Year 2 in primary school, he had a friend he sometimes played with, called David. One afternoon, around school closing time, my wife was doing some work in the front garden when David's mother walked past and stopped for a chat. The conversation turned to school, and David's mother started complaining about some of the other children in Joel and David's classroom. Eventually she got around to voicing what was really bothering her – the fact that there were some Aboriginal children in the classroom, and that she 'didn't want any child of hers sitting next to no snot-faced coon'. David's mother had grown up in a large country town in Western Australia. She was also a devout Christian, attending service every Sunday, and devoting large amounts of her time to the Salvation Army.

This vignette neatly encapsulates many of the issues we will address in this chapter. David's mother was expressing strong sentiments about another group, but in the absence of that group; in other words, she was engaging in intergroup behaviour even though there were no groups physically present. Her sentiments had been mostly, if not entirely, imported to the local context. Her views on race apparently conflicted with other fundamental beliefs she held, such as the Christian injunct to love thy neighbour, but she felt no psychological contradiction. There were, to our knowledge anyway, no problems at school involving race. Why, then, did David's mother think, feel and act the way she did?

David's mother is not an oddity in Australia. Racism is endemic, although its expression is not as blunt as it once was. The report of the National Inquiry into Racist Violence in Australia chronicles case after case of reports to the Inquiry of incidents of violence against

Aborigines (115 reports spanning the five years from 1986 to 1990), of violence against Asians, of violence against people from the Middle East, of violence against Jews, of violence against non-English speakers, and of violence against people who support anti-racist policies or beliefs (National Inquiry into Racist Violence in Australia, 1991). Racism is not just an individual phenomenon, though. It operates in social, cultural and institutional spheres too. For example, Aboriginal health, employment rates, access to education and mortality rates and life expectancy are all more akin to those of an impoverished third world country than an 'advanced' industrialized first world country (see Callan, 1986; Hunter, 1991).

Stereotypes are conventionally defined as mental representations of a group and its members. They derive from the cultural constructions of social groups, are moulded by and reflect the actual social positions of groups, and operate in basic, psychological ways. Stereotypes act as schemas, directing mental resources, guiding the encoding and retrieval of information. As schemas, stereotypes serve to generate behavioural expectancies which often function as self-fulfilling prophecies, and to provide explanatory accounts of events in the social environment. Stereotypes are both a cause and a consequence of prejudice. Prejudice is defined as an evaluation of an outgroup and its members. Negative prejudices provide the pernicious, affective punch to stereotypes. Both stereotypes and prejudice make discrimination against an outgroup and its members more likely, but discrimination may also occur for other reasons, often in the absence of individual stereotypes and prejudice. When applied to the context of race relations, a particular constellation of negative stereotypes, prejudice and discrimination can be identified as racism. According to some accounts, at the core of racism is the fundamental belief in the constitutional superiority of one's own race over other races.

STEREOTYPES AND STEREOTYPING

What is a stereotype?

A stereotype is a mental representation of a social group and its members (Hamilton and Sherman, 1994; Stangor and Lange, 1994). It is a 'picture in the head' (Lippmann, 1922). But, more than just a picture in the head, a stereotype is a cognitive structure with mental life. A stereotype is a schema, with all the properties of schemas as discussed in Chapter 3 – it organizes and integrates incoming information; it directs attention to particular events and away from others; and it colours the retrieval of information. But if that's all stereotypes were, social psychologists would not have accorded them special status and attention. Stereotypes differ from most other schemas because of their social consequences. Stereotypes derive their form and content from the social context surrounding the individual, and their operation leads to social injustice. Indeed, stereotypes can be thought of as social representations, as described in Chapter 6, since they are symbolic and affective, political and ideological. Many social stereotypes operate as objectified knowledge structures in collective and social life. Unfortunately, the mainstream social psychological study of stereotypes has been overly concerned with a cognitive analysis, and has neglected the symbolic and ideological nature of stereotypes.

The term 'stereotype' was introduced to the social sciences by Walter Lippmann (1922), who, as a journalist, borrowed the phrase from the world of printing. In printing, a stereotype is the metal cast that is used to make repeated and identical images of a character on paper. Lippmann used the term by analogy to refer to the ways in which people apply the same character to their impression of a group and its members. When someone, say a white Anglo-Saxon Protestant, views all blacks as stupid, or all Jews as venal, or all Aboriginal children as 'snot-faced', they are applying the same cast to their impression of all members of the particular group.

In many ways, Lippmann was several decades ahead of cognitive psychology. The psychology of Lippmann's time saw cognition of the world as a relatively passive, veridical and 'cold' process which allowed the human perceiver to apprehend a more-or-less true picture of 'reality' (for an example of an occasional exception, see Bartlett, 1932b). It was not until the so-called 'new look' in perception arose in the 1950s (for example, Bruner, 1958; Bruner, Goodnow and Austin, 1956) that perception was seen as a much more active, motivated and 'hot' process. But this was Lippmann's view 30 years prior: perception of the social environment is shaped by the 'mental pictures' we have of the objects of our perception. Furthermore, Lippmann saw that a stereotype was more than just a neutral mental picture, clung to because it is an easy way of perceiving the world, requiring little effort. Stereotypes bind us to our world, and they are highly charged. Thus, he writes:

> An unfamiliar scene is like the baby's world, 'one great, blooming, buzzing, confusion' [citing John Dewey's famous quote]. . . . For the most part we do not first see, and then define, we define first and then see. In the great blooming, buzzing confusion of the outer world we pick out what our culture has already defined for us, and we tend to

perceive that which we have picked out in the form stereotyped for us by our culture. (Lippmann, 1922: 95–6)

There is another reason, besides economy of effort, why we so often hold to our stereotypes when we might pursue a more disinterested vision. The systems of stereotypes may be the core of our personal tradition, the defenses of our position in society. They are an ordered, more or less consistent picture of the world, to which our habits, our tastes, our capacities, our comforts, and our hopes have adjusted themselves. . . . No wonder, then, that any disturbance of the stereotypes seems like an attack upon the foundations of the universe. It is an attack upon the foundations of our universe, and, where big things are at stake, we do not readily admit that there is any distinction between our universe and the universe. A pattern of stereotypes is not neutral. It is not merely a way of substituting order for the great blooming, buzzing confusion of reality. It is not merely a short cut. It is all these things and something more. It is the guarantee of our self-respect; it is the projection upon the world of our own sense of our own value, our own position and our own rights. The stereotypes are, therefore, highly charged with the feelings that are attached to them. They are the fortress of our tradition, and behind its defenses we can continue to feel ourselves safe in the position we occupy. (Lippmann, 1922: 102–3)

Stereotyping refers to the process of activating and using a stereotype. It is useful to distinguish between *social* and *individual* stereotypes. Stereotypes and stereotyping are inherently social. They cannot be anything but social, since they are of a social category, and they are shared. The social or cultural representation of a group is a social stereotype. Social stereotypes are shared and, more or less, universally identifiable by all the members of a culture. Thus, most people in Australia can easily describe the stereotype of Aborigines, precisely because the social stereotype of Aborigines has a social life, existing in the cultural atmosphere beyond the individuals and groups who expound them. For the same reason, most Australians are unable to identify the stereotype of Mauritians or Zulus or Aberdonians. These groups do not have social life in Australia. But being able to identify and reproduce a social stereotype does not necessarily mean that one believes that stereotype. The stereotype that any one person has of a social category is known as an individual stereotype. Undoubtedly, there are strong associations between social and individual stereotypes, but it is too simple to assume they are identical.

'Whether favorable or unfavorable, *a stereotype is an exaggerated belief associated with a category. Its function is to justify (rationalize) our conduct in relation to that category*' (Allport, 1954: 191; original emphasis). Allport was talking, of course, about individual stereo-types. His view was extremely influential for two or more decades: social psychology thought of stereotypes as wrong, or inadequate, or exaggerated, mental depictions of a social group. They were more than just Lippmann's 'pictures in our heads'; they were *inaccurate* pictures. Allport emphasized, though, that stereotypes sometimes do bear some resemblance to the world as it is; that is, that stereotypes sometimes contain a 'kernel of truth'. This notion has been vexing for social psychology, and indeed for social psychol-ogists, for a long time, and we will return to the issue later in this chapter.

Allport's notion of a stereotype as an excessive and inaccurate generalization was gradually extended into an almost completely cognitive notion, so that by the mid-1970s social psychology had largely accepted Lippmann's contention that stereotypes help us to cope with a social reality too full and complicated, too blooming and buzzing, for us to apprehend fully, and had largely forgotten the rest of Lippmann's (and Allport's) analysis. The social origins and consequences of stereotypes were largely neglected. The concept of stereotype, like that of attitude discussed in Chapter 2, had lost its social-ness, and had become entirely an individual and individual-istic construct. In the cognitive hegemony of social psychology, stereotyping was seen almost as a prototypical example of the principle of the 'cognitive miser' (Fiske and Taylor, 1984, 1991; see Chapter 3). Thus, the social origins of stereotypes discussed by Lippmann and Allport have been forgotten and supplanted by an account which sees their origin entirely within the normal, day-to-day routine of cognitive life.

The cognitive analysis of stereotypes dominated social psychology until as recently as the early 1990s (for excellent examples of the cognitive approach, see Hamilton and Sherman, 1994; Stangor and Lange, 1994; and Stephan, 1985). Three recent developments augur for a change in social psychology's understanding of stereotypes. Hearkening back to the second sentence in Allport's definition given above, the first development reintroduces the idea that stereotypes serve social functions, notably the justification of the social position of the stereotyped group and of the system that produces that position (for example, Jost and Banaji, 1994). We have more to say about the system-justification functions of stereotypes later in this chapter when discussing intergroup attributions, and also in Chapter 11 on ideology, where we argue that stereotypes are essentially ideological representations. The second development is the reintroduction of affect associated with the cognitive represen-tation of a social group (for example, Mackie and Hamilton, 1993).

The third is the grounding of stereotyping in social identity and self-categorization theories (Oakes et al., 1994). We briefly consider these last two developments here.

Recent work has related stereotypes and affect in two different ways. First, several researchers have examined the effects of different affective states on the activation and use of stereotypes. Thus, for example, Esses and Zanna (1989) report that English Canadian subjects accentuated their negative judgements of Pakistanis and Native Indians after they had been subjected to a negative mood induction procedure. Their evaluations of other groups (Jewish, Chinese and Arabic people) were not affected by mood state, except that subjects' evaluations of their own group (English Canadians) were more positive in both negative and positive mood conditions when compared with their evaluations in the neutral mood condition. Negative mood, therefore, appears to make more extreme the negative evaluations of at least some minority groups, and any mood, either positive or negative, appears to enhance the positive evaluation of the ingroup (Esses, Haddock and Zanna, 1994). On the other hand, Bodenhausen, Kramer and Susser (1994) have shown that when subjects are made to feel happy, they too demonstrate greater use of stereotypical thinking. The relationship between affective state and stereotypic thinking is thus far from clear.

The second way in which stereotypes and affect have been examined in recent research has altered our understanding of stereotypes. An earlier view of stereotypes sees them as stores of knowledge contained in memory, with patterns of activation following tracks of semantic association between nodes in this knowledge store. The revised version sees relations among the knowledge elements contained within a stereotype as being linked through, and activated by, patterns of affective, rather than semantic, association. Recent experiments by Augoustinos, Ahrens and Innes (1994) and by Locke, MacLeod and Walker (1994) show that, for people high in prejudice at least, when they are asked to judge a target outgroup, a general store of negative information may be activated, whether that information is related to the stereotype of the target group or not. These results imply that stereotype activation is a process of affective arousal in which a cognitive task elicits an affective reaction, which in turn is responsible for directing judgements and evaluations.

Reintroducing affect into the analysis of stereotyping is one of two recent important developments in the study of stereotypes. The other is the application of self-categorization theory to stereotyping (Oakes et al., 1994). Recall from Chapter 5 on social identity that self categorization theory (SCT) is an elaboration of aspects of social identity theory. SCT proposes that the social world is always and only ever perceived through the process of categorization. There are always many different categorial possibilities that may be applied in any one situation. The choice of one over another depends on the meta-contrast principle. Self, as with all other objects of social perception, must be perceived categorially. Through this process, self is perceived as belonging to some categories, and not belonging to others. Categories of perception can be ordered vertically, from subordinate, relatively exclusive categories at the bottom, through intermediate categories, to superordinate, relatively inclusive categories at the top. Crucially, perception of the social world, and choice of one categorial possibility rather than another, always depends on the comparative context.

When applied to the process of stereotyping, SCT suggests that stereotyping is an outcome of categorial perception. Objects, including self, which are perceived as members of social categories are perceived stereotypically. The categorization process naturally produces an accentuation of intracategory similarities and of intercategory differences. Stereotyping is thus a matter of perceiving people, including self, in terms of categorial memberships. Since the choice among categorial possibilities depends wholly on the comparative context and on the meta-contrast principle, stereotyping itself is not the result of *individual* cognitive processes. Rather, it is a natural, fluid and contextualized outcome of *social* perception.

The measurement of stereotypes

In social psychology, stereotypes have traditionally been measured using one form or another of an adjective checklist. Katz and Braly (1933, 1935) pioneered this technique when they asked Princeton University undergraduates to nominate five adjectives from a list of 84 adjectives to describe, in turn, each of several different social groups. The adjectives used most commonly for any one group were taken to define the stereotype of that group. Thus, in their 1933 study, 75 per cent of the white undergraduate subjects selected 'lazy' as an adjective that describes 'Negroes', and the five most commonly nominated characteristics of Negroes were superstitious, lazy, happy-go-lucky, ignorant and musical. The category 'Americans', on the other hand, was described as industrious, intelligent, materialistic, ambitious and progressive. The adjective checklist method allows the content of social stereotypes to be assessed, as well as the degree of consensus about the content. It does not lend itself easily to examination of the content of individual stereotypes or of the strength of elements within an individual's stereotype.

Using the Katz and Braly technique, several studies have documented the changing content and degree of consensus of the stereotypes of certain groups in the United States over the past six decades (Dovidio and Gaertner, 1986; Gilbert, 1951; Karlins, Coffman and Walters, 1969). Dovidio and Gaertner (1986), for example, show that only 13 per cent of their sample of white undergraduates thought 'lazy' described blacks, and the five most commonly ascribed traits were loyal to family, musical, very religious, pleasure-loving and aggressive. These three studies all show that the content of stereotypes of particular groups has changed, sometimes markedly so, over the years, and that this change is often precipitated by a change in the objective social relations between groups. For example, the five characteristics rated as most typical of Japanese in Katz and Braly's (1933) study are intelligent, industrious, progressive, shrewd and sly. Almost two decades, and one world war, later, Japanese were described as imitative, sly, extremely nationalistic, treacherous and shrewd (Gilbert, 1951), but by the mid-1960s the stereotype had returned to a generally positive one marked by industrious, ambitious, efficient, intelligent and progressive (Karlins et al., 1969). The content of the stereotype of Japanese held by Americans changed dramatically, and in ways that presumably reflected the changing relations between the two countries. A further point indicating how stereotypes have changed is the fact that all of Katz and Braly's subjects completed the adjective checklist without question, but a substantial proportion of the subjects in the Karlins et al. experiment refused to do the task. Stereotyping is seen today as 'old-fashioned', and not something one should do.

The Katz and Braly technique is problem-ridden and rarely used these days (but see Haslam and Turner, 1992; Haslam, Turner, Oakes, McGarty and Hayes, 1992, for examples of current research which uses the technique). Aside from being cumbersome and not easily amenable to quantitative manipulation, the technique forces subjects to make a judgement which implicitly applies to *all* the members of one group. The instructions given to subjects ask them to choose adjectives which are 'typical' of the group being judged. Brigham (1971) recognized this difficulty, and suggested that a better measure would be one in which subjects were asked to indicate what *percentage* of the target group could be described by each particular adjective. McCauley and Stitt (1978; McCauley, Stitt and Segal, 1980) further refined this technique by relating the percentage estimates provided for each adjective for the target group to a base-rate frequency for 'all the world's people'. With Brigham's method, someone could indicate that 70 per cent of blacks are lazy. But this rating alone does not tell us that that person is indicating that laziness describes blacks more than anyone else. Rather, the 70 per cent rating only makes sense relative to a judgement by the same subject of the percentage of 'all the world's people', or at least of whites. In McCauley and Stitt's method, these two estimates are expressed as a ratio (black rating/rating of all the world's people). If the ratio equals one, the adjective does not discriminate between the two groups being judged; if the ratio exceeds one, the adjective describes the target group more than it does 'people in general', and if the ratio is less than one, the adjective is less typical of the target group than of 'people in general'. The ratio of the two percentage estimates is known as a *diagnostic ratio*, because the more the ratio diverges from one, the more the trait being rated diagnoses group membership. The McCauley and Stitt technique introduces the possibility that a trait can be, in a sense, negatively stereotypic – a stereotype can be defined by the *absence* of a characteristic as well as by its presence. McCauley and Stitt (1978), for example, found that the terms efficient, extremely nationalistic, industrious and scientifically minded all had diagnostic ratios greater than one when American subjects rated Germans. But the terms ignorant, impulsive, pleasure-loving, superstitious and tradition-loving all produced diagnostic ratios less than one, indicating that those terms are seen as relatively *less* typical of Germans than they are of people in general.

Other techniques are available to assess the content of stereotypes. For example, several studies have asked respondents to *rate* the descriptiveness of traits using some form of Likert-type scale (for example, Triandis, Lisansky, Setiadi, Chang, Martin and Betancourt, 1982), and other studies have asked subjects to describe a *prototypical* group member (for example, Jonas and Hewstone, 1986; Stephan, Ageyev, Stephan, Abalakina, Stefanenko and Coates-Schrider, 1993). Marjoribanks and Jordan (1986) examined the autostereotypes (stereotype of the ingroup) and heterostereotypes (stereotype of the outgroup) held by Aboriginal and Anglo-Australians. High school students in Adelaide, South Australia, rated the two groups 'Aboriginal Australians' and 'Anglo-Australians' on several dimensions (for example, reliable, clean and tidy, friendly). About one-quarter of the students were Aborigines. The 'mental pictures' of the two groups held by the Anglo students differed sharply. These students saw Anglos in overwhelmingly positive terms, rating the ingroup more favourably on all dimensions but one, and rated Aborigines in strongly negative terms. The Aboriginal students did not show this pattern of outgroup devaluation and ingroup enhancement, though. These students had a favourable image of Aborigines (the ingroup), but this was much less favourable than their image of Anglos (the outgroup). Thus, ingroups are not always positively differentiated from outgroups. The relative ingroup devaluation shown by the Aboriginal students in the Marjoribanks and Jordan study is not uncommon in minority groups (see, for example, our discussion of the results of the Clark and Clark [1947] doll preference study in Chapter 5 on social identity).

Whether the Katz and Braly technique, the diagnostic ratio or a Likert-type approach is used, what is being assessed is the content of *social* stereotypes. In contrast, *individual* stereotypes are usually accessed using the techniques of cognitive psychology. In this approach, a stereotype is taken to be a schema. Research in this tradition is not usually concerned with describing the particular details of the content of a stereotype, but, rather, focuses on what stimulates stereotypes into activation, and on how stereotype activation affects subsequent information processing, person perception and interpersonal judgements. Stereotypes themselves are not measured. Instead, response latencies, priming effects and other assorted tricks of the cognitive psychology trade are used to examine the on-line processing of stereotypic information. To provide an example of such research, we describe two of the three studies reported in a paper by Perdue et al. (1990).

In the first study, the authors used classical conditioning techniques to pair generic ingroup and outgroup designators (for example, us and them, we and they, ours and theirs) with neutral nonsense syllables (for example, xeh, yof, laj). The nonsense syllables were selected on the basis of prior ratings by subjects which showed them to be affectively neutral. Over many trials, each nonsense syllable was consistently paired with either an ingroup or an outgroup word, or, for the control presentations, with a personal (non-group) pronoun (for example, he, she, his, hers). Pairs were shown to subjects on a tachistoscope, and on each trial subjects had to indicate whether the real word was on the left- or the right-hand side of the screen. After completing 108 such trials, subjects rated each nonsense syllable on a scale with endpoints labelled *pleasant* and *unpleasant*. The results of comparisons between the pleasantness ratings of the three groups of nonsense syllables were marked: nonsense syllables which had been paired with ingroup designators were evaluated positively (that is, as pleasant); nonsense syllables which had been paired with outgroup designators were evaluated negatively; and nonsense syllables paired with personal pronouns were rated neither positively nor negatively. Since the nonsense syllables were previously neutral, the only explanation for the different ratings given for the three groups of nonsense syllables can be that they acquired their evaluation through their repeated association with ingroup, outgroup or neutral designators, and hence that the ingroup designators are themselves evaluated positively and the outgroup designators negatively. The conclusion must be that simple generic group descriptors such as *us* and *them* carry evaluative connotations which affect cognitive processing of information associated with them. In other words, the most basic, minimal element of a schema of group belongingness – a simple division into ingroup and outgroup – is laden with affect.

The second experiment reported by Perdue et al. (1990) used a priming paradigm, rather than a classical conditioning paradigm. Subjects were told to read words presented one at a time on a computer screen, decide whether the word was positive or negative, and then indicate their decision by pressing one of two keys. There were 36 words; half were positive and half were negative. Before each word was presented on the screen it was preceded by a prime. The prime was one of six words, chosen on each trial at random. Half the primes were ingroup designators (us, we, ours), and half were outgroup designators (them, they, theirs). Each prime was presented for only 55 ms before it was overwritten by the target word. This exposure time is so short that conscious recognition of the stimulus is prevented. On the whole, subjects did a good job in deciding whether each target word was positive or negative. But these decisions were really irrelevant to the main aim of the experiment, which was to examine the reaction times taken by subjects in coming to their decision, as measured by the time between the onset of presentation of the target word and the subject pressing a key to respond. Perdue et al. report a significant interaction between the type of prime (ingroup or outgroup) and the valence of the target word (positive or negative) in determining subjects' response times. Subjects were faster in making a decision about a positive target word when it was preceded by an ingroup prime than when it was preceded by an outgroup prime. Conversely, subjects were faster in deciding about a negative target word when it was preceded by an outgroup prime than an ingroup prime. These results imply that ingroup and outgroup primes alter the accessibility of stores of positive or negative trait information. Since the prime was presented subliminally, this differential priming effect of generic ingroup and outgroup descriptors must occur automatically, or unconsciously. Automatic processes are mental processes which are unavoidable; they are not amenable to conscious manipulation (Bargh, 1984, 1994; Fiske and Taylor, 1991).

The Perdue et al. (1990) studies demonstrate how stereotypes are investigated from the perspective of contemporary social cognition. These particular studies suggest the provocative conclusion that even the most minimal categorization of the social environment into *us* and *them* generates outgroup devaluation and ingroup enhancement as automatic cognitive consequences. This obviously hearkens back to the results of the minimal group experiments described in Chapter 5 on social identity. Since some form of categorization is a *necessary* part of social perception, the conclusion from this perspective must be that ingroup–outgroup differentiation in favour of the ingroup is a necessary and unavoidable part of social life. However, since many minority groups accept derogatory ingroup stereotypes, as the Aboriginal students did in the study by Marjoribanks and Jordan (1986), perhaps the automatic cognitive enhancement demonstrated by Perdue at al. (1990) only applies to majority group members, or to members of positively stereotyped groups.

Stereotypes as schemas

We argued in Chapter 3 that stereotypes are schemas; that is, they direct mental resources, guide encoding and retrieval of information, and save cognitive energy. The underlying notion is that stereotypes only demonstrate these properties once they are activated. If a stereotype, or any schema, is not activated, it is of no consequence. The consequences may follow automatically and unconsciously, though. Stereotypes become activated usually by having stereotype-related information presented to the stereotype holder. Information can be relevant to a stereotype by being either stereotype-consistent or stereotype-inconsistent. Either way, once such information is presented the stereotype is activated. Some of the schematic properties of stereotypes are briefly described here.

Stereotypes direct attention   Of all the stimuli in the vast and complex array of information constituting the social environment we only attend to a small handful. It is impossible to do otherwise. Furthermore, we often do not attend to particular stimuli as if they were unique. Instead, we categorize them and process information about them in a categorial, rather than piecemeal, fashion. We attend to some stimuli and ignore others in an orderly, not random or whimsical, manner. Our attention is directed to some stimuli over others, for reasons to do with the stimulus and its context, and with our own mental preparedness.

Stimuli are often selected for our attention because they are either vivid or salient (see Fiske and Taylor, 1991: 247–57). The vividness of a stimulus refers to its inherent attention-grabbing properties. A loud or fast-moving stimulus is vivid. Salience is a kind of context-dependent vividness. A stimulus which stands out relative to its setting is said to be salient. In practice, the distinction between salience and vividness is often difficult to maintain, and the effects of the two appear to be similar.

From the point of view of stereotypes, it can be said that, once activated, a stereotype will guide which stimuli of the array of possible stimuli will be attended to, but only in contexts where the stereotype is relevant to the stimuli being cognized. The experiment by Taylor et al. (1978), described in Chapter 3, showed that when subjects were asked to identify which member of a small group made up of equal numbers of men and women or of black and white people made a particular comment, the errors were far more often within-subgroup rather than between-subgroup. Thus, subjects were able to remember that it was a woman, or a black person, who made a particular remark, but not necessarily which woman, or which black person. Subjects' attention was focused on category memberships, not on individual members of the categories; subjects' attention was being directed by the category-based stereotype. Similar results have been shown by Howard and Rothbart (1980), and Erdley and D'Agostino (1988) showed that stereotypic information can be presented to subjects subliminally and the effect persists.

Stereotypes guide encoding of information   Once attended to, information must be encoded in memory if it is to have any persisting effect, otherwise it is lost. Encoding, then, refers to the process by which information from the external environment is internalized, or represented within the cognitive system of the perceiver. Encoding usually occurs more or less automatically, without us having to pay attention to how we are to encode any particular piece of information. Once encoded, the information is linked within the perceiver's cognitive system by an associative web formed by semantic and affective ties. Stereotypes often function to assist the process of encoding information, and the encoded information comes to reside within the cognitive system with semantic and affective links to the stereotype.

A good example of how stereotypes influence the encoding of behaviour is provided by a study by Duncan (1976), which is described in detail later on in the section on intergroup attributions. For present purposes, Duncan showed white subjects an interaction between two actors in which an argument developed and eventually one actor shoved the other. When the actor who shoved the other was black, the behaviour was categorized – encoded in memory – as an aggressive or violent act, but when the shove was done by a white person the behaviour was categorized as just playing around or being overly dramatic. The behaviour was ostensibly the same, but it was seen and encoded differently depending upon the race of the actor, and, presumably, upon the stereotype of blacks as, among other things, being aggressive and violent.

Stereotypes guide retrieval of information   Several studies have reported that subjects remember more information about target individuals and about target groups when that information is consistent with their prior impressions than when it is inconsistent (for example, Rothbart et al., 1979). Most of these studies, though, use artificial, fictitious groups in an experimental paradigm that requires subjects to 'form an impression' about the target being described. Rarely, studies report effects using real groups as targets. One such study is reported by Cano, Hopkins and Islam (1991). In this study, subjects in one condition were presented with adjectives about one of three real groups (football fans, salesmen or Japanese). The adjectives were either congruent with the stereotype of the group, incongruent with the stereotype or irrelevant to the stereotype. In the other experimental condition, subjects were provided with the same adjectives as those used for the subjects in the first experimental condition, but were told only that they described a group identified by a letter (group A, B or C). After being presented with these adjectives, subjects were asked, among other things, to recall as many of the adjectives as possible. In the artificial group condition, the number of congruent adjectives recalled was slightly more than the number of irrelevant adjectives, which in turn was more than the number of incongruent adjectives. In the real group condition, subjects recalled many more congruent adjectives than incongruent adjectives, and recalled even fewer irrelevant adjectives. Thus, the degree to which information about a target group fits with the previously held stereotype of the group influences the degree to which that information will subsequently be recalled. Further, the size of this effect, and the relative amounts of stereotype-incongruent and stereotype-irrelevant material recalled, depend on whether the stereotyped group is artificial or real. This last point perhaps suggests a limit to the extent to which results from contrived experimental paradigms using artificial groups and individuals – usually for reasons to do with maintaining tight experimental control – can be generalized to the processing of information about real groups in real social contexts.

Stereotypes save cognitive energy   A central tenet of any model which conceptualizes stereotypes as schemas is that they function to conserve mental energy, that their use frees up cognitive resources for other tasks which otherwise would have had to be spent processing information about the objects of the stereotype in a piecemeal fashion. It is surprising, then, that such a central tenet has largely gone untested. In one recent study, though, Macrae et al. (1994, Study 1; discussed previously in Chapter 3) used a dual-task paradigm to get subjects to form an impression of several target persons from trait terms presented on a computer screen while also doing another unrelated task (listening to a passage of prose played on a tape recorder). Subjects were told that after the tasks they would be asked about the impressions they had formed as well as about the prose they had listened to. The prose passage consisted of a series of facts about the economy and geography of Indonesia, a subject the Welsh undergraduate subjects knew nothing about. The person impression task consisted of a target person's name being presented to subjects on the upper half of a computer screen, with a trait word presented on the lower half. There were four target persons, and each was described throughout the experiment by 10 adjectives. For half of the subjects, the target person was also introduced with a category label (either doctor, artist, skinhead, or estate agent). For each target person, half of the 10 adjectives were stereotype-consistent (for example, caring, honest, reliable, upstanding and responsible for the doctor, and rebellious, aggressive, dishonest, untrustworthy and dangerous for the skinhead) and half were stereotype-neutral (for example, unlucky, forgetful, passive, clumsy and enthusiastic for the doctor, and lucky, observant, modest, optimistic and curious for the skinhead).

The first result to note from this study is that those subjects provided with category labels for the target persons subsequently recalled twice as many stereotype-consistent adjectives as did the subjects not provided with the labels, but the two groups of subjects did not differ in their ability to recall the stereotype-neutral adjectives. This indicates that the stereotypes were functioning schematically by facilitating either encoding or recall of stereotype-consistent information.

The second result shows that those subjects provided with, and presumably using, a stereotype label remembered more facts about Indonesia's geography and economy than did those subjects not provided with such a label. Thus, the stereotype apparently functioned to free up some of the subjects' cognitive resources so they could better attend to the second, but simultaneous, experimental task.

In a second experiment, Macrae et al. (1994) repeated the procedure of the first experiment, but presented the stereotype labels to subjects subliminally. This was achieved by showing the label for 30 ms, and then masking the label with a neutral stimulus. The effect of the stereotype label was still apparent, even though subjects could have had no conscious access to the label. Subjects in the stereotype-present condition remembered more of the targets' traits than did those subjects in the stereotype-absent condition, and they also recalled more information about Indonesia. Thus, the schematic consequences of stereotype activation – facilitated encoding and recall of information about the target person, and the liberation of attentional resources for deployment on other tasks – do not depend on the conscious awareness of the stereotype label.

Stereotypes as social representations

So far in this chapter, we have described the information processing functions of stereotypes. From this highly cognitive and individual-istic perspective, stereotypes can be easily viewed as social schemas: they are theory-driven, stable knowledge structures in memory, they have internal organizational properties and are learned by individuals usually during their early years. This has been the dominant con-ceptualization of stereotypes within the social cognition literature. Relatively scant attention has been paid to the symbolic, political and ideological nature and functions of stereotypes. In contrast, we propose that stereotypes are more than just cognitive schemas. Stereotypes are social representations: they are objectified cognitive and affective structures about social groups within society which are extensively shared and which emerge and proliferate within the particular social and political milieu of a given historical moment. Stereotypes do not simply exist in individuals' heads. They are socially and discursively constructed in the course of everyday communication, and, once objectified, assume an independent and sometimes prescriptive reality. It is naïve to argue that stereotypes are simply the by-product of the cognitive need to simplify reality. For what gives stereotypes their specific form and content? Why are stereotypes group-serving and, in many cases, system-serving? Why do members of minority groups often internalize negative social stereotypes of their ingroup? A schematic or cognitive account of stereotypes and stereotyping has enormous difficulty answering such questions. It is only when stereotypes are conceptualized more as social representations, or, as we argue in Chapter 11, as ideological representations, that the inherently social and political nature and function of stereotypes can be understood. We have much more to say about this in Chapter 11.

Is stereotypic thinking normal or inevitable?

Social psychology's original thinking about stereotypes construed them as faulty, inflexible and inaccurate. They were a sign of aberrant and abhorrent thinking, a kind of thinking to be remedied by full consideration of the *individual* being perceived. This notion, that stereotypes and stereotypical thinking are abnormal or wrong, is not an unusual one. It resonates with the contemporary common understanding of stereotyping, and it has a long tradition in social psychology. Questions about whether stereotyping is abnormal or wrong, or, as is currently the dominant view in social cognition, inevitable, should really be considered separately. The *'normality'* of stereotyping refers to its prevalence in the community, and is an issue that can be addressed empirically. Whether it is *wrong* to stereotype, though, is and always will be a moral question. Empirical research is of no help. However, the dominant morals of our times certainly are opposed to stereotyping to the extent that it creates social injustices and denies people, individually and in groups, certain legal and moral rights. Social psychology, by and large, accepts this common morality. Finally, the *inevitability* of stereotyping is a theoretical question, about which social psychology should have much to say.

It was Gordon Allport, in his classic *The Nature of Prejudice* (1954), who led the charge away from the idea that stereotyping is a sign of a sick mind, something that could be avoided with the proper mental effort, and toward the notion that stereotypes and stereotyping are a normal and necessary part of the way we perceive the world. The fundamental process of categorization, suggested Allport, is the basis of stereotyping. It is a normal and unavoidable part of cognitive life. In this sense, Allport presaged much of what social cognitive theorists were to contribute three decades later. Allport, like Lippmann before him, accepted that categorization is an essential part of the process of simplifying the social environment, thus predating the metaphor of the cognitive miser (Fiske and Taylor, 1984, 1991).

This view was taken to its limits by Tajfel (1969). Research on the principle of categorization, discussed in Chapter 5 on social identity, illustrates how categorization underlies stereotyping. The accentuation effect holds that when a salient and useful classification is systematically imposed upon a range of stimuli, intraclass similarities and interclass differences are accentuated. When this is applied to the perception of social groups the accentuation effect is essentially the process of stereotyping. If perception without classification is practically impossible, and if the accentuation effect follows necessarily from classification-based perception, then stereotyping is a normal, and indeed inevitable, consequence of the perception of social groups.

A more social perspective affords a different view about the inevitability of stereotyping. While admitting the undeniable prevalence and vehemence of many stereotypes, a social perspective also considers the fact that stereotypes are functional for society, or at least for some potent groups in society, as well as for cognitively slothful individuals. Stereotypes provide a system-justificatory function (Jost and Banaji, 1994; see also Chapter 11 below). Stereotype content is determined by the relative social and economic positions of groups, not by any properties intrinsic to the members of those groups. A social perspective also highlights the fact that stereotypes serve social identity functions as well as cognitive functions, and that they often elaborate an impoverished social environment as much as they simplify an overwhelming one. For these, and other, reasons, a social perspective on stereotypes rejects any suggestion that stereotyping is the inevitable consequence of humans' cognitive hard-wiring or of their cognitive sloth.

The veracity of stereotypes

The idea that stereotypes contain a kernel of truth, and indeed exaggerate that kernel, has long been accepted, and has long been a source of concern for many social psychologists (Judd and Park, 1993; Levine and Campbell, 1972; see Oakes et al., 1994: 19–24, for a good historical overview of the idea of a kernel of truth). Partly because of the political implications of this idea, social psychology has been reluctant to tackle it head on. But implicitly at least, most views of stereotypes which accept the cognitive miser notion, or which accept that stereotypes are a kind of schema, also accept the premise that stereotypes are cognitively functional; that is, stereotypes simplify the inherent complexity of social life. However, many social psychologists have gone further and have argued that since stereotypes are schemas, and hence adaptive and reality-orienting, they must have some basis in reality. It is arguable that any conception of stereotypes as schemas must have the kernel of truth idea lurking somewhere near its core.

The study by McCauley and Stitt (1978) described in the section on measuring stereotypes, in which the diagnostic ratio (DR) technique for measuring stereotypes was formulated, also contains a direct attempt to evaluate the kernel of truth argument. McCauley and Stitt collected DR estimates for seven different characteristics as they

Table 9.1 Actual and estimated diagnostic ratios
(percentage of black Americans/percentage of all Americans)

Characteristic	Actual DR	Mean estimated DR
Completed high school	0.65	0.69
Illegitimate	3.1	1.96
Unemployed last month	1.9	1.98
Victims of crimes	1.5	1.77
Welfare	4.6	1.82
Four or more children	1.9	1.43
Female head of family	2.8	1.77

Source: Adapted from McCauley and Stitt, 1978: 937, Table 2

applied to black Americans when the study was done, and then compared these DRs with actual DRs obtained from official government documents. The two sets of DRs are presented in Table 9.1. The actual and the estimated DRs correlate .62 with one another. McCauley and Stitt point out that the stereotypes being expressed by their subjects would seem to contain more than just a kernel of truth: the subjects seem well able to predict the actual DRs. Further, the estimated DRs fail to exaggerate the criterion information, being either reasonably accurate or an *under*estimation. On the basis of these results, McCauley and Stitt claim that stereotypes can be, and in this case are, veridical.

McCauley and Stitt's (1978) study seems to provide strong evidence that stereotypes help orient the stereotyper to a set of objective conditions in the real world; that is, that stereotypes have a basis in the objective nature of social groups, and therefore are, in a sense, justified. Several reasons mitigate against interpreting McCauley and Stitt's data this way. First, the characteristics rated by their subjects are not usually the stuff of stereotypes. The stereotype of blacks in the United States may well contain knowledge elements concerning higher rates of illegitimacy and unemployment, and lower rates of completing high school, but these elements are not to be found at the core of the stereotype. Second, the sorts of characteristics which constitute most of the potent stereotypes about minority groups in most societies are not the sorts of characteristics which can be easily quantified and maintained as government statistics. A characteristic such as 'lazy' is not a characteristic counted in most censuses. Yet it is these characteristics, impressionistic and unquantifiable, which define most stereotypes. There is no yardstick against which a stereotypic element such as 'lazy' can be measured, so the veracity of such stereotypic elements is forever unknowable.

The fact that the veracity of stereotypes cannot usually be assessed is not a fact accepted in the common sense of our society, even among people who ought to know better. For example, Murdoch University's policy on non-discriminatory language contains the sentence: 'Discriminatory language is that which refers in abusive terms to gender, race, age, sexual orientation, citizenship or nationality, ethnic or language background, physical or mental ability, or political or religious views, or which stereotypes groups in an adverse manner that is *not supported by evidence'* (emphasis added). Murdoch University is not unusual in how it considers stereotypes. The fact that most stereotypic characteristics can never be supported or refuted by evidence renders the policy moot.

A third argument against McCauley and Stitt's position is that the characteristics they measured are purely descriptive, yet one of the features of stereotype function is that they are *explanatory*. To believe that black Americans do not complete high school at the same rate as other Americans, or that black Americans are more likely to be illegitimate, is, psychologically, as bland as believing that black Americans have darker skin complexion, or have fuzzier hair, than other Americans. These statements all only serve to mark the target group. Yet the invidious part of stereotypes is that they *attribute* fixed and constitutional qualities to the target group and its members; that is, that they function as *explanations* as well as descriptions. A stereotype contains not only the phenotypic, descriptive characteristic that blacks do not complete high school at the same rate, but also the genotypic ascription of laziness and stupidity as an explanation of why blacks fail to complete high school at the same rate. In one large American study, Apostle, Glock, Piazza and Suelze (1983) show that it is *how* whites explain perceived differences between blacks and whites, and not the recognition of differences *per se*, that serves to determine how those whites evaluate blacks and evaluate government programmes designed to aid blacks.

A fourth point against a position maintaining the veracity of stereotypes is that such a view tends to ignore the role of social status in determining stereotypes. Stereotypes of different groups occupying the same social position are remarkably similar. For example, Bonacich (1973; Bonacich and Modell, 1980) has described the so-called 'middleman minorities': those groups prepared to occupy the economic position filled by occupations such as bankers, merchants and money-lenders, which other traditional groups in a society are unwilling to fill. Although the middleman position has been filled around the world by, among others, Jews, Scots, Chinese and Greeks, the predominantly negative stereotype and social evaluation of groups occupying the middleman position are similar wherever and whenever they occur, and are shared by groups on both sides of the middleman position. It is the social position and function of these groups which determines the stereotype which evolves of them, not any intrinsic qualities of the group itself. Thus, as far as the veracity argument goes, there is a sense in which the stereotype of Jews as venal, or of Scots as thrifty, may contain a kernel of truth. But whatever kernel of truth exists, to whatever degree, is due not to the constitutional venality of Jews or thriftiness of Scots, but rather to the social and economic position occupied by these groups. Another example is provided in a letter purportedly written by Cicero to Atticus during the time of the Roman occupation of Britain, in which he reports, 'Do not obtain your slaves from Britain, because they are so stupid and so utterly incapable of being taught that they are not fit to form a part of a civilized household.' Given the role of Britain in enslaving many of the world's peoples, and of British psychology in developing racist ideology (Gould, 1984), this quote presents a nice irony. It serves to demonstrate how the social qualities attributed to a group change through time and with changing social and economic position.

The question of the veracity of stereotypes has recently been considered from a different viewpoint. Extending self-categorization theory (SCT), Oakes et al. (1994) argue in favour of stereotype veracity, but on the grounds that stereotype content has psychological and social validity, rather than on the grounds that it can be matched veridically with an objective reality; that is, that stereotypes reflect the nature of the intergroup context at that particular time. Rejecting the idea that stereotypes are 'pictures in the head', fixed and unchanging, waiting to be 'turned on' by appropriate environmental cues, they argue that stereotypes, as social perceptions, are fluid and contextual. All social perception is categorial. Which perceptual categories are used on any one occasion depends on the meta-contrast principle and on the principle of perceptual fit. The stereotype of a particular group depends, then, on the comparative context. The stereotype of social psychologists used by other people and by social psychologists themselves depends on whether the comparative context is a meeting of the Psychology Department in which there is only one social psychologist among a collection of hard-nosed cognitive and physiological psychologists, or is a committee meeting of the faculty of arts attended by sociologists, political scientists, historians and a lone psychologist, or is a party attended by people who mostly never have anything to do with psychology or universities. The point is that in each of these comparative contexts the pattern of self and other categorizations varies, and consequently so too does the pattern of stereotypic representations of self and others. But in each case the form of self and other categorization has a psychological validity for each person.

It is often tacitly implied that stereotypes are bad because they deny the individuality of the person who is stereotyped – the dual-process and continuum models of person perception discussed in Chapter 3 make this assumption, for example. If only people would not see group memberships, and would see the individual as an individual, then stereotypes and prejudices would vanish, or so the story goes. For SCT this is a nonsense. Individual-level categorizations instead of group-level categorizations are still categorial, just at a different level of categorial inclusivity. To deny or devalue the validity of group-level knowledges is to deny or devalue the psychological and social reality of groups as groups, not as aggregates which can be reduced to, and understood in terms of, the individual constituent members. Groups *are* real. Individual-level stereotypes are no more valid than group-level stereotypes.

All this is not to say that Oakes et al. accept that group stereotypes are socially acceptable. The question of their social validity is a political question, not a question of the degree to which they isomorphically mirror the world as the gods see it.

The position taken by Oakes et al., based on SCT, has much merit. However, their consideration of the veracity of stereotypes addresses the issue in a way which is little related to how the question has traditionally been formulated. Their argument that stereotypes are veracious has a different meaning to the meaning that most social psychologists would accord that answer. Veracity and validity are not synonymous, and to argue that the personal validity of stereotypes makes them veracious confuses the issue, and borders on tautological anyway. While stereotypes are contextual, and while they may have personal validity which directs the stereotyper to act as though the stereotype were a true and accurate representation of a group and its members, it is misleading to claim that stereotypes are therefore veracious. We also take issue with the SCT analysis on the point of the stability of the representation, of the 'picture in the head'. Oakes et al. argue against the metaphor of pictures in the head. So too do Potter and Wetherell (1987) in their non-cognitive approach to social psychology which will be discussed in Chapter 10. While it is only a metaphor, and argument by metaphor or analogy is never fully convincing, we believe that many social cognition studies clearly demonstrate that stereotypes *do* act as if they were pictures in the head, that some stereotypes *are* relatively inflexible, and that the content of stereotypes is often activated in a generic, context-independent fashion. Studies on stereotype auto-maticity, described below in the section on stereotypes and prejudice, provide strong evidence that stereotypes can act in these ways. Further evidence for these conclusions can be furnished by examining any of the strong and persistent stereotypes of disliked minority groups in our – or any – society. Consider as an example the stereotype of Australian Aborigines held by someone like David's mother, described at the start of this chapter. Like many indigenous populations of countries colonized by Britain and other European nations, Aborigines occupy the least respected position in society. The stereotype of them is strong and overwhelmingly negative, and Aborigines are actively and strongly disliked by many white Australians. David's mother not only knows the social stereotype of Aborigines which pervades Australian society, but she also personally accepts that stereotype. She believes it to be a true and accurate depiction of Aborigines as a group. If she were asked to do so, she could easily provide many examples of how and why the stereotype is veracious. It is unlikely that the stereotype David's mother has of Aborigines would ever vary much from one situation to another, from one time to another, from one comparative context to another. It would not matter if David's mother self-categorized at an individual level, or if she self-categorized at a national level as an Australian. Across all these settings, the stereotype of Aborigines held by David's mother would persist. She may make occasional exceptions of individuals such as Cathy Freeman competing for Australia at the Commonwealth Games, but only to preserve the stereotype. David's mother, as well as the subjects in experiments examining the automatic activation of stereotypes, argues for the persistence of a relatively stable 'picture in the head'.

We can imagine how SCT can accommodate the performances of subjects in automatic activation experiments, and can accommodate David's mother. These data and anecdotes do not fundamentally contradict SCT, but they mitigate against the position claimed by Oakes et al. Their position accounts for the data they examine (for example, Haslam and Turner, 1992; Haslam et al., 1992), but those data come from studies which examine tame, bland stereotypes of residents of Perth vs Canberra, or of Americans vs Australians, as they are manipulated by the comparative context (including Detroit or Sydney, or including Great Britons or Iraqis). Social psychology has, quite rightly, not been greatly concerned with such stereotypes. Of greater concern are the pernicious, prevalent, potent stereotypes based on race, ethnicity, gender and religion. Just as social identity theory stumbles when it wanders from the comfort of a minimal group experiment into the complexities of real groups, so too does SCT when it is generalized to the stereotypes which lie at the guts of intergroup hatreds.

PREJUDICE

Prejudice is an attitude. Recall from Chapter 2 that an attitude 'is represented in memory by (1) an object label and rules for applying that label, (2) an evaluative summary of that object, and (3) a knowledge structure supporting that evaluation' (Pratkanis and Greenwald, 1989: 249). When the attitude object is a social group the attitude is a prejudice. Prejudice is usually negative, although by definition it is not necessarily so. The object label, rules for applying the label, and the knowledge structure supporting the evaluation of the object are all cognitive elements of the attitude. In the case of prejudice, they are the stereotype of the group. The heart of the prejudice concept, though, and of the attitude concept too, lies in the evaluative summary of the object. Prejudice is, at its core, an evaluation of a social group. It is a depiction of a group as good or bad, positive or negative, an object to be approached or to be avoided. Almost always, social psychology, and society for that matter, has only been concerned with negative prejudices. It is the same for us here.

Prejudice and racism

When the social group that is the object of prejudice is defined by race, prejudice is almost synonymous with racism. Racism is more than just a negative evaluation of an outgroup, though. It includes a fundamental belief in the inherent, biological inferiority of races other than one's own (Katz and Taylor, 1988).[1] Race and racism are relatively recent terms, racism being used only since the 1930s (Miles, 1989). It is important to stress that the term 'race' is a social construct, used to identify and categorize people on the basis of physical characteristics such as skin colour. The way race is used by most people, including many social psychologists, does not correspond with scientific and genetic definitions of the term. What is important for our analysis is not whether the term refers to any fundamental part of nature, or that scientists and laypeople do or do not agree, but the fact that people act as if race were a given. One of the ways in which they express this is through behaviour, attitudes and discourse which rely on the premise of racial superiority, or, more generally, which negatively discriminate against members of some group.

Jones (1972) demarcates three kinds of racism. *Individual racism* refers to the belief that one's own race is constitutionally superior to other races, and to the negative evaluations and negative behaviours following from that belief. *Institutional racism* refers to practices and policies of society's institutions which discriminate against members of one race. The discrimination may be intentional or may be spurious. Either way, it is the effects of the practice which define it as institutional racism. Importantly also, institutional racism may occur regardless of the particular beliefs of the individuals working in that institution. Finally, *cultural racism* refers to the belief that the cultural heritage of one's race is superior to that of another. The expression of cultural racism can overlap both individual and institutional racism.

Examples of each of Jones' three kinds of racism are all too easily found in contemporary Australian society. Jack van Tongeren, the jailed leader of Perth's Australian Nationalist Movement, is a prototypically racist individual. Following closely Hitler's *Mein Kampf*, he and his followers believe that Asians do not belong in Australia, and enact that belief by, for example, fire-bombing Chinese restaurants. It is ironic that van Tongeren is himself an immigrant to Australia, and that his father is half Indonesian. Institutional racism was (and occasionally still is) exemplified by pubs which either refuse to serve Aborigines, or charge Aborigines different prices for alcohol, or segregate Aborigines from white patrons. All of these examples can occur regardless of the personal views of any individual bar worker. Banks which systematically refuse housing loans to Aborigines, putatively because they do not satisfy all the lending requirements, provide another example of institutional racism. Employers who refuse bereavement leave to Aborigines to attend funerals, because the deceased is not a member of the immediate family, give yet another example, wherein the Aboriginal definition of, and obligations to, 'family' are different from that in Anglo-Australia. Finally, schools which fail to acknowledge Aboriginal history in their teaching of Australian history are practising cultural racism: what is Aboriginal is devalued to the point of exclusion. It can also be argued that educational systems requiring Aboriginal children to learn in traditional Anglo ways, and which ignore or discount evidence that Aboriginal learning occurs in different ways, practise cultural racism (Goodnow, 1976; Kearins, 1976).

Racism used to be simple. To be racist, either in Australia or in the United States or in probably most other western countries, used to involve a straightforward rejection of, and hostility toward, a minority group.[2] This kind of racism, sometimes called 'old-fashioned racism' (Sears, 1988), was segregationist, and overtly accepted and advocated white supremacy. It was once the dominant, acceptable and normative view of race. In the United States, Australia, New Zealand, the United Kingdom, Canada, South Africa to a lesser extent, and probably many other countries, the normative view of prejudice and racism has changed markedly in recent times. It is now no longer as socially acceptable to believe in racial superiority, or to express prejudice. The norm of egalitarianism is now much stronger. This is not to say that racism has disappeared. The case of David's mother at the beginning of this chapter is but one of countless examples of prejudice which occur on a daily basis. Rather, the form of racism has changed. Old-fashioned racism has been replaced with a more subtle variant, known as modern, or symbolic, racism (Kinder and Sears, 1981, 1985; McConahay, 1986).

Modern racism, like old-fashioned racism, involves a rejection of blacks and recent black gains. However, this is based around values and ideology rather than a straightforward dislike. Kinder and Sears define symbolic racism as

> a blend of antiblack affect and the kind of traditional American moral values embodied in the Protestant Ethic. Symbolic racism represents a form of resistance to change in the racial status quo based on moral feelings that blacks violate such traditional American values as individualism and self-reliance, the work ethic, obedience, and discipline. Whites may feel that people should be rewarded on their merits, which in turn should be based on hard work and diligent service. Hence symbolic racism [would express itself in opposition to] political issues that involve 'unfair' government assistance to blacks; welfare ('welfare cheats could find work if they tried'); reverse discrimination and racial quotas ('blacks should not be given a status they have not earned'); forced busing ('whites have worked hard for their neighborhoods, and for their neighborhood schools'). (1981: 416)

Thus, symbolic racism emphasizes a resentment of blacks which is embedded within wider moralistic American values such as the Protestant ethic.

Kinder and Sears found that political behaviour such as voting preferences for mayoral candidates in elections involving black candidates were better predicted by measures of symbolic racism than by perceived 'realistic' threats by blacks. This was true for people for whom direct threats to 'the good life' were tangible (in terms of jobs and schools) *and* for people who stood to lose little from black gains. Kinder and Sears conclude that racial prejudice is motivated more by symbolic resentments than by tangible threats.

More recently, Katz and Hass (1988) have argued that the racial attitudes of whites toward blacks have become complex and multidimensional. They suggest that ambivalence is a pervasive feature of racial attitudes – pro- and anti-black attitudes often exist side by side within the one (white) individual. Further, they argue that these sentiments are rooted in two core independent American values. Pro-black attitudes reflect humanitarian and egalitarian values which emphasize the ideals of equality and social justice. On the other hand, anti-black attitudes reflect values embodied within the Protestant ethic, such as hard work, individual achievement and discipline. Katz and Hass (1988) report a study demonstrating that both pro- and anti-black attitudes co-existed in their white student samples, and that anti-black attitudes were positively correlated with values embodied within the Protestant ethic and pro-black attitudes were positively correlated with values within an egalitarian-humanitarian perspective. These results have important social and theoretical implications. They suggest that the enduring nature of racism and anti-black prejudice may be due to the link to core, central values, embedded deep within American culture. They also suggest that attempts to strengthen pro-black attitudes in the community may succeed without having any effect on anti-black attitudes. Theoretically, the results highlight the inadequacy of unidimensional, bipolar conceptions of attitudes – in this case, racial attitudes.

Evidence from the United States (Kinder and Sears, 1981; McConahay, 1986), from Australia (Augoustinos et al., 1994; Locke et al., 1994; Walker, 1994) and from South Africa (Duckitt, 1991) indicates that indeed many people – not just in the United States – do appear to express views consistent with the modern racism concept. However, at least in Australia, there is still evidence that many people are not unhappy with expressing old-fashioned racist beliefs (Walker, 1994). The concept of modern racism is not without its critics, and it is far from clear exactly what is being measured by scales developed to assess the concept (Bobo, 1983; Sniderman and Tetlock, 1986a). However, for our purposes, the distinction between old-fashioned and modern racism is a useful one to retain, if for no other reason than to acknowledge the facts that nowadays respondents typically give more tolerant responses when asked directly about their racial beliefs than they do if their behaviours are indirectly assessed (Crosby, Bromley and Saxe, 1980), and that white subjects show strong signs of ambivalence when their racial attitudes are made salient by experimental procedures (Hass, Katz, Rizzo, Bailey and Moore, 1992). Finally, we do not want to suggest that modern or symbolic racism is any less invidious or odious than its old-fashioned, more explicit, counterpart. Indeed, we agree with others who have argued that this form of racism is more insidious, entrenched and resilient because of its subtlety and apparent egalitarianism.

Prejudice and personality

✓Prejudice is often thought to be the manifestation of a particular kind of personality. We are all familiar with the bigot – the person who rejects any and all outgroups, who believes in the prime importance of his or her own group, who is intolerant, who is hostile to individual members of outgroups, who often is servile to his or her superiors, and who, depending on our own stereotypes, is male, blue-collar or unemployed, poorly educated, and has not travelled. The bigot is a clearly identifiable personality type, or so we tend to believe. But if you were to ask for all the bigots in a crowd to raise their hand, no one would. We all know bigots, but no one identifies him/herself as a bigot.

The idea of a bigoted or prejudiced personality has widespread intuitive appeal, and social psychology has searched for nearly half a century to uncover the bigot and how the bigoted personality is predisposed to prejudice (for example, Adorno, Frenkel-Brunswik, Levinson and Sanford, 1950; Altemeyer, 1981, 1988; Stone, Lederer and Christie, 1993). The evidence of almost half a century stands against any explanation of prejudice couched solely in terms of individual personality structure and function.

How and why is it that the intuitively appealing notion of a prejudiced personality fails as an explanation of prejudice and discrimination? First let us briefly review work on the *authoritarian personality* as a prototypical example of this kind of research. The rise of fascism in Germany provided the impetus for a group of workers at the University of California at Berkeley to examine the psychological factors which allow fascist regimes to operate. Through extensive survey and interview research, and being guided by a psychodynamic theoretical approach, these researchers developed a portrait of the 'authoritarian personality' (Adorno et al., 1950). This personality was defined by several dimensions, including *conventionalism* (rigid adherence to conventional social values and mores), *authoritarian submission* (an unquestioning subservience to one's moral and social superiors) and *authoritarian aggression* (a vigilance for, and hostile rejection of, those who violate conventional social values and mores). Authoritarian personality types become that way, according to Adorno et al., because of particular patterns of family structure and child-rearing. Authoritarian families are hierarchically organized around a stern, strict father who uses physical punishment capriciously. Authoritarianism was regarded as a personality dimension, and those high on the dimension (authoritarians) are more prone to prejudices of all kinds. Adorno et al. also developed a Likert-type scale called the F-scale (the F representing fascism), which has been used in countless hundreds of research articles since its publication.

The authoritarian personality work has been extensively critiqued on both theoretical and methodological grounds (see Billig, 1976; Brown, 1965; Christie and Jahoda, 1954, for examples). After a long period of relative neglect, the construct has recently been revived and revamped. Altemeyer (1981, 1988), in particular, has developed scales to measure right-wing authoritarianism which are psychometrically sound, and has reformulated the theory, basing it on social learning theory rather than psychodynamic theory. Interestingly though, he has arrived at the conclusion that three aspects of authoritarianism define the construct: conventionalism, authoritarian submission and authoritarian aggression – the three most important factors identified by the earlier researchers.

Adorno et al. were not the first ever to describe the set of characteristics that they label the authoritarian personality. Brown (1965: 477–8) points out that in 1938 E. R. Jaensch, a German psychologist (and also a Nazi), described two personality types: the S-Type and the J-Type. We would describe the former type today as a liberal; one who favours nurture over nature as an explanation of behaviour, one who is tolerant, one who does not favour capital or corporal punishment. The latter, the J-Type, is almost identical with Adorno et al.'s authoritarian personality type: rigid in outlook, definite in judgement, firm and stable. The behaviours described by Adorno et al. and by Jaensch are the same; the values placed upon those behaviours are opposite. What for Adorno et al., and probably for most Australians, Americans, Canadians and Britons, is rigid and inflexible is reliable and stable for Jaensch; what is tolerant and understanding is flaccid and weak. Duckitt (1992) cites a similar example of work done in South Africa by MacCrone, describing a 'frontier' personality type which closely resembles the authoritarian personality type. Brown's (1965) example highlights the ease with which cultural values are transmitted into 'objective' social scientific research, and the dangers of failing to recognize this.

If prejudice and discrimination were the product mostly of personality factors such as authoritarianism, there ought to be greater authoritarianism in societies and areas where there is greater prejudice. This is not the case, though. Research by Pettigrew (1958, 1959, 1960, 1961) demonstrated that authoritarianism was no greater south of the Mason–Dixon line in the United States than north of it; nor was it greater in white South Africans than in white Americans. Since there is strong regional variation in prejudice, and since there is no such regional variation in authoritarianism, the latter logically cannot account for the former. What, then, can account for regional differences in prejudice?

Pettigrew suggested that in the Southern United States and in South Africa there is a tyranny of 'whites on whites'. There are strong norms in both regions which support a prejudiced outlook, and strong sanctions are imposed on anyone who violates those norms. In other words, prejudice is a function of normative compliance, not of personality predispositions. Following from this argument, it can be concluded that those individuals with a greater propensity to comply with norms (including authoritarians), and those who have had greater exposure to a culture's norms, ought to display more prejudice. This appears to be the case (Middleton, 1976; Orpen, 1975; Pettigrew, 1958), although the evidence is far from being as unequivocal as it is normally assumed to be. Duckitt (1988) presented evidence that normative exposure was unrelated to prejudice level in a sample of South African whites, but authoritarianism and cognitive sophistication were. Duckitt (1992) sets out clearly the limits of the evidence in favour of the normative compliance explanation, and offers a reinterpretation. Also recently, but supporting the normative compliance explanation, Blanchard, Lilly and Vaughn (1991) demonstrate that situation-specific norms can be changed experimentally and these subsequently affect the expression of racial opinions by people in those situations.

Social psychology has tended to adopt the normative compliance explanation of prejudice more than any other, partly because it fits the general situationist perspective of social psychology (Ross and Nisbett, 1991). This perspective also allows for greater optimism about reducing prejudice than does any explanation that roots prejudice in individual personality structure and functioning. If prejudice stems from personality, then attempts to reduce the expression of prejudice must focus on changing personalities, which is not an easy task. It is easier to change a norm than to change a personality. On a final note, Altemeyer (1994) reports that there may not be good reason for dismissing authoritarianism altogether in accounting for prejudice. He reports that high right-wing authoritarians demonstrate greater proneness to a range of cognitive mechanisms such as ingroup favouritism. These mechanisms are usually thought to operate in all individuals, and, combined with broader social factors, are generally accepted as leading to prejudice. The role of personality factors may thus be more subtle than earlier research allowed. And by using social learning theory, rather than a psychodynamic approach, to account for the development of right-wing authoritarianism, Altemeyer dispels the main cause of pessimism normally associated with work on authoritarianism and prejudice.

Stereotypes, beliefs and prejudice

A part of the lay understanding of prejudice is the belief that those individuals who hold strong stereotypes of minority groups will, by doing so, be led to be prejudiced against them. This is an intuitively appealing, and straightforward, notion. Does social psychological research support it, though? There is some evidence of a link between the two, but also some evidence that it is prejudice against a group which leads to the development of a negative stereotype about that group, rather than the other way around (Aboud, 1988). What is most remarkable about research investigating the links between stereotypes and prejudice, though, is its absence. There are large research literatures in both areas, but very little which relates the two. In a review of the stereotyping literature more than two decades ago, Brigham (1971) stated that his analysis of the relationship between stereotyping and prejudice must remain 'essentially speculative'. Unfortunately, the comment applies equally well today. In some ways, the question of a link between the two is a matter of definition. Negative stereotypic elements are evaluative; the evaluation being contained within the negativity. It is, therefore, impossible to maintain a negative stereotype about some group without also being prejudiced toward that group. However, stereotypes and prejudice are usually thought of separately, even though the dominant social cognitive position often sees prejudice as the *inevitable* consequence of categorization and stereotyping.

Recent evidence suggests that stereotypical thinking can be prompted unconsciously and automatically. Thus, in the second study by Macrae et al. (1994) described in the section on stereotypes, subjects were presented with a group label for just 30 ms. This exposure period is too brief for subjects ever to be aware of having seen the label. Yet the label had demonstrable effects on subsequent recall of stereotype-related information (indicating an encoding effect) and on performance on an ancillary, parallel task (demonstrating a processing effect of release of cognitive resources). These effects of the group label happen *automatically*.

Automaticity has a particular and narrow meaning in cognitive psychology. It can be used to refer to cognitive processes or to cognitive effects. The encoding effect demonstrated by Macrae et al. (1994) is an example of an automatic process. Subjects were not aware of how they were encoding information or of how their encoding was affected by a group label presented to them subliminally. Indeed, most people are typically unaware of the processes their cognitive systems are engaged in. An example of an automatic effect is provided by the initial reaction of a person to a member of a disliked outgroup. Usually, the store of information a person has about a particular social group – that is, the social stereotype of that group – is activated automatically when the person is confronted by a member of that group or by a symbol of that group. Research examples of the automatic activation of stereotypes are given below.

A cognitive process or effect is considered to be automatic if it satisfies one of several criteria (Bargh, 1984, 1989; Hasher and Zacks, 1979; Schneider and Shiffrin, 1977). It must not require conscious intention, attention or effort; or it must be resistant to intentional manipulation; or it must happen beyond any awareness. Automatic processes and effects happen rapidly, and do not use cognitive processing capacity. If a process or effect fails to satisfy these criteria, it is considered to be controlled. Controlled processes are susceptible to conscious intervention, require cognitive effort and are amenable to consciousness.

There is now ample evidence that stereotypical trait information about a group can be automatically activated by exposure to a group-related stimulus (Augoustinos et al., 1994; Devine, 1989a; Gaertner and McLaughlin, 1983; Locke et al., 1994; Macrae et al., 1994; Moskowitz and Roman, 1992; Perdue and Gurtman, 1990). Since most stereotypes of real groups are predominantly negative, the automatic activation of such stereotypes does not augur well for attempts to lessen any pernicious effects of those stereotypes. One recent and influential model of how automatic and controlled processes in stereotyping are related to prejudice has been proposed by Devine (1989a, 1989b). An outline of the model is sketched here.

There is a social stereotype attached to most, if not all, of the major groups in our society. These stereotypes have a life outside any one individual, being a part of our common cultural heritage, existing as icons or consensually defined representations of these groups. As members of our society, we are each exposed to these social stereotypes so often through the course of our socialization that we acquire an internal, mental representation of the social stereotype. This knowledge of the social stereotype is possessed equally by all members of society, and is rehearsed so often that it becomes *automatically* associated with the group it represents. This is not to say that all members of society will equally endorse the social stereotype. Individuals differ in their level of prejudice against the target group: some people are high, and some are low, in prejudice. Whereas previous models, and 'common sense', suggest that individual differences in stereotyping are associated with individual differences in level of prejudice, Devine's model suggests that all members of society have equal access to the social stereotype of well-known groups, and consequently the mental representation of that stereotype will be automatically activated upon presentation of any group-related symbol. This activation will occur equally for individuals high and low in prejudice. Only once the stereotype's content has been activated for long enough to become amenable to conscious intervention will differences between high- and low-prejudice individuals emerge. High-prejudice individuals will allow the automatically activated stereotype content to persist, but low-prejudice individuals will intervene in the on-line processing of this information, deliberately inhibiting that automatically activated material and deliberately activating other, more positive material. Thus, Devine's model provides cause both for optimism and pessimism compared to the prior models and compared to 'common sense': the former because she removes the earlier assumption that stereotypes inevitably lead to prejudice; and the latter because everyone, regardless of their beliefs and level of prejudice, has a store of stereotypic negative information which is automatically activated by a group-related stimulus.

To support her position that stereotypes and prejudice are separate cognitive structures, and that the path from stereotypes to prejudice is mediated by personal beliefs, Devine (1989a) presents three separate studies with American subjects, which we briefly outline here. The first study examined the suggestion that white subjects high or low in prejudice against blacks will be equally knowledgeable of the stereotype of blacks. Subjects were asked simply to list all the aspects of the social stereotype of blacks that they could think of. They then completed a measure of prejudice (the Modern Racism Scale of McConahay, Hardee and Batts, 1981), which allowed them to be classified as either high or low in prejudice. Responses from the thought-listing task were sorted into one of 15 different categories (for example, poor, aggressive/tough, criminal, low intelligence, etc.). The low- and high-prejudice groups did not differ in the frequency with which they generated responses in any of the categories. Thus, there is *prima facie* evidence that white subjects have equal accessibility to, and knowledge of, the social stereotype of blacks, regardless of their prejudice level.

Study 2 was designed to examine the automatic effects of activating white subjects' stereotype of blacks. Once again, subjects completed the Modern Racism Scale to measure their anti-black prejudice, but did so six months before the start of the second part of the experiment. The second part of the experiment used a method developed earlier (Bargh and Pietramonaco, 1982), in which words are presented to subjects parafoveally (that is, outside of the normal focal area of the eyes), for a short duration (80 ms), and are then masked. This all serves to prevent the stimulus word entering each subject's consciousness. Each subject was presented with a set of 100 words, either 80 per cent or 20 per cent of which were related to the stereotype of blacks (the remainder in each set being neutral). The task for subjects was to indicate in which of the four visual quadrants each stimulus appeared. After completing the 100 judgements, subjects were then asked to participate in ostensibly a separate procedure, in which they read a description of a character's behaviour and then rated that behaviour on several dimensions. The behaviour was deliberately described ambiguously, and the character's race was not mentioned. The crucial rating for Devine's hypothesis concerns how hostile the character's behaviour was judged to be, since hostility (and aggression and violence) was prominent in the descriptions of the stereotype of blacks in Study 1. Ratings of hostility were more extreme in subjects in the 80 per cent condition than in subjects in the 20 per cent condition. Ratings on 'non-hostile' scales were unaffected by the priming manipulation. These effects did not differ between the high- and low-prejudice groups of subjects.

Devine's third study again used white subjects, and asked them to list all of their thoughts in response to the social group 'Black Americans'. Responses were categorized according to whether they were belief statements or trait ascriptions, and whether they were positive or negative. Subjects classified as high in prejudice used trait terms more than belief statements, and low-prejudice subjects used more belief statements than trait terms. High-prejudice subjects listed more negative than positive thoughts, and low-prejudice subjects listed more positive than negative thoughts.

From her three studies, Devine concludes that low- and high-prejudice white subjects do not differ in how well they know the social stereotype of blacks, that low- and high-prejudice white subjects do not differ in how automatically activated stereotypical information affects their ratings of how hostile a target's behaviour is when the race of that target is not specified, and, finally, that low- and high-prejudice white subjects do differ when they are asked to list their own thoughts related to blacks. Devine takes these three conclusions as evidence for her model relating stereotypes to prejudice, through the mediating influence of personal beliefs.

Although Devine's model has some intuitive appeal, and has been widely accepted, several problems with her studies limit the extent to which they support the model (Augoustinos et al., 1994; Banaji and Greenwald, 1994; Locke et al., 1994). Her studies only examine *negative* stereotype content. It is possible that differences may exist at both the automatic and controlled levels of processing between high- and low-prejudice subjects when positive stereotype content is considered. Her model is about on-line processing within an individual, and how activated stereotype content passes from automatic to controlled processing, and then perhaps influences the expression of prejudice. Yet the data to support this on-line processing model come from different subjects in different experiments. Her studies and her model do not allow room for non-cognitive factors to play a role. Perhaps low- and high-prejudice subjects differ in the extent to which they automatically activate generic sets of positive and negative (that is, affective) information. And finally, her first and third studies are susceptible to social desirability response biases.

Augoustinos et al. (1994) examined Devine's model in the context of Aboriginal–white relations in Australia. In the first of two studies, subjects (people on the street) were asked to list all the aspects of the social stereotype of Aborigines they could think of, in the same way that subjects in the first of Devine's studies were asked. Responses were classified into one of 19 different categories. Subjects also completed a measure of prejudice (a version of the Modern Racism Scale used by Devine, but adapted for Australian conditions). As in Devine's study, there were hardly any differences between those people low in prejudice and those high in prejudice in their ability to list elements of the social stereotype. Augoustinos et al. note, though, that there was a noticeable difference in *style* of response between the two groups: high-prejudice subjects tended to give unqualified pejorative responses, whereas low-prejudice subjects qualified their responses and tended to distance themselves from those responses. Regardless, the first study of Augoustinos et al. clearly establishes, as does Devine's first study, that all people, whether high or low in prejudice, have knowledge of and are able to produce the defining elements of a strong social stereotype.

In their second study, Augoustinos et al. asked subjects to indicate whether each of a series of words presented on a computer screen accurately described Aborigines. Subjects' response latencies were recorded. Subjects again completed a modified version of the Modern Racism Scale. The words judged by subjects were either positive or negative, and either belonged to the stereotype of Aborigines or did not belong (for example, artistic and easy-going were positive, stereotype-related words; cheerful and happy were positive, stereotype-unrelated words; bludgers and dirty were negative, stereotype-related words; and conceited and dishonest were negative, stereotype-unrelated words). Another set of words described situational or sociological qualities (for example, alienated, dispossessed, oppressed). Because subjects had to make a conscious judgement about each word, the experiment was tapping controlled rather than automatic processing.

Low-prejudice subjects endorsed more of the sociological terms than did the high-prejudice subjects, but took the same length of time to make their decision. The most interesting results, though, indicated that all subjects were quicker at endorsing stereotypic descriptions than non-stereotypic descriptions, highlighting again the information processing advantages of schematic representations of groups. Furthermore, high-prejudice subjects were faster to endorse negative descriptions than were low-prejudice subjects, and this difference in speed of processing did not depend on whether the words were related to the stereotype. Low-prejudice subjects, on the other hand, were significantly faster in responding to positive descriptions than negative ones. Low-prejudice subjects also endorsed more of the positive elements of the stereotype than did high-prejudice subjects, who in turn endorsed more of the negative elements.

The results of the two studies by Augoustinos et al. support Devine's argument for separating stereotypes from personal beliefs about a target group, but they modify the links between knowledge of the consensual social stereotype and the activation and suppression of stereotypic knowledge. Devine suggests all people automatically activate the stereotype of a group when confronted with a group-related stimulus, and that those low in prejudice toward the target group subsequently inhibit that information while those high in prejudice allow the information to continue to be processed. The results of the second study by Augoustinos et al., while saying nothing about what is automatically activated, suggest that people low in prejudice against Aborigines activate many more positive stereotypic elements than do those high in prejudice, and that those high in prejudice tend to activate anything negative, whether it belongs to the stereotype or not. This suggests that affect (positive or negative evaluation of the target group) plays a central role in stereotype activation (see also Stangor, Sullivan and Ford, 1991). All this implies that high- and low-prejudice people do differ in their individual mental representations of the group 'Aborigines', even though the two groups may be equally able to identify the social stereotype of Aborigines.

The qualifications to the Devine model suggested by Augoustinos et al. are also supported by another Australian study (Locke et al., 1994). This study examined automatic and controlled processes as they occur on-line within the same subjects. Again, the target group was Aborigines. Two groups of subjects were used: a sample of white Australian students, and a sample of Singaporean students who had been in Australia less than three months. According to Devine's model, the former group should have a well-rehearsed knowledge of the social stereotype of Aborigines, and should thus display automatic activation of the stereotype. While the Singaporean students may have knowledge of the stereotype of Aborigines, they will not have been exposed to that stereotype sufficiently often for it to become automatically activated in the presence of a group-related stimulus. The two groups of subjects were sorted into high- and low-prejudice groups, according to their score on the Modern Racism Scale, as modified by Augoustinos et al. (1994).

The results from this study contradict Devine's model in two important ways. At its core, this model proposes that stereotype activation will occur at an automatic level to an equal extent for high- and for low-prejudice subjects, and that low-prejudice subjects will subsequently inhibit that activated material. Contrary to this, Locke et al. found that high-prejudice Australian subjects automatically activated only stereotype-related information. Low-prejudice subjects, on the other hand, automatically activated a range of information both related and unrelated to the stereotype. When the information passed into controlled processing, neither high- nor low-prejudice subjects appeared to engage in any information inhibition. Thus, noticeable differences between those high and those low in prejudice do not follow from the low-prejudice person's inhibition of negative stereotype-related information, but from the fact that low-prejudice people automatically activate positive and negative stereotypical information, whereas high-prejudice people automatically activate only negative information. These differences then persist as the information becomes amenable to conscious intervention.

The second way in which the Locke et al. study contradicts the Devine model relates to the Singaporean subjects. High- and low-prejudice Singaporean students may have been exposed to information about Australian Aborigines, but would not have rehearsed this information sufficiently for it to become automatically activated. The finding that high-prejudice Singaporean subjects automatically activate a generic set of negative information, whether or not it is related to the stereotype of Aborigines, and the low-prejudice Singaporean subjects do not is thus at odds with Devine's model. The result implies that high-prejudice individuals perhaps automatically activate a negative evaluation of any outgroup, whether they have a detailed mental representation of the outgroup or not; that is, that stereotype activation is mediated by affective reactions, not just cognitive processes. This conclusion mirrors the results from the Augoustinos et al. study.

To end this section on the relationship of stereotypes to prejudice, we can conclude that presentation of a group-related stimulus triggers an automatic – an effortless, unconscious and unstoppable – reaction in people. An automatic reaction remains automatic for only a brief part of a second, when it then becomes amenable to conscious manipulation. Devine (1989a) proposed a model in which all people, regardless of prejudice level, automatically activate the same store of group-related information, and subsequently low- and high-prejudice people only differ because low-prejudice people deliberately inhibit the stereotypic information. Studies by Augoustinos et al. (1994) and Locke et al. (1994) contradict this model, and suggest an alternative. In this revised model, any group-related stimulus will still trigger an automatic activation of information. However, the information activated is not the same for all people. High-prejudice people with a detailed cognitive representation of the target group will activate a store of predominantly negative, stereotypic information. Low-prejudice people will activate both positive and negative infor-mation. In other words, the mental representations the two groups of people possess are different. Underlying this difference, high-prejudice people lacking a detailed cognitive representation of the target group will still automatically activate a set of negative information, but that set is a generic set, defined by, and activated because of, its negativity, not because of any fundamental relation-ship with the target group. This is a kind of neuronal ethnocentrism, in which the cognitive system of a high-prejudice person auto-matically rejects and derogates *any* outgroup. Once the activated information proceeds on-line until it is amenable to conscious manipulation, high-prejudice subjects perceive no need to modify it, because it does not conflict with any personal belief systems they hold or with any sense of social identity they possess. For low-prejudice subjects, though, the negative parts of the set of positive and negative information which was automatically activated do contradict their personal beliefs and their social identity as a tolerant, prejudice-free person. Although they will not always inhibit this negative information, they will be motivated to do so when they are made aware of it. Thus, low-prejudice subjects in the first study by Augoustinos et al. (1994) acted to distance themselves from their utterances reflecting what they knew of the social stereotype of Aborigines but which they found distasteful. However, when the attention of low-prejudice people is not brought to bear upon activated stereotypical information, it is likely the information will persist in processing, and will influence judgements in the way of all schematic processing.

Behavioural expectancies

A potent path linking stereotypes to prejudicial behaviour is through expectancies. Stereotypes act as a kind of cognitive anchor for expectations about what another person or group of people is likely to do. Once activated, these behavioural expectancies act as self-fulfilling prophecies, confirming the initial stereotype. The self-fulfilling nature of stereotype-based expectancies renders stereo-types particularly difficult to change. Ask a bigot why he or she believes all Aborigines are lazy and the reply will be that that is how they are, the behavioural evidence is there for all to see. Not only do such people interpret behaviours of others in ways that support their schematic knowledge of the world, but they actually elicit the very behaviours they expect others to perform. An example will help illustrate the phenomenon and how it operates.

Drawing upon the sociological analysis of how a false definition of a situation can come to be true through the actions of the perceiver (Merton, 1948), and upon earlier work in social psychology on how classroom teachers interact with schoolchildren to confirm labels given to those children as 'late bloomers' (Rosenthal and Jacobson, 1968), Word, Zanna and Cooper (1974) conducted a two-stage study to demonstrate how cross-race expectancies generate behaviour which confirms the original expectancies. Subjects in the first study were all white undergraduates at Princeton University who volun-teered for an experiment on group decision-making. Each subject participated in a group on a joint project to design a marketing campaign. The other members in their group were all confederates of the experimenters. Each subject was 'randomly' allocated the task of interviewing four people for a job in the marketing campaign. The people who were interviewed were also confederates of the experimenters, and were all trained to act in the same way during the interview. The first interviewee was always white. Half the time, the second interviewee was white, and the third black; for the other half, the second interviewee was black, and the third white. The fourth interview was never conducted, and the first interview was treated as just a 'warm up' and the data never used. Thus, each white subject interviewed one white and one black interviewee. The experimenters recorded several measures of the quality of the interview. The results showed that the white subjects sat further away from black than from white interviewees, that white interviewees were given an interview almost a third longer than were black interviewees, and that white interviewees made about 50 per cent more speech errors per minute when the interviewee was black rather than white. In sum, the black interviewees were given a shorter and colder interview than were the white interviewees.

The second experiment is what powerfully demonstrates the self-fulfilling nature of expectancies. In this experiment, the confederates were the job interviewers, and the real subjects were the interviewees. All the subjects were white, as were the confederate interviewers. Subjects were interviewed in one of two conditions: either in an 'immediate' or a 'non-immediate' condition, mirroring the two styles of interpersonal immediacy the white interviewer subjects had displayed in the first experiment, depending on whether they were interviewing blacks or whites. In the immediate condition, the confederate interviewers were trained to act as the interviewers had acted in the first experiment when they were interviewing whites; that is, to sit relatively closer, to give a longer interview, and to make relatively few speech errors. In the non-immediate condition, the confederate interviewers were trained to act as the interviewers had acted in the first experiment when they were interviewing blacks – to sit further away, to avoid eye contact, and to make many speech errors. About five minutes into the interview, the experimenter entered the room and, after concocting a plausible story for the subjects, removed the subject's chair and provided another one. The major variables of interest were the performance of the subject interviewees (rated after the experiment by independent judges using videotape of the experimental sessions), the distance away from the interviewer that subjects repositioned their chair, and their satisfaction with their performance and with the interview.

The performances of all subjects in both conditions were judged by independent raters ignorant of the aims of the experimenter and of the condition each subject was in. Subjects in the non-immediate condition (the 'black' interview style) were judged to be less adequate for the job than were subjects in the immediate condition. They were also judged to be less calm and composed. When subjects were provided with the chance to move their chair closer to, or further away from, the interviewer, subjects in the immediate condition chose to sit almost 40 cm closer to the interviewer than did the subjects in the non-immediate condition. Subjects in the non-immediate condition made about two-thirds more speech errors per minute than did subjects in the immediate condition, and judged their mood after the interview, the interviewer's friendliness and the interviewer's adequacy all to be much lower than did the subjects in the immediate condition.

The results from these two experiments illustrate clearly the processes involved in the self-fulfilling prophecy. When white subjects interviewed black interviewees, they acted in a cold, hesitant, and distant manner, in comparison to their actions toward white interviewees. Presumably, these actions reflect an unease with, and perhaps a dislike of, black people on the part of the white subjects. The self-fulfilling prophecy suggests that these behaviours are likely to elicit behaviours from the black interviewees which will confirm the original unease held by the white subjects; that is, that the black interviewees will perform less well, will appear less able, and will dislike the interview, and that these are the very behaviours on which the white interviewees' initial sentiments are based. Thus, the white interviewees' stereotypes and prejudices toward black people cause them to act in a way which draws out of the black interviewees the very behaviours which the white interviewees expected, thus confirming those initial expectations. The self-fulfilling nature of the stereotype-based expectancies is shown in the second experiment. Naïve white subjects who were interviewed by white interviewers trained to act as the original naïve white interviewers had done when interviewing blacks performed less well (as judged by independent observers) than their counterparts interviewed by white interviewers trained to act as the original naïve white interviewers had done when interviewing whites. They also disliked the interview and the interviewer more than their counterparts.

The self-fulfilling nature of interpersonal expectancies, whether based in stereotypes or not, has been well documented as a robust phenomenon. Snyder, Tanke and Berscheid (1977) showed that men who were conversing with a woman they were led to believe was beautiful behaved differently, and elicited more 'beautiful' behaviour from their interaction partners, than did men who believed they were talking with a plain woman – even though the interaction took place over a phone and there was no face-to-face interaction. Extensive reviews of research on how initial expectancies elicit expectancy-confirming behaviours are provided by Hamilton, Sherman and Ruvolo (1990), Jussim (1986, in press), Neuberg (1994) and Snyder (1984, 1992). The general conclusion, though, is that stereotypes are a singularly strong source of expectancies about others' behaviour. Those expectancies influence the stereotype-holder's own actions in such a way that they elicit behaviours from the target of the stereotype which confirm the original expectancies. This process of self-fulfilment only makes the original stereotypes stronger, and makes all the harder any attempt to dilute the potency of stereotypes, especially by encouraging interaction between the holder and the target of the stereotype.

INTERGROUP ATTRIBUTIONS

Positioned perceptions

As this chapter is being written, the IRA-proclaimed ceasefire in Northern Ireland is just a week old and is persisting despite the best attempts of the Unionists to provoke the IRA into armed retaliation for Unionist violence. It is clear that many Unionists interpret the actions of the IRA suspiciously, not believing that the cause of the IRA's ceasefire lies in a dedication to ending the troubles and restoring peace. They also doubt the causes of the actions of the governments in London and in Dublin, with Unionist leaders such as the Reverend Ian Paisley decrying London's treasonous betrayal to the Papists. On the other side, Gerry Adams, the leader of Sinn Fein, insists that the IRA is sincere in its intentions to end the violence of a civil war a quarter of a century old. The situation is a clear example of how ostensibly the same act can be interpreted in opposite ways.

Hunter, Stringer and Watson (1991) recently published a simple study which illustrates the social psychological processes underlying the markedly different perceptions of the IRA's ceasefire. In this study, Hunter et al. gathered newsreel footage of Catholic and Protestant violence in Northern Ireland. One scene showed a Protestant attack on a Catholic funeral, and the other showed two soldiers in a car being attacked by a group of Catholics. To ensure that the two news clips were not different in their violent content, they were rated by Spanish and German foreign exchange students. The scenes in the clips were both judged to be very violent. Assured that the two clips were equally violent, Hunter et al. then showed them to Catholic and Protestant students at the University of Ulster. These students were asked to 'explain in their own words what they thought was happening in the videos, and why they thought those involved had behaved as they had' (Hunter et al., 1991: 263). Subjects' reasons for the behaviour of the people shown in the video were coded as either an internal or an external attribution. The pattern of attributions was clear, and is shown in Table 9.2.

Clearly, Catholic subjects saw the causes of violent acts committed by Catholics as residing somewhere in the situation, but saw acts of violence committed by Protestants as being caused by dispositional factors. Protestant subjects behaved the same way, seeing Catholic

Table 9.2   Pattern of internal and external attributions
made by Catholic and Protestant subjects for acts of
violence committed by Catholics and Protestants

| | Catholic violence | | Protestant violence | |
	Catholic subjects	Protestant subjects	Catholic subjects	Protestant subjects
Attribution				
Internal	5	15	19	6
External	21	6	5	15

Source: Hunter et al., 1991: 263

violence as being due to the Catholic actors and explaining
Protestant violence away to the situation. Yet the two groups of
subjects were witnessing the same acts; acts which had previously
been judged by presumably impartial Spanish and German subjects
to be identically violent. It is little wonder that the search for a
peaceful resolution to the troubles in Northern Ireland has been so
long and has produced so few gains.

The behaviour of the subjects in the Hunter et al. experiment is not
unusual. Experiments from around the world have demonstrated
what may be a universal, certainly a pervasive, egocentric and
ethnocentric pattern in the way we see and explain the events
around us. Almost 30 years before Hunter and his colleagues
reported their results, Hastorf and Cantril (1954) conducted a similar
study. This time, though, the protagonists were supporters of the
Princeton and the Dartmouth football teams in the United States.
The game between the two teams at the end of the 1951 season was
the last of the season and was particularly emotional and hostile. The
game was won by Princeton, completing an undefeated season, and
during the game Princeton was penalized 25 yards and Dartmouth
70 yards. Hastorf and Cantril obtained a film of the game and
showed it to groups of students at Princeton and at Dartmouth. The
students were asked to record all the rule infringements they
witnessed in the game and to classify each infringement as either
mild or flagrant. The Dartmouth students thought the two teams
committed as many infringements as each other, and that both sides
were equally to blame for the 'rough but fair' game. Princeton
students, on the other hand, counted the Dartmouth team commit-
ting twice as many fouls as the Princeton team, and twice as many as
the Dartmouth students counted for their own team. They also saw
the game as 'rough and dirty', and thought that the Dartmouth team
started the rough play.

In both the Hunter et al. experiment and in the Hastorf and Cantril study, what is ostensibly a single social event – an act of violence or a football game – is seen and explained completely differently depending on one's position relative to the event. The results from these two studies have been produced in many studies (see Lord, Lepper and Ross, 1979; Nisbett and Ross, 1980, Ross and Lepper, 1980; and Vallone, Ross and Lepper, 1985, for further examples). Several implications can be drawn from all this research. First, social perception, especially in situations involving partisanship, is rarely, if ever, neutral and dispassionate. Second, the possibility of ever being able to apprehend a single 'true' account of social 'reality' is questioned. And third, the patterns of interpretations and attributions produced by subjects in all these experiments highlight the inadequacy of attribution theories as they are normally constructed. It is to this third point that we now direct our attention before going on to consider research on intergroup attributions.

Levels of analysis

Theories of attribution processes and biases discussed in Chapter 4 proceed as though people make attributions about self and others *qua* individuals. This is too simple. Indeed, it is simple-minded. As we all know, social life in all its intricate complexity is a mass of individuals, couples, groups, sects, ethnicities, nations, all interacting and negotiating an ever-changing social reality which exists 'out there' and which is reproduced, represented, reconstructed, within our heads and hearts. None of us interacts with any one other person as if that person were an abstracted, fixed and given *individual*. We all are social, contextualized, and cannot interact with, or even perceive, an other as if we or they were otherwise. Yet attribution theory, as with so much of the rest of psychology, persists in theorizing the asocial, decontextualized fiction called the individual. Several theorists and researchers have recognized this and attempted to develop a more social account of attributions.

Drawing on earlier work by Doise (1986), Hewstone (1988, 1989a) has articulated four 'levels of analysis' on which attribution theory has developed. The first two levels, the *intrapersonal* and the *interpersonal*, characterize the bulk of attribution research. The intrapersonal level of analysis examines processes and functions within the individual. Kelley's (1967) covariation model of attribution, discussed in Chapter 4, is a good example. In this, an individual perceives an event – usually a behaviour enacted by another individual – and engages in a mental calculus estimating the consistency, consensus and distinctiveness of that event, before arriving at a conclusion regarding the cause of the event. The attributer turns only inward in this attributional search, and the search presumably proceeds in the same manner regardless of who or what did the behaving or of the relationship between the attributer and the actor. Everything apart from the event which triggered the attributional search takes place between the attributer's ears; it is all intrapersonal.

The second level of analysis, the interpersonal, allows for facets of the relationship between two individuals to affect the attributions each makes about the other's behaviour. The actor–observer effect and the fundamental attribution error are examples of attribution research which can be called interpersonal. Even here, though, the individuals in the interaction come to the interaction strictly as individuals. In terms of attribution theory operating at this level of analysis, the individuals have no history, no power or status differentials, no social context. They are interchangeable, asocial, decontextualized, often disembodied individuals.

The third level of analysis addressed by Doise and Hewstone is the *intergroup* level. Research and theory at this level examine how social categorization, group memberships, social identity and intergroup relations affect how, and what sorts of, attributions are made. The study of Hunter et al. in Northern Ireland is an example of intergroup attribution research. Finally, the fourth level of analysis – the *societal* level – is concerned with social representations and ideology, and with how these affect attribution processes and outcomes. This is dealt with in Chapters 8 and 11.

Explaining group behaviours   In Chapter 4 we discussed the fundamental attribution error (FAE), or the 'tendency for attributers to underestimate the impact of situational factors and overestimate the role of dispositional factors in controlling behavior' (Ross, 1977: 183). The FAE is expressed at the second of Hewstone's four levels of attribution research: it deals with how attributions depend on one's position in the actor–observer couplet. As far as the FAE is concerned, it matters not what relationship might exist between the actor and the observer, or what groups each might belong to, or what history might tie the two together. The results of the study by Hunter et al. (1991), and of other similar studies, demonstrate unambiguously that the FAE *does* depend on group relationships. Essentially the same violent behaviour committed by some other person is explained entirely differently by an attributer depending on the social positions (Catholic or Protestant, Dartmouth or Princeton supporter) of the attributer and the actor. It is not just a simple case of the attributer overestimating the role of dispositional factors in controlling behaviour.

Pettigrew (1979) extended the FAE to an analysis of intergroup attributions. In a joke about the rather grand title Ross gave his effect (it is unlikely anything in the social sciences deserves the epithet 'fundamental'), Pettigrew coined the term 'ultimate attribution error'. It is perhaps telling that the editors of the journal which published his paper missed the punch-line. If nothing in the social sciences is fundamental, there certainly is nothing which is ultimate. But the ultimate attribution error (UAE) it is, and so we shall call it.

Pettigrew integrated Ross's FAE into Allport's (1954) classical analysis of intergroup relations to formulate an analysis of how prejudice shapes intergroup 'misattributions' (Pettigrew, 1979). When a person is confronted with an unambiguously positive behaviour committed by a member of a disliked outgroup, that person will have trouble reconciling the information provided by that behaviour with their stereotype of the outgroup, and is unlikely to make a dispositional attribution in the manner of the actor–observer effect or the FAE. Given that it is difficult – though far from impossible – to deny the positive behaviour ever happened, or to re-evaluate it negatively, the perceiver is most likely, according to Pettigrew's analysis, to explain away the behaviour. It is possible, though extremely unlikely, that the perceiver will attribute the positive behaviour to the outgroup actor's disposition and consequently revise his or her stereotype of the outgroup. More likely, though, the stereotype will be preserved, even strengthened, and the positive behaviour discounted or dismissed.

How can a perceiver 'explain behaviour away'? There is probably no limit to the inventiveness of people in this regard, but Pettigrew suggested four strategies are likely. These each represent one of the cells in a 2 × 2 matrix formed by crossing *perceived locus of control* (the behaviour is seen as caused by factors internal or external to the actor) and *perceived degree of controllability* (the actor has high or low control over the behaviour). When the cause is external, the positive behaviour will be attributed to *luck* or *special advantage* if controllability is low, and to manipulable *situational context* if controllability is high. Minority group members often attribute the behaviours of majority group members to the advantages and privileges their group status confers upon them. Conversely, majority group members often attribute the successes of minority group members to affirmative action programmes. Both of these are examples of attributions to special advantage. Attributions to manipulable social context are akin to the situational attributions described in correspondent inference theory, except now they are applied to the actor by an observer. Positive actions by an outgroup member are seen as solely the product of situational pressures to perform those actions. Note, though, that Jones and Davis (1965) view such actions as relatively uninformative; here, on the other hand, the positivity of such actions *is* informative because of the contrast with the negativity of the stereotype.

For positive actions judged to be internally caused, the actor is likely to be judged to be an *exceptional case* if controllability is low, but when controllability is high the resultant attribution will likely emphasize the *high motivation* and *effort* of the actor. Making an exception to the stereotypical rule is one of the easiest attributional escapes to make, and its ease of use renders stereotypes difficult to change. In fact, because making an exception to the stereotypical rule almost, psychologically speaking, proves the rule, using such an attribution confirms and strengthens the original stereotype. Similar to the exceptional case, positive behaviours committed by a member of a disliked outgroup can be seen as caused by the particularly keen motivation of that person.

The discussion so far has only considered *positive* behaviours performed by disliked outgroup members. When the behaviour is *negative*, the resultant attribution will be dispositional. In the case of racism, the disposition seen to be causing the behaviour is a biological or genetic inferiority. Dispositional attributions for negative behaviours are easy, and are not qualified by dimensions such as locus of control.

Pettigrew suggested that these attributional patterns will be stronger in prejudiced individuals, which suggests they will still be present in less prejudiced individuals. He also suggested that the UAE is more likely when group memberships are salient, when the perceiver believes he or she is a target of the behaviour in question or is otherwise highly involved in the behaviour, when the groups involved have histories of intense conflict and have strong stereotypes of each other, and when group memberships coincide with national and socio-economic status differences.

Perhaps the earliest direct demonstration of group effects on attributions was a study carried out by Taylor and Jaggi (1974), who presented Hindu office workers in India with a series of vignettes describing several behavioural episodes. Half of the episodes described a positive behaviour – stopping to help someone, for example – and the other half described a negative behaviour – going past someone who needed help. Crossed with the positivity or negativity of behaviour was the religion of the actor – half the actors described were Hindu, and half were Muslim. When the Hindu subjects were asked to make attributions about the cause of the

Table 9.3 Proportion of all attributions which were internal in Hewstone and Ward's (1985) two studies

| | Chinese subjects | | Malay subjects | |
	Positive behaviour	Negative behaviour	Positive behaviour	Negative behaviour
Malaysian samples				
Chinese actor	0.39	0.54	0.27	0.46
Malay actor	0.57	0.24	0.66	0.18
Singaporean samples				
Chinese actor	0.40	0.49	0.39	0.44
Malay actor	0.48	0.37	0.70	0.27

Source: Hewstone and Ward, 1985: 617 and 619, Tables 1 and 3

behaviour described in the vignette they read, they behaved in just the way Pettigrew's UAE predicts they ought to. Positive behaviours performed by a Hindu (ingroup) actor were attributed to the actor's disposition, whereas negative behaviours performed by a Hindu actor were attributed externally. The opposite pattern was observed when the actor was described as a Muslim.

A number of studies together now show that attributing a positive or negative, successful or unsuccessful, behaviour to something about the actor or something about the actor's situation is not simply an individual process (Greenberg and Rosenfield, 1979; Mann and Taylor, 1974; Stephan, 1977). The group memberships of both the attributer and the actor are important in formulating attributions about the causes of behaviour. The studies do not provide unequivocal support for Pettigrew's notion that attributions will always favour the ingroup, though. Two studies by Hewstone and Ward (1985) highlight how broader societal factors, as well as group-level factors, are important in determining patterns of attributions.

Hewstone and Ward's first study attempted to replicate the findings of Taylor and Jaggi (1974), using Chinese and Malay subjects in Malaysia. Using the standard method, subjects were presented with a vignette description of a positive or negative behaviour performed by either a Chinese or a Malay actor, and attributions of the cause of the behaviour were gathered. Examining the proportion of all attributions which were internal reveals that the Malay subjects made the typical ingroup-favouring set of attributions, but the Chinese subjects did not produce attributions favouring the ingroup. Instead, their attributions tended to resemble those of the Malay subjects. The results of Hewstone and Ward's first study are presented in Table 9.3.

Hewstone and Ward then replicated their study with Chinese and Malay subjects in Singapore. Once again, the Malay subjects produced attributions favouring the ingroup, and the Chinese subjects showed only a slight tendency to favour the outgroup. Clearly, then, group effects on attributions are not consistently in favour of the ingroup at the expense of the outgroup. Hewstone and Ward argue that the different effects of group membership on attributions demonstrated by the Malayan and Chinese subjects in their Singaporean and Malaysian samples reflect the actual social positions of the two groups in the two societies. The Chinese in Malaysia have a devalued minority group status, occupying a 'middleman' position in the economy. This position is strengthened by the Malaysian government's policies. In Singapore, even though the Chinese also occupy a 'middleman' position, the society is much more openly plural, and there is no government policy promoting any one particular ethnic group.

All the studies described above have relied on ethnicity or race to demonstrate group effects on attributions. Such effects are also apparent in studies using other social groups. A large body of research on intergroup achievement attributions has found a significant tendency for perceivers to make more favourable attributions for males than for females when explaining success and failure. Deaux and Emswiller's (1974) study is one of the most well known of these. These authors found that on a stereotypically masculine task (identifying mechanical tools) a male actor's success was more likely to be attributed to ability than the same success by a female actor. However, on a stereotypically female task (identifying household utensils) no differences were found in attributions for male and female success. As with studies using race or ethnicity, a large number of studies have now documented the prevalence of an attributional pattern of male enhancement and female derogation on tasks leading to success and failure, and that this pattern is found in women as well as men (for example, Etaugh and Brown, 1975; Feather, 1978; Feather and Simon, 1975; Feldman-Summers and Kiesler, 1974, experiment 2; Garland and Price, 1977; Nicholls, 1975; and Sousa and Leyens, 1987). Not all studies have found the effect, though (Feldman-Summers and Kiesler, 1974, experiment 1; Terborg and Ilgen, 1975), but the pattern across studies seems to be convincing.

These studies point to an enigma in social psychology's understanding of intergroup attributions; namely, that members of a minority group (in this case, women) appear to internalize negative stereotypes of themselves, and this leads to different expectations and to different explanations of success and failure. Such behaviour is clearly not ingroup-serving. However, it is worth noting that most of the studies demonstrating gender effects in attributions for success and failure were conducted in the 1970s, and their results may not hold true today.

There is, thus, a considerable body of evidence demonstrating that attributions depend on the relative group memberships of the person making the attribution and the target of the attribution, whether the group be based on race, ethnicity, gender or even social class (Augoustinos, 1991a; Hewstone et al., 1982). However, as Hewstone (1990) concludes after reviewing 19 published studies examining the UAE, the effect is not consistent in a simple way. The UAE is formulated in terms of ingroups and outgroups, and posits that attributions will be group-serving. The 'error' appears to operate in more subtle and complicated ways than a simple reliance on an ingroup–outgroup classification. All the studies cited above which include as subjects members of both majority and minority groups in the society in which the study takes place find that minority group members do not attribute in a way which favours the ingroup. The kinds of attributions majority and minority group members make, then, appear to reflect not only an underlying motive to favour the ingroup, but also the broader social stereotype and social status of the groups in question.

The fact that attributions vary depending on the social group memberships of the attributer and the target is one thing, but the importance of this lies not in the fact that it happens but rather in its social consequences. Intergroup attributions rely on stereotypes or cultural representations of groups, and, once made, they lend a pernicious bite to intergroup interactions. Two studies will be described here to demonstrate the relationship between attributions and stereotypes. The first is the Hewstone and Ward (1985) research described earlier. In each of their Malaysian and Singaporean samples, Hewstone and Ward collected subjects' ratings of whether each of a list of 17 trait terms described each of the two groups 'Malays' and 'Chinese', and also asked subjects to rate how good or bad each trait term was. A trait term was only considered stereotypical if it was endorsed by at least half of the subjects in either ethnic group. The Malay subjects favoured their ingroup and derogated the outgroup when they were making attributions for positive and negative behaviours. Similarly, the Malays' autostereotype was positive, including the terms hospitable, honest, emotional, friendly and polite; and their stereotype of the Chinese was almost uniformly negative, including the terms industrious, verbally violent, sly, deceitful, stingy and suspicious. The Chinese subjects tended to agree with their Malay counterparts on the stereotype of the

Chinese, indicating that industrious, verbally violent, stingy and suspicious were important elements of the stereotype. The Chinese subjects produced no stereotype of the Malays, though. The stereotypes produced by subjects in Singapore were less broad, but similar in content. The Malay subjects agreed that they were hospitable, and that the Chinese were verbally violent, sly, industrious and suspicious. The Chinese subjects believed Malays were slovenly and that the Chinese were industrious. The content of the stereotype thus appears to persist across national boundaries. This persistence, and the fact that the Chinese subjects agree with the Malay subjects that the Chinese can be described by a host of pejorative terms does not necessarily mean that the stereotype of the Chinese has a kernel of truth, though. As we described earlier in this chapter in the section on stereotype veracity, the stereotypical characteristics applied to the Chinese in both studies by both groups of subjects resembles the stereotype often applied to 'middlemen' groups in different economies around the world. The group most often the victim of a stereotype built around the traits sly, deceitful, stingy and suspicious is the Jews (Adorno et al., 1950). The fact that both the Jews and the Chinese in Malaysia and Singapore occupy similar social and economic positions is a strong indicator that the content of the stereotype is dictated more by social and economic position than any qualities inherent in being either Chinese or Jewish.

Hewstone and Ward's study can only suggest the relationship between stereotypes and attributions. More direct evidence comes from a study by Duncan (1976). Duncan recruited subjects for an experiment on 'interpersonal behavioural research'. The subjects were all white, and the experiment took place in southern California. Subjects were told they would be viewing an interaction between two people, and afterwards would be asked to give ratings of the interaction on a new system for categorizing behaviour. What subjects actually saw was a videotaped interaction carefully scripted so that the two interactants started a discussion which quickly led to a disagreement and then ended when one shoved the other. Subjects were asked to code the 'shoving' behaviour into one of several different categories, and then were asked to provide answers to several questions about different internal or external causes of the 'shove'. Responses to these questions were summed to produce two indices, one of the extent to which the subject saw the behaviour as caused by dispositional factors and one of the extent to which the behaviour was seen as caused by situational factors.

Although all the subjects were white, the race of the two actors was varied. Sometimes the interaction was between two white actors, sometimes between two black actors, sometimes a white

Table 9.4 Frequencies of categorizations of 'shoving' behaviour

| | Harm-doer–victim race pairings | | | |
Behaviour	Black–black	White–white	Black–white	White–black
Playing around	0	3	1	8
Dramatizes	1	7	2	12
Aggressive behaviour	4	4	5	8
Violent behaviour	11	2	24	4

Source: Adapted from Duncan, 1976: 595, Table 1

person shoved a black person, and sometimes a black person shoved a white person. How the subjects categorized the 'shove' is summarized in Table 9.4, which adopts Duncan's terminology of 'harm-doer' to refer to the person who shoved the other, and 'victim' to refer to the person who was shoved.

Comparing the first two columns of this table shows that ostensibly the same behaviour – a 'shove' after a gradually increasing disagreement – is 'seen' quite differently depending on the race of the actors. When a white person shoves another white person, the shover is likely to be seen as just playing around or being dramatic; but when the shover and the shoved are both black, the behaviour is likely to be seen as either aggressive or violent. The effect is more stark when we consider the last two columns of the table, representing categorizations of behaviour in cross-race dyads. Almost two-thirds of the respondents who saw a white person shove a black person categorized that behaviour as either playing around or being dramatic; but almost all of the subjects who witnessed a black person shove a white person classified the shove as a violent act. The lesson from the Hastorf and Cantril study, and countless other studies, is once again demonstrated – what is apparently a single behavioural act is seen and interpreted almost completely differently depending on the position and the group memberships of the witnesses.

The first part of Duncan's study illustrates how the race of two actors influences the encoding of behaviour. The second part illustrates just as graphically how the behaviour, once encoded, is explained differently. Duncan recorded dispositional attribution scores as well as situational attribution scores for each subject. Scores on each index could vary from zero to eight, with high scores on each index representing a greater causal role. The mean scores on each

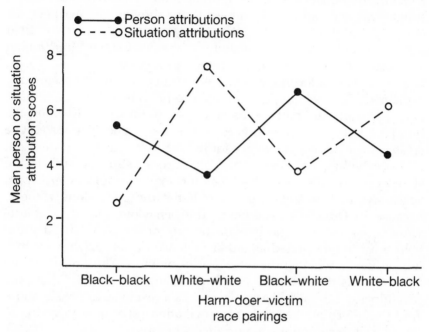

Figure 9.1 Mean dispositional and situational attributions in each harm-doer–victim race pairing (Duncan, 1976: 596, Figure 1)

index for the four harm-doer/victim race pairings are shown in Figure 9.1.

Figure 9.1 shows more clearly than almost any other research in attribution theory how dispositional and situational attributions can vary ipsatively – as scores on one index increase, scores on the other decrease. More importantly, though, the figure shows that the 'shove' is seen to be caused by factors associated with the actor when the actor is black, but is seen to be caused by factors in the actor's situation when the actor is white.

Duncan's study shows clearly that the race of an actor affects how the actor's behaviour is encoded, and then, once encoded, how the behaviour is explained. Why should the attributions made by Duncan's subjects vary depending on the race of the actor? The answer appears to lie somewhere in the cultural stereotype of blacks prevalent in the United States (or at least in southern California in the mid-1970s). The content of the stereotype of blacks in the United States was once marked as superstitious, lazy, happy-go-lucky, ignorant and musical (see our discussion earlier in this chapter on the measurement of stereotypes). But the content has shifted, and has come to include 'aggressive' and 'violent' as central components

(Devine, 1989a; Dovidio and Gaertner, 1986). Thus, when Duncan's subjects were confronted by a black actor shoving another person – and especially when that other person was also black – their stereotype of blacks was activated. Once activated, and functioning as a schema, the stereotype then affected how the witnessed behaviour was interpreted, encoded in memory and subsequently explained. The stereotype functioned to provide a ready, automatic and easy explanation of events, and also, importantly, to *distort* the interpretation of those events to fit the stereotype. The stereotype created the evidence necessary for its own confirmation. It does not matter whether there is a kernel, or even a fistful, of truth to the stereotype in this case. It does not matter if blacks *are* more aggressive and violent in the world that the gods alone witness, because in Duncan's experiment the behaviour that the subjects witness is identical regardless of the race of the actor. An identical behaviour is interpreted as either violence or just playing around, depending on whether the actor is black or white. The violence of the black actor is then seen as an expression of that actor's nature; the playfulness of the white actor is seen as a response to the situation. And the interpretation and the explanation serve only to verify, to justify and to reproduce the original stereotype.

To conclude this section, let us return to the case of David's mother that we described at the beginning of the chapter. David's mother has a strong stereotype of Aborigines. The content of her stereotype will influence what behaviours she attends to, how she interprets those behaviours, and finally how she explains those behaviours. It is unlikely she will ever notice behaviours which violate her stereotype, and if she does, it is likely she will either encode the behaviours in a particular way and/or explain them away by attributing them to the situation rather than to the individual actor or the social category 'Aborigines'. Thus it is that she will more likely notice a 'snot-faced' Aboriginal child than a 'snot-faced' Anglo child. She will also be more likely to interpret a runny nose as a case of being 'snot-faced' than of just having the sniffles. And she is more likely to attribute the Aboriginal child's 'snotty face' to something about the child or his or her family – it is just another example of how Aborigines are dirty and unhygienic – than she is to attribute the behaviour to something situational. She is unlikely to attribute an Anglo child's 'snotty face' to the dirty and unhygienic habits of his or her family, preferring instead to explain the behaviour as due to the flu. All of David's mother's actions serve to confirm her stereotype of Aborigines. It is unlikely that any evidence counter to her stereotype will ever penetrate the array of cognitive mechanisms which so well protect her stereotypes. For the same reasons, it is immensely difficult to make headway in reducing intergroup tensions in any situation of intense intergroup conflict, be it between Catholics and Protestants in Northern Ireland, Arabs and Israelis in the Middle East, Serbs and Muslims in the Balkans, blacks and whites in the United States or in the United Kingdom or in Australia. Social psychology has invested a great amount of energy into researching ways of changing stereotypes and prejudicial behaviour. Unfortunately, space prohibits us considering this research here. Interested readers are referred to Hewstone and Brown (1986).

SUMMARY

The chapter has examined the interplay between stereotypes, beliefs, personality, behavioural expectancies, attributions and prejudice. We have argued that stereotypes are relatively persistent mental representations of a group and its members, and that they have their origin in the social and economic positions of groups rather than any inherent properties of the members of those groups. Stereotypes serve to generate behavioural expectancies and to colour how behaviours are interpreted and explained. Thus, they facilitate prejudice, and serve a social justificatory role through their own reproduction. The orthodox treatment of stereotypes and prejudice by social cognition researchers was criticized throughout the chapter for its excessive emphasis on individual, cognitive explanations, and for ignoring the social, representation and ideological origins and consequences.

NOTES

1 Work on 'modern' or 'symbolic' racism (discussed later in this chapter) argues that such racism does not rely on a belief in biological superiority. It may be better to reserve 'racism' for those cases which rely on belief in racial supremacy, and think of modern or symbolic racism as a form of prejudice which is not necessarily racist. However, in keeping with contemporary usage, we will refer to modern or symbolic *racism*.
2 The terms 'minority' and 'majority' group are used in this book to refer to groups marked by their relative social, economic and political status (see Simpson and Yinger, 1985). The terms do not refer to the numeric size of a group. Thus, in Australia, the black population is a minority group both in status and in size, but in South Africa the black population is a minority group in terms of status only.

10
POSTMODERN CHALLENGES TO SOCIAL COGNITION

All of the socio-cognitive approaches we have considered thus far adhere to the notion of internal mental representation. The basic philosophical presupposition underlying those approaches is that there is a cognitive life world to be explored and delineated, both its content and associated mental mechanisms. From this perspective, cognition is conceptualized as prior to language. Language is viewed primarily as a communication medium through which cognition finds expression. While the theoretical approaches we have considered vary in the extent to which they emphasize the constructivist nature of human thought, all subscribe to a realist epistemology: that there is a knowable domain of facts about human experience and consciousness which can be discovered through the application of reason and rationality (science) or through hermeneutic interpretative methods. The emergence of poststructuralist and postmodernist social theory within a variety of disciplines has challenged this realist epistemology. This challenge can be attributed to the increasing interest in the role and function of language as a socially constitutive force in consciousness and experience. The 'turn to language' is reflected in the burgeoning development of discourse analytic research within social psychology. In this chapter we will consider this tradition of research and the radical critique it has directed toward many of the central concepts in social cognition theory and research.

POSTMODERNISM

'Postmodernism' is not easily defined and categorized. It is often used, however, as an umbrella term to refer to recent conceptual developments in artistic, intellectual and cultural spheres (Feather-stone, 1988). 'Postmodernity' refers to the contemporary nature of western industrialized culture and society. Social theorists argue that we have entered into an historical era which is qualitatively different from the past. In contrast to previous liberal and organized forms of capitalism, a 'disorganized' and postindustrial state of capitalism has emerged which transcends the boundaries of the nation state (Lash and Urry, 1987).[1] Most writings on postmodernity are essentially commentaries on the contemporary nature of social and cultural life. While we have little space to consider these commentaries and the social psychological implications that emanate from these descriptions of contemporary life (see Michael, 1991), we will, instead, consider the central epistemological and philosophical foundations of postmodern perspectives on knowledge.

Postmodernism is associated with a wave of critical thought and philosophy which seeks to

> deconstruct or question modernist beliefs about truth, knowledge, power, individualism, and language. . . . Postmodern philosophers challenge the assumption that reason can provide an objective and universal foundation for knowledge or that a knowledge based on reason will be socially beneficial and ensure progress. (Collier, Minton and Reynolds, 1991: 267)

The modernist view that reason, through science, will lead to the discovery of knowledge which can be utilized for the benefit of society was at the very core of the Enlightenment. Postmodernists have rejected the capacity of a positivist philosophy of science to achieve this end. They have questioned the notion of a knowable reality by emphasizing the socio-historical and political nature of all knowledge claims. By analysing the socio-historical determinants of concepts and theories, especially those in the social sciences, postmodern analysts have been able to demonstrate how specialist disciplines of knowledge maintain and reproduce the dominant social relations and institutions of society; relations and institutions which are shaped by capitalism, patriarchy and racism.

Some components of this critique are not unique to postmodern or poststructural theory and analysis. Indeed, the 1970s witnessed a similar wave of radicalism, but one that was more influenced by the historical materialist philosophy of Marxism. Within psychology, critical theorists such as Buss (1976) and Sampson (1977) demonstrated the socio-historical and ideological origins of many of the discipline's central theories. As we discussed in earlier chapters, social psychology did not escape this critical onslaught. Most notable and influential was Gergen's (1973) critique which emphasized the historically, culturally specific and individualistic nature of social psychological theories. Throughout this book, we have made similar criticisms of many of the social cognitive approaches we have presented.

While this tradition of critique pointed to the complex interplay between society's ideological structure and the social determination of knowledge, many of these critics were realists who maintained that a 'true' version of reality, while difficult to identify through the mystifying layers of ideology, could be ascertained. In stark contrast, postmodernism attacks the very notion of 'reality' itself. In part, the questioning of the existence of a fixed discoverable reality emerges from a particular philosophical view of language.

While positivism treats language as a 'mirror of reality', reflecting a world 'out there' (Agger, 1991), postmodernists stress that words and language do not have independent objective meanings outside the social and relational context in which they are used. Derrida is perhaps the strongest advocate of this position, arguing that no text has a single fixed meaning: all texts are subject to pluralistic and therefore differing interpretations. Surface meanings conceal layers of meaning which are not always immediately evident. Definitional categories presuppose cultural and social assumptions which emerge with different readings and interpretations. Sometimes what is absent from the text can convey as much meaning as what is present. For Derrida, all categories and all texts deconstruct themselves. These views have led to a critical Derridean method of deconstruction which has become popular in literary theory and practice but which has also been used to deconstruct positivist science as a dominant 'text' or discourse. As Agger puts it, Derrida's views suggest that 'There is no royal road to meaning except through the meaning-constitutive practices of language that, in turn, provoke new confusions, contradictions, and conflicts' (1991: 114).

An important philosophical precursor to this relativist view of language is the later work of Wittgenstein (1953). Wittgenstein emphasized the interactive and conventional nature of language. As a social practice, language has no fixed meaning outside the context in which it is used. Our perception of the world is shaped by the language we use to describe it: objects, activities and categories derive their epistemological status from the definitions we create for them. Within this view, thought and language are no longer separated. 'When we think in language, there are not "meanings" going through our mind in addition to verbal expressions. The language itself is the vehicle of thought' (Collier et al., 1991: 277).

The social constructionist movement (Gergen, 1985) was among the first 'schools' of psychology to embrace the postmodernist critique of positivist-empiricist science and its conception of truth and knowledge. Representing a loose association of critics from differing intellectual backgrounds (feminists, hermeneuticists, ethogenicists and critical theorists), social constructionism regards psychological knowledge as socially constructed via the negotiated socio-cultural meanings which are historically prevalent. Deconstructing this knowledge by elucidating its cultural and often political foundations has been a major concern for social constructionism. For example, feminist critiques of psychology have highlighted the androcentric bias implicit in many psychological theories and practices, which, in turn, have had the net political effect of supporting and maintaining patriarchal forms of oppression within the discipline as well as in society in general.

While components of postmodernism and social constructionism sit comfortably with some socio-cognitive perspectives (especially social representations theory, which emphasizes the social construction of everyday knowledge), the more relativist and non-cognitivist variants of this position are not always easy to accommodate. It is perhaps the newest branch of social psychology, known as 'discourse analysis', which has taken up these issues seriously. It is these to which we now turn.

DISCOURSE ANALYSIS

Given the contemporary philosophical and epistemological climate described above, the 'turn to language' (Parker, 1991), as exemplified in discourse analytic approaches which have developed recently in social psychology, is perhaps not surprising. Talking, listening, having conversations, are central human activities in which people are engaged for most of the time. Even when alone, we are not free from the 'constant chatter' which goes on in our heads in the form of self-talk and reflection.

There are a number of discourse analytic approaches which differ philosophically from each other (Burman, 1991; Potter and Wetherell, 1987). 'Discourse analysis', in a generic sense, describes a number of social psychological approaches which are predominantly concerned with analysing the socially constitutive nature of language. However, we will rely heavily on Potter and Wetherell's (1987) *Discourse and Social Psychology: Beyond Attitudes and Behaviour*, and their more recent book, *Mapping the Language of Racism* (Wetherell and Potter, 1992) as points of reference because these provide the clearest expression of the differences between their brand of discourse analysis and social cognitive approaches in social psychology. We will also refer to Ian Parker's approach to discourse analysis in order to highlight some of the contested issues within the discursive approach.

Potter and Wetherell (1987) utilize the theoretical and empirical foundations of speech act theory, ethnomethodology and semiology to arrive at their own approach to the analysis of discourse. Based on Austin's speech act theory, a central emphasis running through their approach is that people use language 'to do things', to achieve certain ends. Words are not simply abstract tools used to state or describe things: they are also used to make certain things happen. People use language to justify, explain, blame, excuse, persuade and present themselves in the best possible light. Thus language is functional. Potter and Wetherell are interested in how people use language to understand and make sense of everyday life. Like ethnomethodology, the focus is on the ordinary everyday use of talk which has practical consequences for participants. Language is viewed as reflexive and contextual, constructing the very nature of objects and events as they are talked about. This emphasizes the constructive nature and role of language. Furthermore, words do more than just name things; there are complex relations of meaning which are taken for granted in the words and language that we use. Semiologists have studied the underlying culturally constructed meanings with which words are imbued, emphasizing that meaning is often realized by the words which are both present and absent.

A pervasive theme in Potter and Wetherell's work is the variability of people's talk. What people say depends on the particular context in which it is spoken and the function it serves. In the ebb and flow of everyday life the context within which talk occurs and its accompanying function continually shifts and changes. As people are engaged in conversation with others, they construct and negotiate meanings, or the very 'reality' which they are talking about. In contrast to most traditional approaches in social psychology and social cognition research which look for stability, consistency and order in people's attitudes and accounts, Potter and Wetherell stress the inherent variability of what people say. In fact, from a discourse perspective, people are expected to demonstrate considerable variability and inconsistency, as content is seen to reflect contextual changes and functional purposes of the immediate moment. Moving from a traditional realist view which treats language as merely descriptive and reflecting a stable and presupposed world 'out there', discourse analysis is not attempting

to recover events, beliefs and cognitive processes from participants' discourse, or treat language as an indicator or signpost to some other state of affairs but looking at the analytically prior question of how discourse or accounts of these things are manufactured. (Potter and Wetherell, 1987: 35)

Potter and Wetherell argue that social psychological theories have not taken the issue of variability seriously. We have already discussed in Chapter 6 how social representations theory has been criticized for valorizing consensus over variability. Potter and Wetherell argue that through traditional quantitative and qualitative methods of research variability in people's attitudes, representations and accounts has been suppressed. The use of aggregating quantitative methods and the use of gross categories to code qualitative data conceals variability, which constructs an oversimplified picture of people's attitudes and representations. The statistical use of mean results in questionnaire data says little about the inconsistent, ambivalent or context-dependent views that people may have. As Billig (1982) and his colleagues (Billig et al., 1988) have documented, many social psychological theories have assumed an inherent human motivation for cognitive balance and consistency. There has been surprisingly little interest in theorizing the ambivalent and 'dilemmatic' nature of people's thoughts and opinions.

More importantly, Potter and Wetherell challenge the epistemological status of the 'attitude' concept itself. The theoretical notion of an attitude and the assumption that it can be encapsulated by how a person responds to a questionnaire scale assumes the existence of internal cognitive entities which are relatively enduring. Their discursive approach suggests that people may make different evaluations depending on the specific context at hand. The view that something like an attitude can be identified and located assumes that there exists an internal cognitive world. In this view, language simply reflects this internal and mental world. Potter and Wetherell argue that such cognitive assumptions are problematic. They prefer to suspend and refrain from cognitivist assumptions by analysing what people have to say discursively about particular issues paying attention to the variability in their language and the function that this variability serves. Their approach to the functional and contextual nature of discourse is summarized thus:

We do not intend to use the discourse as a pathway to entities or phenomena lying beyond the text. Discourse analysis does not take for granted that accounts reflect underlying attitudes or dispositions and therefore we do not expect that an individual's discourse will be consistent and coherent. Rather the focus is on the discourse *itself*: how it is organized and what it is doing. Orderliness in discourse will be viewed as a product of the orderly *functions* to which discourse is put. (Potter and Wetherell, 1987: 4; original emphasis)

In place of the attitude concept, and indeed, the concept of social representations, Potter and Wetherell put forward the notion of 'interpretative repertoires'; defined as a set of metaphors, arguments and terms which are used recurrently in people's discourse to describe events and actions. Later in this chapter we will be illustrating the implications of this discursive approach for the analysis of prejudice and intergroup relations, and will contrast it with the socio-cognitive approaches to prejudice we have already discussed.[2]

Categories in discourse

A central concept in most of the theoretical approaches we have discussed in this book is categorization. The use and application of social categories is assumed to be a pervasive cognitive tendency which serves to simplify an overly complex world. In this sense, categorization is viewed as highly functional and, indeed, necessarily adaptive if we are to protect ourselves from cognitive overload. However, we have also documented some of the associated cognitive consequences of categorization, consequences such as objectification, distortion, bias, stereotyping and prejudice, all of which have been lamented by social psychologists and others. In contrast, Potter and Wetherell introduce an entirely different approach to the study of categorization. While their discursive approach does not deny that people use social categories to talk about the world, they deny that social categories are rigid internal entities which are used inflexibly. Furthermore, they do not regard categories as cognitive phenomena located in people's heads – preformed static structures which are organized around prototypical representations of the category. Rather, they are more interested in how people discursively constitute categories to do certain things.

> Instead of seeing categorization as a natural phenomenon – something which just happens, automatically – it is regarded as a complex and subtle social accomplishment . . . this . . . emphasizes the action orientation of categorization in discourse. It asks how categories are flexibly articulated in the course of certain sorts of talk and writing to accomplish particular goals, such as blamings or justifications. (Potter and Wetherell, 1987: 116)

Previous chapters have highlighted the extensive social cognitive research on stereotypes of minority groups. Stereotypes have been conceptualized as a stable set of descriptions and attributes of a particular social group which are highly consensual, pervasive and resistant to change. If the stereotype concept (as a cognitive structure) has any ecological validity, then one would expect a set of core descriptions and adjectives to emerge readily from people's talk of a particular category of people. Potter and Wetherell argue that in their research on white middle-class New Zealanders' discourse on Maoris they were unable to find a consensual and consistent core of descriptions which could readily be identified as a Maori prototype or stereotype. Rather, people's descriptions were inconsistent, highly variable and context-dependent. People used descriptions selectively, so that the same person could describe Maoris as a 'lazy race' and at another point in the interview refer to them as 'such hard-working people'. Discourse analysis tries to make sense of these inconsistencies by emphasizing what people are trying to do and what effects they are trying to produce with their talk at different points in time.

While social cognitive researchers regard stereotypes as distorted and biased descriptions of social groups, the social categories themselves are regarded as reflecting real and valid group entities in the social world. Categories such as man–woman, black–white, young–old, rich–poor, are treated as uncontested and non-problematic social objects which are perceived directly through identifiable physical and social features. While social identity theory and social representations theory are more inclined to emphasize the socially constructed nature of these categories, they too tend to treat social categories 'as static features of a predefined macro-sociological landscape' (Wetherell and Potter, 1992: 74). We discussed this particular criticism of social representations research in Chapter 6, the charge being that most studies to date have used pre-defined 'naturally occurring' groups, without investigating their socially negotiated construction.

In contrast, Wetherell and Potter are interested in 'how categories become constructed in different social contexts and how the method of construction creates a subjectivity for oneself and for those defined as Other' (1992: 74). For them, categorization is not simply a cognitive, internal process based on direct and veridical perception, but a 'discursive action' which is 'actively constructed in discourse for rhetorical ends' (1992: 77). Likewise, Edwards describes categorization as 'something we do, in talk, in order to accomplish social actions (persuasions, blamings, denial, refutations, accusations, etc.)' (1991: 94; original emphasis). Moreover, some constructions are so familiar, pervasive and common-sensical that they 'give an effect of realism' or fact. People therefore come to regard some constructions not as versions of reality, but as direct representations of reality itself.

Edwards (1991) argues that the experiential basis of categories is what makes them appear to be direct, perceptual and objective descriptions of reality. In this way, experiential realism operates as a rhetorical device in making claims about reality.

In *Mapping the Language of Racism*, Wetherell and Potter (1992) investigate the way in which Pakeha (white) New Zealanders use the particular categories of 'race', 'culture' and 'nation' in their talk of Maori–Pakeha relations and how these rhetorical constructions are used to legitimate the existing social order of inequality and Maori disadvantage. Wetherell and Potter argue that it is through the dynamic process of discursive interaction that a particular individual's subjectivity and the social objects of the discourse are defined and constructed. For example, the categories of 'race' and 'culture' were used by the Pakeha respondents as contrastive categories to define the Maori people as a distinct biological group of people who shared similar physical characteristics, values and personality characteristics. These categories were used predominantly to contrast Maoris with the Pakeha majority who were represented as the 'norm' of New Zealand society. While Pakeha society represented civilization, progress and modernism, Maoris were the repository of 'culture'. In this way, the Maori people were always constructed as the 'Other': exotic, steeped in culture and separate. While many of the respondents spoke favourably of a Maori cultural identity, ultimately this identity was viewed as secondary to a homogeneous and unifying 'national' identity. The category of 'nation' was used in Pakeha talk to limit and constrain the aspirations of a Maori identity, which in its 'radical' form was seen to undermine and threaten national unity.

The discourse of prejudice and racism

Wetherell and Potter's unique social psychological approach to the study of racist discourse in New Zealand emphasizes how people strategically and rhetorically organize what they say in order to avoid being evaluated and labelled as racist. Indeed, all of the respondents were proficient at using a range of liberal and egalitarian principles such as freedom, fairness and equal opportunity to argue for outcomes which Wetherell and Potter describe as 'illiberal': arguments and rhetoric which justified and sustained the existing inequitable social relations in New Zealand. Wetherell and Potter identify 10 common 'rhetorically self-sufficient' or clinching arguments that respondents used in their discourse to this effect. These include:

1. Resources should be used productively and in a cost-effective manner.
2. Nobody should be compelled.
3. Everybody should be treated equally.
4. You cannot turn the clock backwards.
5. Present generations cannot be blamed for the mistakes of past generations.
6. Injustices should be righted.
7. Everybody can succeed if they try hard enough.
8. Minority opinion should not carry more weight than majority opinion.
9. We have to live in the twentieth century.
10. You have to be practical. (Wetherell and Potter, 1992: 177)

While these 'rhetorically self-sufficient' arguments were used extensively in Pakeha discourse, Wetherell and Potter emphasize that they were used in a flexible and often contradictory manner. They stress that these maxims should not be viewed as cognitive templates or schemas that structured and organized Pakeha discourse, but rather as 'tools' or 'resources' which were combined in variable ways by the respondents to do certain things, most notable of which was to avoid a 'racist' identity and to justify existing Maori–Pakeha relations. Like Billig et al. (1988), Wetherell and Potter argue for the fragmentary, dilemmatic and contradictory nature of people's views, an approach which is considerably different from the social psychological concept of attitude as an enduring, stable and consistent cognitive entity.

The 'appropriation' and use of liberal and egalitarian principles to argue for 'racist' and discriminatory practices is, of course, a central feature of contemporary theories of modern racism. As described in Chapter 9, these theories argue that, unlike 'old-fashioned' racism, which is predominantly characterized by white supremacist beliefs, contemporary racism is more subtle and insidious. While extreme negative affect toward black Americans has been tempered by egalitarian values, this negative affect (conscious or unconscious) has not been entirely eradicated and persists in the American psyche. The contradiction between this affect and liberal values produces considerable psychological ambivalence so that individuals struggle between their emotions and their beliefs. Moreover, the modern racist denies that he or she is prejudiced; any conscious and obvious negative feelings and attitudes are justified by 'matter of fact' observations that blacks transgress central American values such as hard work, thrift and self-reliance.

While theories of modern racism bear elements of similarity to Wetherell and Potter's findings of conflicted and contradictory discourse on Maori–Pakeha relations in New Zealand, there is an important difference between the two approaches that these authors are at pains to point out. Theories of modern racism do refer to the wider socio-historical and ideological factors that have influenced and shaped the content and form of racism and prejudice over the years. However, these theories and the questionnaire research methods which have been used to investigate variants of racism primarily view racism as an individual and psychological problem. The ambivalence and contradictions which are manifest both in questionnaire responses and in people's talk are located 'within the emotional and cognitive domain of the individual' (Wetherell and Potter, 1992: 197). The discourse analytic approach

> locates the conflicts and dilemmas within the argumentative and rhetorical resources available in a 'liberal' and 'egalitarian' society such as New Zealand. The conflict is not between a feeling and a value, between psychological drives and socially acceptable expressions or between emotions and politics, but between competing frameworks for articulating social, political and ethical questions. These conflicts and dilemmas could be said to be realized in a 'psychological' form when the members of society begin to discuss, debate, explain, justify and develop accounts in the course of social interaction and everyday life. (Wetherell and Potter, 1992: 197)

From this perspective, racism or prejudice ceases to be an individual or psychological state but a structural feature of a society which is 'organized around the oppression of one group and the dominance of another group' (Wetherell and Potter, 1992: 198). Individuals utilize whatever ideological resources a society makes available to justify and legitimate racist outcomes, but this is always viewed primarily within the context of oppressive structural arrangements which need to be continually justified and legitimated for their maintenance and reproduction.

By locating prejudice primarily within the individual rather than in society, social psychological theories have colluded in conceptualizing prejudice as an individual pathology. In doing so, the categories of the 'prejudiced individual' and the 'tolerant individual' have been constructed and reified as real entities with clear definitional boundaries. 'Prejudice remains a personal pathology, a failure of inner-directed empathy and intellect, rather than a social pathology, shaped by power relations and the conflicting vested interests of groups' (Wetherell and Potter, 1992: 208). Prejudiced individuals are seen to be irrational and illogical, requiring some kind of attitudinal and moral 'rehabilitation'. The development and implementation of widespread anti-racist workshops are interventions which reflect the view that prejudice is a 'state of mind' which requires change through education and training. Politically, this has the effect of deflecting attention from the political necessity of societal and structural change.

Problems with the discursive approach

The above summary of Wetherell and Potter's social psychological approach to discourse is not intended to be exhaustive. We believe their approach introduces a very different, unique and exciting perspective to contemporary social psychology and that their empirical focus on everyday discourse engages seriously with Moscovici's emphasis on the centrality of the everyday chatter and conversations in which we engage. We also welcome their challenges to the social categorization research, moving such research away from the study of static and idealized objects which supposedly exist 'out there' in an extra-linguistic reality, to the investigation of the dynamic way in which people construct social categories discursively and interactively. Their research on racist discourse also challenges the oversimplified conceptualization of racist attitudes and the 'prejudiced identity'. We also agree that despite the politically motivated concern of most social psychological approaches to prejudice and racism, such approaches have, paradoxically, led to the individualization of prejudice. Prejudice has undoubtedly been predominantly constructed as a cognitive and psychological phenomenon and few psychologists have looked to the inherent contradictions of a racist society.

However, we do see certain difficulties with Wetherell and Potter's discursive approach. First, we would like to make a number of observations about their claim that the inherent variability of what people say stems largely from what they want to do with their talk. Wetherell and Potter clearly document and illustrate contradictory and inconsistent views that individuals give during interviews, demonstrating the context-specific and functional nature of discourse. They make much of this inconsistency, pointing to the inherent problems of categorizing individuals as being 'racist' or 'prejudiced' as opposed to being 'non-racist' or 'non-prejudiced': categorizations which most social psychological theories and measures of prejudice produce with apparent simplicity. Rather, in a more naturalistic conversational setting, respondents articulate a complex set of positions which blend egalitarian and tolerant views with discriminatory and prejudiced ones. Moreover, many respondents are proficient at using liberal-egalitarian principles to justify and rationalize their discriminatory views.

We have few problems with Wetherell and Potter's arguments and are convinced that contemporary racism is indeed a complex blend of both egalitarian and non-egalitarian principles, which makes it all the more resilient and pervasive throughout society. However, we are not totally convinced that individuals' discourse or talk cannot be differentiated or categorized. We accept that the most dominant form that racist talk takes is that of a contradictory meshing of liberal and illiberal arguments, making it difficult to differentiate the racist from the non-racist. In contrast, however, there are some individuals whose views are less complex and reflect blatant and obvious forms of prejudice, the sort which is characteristic of biological racism and white supremacist beliefs. Indeed, Wetherell and Potter refer to such views, but do not discuss this type of discourse in great detail. Likewise, they make only a cursory reference to a few individuals who utilized a 'counter-ideological' discourse, drawing from socialist and feminist frameworks to argue against racism (1992: 219). We would have been interested in the kind of discourse these people produced, and, indeed, some discussion regarding the criteria used to differentiate the discourse of these individuals from that of others. It is unclear whether these accounts were just as fragmentary and contradictory as the ones Wetherell and Potter chose to document and discuss in detail.

While we accept that discourse is fragmentary, dilemmatic and contradictory, we suggest that, despite this, there is often an identifiable 'coherence' in what people say. Instead of selecting bits and pieces of discourse at different points of an interview, when an individual's entire discursive account is reproduced is there an underlying sense of coherence, is there a 'position' which can be discerned and delineated? We are not able to determine this because of the selective nature of the empirical data which is reproduced by Wetherell and Potter. We are not trying to argue so much for the existence of certain 'types' of individuals who can be differentiated by their discourse. We agree that the construction of such typologies is problematic given the complex and contradictory nature of what people say. However, we are suggesting that Wetherell and Potter may be overemphasizing the extent to which there is variability in what people say, and that if an individual's entire account is considered, without selective editing, a more coherent and consistent story may emerge. Paradoxically, we are suggesting that there may be both consistency *and* variability in what people say and that whether an account is labelled consistent or inconsistent depends on what the researcher is looking for. Variability will undoubtedly be found, in part due to the functional and purposive nature of language, but also because many people do not hold views that are always internally consistent. Nevertheless, despite the fluidity and variability, an overall coherence and structure in accounts may emerge. Indeed, Wetherell and Potter's research puts a strong case for the existence of a 'dominant' kind of racist discourse which utilizes egalitarian and social reformist principles to legitimate discriminatory practices and the existence of inequalities between social groups. This discourse is used flexibly, depending on the rhetorical purposes to which it is put, but this flexibility is shaped by some overall cognitive coherence and order. For example, the desire to appear non-racist and non-discriminatory (a motivation repeatedly referred to by Wetherell and Potter) in itself provides shape and coherence to what is said and not said during talk. Moreover, it is difficult not to view self-presentation and impression management as underlying cognitive and evaluative motivations which determine what is said and not said (Giles and Coupland, 1989).

The variability argument is also at the core of Wetherell and Potter's criticisms of the prototype and stereotype concepts. The argument that these phenomena do not exist because people contradict themselves in talk is far from convincing. Despite the reactive limitations of the use of rating scales and the application of categories in qualitative research, a core set of consensual descriptions to describe social groups is one of the most robust findings in the social psychological literature. This research does not suggest that a stereotype is always applied, consistently and in every context, but that it is a particular kind of 'cognitive resource', or, alternatively, an 'interpretative repertoire' which is relatively stable, shared and identifiable. Even if stereotypes are artefacts of the reactive methods which are used to measure them, their consensuality and the relative ease with which people can identify and describe them, suggests that they are some kind of cognitive and symbolic phenomenon to be reckoned with. As we make clear in previous chapters, we would qualify this by arguing that the content of stereotypes is subject to considerable change given differing socio-historical contexts. Nor do we share the view of some theorists that stereotypes are inevitable because of the functional need to categorize. Stereotypes function as ideological mechanisms by justifying and legitimating the oppression of certain groups within society. We will be saying more about the system justification function of stereotypes in the following chapter.

For us, one of the strengths of Wetherell and Potter's discursive approach is their empirical demonstration of the way in which people construct and use categories in discourse and the ideological effects and consequences some uses and constructions have. This is quite different from the usual social cognitive approach which treats categories as fixed social entities which exist 'out there' in the real world as discrete cognitive entities in people's minds. It emphasizes the social constructionist nature of social categories and identities. Consistent with their views on the variability and fluidity of discourse, they have also emphasized the contextual and functional way in which categories are constructed in discourse. Categorization is viewed as a situated discursive practice (Edwards, 1991). Most of the empirical work Wetherell and Potter discuss focuses almost exclusively on the way in which categorization functions to 'fix' reality in discourse (even if momentarily): '. . . the discursive act creates groups, interests, emotions, similarities and differences, a social landscape, an anthropology, a psychology of identity and even a geography' (1992: 146). Paradoxically, by so clearly demonstrating the constructivist and ideological effects of category use, Wetherell and Potter reinforce the cognitivist arguments regarding categorization; its centrality to human thought (in this case, discourse), its functional nature (defining parameters of inclusion and exclusion) and its resultant 'effects' (for example, generalization, evaluation). As Edwards (1991) suggests, the work on categorization is not totally incompatible with a discursive approach, for both research traditions demonstrate the capacity of categories to provide meaning and definition. Indeed, we are uncertain as to the extent to which the discursive approach challenges cognitivist assumptions about the human functional need to order and simplify perception. We will return to this issue later.

A particularly problematic aspect of Wetherell and Potter's discursive approach to understanding human social and psychological life is that, at times, the individual purposive-agent appears absent in their discussions. In deliberately avoiding any suggestion that there is an essentialist psychological 'self', subjective experience such as social interaction, social identity and discourse is made so context-dependent, so fluid and flexible, that there seems to be little beyond a personal psychology which is a moment-to-moment situated experience. Sometimes the individual is seen to be totally subject to and determined by societal forces and processes. For example, in locating prejudice and racism totally within the socio-political structures of a society, Wetherell and Potter strip the individual agent of any personal 'ownership' of his or her views (racist or otherwise) and thus moral accountability and responsibility for his or her 'attitudes'. People are cast as helpless victims who are subject to the contrary ideological themes which proliferate within society. This is most evident in Wetherell and Potter's critique of anti-racist training programmes, intervention strategies which attempt to educate and reform. These are viewed critically as individual cognitive strategies which make a negligible contribution to the fight against racism. For Wetherell and Potter, the proper and most legitimate site for action is at the socio-political level. We would prefer to suggest that the fight against racism should take place at all levels, from the societal and institutional, to the individual and personal, and that strategies at different levels can complement and reinforce each other. Nevertheless, we do agree that programmes which are marked for individual attitude change are unlikely to succeed without appropriate interventions at the socio-political and structural level.

While Wetherell and Potter acknowledge some of the problems to which we refer, they are, nevertheless, committed to not making any sharp distinctions between the individual and the social, and so refrain from speculations about any internal psychological realm. However, like others, we have found the absence of any psychological model of the person, their 'black box'[3] approach to discourse, unsatisfying. In contrast, Parker (1991) confronts this issue more directly. Before discussing individual psychological approaches which Parker believes can complement discourse analysis, we want first to say a little about his approach to discourse and how it contrasts with Wetherell and Potter's work.

Interpretative repertoires or 'discourses'?

In contrast to Potter and Wetherell's ethnomethodological approach to discourse analysis, Ian Parker (1990) has developed an approach to the study of discourse which has been informed by French poststructuralist writers such as Foucault and Derrida. Parker is more interested in locating and describing the variety of 'discourses' which proliferate within society and which inform, shape and construct the way we see ourselves and the world. In place of Potter and Wetherell's concept of 'interpretative repertoire', Parker prefers to call a recurrently used 'system of statements which constructs an object' a *discourse* (1990: 191). So, for example, within western societies there exist a number of dominant discourses which inform and shape various aspects of our lives. We have a medical discourse which informs our understanding of anything to do with health and illness; we have a legal discourse which provides us with certain codes of conduct and rules for behaviour; we have a familial discourse which buttresses views about the sanctity and importance of the family, etc. While Parker defines discourses as 'coherent systems of meaning', contradictions and inconsistencies within discourses are common, as are alternative discourses which compete with dominant ones for recognition and power. Often discourses are related to or presuppose other discourses or systems of meaning. Discourses primarily function to bring 'objects into being', to create the status of reality with which objects are endowed. They also position us in various 'subject' positions, so that discourses invite us, even compel us, to take on certain roles and behaviour. For example, an advertising discourse positions us in the role of 'consumer'. Often, however, this is achieved by addressing us by virtue of our status and identity as a woman, a parent, a worker, etc. Parker does not restrict discourse to just spoken and written language. Discourses can be found in all kinds of 'texts', such as in advertising, popular and high-brow culture, non-verbal behaviour and instruction manuals.

As coherent meaning systems, Parker argues that discourses have a material and almost 'physical presence'. Like social representations (as defined by Moscovici), discourses, once created, proliferate within society. Importantly, however, Parker does not view discourses in idealist terms but sees them as grounded in and shaped by historical and political (material) 'realities'. Thus he does not subscribe to the linguistic and political relativism which is associated with some approaches to discourse analysis – the view that all meaning is constituted by semiotic systems. It would be fair to call Parker a 'critical realist', whose goal is to develop an approach to discourse which is sensitive to the material and socio-structural conditions from which discourses emerge and take shape. The political edge to Parker's approach is that some discourses function to legitimate and buttress existing institutions, reproduce power relations and inequities within societies, and have certain ideological effects (Parker, 1990). Thus, '[d]iscourse analysis should become a variety of action research, in which the internal system of any discourse and its relation to others is challenged. It alters, and so permits different spaces for manoeuvre and resistance' (Parker, 1990: 201).

While Parker's approach to discourse analysis shares features with that of Potter and Wetherell's work, his notion of 'discourses' has been criticized for its reified and abstract status. For him discourses, as entities, exist independently from the people who use them. In contrast, Potter and Wetherell's approach to the analysis of discourse is attuned to the context-specific and functional ways in which talk or discourse is mobilized in specific situations. For them, defining discourse as a 'situated practice' provides a more social psychological focus to discourse analysis (Potter, Wetherell, Gill and Edwards, 1990).

INDIVIDUAL PSYCHOLOGICAL APPROACHES CONSISTENT WITH DISCOURSE ANALYSIS

Despite this social psychological focus, discourse analytic 'research repeatedly begs the question: what is going on inside human beings when they use discourse? ' (Parker, 1991: 83). Parker suggests two conceptual approaches which would complement the theoretical and moral goals of discourse analysis, and also provide some link between discourse and individual subjectivity: poststructuralist psychodynamic theory and Gibson's ecological theory of perception.

Recourse to psychodynamic perspectives to furnish us with a model of the individual person may appear a strange choice, but, as Parker (1991) makes clear, recent psychodynamic writings by Lacan and Habermas pay particular attention to the role of language in human consciousness and reflexivity. The capacity to be reflexive is at the core of human agency and understanding and it is this capacity to be reflexive which Parker argues is 'the point of connection between the individual and the social' (1991: 105). Reflexivity is also a central concern in discourse analytic research and Parker turns to psychodynamic models to throw light on how the process of reflection can elucidate both manifest, latent and distorted meanings in discourse. While we are prepared to agree with Parker that certain psychodynamic perspectives have important contributions to make in understanding human agency and behaviour, we find more difficulty in accepting his position that there is nothing cognitive 'going on'. While the capacity for self-reflection and reflection of others is itself embedded in language and is therefore social and symbolic in nature, it seems to us difficult to deny that reflexivity is, at some level, a cognitive activity. This leads us to consider, in more detail, the Gibsonian ecological approach, for Gibson's work has invariably been associated with alternative and non-cognitive accounts of human experience and behaviour (Costall and Still, 1987; Shotter, 1984).

Gibson's ecological theory of perception

The increasing disenchantment with cognitivism has led to a renewed interest in the work of J. J. Gibson and his theory of perception. While Gibson has been branded as an anti-cognitivist, it is more accurate to depict his ecological approach to perception as questioning the taken-for-granted assumption that *all* psychological processes are mediated by mental representation and mental rules (Still and Costall, 1987). Reed argues that:

> It is virtually a dogma of modern psychology that all meaningful perception is indirect, and is in some ways analogous to language and the use of symbols and representations. . . . Simply put, the idea is that perception of the world is based on sense inputs. We have direct access to the sense inputs, but these are not meaningful in themselves, they become meaningful only after a complex form of quasi-grammatical or computational processing. . . . On this theory there is no direct experience that is truly meaningful. (1987: 153–4)

While conventional theories argue that perception is the product of the internal and mental elaboration of sensory experience, Gibson argues that perception is a direct apprehension of the information contained within the environment at a particular point in time. The human mind does not need to impose meaning upon what is seen or heard because ecological objects themselves contain sufficient information to be directly perceptible and knowable. 'Gibson's epistemology is a theory of *direct cognitive contact with existents*' (Reed, 1987: 101; original emphasis). Importantly, unlike most cognitive theories, Gibson's fundamental unit of analysis is not the individual person abstracted from the environment. Rather, the person and environment are seen to be an integral unit, each co-determining the other in a direct and unmediated manner. Both the person and environment 'move' together in an integral and coordinated way. Furthermore, perception is seen to extend beyond static objects in the environment, by embracing dynamic and fluid events. This is in sharp contrast to the way in which perception and cognition have been studied experimentally via the use of static and fixed objects in the laboratory.

According to Gibson, not only do we 'see' ecological objects and events as they really are, but humans have evolved nervous systems to perceive 'affordances' for behaviour. Human behaviour, and, for that matter, animal behaviour, is shaped by the affordances which exist in the environment.

> The *affordances* of the environment are what it *offers* the animal, what it *provides* or *furnishes*, whether for good or ill. . . . I mean by [affordance] something that refers to both the environment and the animal in a way that no existing term does. It implies the complementarity of the animal and the environment. (Gibson, 1979: 127; original emphases)

Organisms are attuned to perceive information selectively in the environment, and this selectivity is in turn determined by what is useful to the organism's immediate goals and needs. Indeed, one of the central premises of Gibson's (1979) work is that 'perception is for doing'. Perception therefore serves an important adaptive function.

According to Gibson, the environment is perceived directly and without recourse to cognitive or mental processing. Moreover, because the environment contains rich ecological information, knowledge of the environment is public and available to all. As a shared resource, humans come to perceive common affordances and, as such, human activities and interactions are coordinated and shaped by these affordances. The selectivity of perception and its orientation to action emphasizes that perception is not simply the passive reception of sensory information.

In contrast to the direct realism of his theory of perception, Gibson also acknowledged the role of mediated or indirect cognition, but this was reserved solely for the forms of human symbolic activity such as language. The role and function of indirect cognition, however, is not to make sense of the world, but primarily to share and communicate knowledge to others (Reed, 1987). While symbol systems (writing, drawing, etc.) are historically and culturally determined, they are also grounded in ecological information. In this way, mediated and unmediated cognition, 'the cultural and the individual (natural) processes are thoroughly mixed' (Reed, 1987: 162). While Gibson acknowledges the role of language in enhancing our awareness of the world, Noble (1987) argues that one of the problems with Gibson's ecological approach is that it fails to make explicit the connections and interactions between language and perception. More specifically, while direct perception of the world is a useful starting point as a model of human perception, it does not adequately recognize that perception, in the case of humans, is mediated by language. We use language to label, identify and thus communicate what we perceive to others. In turn, the labels and names we use are part of an historical and cultural matrix which signifies normative rules for how to behave in relation to objects and events in the environment. Language can also, in itself, be the object of our perceptions (Noble, 1987).

Parker (1991) engages directly with these criticisms of the ecological approach by emphasizing the role of language and symbolic meaning in perception. He argues that just as individuals are embedded in the physical environment, so too are they embedded in language and meaning. Parker extends Gibson's notion of direct and unmediated perception of the physical world to argue for a theoretical model which views the individual as perceiving the social world through the direct and unmediated use of language and discourse. Parker uses Gibson's notion of the 'organism–environment system' to avoid the dualist tendency of separating the individual from the social. Just as individuals directly perceive affordances in the environment for action, so too do they directly perceive affordances for employing certain discourses or 'symbolic arrays of meaning'. Consistent with his realist epistemology, Parker describes the individual as a 'realist subject' who

> directly perceives the world, engages with physical and social material as real opportunities for (and constraints on) action. When deconstructed, the agency of the person is no longer seen as 'inside' seeking expression against an imperfectly known 'outside', but as the exercise of power (and resistance) realised moment to moment in movement through the world. Aspects of this movement are physical, practical, and here the biological structure of the person as organism resonates with material niches. Other aspects of this activity are symbolic, expressive, and here the individual moves through the world as a reader of texts. Collections of texts define symbolic arrays which are the cultural niches we inhabit, and discourse analysis traces the threads which run through those niches meshing them together into 'society'. (1991: 96)

For Parker, the extension of this ecological approach to the perception of the social and symbolic circumvents the need to posit forms of cognitive mediation or representation. The direct apprehension and use of discourse, such as the reading of 'texts', is like the physical environment, ever-present, enveloping and constitutive of individual subjectivity. While the image of people flowing or 'moving' rather effortlessly through everyday life has a nice mystical and romantic appeal, the direct and unmediated apprehension of the material and symbolic world is no doubt a plausible alternative to cognitivism. However, we do not regard Gibson's ecological theory of perception as a *definitive* alternative to cognitivism. Those pushing the ecological view are themselves keen to emphasize that Gibson did not totally rule out cognitive mediation or representation. Rather, he was critical of the unchallenged assumption that it was the most common form of perceptual experience (Costall and Still, 1987). If one accepts that perceptual experience can be both mediated and unmediated by cognition, and in a number of instances it would be difficult denying that anything resembling cognition is taking place (for example, reflection, learning, deductive reasoning), the question then becomes; when is perception mediated and when is it not? Under what conditions are cognitive processes required to elaborate upon what is being perceived and why? Furthermore, the Gibsonian ecological approach is not immune from a highly reductionist application. For example, McArthur and Baron's (1983) ecological treatment of social perception resembles a socio-biological account of perceptual attunement. They suggest that humans have evolved, through the necessity of species survival, a selective tendency to perceive certain properties of social stimuli over others, that is, a hierarchy of perceptual information in the environment important to adaptation and survival.[4] They use this 'Darwinian' rationale to explain empirical effects demonstrated in the social cognition literature such as the fundamental attribution bias. It seems, then, that the ecological approach cannot only be appropriated to complement a discursive analysis, but, in giving it an essentialist and biological appeal, it can also be appropriated by the mainstream!

CAN THE DISCURSIVE AND SOCIO-COGNITIVE APPROACHES BE RECONCILED?

It would be remiss of us not to consider whether the discursive and socio-cognitive approaches considered thus far can be reconciled. Aside from the conceptual and philosophical objections some may have to the very idea of integration, we feel that our relative unfamiliarity with the 'nitty gritty' of discourse analysis does not equip us adequately to attempt such a feat. The 'turn to language' associated with the poststructural and postmodern intellectual traditions does require us, however, to discuss whether there is any conceptual utility in abandoning the notion of cognition altogether. If thought is no more and no less than language itself, then a substantial component of psychological inquiry and scholarship has been misplaced in its quest to identify, operationalize and measure underlying cognitive mechanisms and processes.

While Wetherell and Potter describe their discursive approach as a non-cognitive alternative to the work on attitudes, categorization, social identity and social representations, they nevertheless acknowledge some of the useful insights this work has produced. In contrast, Parker is uncompromising in his critique of cognitivism. Parker warns of the inherent 'perils' and 'dangers' of any kind of cognitivism creeping into discourse analysis. For him, any notion of internal representation or model which assumes cognitive mediation is incompatible with a discursive approach. At times, however, he is more circumspect, acknowledging that cognition may be necessary for some forms of perception. Ironically, he attributes the probable 'reality' of representation and cognitive entities such as attitudes, stereotypes, attributions and schemas to the dominant cognitivist discourse within psychology and related disciplines which, through its proliferation and dissemination throughout society, has the power to create the very forms of thinking that it attempts to identify. For Parker, 'that is all the more reason to challenge cognitivist discourse inside psychology' (1991: 103).

While it is true that much of social cognition research has been shaped by an individualistic, mechanistic and sometimes dehumanizing model of the person, we believe it is possible to argue for a thoroughly socialized or 'reconstructed' notion of cognition which is compatible with the political and reflexive concerns espoused by many researchers within the discourse analytic school. For us, there is nothing inherently dehumanizing or mechanistic about the notion of cognition, other than the way it has been traditionally conceptualized and applied. Likewise, as Burman (1991) argues, there is nothing inherently politically progressive or critical in discourse analysis itself. Indeed, because discourse analysis is prone to relativism and there are few criteria by which to evaluate the validity of different readings or interpretations of discourse, analyses can sometimes have the ring of liberal-pluralistic accounts of meaning and difference. Associated with this is the tendency to treat discourse as 'all there is' rather than grounding it within existing socio-structural relations within society – relations which are shaped by individual and group interests.

For many of us the experience of consciousness and thought furnishes us with the self-evident reality of internal cognitive representation, and the very idea that there is little human behaviour and experience which is not cognitively mediated may seem absurd. Using Parker's language, cognitivism is indeed a 'discourse' which is dominant not only within the scientific and academic realm but also in the everyday world where people live out their lives. Cognitive concepts such as attitudes and beliefs are part and parcel of our everyday language and most people talk of their 'attitudes', 'beliefs' and 'opinions'. Whether this simply reflects the capacity that an intellectual discourse has in creating the very things that it believes to exist, or whether some elements of cognitivism resonate with common sense experience is difficult to determine.[5] Representation or cognition should not be defended simply because it makes good sense, but neither should we be happily convinced that it is the 'ultimate illusion' (delusion) that some claim it to be.

While we are prepared to agree with discourse theorists that language is vitally important in understanding how we come to see the world and our place in it, we do not think that it is necessary to argue for a completely non-cognitive social psychology. The employment of categories in talk and thought, the tendency to reify and objectify groups, objects and events, to perceive and interpret information according to cultural expectations and personal needs, and to provide accounts and explanations for events and experiences are all socio-cognitive tendencies which have been researched in the mainstream and which find some calibration when analysing everyday talk. While discourse theorists would claim that these principles have been reified and therefore smack of 'cognitive universalism' (and we would agree), certain general assumptions also flow from the discursive approach about what it is to be human: the need to communicate, to have one's voice heard, to reflect and to understand and explain the world around us.

Whether we subscribe to the view that language is a medium for cognition, or that there is little outside language itself, the recent uptake of discourse analysis does force us to take discursive interaction more seriously in our conceptual and empirical deliberations as social psychologists. Shotter, for example, describes conversation as 'the primary human reality' (1992: 176). A radically transformed and reconstructed notion of cognition needs to acknowledge the centrality of language in psychological experience and social interaction. While many theorists and researchers in the field are happy to agree that cognition is more than just an 'inside-the-head' phenomenon, often this has simply amounted to considering social and cultural factors as additional variables which can be added to basic individual models. As Sampson (1993) suggests, this 'accommodative' strategy does little to transform and overhaul the existing dominant models. Shaped and constituted by interaction, communication and cultural and socio-historical forces, human cognition is *always* socially situated. Here the work of Vygotsky can inform us of the essentially social and cultural nature of cognition. While Vygotsky maintained the distinction between language and cognition, for him mental functioning was always shaped by and situated within social life. Vygotsky's socio-cultural approach to mind (Wertsch, 1991) emphasized the importance of language or 'semiotic mediation' as a psychological tool for both thought and communication. For him, as for many discourse theorists, the point of connection between the social and the individual is the use of semiotic discursive practices. 'On the one hand, particular semiotic practices . . . reflect and help constitute sociocultural settings; on the other hand, they shape the genesis of individual mental functioning' (Wertsch, 1991: 93). More recently, Vygotsky's work has been central to educationalists, anthropologists, semiologists and psychologists who have come to view cognition as being always *socially situated* (Resnick, Levine and Teasley, 1991).

For the time being, the anti-cognitive rhetoric associated with discourse analysis and the antipathy of the mainstream's response to the 'turn to language' (for example, Abrams and Hogg, 1990b) suggests that the discursive and socio-cognitive approaches in social psychology are unlikely to be reconciled soon. It is important to emphasize, however, that not all approaches to discourse analysis are anti-cognitive. For example, van Dijk's (1987) analysis of racist discourse combines both the cognitive and discursive dimensions of prejudice in an insightful and meaningful way. It is perhaps ironic that, consistent with the action-orientation emphasis of discourse analysis (that is, people do things with words), Susan Fiske (1992) has recently stressed that 'thinking is for doing'! Fiske argues that, after a long period of neglect, social cognition research is beginning to investigate the 'pragmatic' nature of social thinking: that thinking is always attuned and oriented to the needs of social behaviour and interaction. Likewise, social representations researchers are arguing that representations are shaped by and tied to everyday *behavioural practices* (Pereira de Sa, 1992; see also Guerin, 1992). Whether this interest in doing and action reflects the beginnings of a pendulum swing away from cognitivism is too early to tell.

What is clear, however, is that the realist epistemological foundations of mainstream social cognition research, the quest for knowledge and truth through the application of positivist methods of science, will always be a bone of contention with the social constructionist and relativist notion of knowledge associated with the discursive approach (though a realist epistemology is not necessarily incompatible with discourse analysis). Thus social cognitive approaches in social psychology remain largely unaffected by the 'postmodern' intellectual challenge to truth and certainty.

SUMMARY

In this chapter we have documented some of the most radical contemporary critiques of social cognitive theories. Consistent with the increasing emphasis on the socially constitutive nature of language within poststructural and postmodern social theory, discourse analysis has emerged as a radical alternative in under-standing the way in which humans function to make sense of everyday life. This tradition of research is critical of traditional social cognitive concepts such as representations, attitudes, schemas, categories, etc., which are hypothesized to be stable mental structures located within the mind. Rather, discourse analytic research emphasizes the contextual and relational nature of every-day talk (discourse) which is inherently contradictory and fragmen-tary. Categories are not viewed simply as preformed static structures which are automatically activated, but as discursively constructed entities which are used in talk to do certain things such as to blame or justify. We contrasted Wetherell and Potter's discursive approach to racism and prejudice with traditional socio-cognitive treatments of these phenomena. In addition to the ethnomethodological application of discourse analysis we also discussed Parker's poststructural treatment of discourse analysis as the identification of coherent meaning systems which proliferate within society and which are used to construct meaning. Central to both approaches is the primacy of language in reality construction and a disdain for cognitivist accounts of this process. We argued that any attempts to reconcile the socio-cognitive and discursive approaches in social psychology require a thoroughly transformed and reconstructed notion of cognition consistent with Vygotsky's socio-cultural approach to mind.

NOTES

1 The view that we have entered the era of 'postmodernity', a stage of postindustrial capitalism which is significantly different from the past, is not a position shared by all – see Callinicos (1989) for a very different perspective.
2 As with the traditional notions of categorization, representations and attitudes, discourse analysts have reconceptualized the cognitive notion of attribution central to attribution theory. We do not have space to consider this work, but see Edwards and Potter (1992) for a comprehensive account.
3 It is perhaps unfair to use the 'black box' metaphor, traditionally associated with behaviourism, to describe Wetherell and Potter's approach to discourse. If one takes the Wittgensteinian view of language seriously, then any internal cognitive realm would be conceptualized as a form of *situated practice*.
4 For example, the perceptual attunement of emotions such as anger and fear, as well as aggressive and threatening behaviour, would take precedence over others, because of their adaptive value and function.
5 Of course no one has actually investigated what common sense meanings and understandings are attributed to concepts such as attitudes and beliefs and whether the ordinary person defines them in the same manner as social psychologists. Do people objectify their own attitudes as stable and enduring entities, or do they view them as fluid and context-dependent?

11

THE SOCIAL PSYCHOLOGICAL STUDY OF IDEOLOGY

In considering the wide range of conceptual and empirical work on the perception and understanding of the social world, we have thus far said little about the role ideology plays in constructing social reality for individuals and groups. This question has been long debated and argued within political and social theory, but has largely been ignored by social psychologists. There have been rare exceptions like Michael Billig, who has not only delineated the relationship between ideology and social psychological theory (1982), but also written extensively about the role of ideology in the everyday life of the ordinary person. To be sure, there have been many attempts to study ideology within social psychology, but, as we will argue, the definition of ideology which has been adopted within this body of research, the study of formal political belief systems, has been restrictive in scope and analysis. We define the social psychological study of ideology as the study of the social psychological processes and mechanisms by which certain representations and constructions of the world serve to legitimate, maintain and reproduce the existing institutional arrangements, social and power relations within a society. Given the breadth and scope of Moscovici's theory of social representations, a theoretical approach highly conducive to the study of ideology, it is somewhat surprising that few social representations researchers have concerned themselves with the contents and functions of ideological representations. This is surprising given the European origins of the theory. European social psychologists have not been as reluctant to move into explicitly political territory as their North American counterparts. In contrast, the discursive and rhetorical approach in psychology has begun to look at this long-neglected area.

THE CONCEPT OF IDEOLOGY

Ideology has been described by many as the most contested and elusive concept within the social sciences. Both McLellan (1986) and Larrain (1979) provide thorough historical accounts of this concept. Indeed, McLellan warns that all attempts to define ideology are ideological in themselves.

Ideology as political belief systems

The dominant approach in the social sciences is to view ideology as a coherent set of political beliefs and values embraced by formal political parties. The empirical tradition linked with this positivist view has involved large-scale surveys aimed at examining the political, economic and social attitudes of the mass public. The primary aim has been to determine the underlying structure of these beliefs in terms of a liberal–conservative political framework. This tradition of research culminated in Converse's (1964) work which concluded that the American public displayed little internal consistency in their political attitudes. People's views on a specific issue do not always predict their views on other related issues. Similarly, McClosky (1964) found that although the American public generally endorsed the principles of freedom and democracy in their abstract form, they were inconsistent in their application of these principles to specific instances. Thus, it was argued that there existed little ideological coherence amongst the American electorate, whose knowledge and understanding of politics was, at best, rudimentary.

Instead of an over-arching belief system that organized large amounts of information, the public were found to have clusters of simple, concrete and personally relevant ideas which displayed little consistency. It was argued that the public, unlike the political élite, did not think 'ideologically'. The public displayed confusion over the meaning of conservative as opposed to liberal ideological dimensions and did not share with political élites a conservative vs liberal conceptual frame of reference by which to structure and organize their political knowledge. Indeed, some surveys found that a substantial number of people were unable to place themselves along a liberal–conservative attitudinal continuum because they had not given the matter much thought (Erikson, Luttbeg and Tedin, 1980)! Thus, Kinder and Sears (1985) concluded that the American public were largely 'innocent' of ideology.

The inconsistency in beliefs among the public has been documented by a considerable body of survey research. The notion that the public is politically uninformed and ideologically inconsistent has formed the paradigmatic core of American political science over the last three decades. Critics of this research have argued that because the public do not structure political beliefs in the same manner as do the political élite, it does not necessarily follow that the content of lay political beliefs demonstrates little in the way of a substantive ideological orientation. The presence or absence of a logical cognitive structure, it was argued, is not necessarily synonymous with the presence or absence of ideology (for example, Bennett, 1977; Marcus, Tabb and Sullivan, 1974). In an effort to salvage the notion that people's political orientations do possess some degree of organization and coherence, Sniderman and Tetlock (1986b) proposed that people organize and structure their attitudes according to a likeability heuristic, that is, by their pattern of likes and dislikes. Sniderman and Tetlock argue:

Affective processes . . . play an especially crucial role in giving mass beliefs what structure they do possess. The building blocks of political coherence, we shall propose, are personal likes and dislikes of politically strategic small groups. Even citizens who know little about political ideas or the political process can put together a consistent political outlook, provided they at least know whom they like and, perhaps more important, whom they dislike. (1986b: 79)

The use of a 'rule of thumb', a determining affective principle, is consistent with the cognitive miser view dominant in social cognition research. Here we are reminded yet again that in understanding the social world people in general are unmotivated to think too deeply about issues. As Sniderman and Tetlock put it, 'the resultant ideological understanding of mass publics may be a crude and simplified one; but so are most effective ways of understanding a complex world' (1986b: 89). We will contrast this view of the person as a limited thinker with that of Michael Billig's portrayal of the person as an 'ideological dilemmatician' later in this chapter.

A more substantial criticism of this research concerns the manner in which the concept of ideology has been defined. Equating ideology with political identifications such as 'liberal' or 'conservative' in North America, 'Labour' or 'Tory' in Britain, and 'Labor' or 'Liberal' in Australia restricts the concept of ideology to formal political belief systems. We believe that this particular conception neglects the link between ideology and everyday life – the role which ideology plays in structuring everyday social reality outside the domain of formal political issues and debates. Moreover, simply equating ideology with political identifications also strips the concept of its critical component (McLellan, 1986; Thompson, 1984). From within this perspective, ideology is primarily used as a descriptive and neutral concept, which refers to any formal belief system. This also has been the predominant use of the concept of ideology by psychologists (for example, Eysenck and Wilson, 1978), and, more recently, by political psychologists (Kinder and Sears, 1985; Sniderman and Tetlock, 1986b; Stone and Schaffner, 1988). While there is nothing inherently wrong with defining ideology in this way, we suggest that restricting the definition of ideology to a coherent system of political beliefs as embodied within the rhetoric of western democratic political parties focuses only upon superficial political conflicts and the formal processes of political decision-making.

Another positivist approach to the concept of ideology is to equate ideology with political extremism and totalitarianism. The decline of Nazism and Stalinism after the Second World War led to many American political scientists declaring the 'end of ideology' (for example, Bell, 1960; Lipset, 1960). Ideology was contrasted with science. Only a rational and positivist approach to the study of society, unfettered by grand political theories such as Marxism, would result in social progress. Indeed, the recent decline of Soviet and East European Communism has led to proclamations that capitalism has been vindicated as a rational, value-free and objective way of organizing society – a social and economic system free of ideology. This view has been argued recently by Fukuyama (1992), who declares liberal democracy to be 'the end of history'. The cessation of the Cold War has also been characterized as ending one of the most significant ideological battles in history. However, we question whether this recent historical event signals the end of the importance of ideology in the way in which people construct and understand their everyday lives. To argue this is to ignore or downplay the inherent ideological currents within liberal democratic societies themselves and within everyday life outside formal politics.

Ideology as system-justification

So far we have described the dominant ways in which ideology has been defined by mainstream social science. This can be contrasted with a more critical approach which views ideology as the means by which relations of power, control and dominance are maintained and preserved within any society. In contrast with earlier historical periods, power and control within western liberal democracies has been wielded increasingly by covert and subtle means and less by the use of overt force. Although different in emphasis, social theorists such as Althusser (1970) and Foucault (1977) have identified symbolic meaning systems and practices as the central means by which relations of power and dominance are maintained and reproduced within contemporary modern societies. Such theoretical perspectives have emerged largely from Marxist accounts of ideology and it is to these we now turn.

Marxist-influenced accounts of ideology are particularly relevant because they have systematically attempted to explain the role of ideology in contemporary liberal democracies. Marx's early writings emphasized the illusory role which ideology plays in portraying society as cohesive and harmonious, whereas his later writings emphasized the role ideology plays in making sense of people's everyday social interactions within a capitalist society. According to Marx, ideology functions to conceal social conflicts by embodying ideas, values and language which justify existing social and economic inequalities. The ideology of freedom and equality within capitalist society is reinforced by the individual's apparent experience of free exchange in the marketplace. Marx viewed ideology as concealing the real relations of dominance and inequality which exist in capitalist societies (Larrain, 1983; McLellan, 1986).

Marx argued that the economic relations of a society, its dominant mode of production and constituent social relations, form the base for a society's ideological superstructure. Not only were the superstructural elements of a society the expression of the dominant material relations but they were also an outgrowth of class domination. In the *German Ideology*, Marx argued that:

> The ideas of the ruling class are in every age, the ruling ideas: i.e., the class which is the dominant material force in society is at the same time its dominant intellectual force. . . . The dominant ideas are nothing more than the ideal expression of the dominant material relationships. (Marx and Engels, 1947: 39)

This dictum is perhaps one of the most well-known and most criticized notions within Marxist social theory. Criticized for being too economically determinist and reductionist, Marxist theory has subsequently emphasized the need to articulate more complex interrelations between economic and non-economic influences which together shape a society's ideological form. Although not Marxist in nature, the more recent work of Foucault, for example, has emphasized that modern power is not always economic in nature nor is it simply embodied and exercised by the economically dominant classes and the institutions of the capitalist state. For

Foucault, modern power is diffused and dispersed throughout all layers of society and is largely exercised through discursive and behavioural rituals which become internalized norms by which people live out their everyday lives. We will come back to some of Foucault's ideas on power later, but for now we discuss Gramsci's notion of hegemony.

Antonio Gramsci's writings on hegemony have been applied to contemporary discussions about the social cohesiveness of western culture and society. The concept of hegemony has been used to understand the widespread perceived legitimacy and support western societies receive from the majority of their citizens. Hegemony refers to the way in which

> a certain way of life and thought is dominant, in which one concept of reality is diffused throughout society in all its institutional and private manifestations, informing with its spirit all taste, morality, customs, religious and political principles, and all social relations, particularly in their intellectual and moral connotations. (Williams, 1960: 587)

Within any society at any given time various conceptions of the world exist which are not structurally or culturally unified. The hegemonic process can be described as the way in which a particular 'world' view or moral philosophical outlook diffuses throughout society, forming the basis of what is described as common-sense knowledge or 'objective truth'. Many factors influence what world view becomes widely shared and dominant. One important factor is the ability of a philosophical outlook to 'make sense' of the structural organization of society: the dominant social, political and economic relations.

Gramsci, however, was highly critical of simple economistic accounts of the development of a society's moral, political and cultural outlook. He emphasized the need to analyse all levels of society, in particular civil society where religious, moral and social patterns of perception emerged and proliferated. It is important to make clear, however, that Gramsci did not view hegemony as being imposed by force by the dominant classes. For Gramsci, hegemony is not achieved through coercion, but, rather, is freely consented to by the people. It is a philosophical and moral outlook that has won the 'hearts and minds of the people' (Bocock, 1986). Gramsci emphasized the common-sense nature of a hegemonic world view, endowing it with an almost 'folklore' quality. Such an outlook becomes powerful and pervasive, Gramsci argued, because it is able to make sense of people's everyday lived experience and is intimately linked to the practices of everyday life. For Gramsci, common sense, the primary resource of human thought, is imbued with philosophy – all people are philosophers.

> It is essential to destroy the widespread prejudice that philosophy is a strange and difficult thing just because it is the specific intellectual activity of a particular category of specialists or of professional and systematic philosophers. It must first be shown that all men [and women] are philosophers, by defining the limits and characteristics of the 'spontaneous philosophy' which is proper to everybody. This philosophy is contained in:
> 1. language itself, which is a totality of determined notions and concepts and not just of words grammatically devoid of content; 2. common sense' and 'good sense'; 3. popular religion and, therefore, also in the entire system of beliefs, superstition, opinions, ways of seeing things and acting, which are collectively bundled together under the name of 'folklore'. (Gramsci, 1971: 323)

There are certain elements in Gramsci's writings on hegemony which have interesting parallels to Moscovici's theory of social representations. Both Gramsci and Moscovici emphasize the centrality of common sense in everyday thinking and in the understanding of social reality. Unlike theories within social cognition which stress the distortions, biases and errors in lay thinking, common sense is not viewed as an impoverished source of knowledge and ideas. It is imbued with moral, philosophical, cultural and political traces. Common sense in both theories is socially and historically contingent, subject to change given political and historical transformations. Furthermore, both Gramsci and Moscovici write about the dissemination of ideas and knowledge from intellectual realms to the rest of society. There are strong similarities between Gramsci's interest in the way in which philosophical ideas articulated by intellectuals trickle their way down into the consciousness of the people and Moscovici's description of how scientific concepts which originate in the reified universe of science diffuse throughout the rest of society, contributing to the stock of common-sense knowledge which people draw upon to make sense of their social world. Gramsci referred to intellectual ideas and scientific knowledge which become a part of everyday common sense as 'organic'. According to Gramsci, ideas and beliefs are organic insofar as they inform the practical consciousness of everyday life. As Billig and Sabucedo (in press) suggest, in many respects Gramsci seems a more suitable intellectual ancestor than Durkheim for the development of social representations theory. This would give social representations theory a political emphasis by linking it to the study of hegemony more generally and ideology more specifically.

Ideological hegemony

Gramsci's notion of hegemony is linked to that of 'ideology'. Gramsci himself did not use the term ideology to refer to a hegemonic outlook. Consistent with the Marxist definition of ideology at the time, ideology referred to distorted perceptions, mystification or false beliefs. However, if one defines ideology as beliefs, representations, discourse, etc., which function to legitimate the existing social, political and economic relations of dominance within a society, irrespective of their 'truth' status (the definition we have preferred to give to ideology), then Gramsci's notion of hegemony can be viewed as referring to a dominant and pervasive ideological outlook within a society. Indeed, many cultural analysts have used the Gramscian notion of hegemony in this way to understand the continual system support which characterizes contemporary western societies, and we shall do the same for the arguments which are to follow.

The question of ideological hegemony or the existence of a cohesive and totalizing 'dominant ideology' has long been debated (Abercrombie, Hill and Turner, 1990). The crude version of hegemony has been used to explain almost anything from the failure of Marxist predictions about the inevitable demise of capitalism, to the acceptance by the masses of capitalist relations of production. The working classes were seen to have failed to recognize their true economic and political interests; worse still, they had internalized the bourgeois values of their oppressors. The German critical theorists such as Adorno, Horkheimer and Marcuse described the acquiescence of the working classes to capitalism as 'false consciousness' (Agger, 1991). Similarly, cultural analysts emphasize the extent to which contemporary western life is characterized by the conspicuous consumption of goods bought for their symbolic value (Baudrillard, 1983), a preoccupation which some argue undermines the development of critical political awareness (Lash and Urry, 1987). While people sometimes embrace attitudes and values which serve the interests of dominant groups at the expense of their own self and group interests, categorizing such beliefs as 'false consciousness' is highly problematic. Our reservations toward the concept of false consciousness will be discussed in more detail later in this chapter.

There is little doubt that some analyses of ideological hegemony are overly simplistic and deterministic. Human agency and autonomy disappears and consciousness is determined and directed by powerful structural forces (Thompson, 1984). While Moscovici (1988) has referred to hegemonic representations, he rejects the view that everyone is always under the sway of a dominant ideology. This crude version fails to acknowledge the constructionist and reflexive capacities of people. Billig (1991; Billig et al., 1988) has also argued against this version of ideological domination which treats people as passive and gullible pawns, duped by an array of ideological managers and institutions which serve the interests of the dominant classes.

Furthermore, empirical studies give only qualified support to the 'dominant ideology' thesis. Rather than a pervasive diffused consensus in people's views about the nature of society, sociological studies have found significant class differences, with the middle classes demonstrating more consensus and cohesion in their views than the working classes (Chamberlain, 1983; Mann, 1970). Indeed, it has been argued that it is this ideological cohesion in the middle to upper classes and ideological disunity among the lower classes which helps maintain the stability within liberal democracies. The hegemony of the dominant classes is maintained by the nature of the fragmented and disparate opposition which exists. Furthermore, Abercrombie et al. (1990) have argued that the cohesiveness of liberal democracy is not so much due to the internalization of legitimating societal values and beliefs (ideology) as to the everyday economic need of lower socio-economic groups to participate in the wage labour system central to capitalist economies.

One of the central themes emphasized by postmodernist commentators in the last decade is the increasing fragmentation and diversification of modern societies (Lyotard, 1984). The pluralism embodied in postmodernism renders the notion of a unified and coherent dominant ideology as unrepresentative of modern contemporary culture. Similarly, Moscovici (1988) has argued that hegemonic representations are more difficult to locate in modern capitalist societies, and are more characteristic of small traditional societies.

So what are we to make of life in the increasingly diversified 'postmodern' world? Are there no beliefs, values, representations, discourses, which bind and unify individuals and groups within the complexity of everyday life? Are there no parameters within which people frame conflicts, questions and answers, and in so doing legitimate and reproduce the power relations within a society? While many more 'voices' (perspectives) are being heard in contemporary life, do all voices have the same capacity of being heard and the same power to persuade? While postmodern accounts of western society have provided interesting and stimulating commentaries, emphasizing the increasing diversity and plurality of contemporary life, we suggest that many of these analyses underestimate the unifying and legitimating features of certain representations and discourses. While ideology may be less important in contributing to the cohesiveness of liberal democracy than some commentators have assumed, it is also rather naïve to suggest that it has no role to play at all (Eagleton, 1991).

While few empirical studies have found evidence of a dominant ideology in modern democracies, there is some evidence of the prevalence of certain ideological themes. The liberal individualist conception of the person as the centre of cognition, action and process has been described by various commentators as a shared representation which permeates all aspects of social life within western industrialized societies (Lukes, 1973). Linked to this conception of the person is one of the few value orientations about which empirical studies do indicate a dominant consensus: individualist values of achievement (Mann, 1970). Some of this research was reviewed in Chapter 7 where we discussed lay explanations for success and failure. Much of this research suggests that personal and individualistic explanations for achievement and social mobility are favoured over situational and contextual explanations. The development of a cultural emphasis upon individual achievement, the causes of which are primarily located within the individual, has been referred to by some theorists as 'possessive individualism' (Macpherson, 1962). Indeed, individualism has been described as the most pervasive ethos characterizing liberal democracies because it has the ability to make sense of the social conditions of a capitalist society. Individual merit and success are largely rewarded in such societies, and competition, which forms the cornerstone of economic relations, is heralded as the most effective and efficient means by which to motivate people in most spheres of social life.

INDIVIDUALISM AND LIBERALISM

As a dominant value orientation, individualism is an inherent feature of liberalism, the political creed around which most western capitalist democracies are structured. Stuart Hall (1986) documents the historically dynamic development of liberalism within England since the seventeenth century. So responsive was liberalism to the changing historical and social circumstances within England that a number of variants of liberalism developed, ranging from the conservative to the more progressive and reformist versions. Throughout the twentieth century recurring experiences of economic crises seriously challenged the classic liberalist emphasis on *laisser-faire* capitalism. Liberalism embraced the necessity for social change by attempting to 'humanize' capitalism. This culminated in increased state intervention in the market economy and the development of the modern capitalist welfare state. Hall argues that liberalism managed to maintain its hegemony because of its ability to accommodate a range of political inflections. While social democratic parties have embraced the more reformist and progressive versions of liberalism which emphasize the need to redistribute wealth and protect the casualties of the system, conservative liberalism has continued to stress the importance of free competition and market economics in combination with the rhetoric of tradition and authority. Liberalism's remarkable flexibility has enabled it to become adopted by different political positions and to serve the interests of different social groups.

Despite the differences and contradictions between social democratic and conservative variants of liberalism, the two strands share a number of core concepts which are fundamental in identifying them as part of a particular ideological discourse. The liberalist conception of the world is premised on the 'sovereign individual'. Liberalism abstracts the individual from society. All individuals possess certain inalienable rights which are viewed to be consonant with the essential character of human nature. The freedom of individuals to maximize self-interest and to take part in social, political and religious activities of their own choosing is regarded as most important. The competition and struggle for material resources is viewed as an expression of a natural human drive. An open meritocracy in which individuals are free to compete and maximize self-interest is regarded as a 'natural' society. A market economy which allows all individuals to compete, sell and buy, accumulate wealth and improve their position in society is regarded as a 'natural' economy. Society and economy organized around market principles are seen to be consistent with the fundamentals of human nature. Indeed, this perspective has gained prevalence since the demise of East European and Soviet Communism and the transition to market economies world-wide (Fukuyama, 1992).

Liberalism has been able to maintain its hegemony not only because it forms the basis of philosophical reasoning for many of the major political parties in liberal democracies, but also because it forms the basis of spontaneous everyday thinking by ordinary people. Hall documents the way in which components of philosophical liberalism have become widely diffused throughout English society, 'informing practical consciousness' and becoming an important component of English common sense.

> So much so that, to many of those who constantly think within its limits, it does not appear to be an ideology at all, but simply an obvious way of making sense of things – 'what everybody knows'. However,

this 'obviousness' is itself a sign that the ideas do belong to a particular ideological configuration – they are obvious only because their historical and philosophical roots and conditions have somehow been forgotten or suppressed. (1986: 35)

While many social theories emphasize the way in which individuals are primarily social beings, and in some way constituted by society, liberalism abstracts and separates the individual from society. 'Liberalism thus played a role in constructing our prevailing common sense or "spontaneous awareness" of ourselves today as separate, isolable and self-sufficient beings' (Hall, 1986: 41).

Billig (1982, 1991) has argued that it is an oversimplification to characterize modern liberal democracies as individualistic, pointing out that both individualist and collectivist values co-exist within contemporary capitalism. Hall also makes this clear in his historical account of variants of liberalism. In a similar vein, as we noted in Chapter 9, the research of Katz and Hass (1988) in the United States has demonstrated the co-existence of two largely independent value systems amongst American college students: humanitarianism–egalitarianism and the Protestant work ethic. While the former emphasizes the importance of political equality and social justice between individuals and groups, the latter stresses the importance of hard work, individual achievement, self-reliance and discipline. In practice, these two core values often lead to feelings of ambivalence toward marginalized groups such as black Americans and the poor. Concern for the welfare and justice of these groups is tempered by beliefs that individuals in such groups transgress cherished values such as hard work and self-reliance. This is based on the assumption that another person's lower social status within a society is a result of personal shortcomings and failures.

Despite the rhetoric of postmodernism, we suggest that liberal individualism continues to exercise ideological constraints on the way people think, live and behave in modern societies. Indeed, as Johnson (1992a) argues, the quintessential postmodernist, Lyotard, has exaggerated the decline of liberalism as a grand narrative within contemporary western society. His focus on the increasing plurality of discourses and fragmentation of consciousness fails to acknowledge the resurging influence of New Right liberalism, elements of which were endorsed not only by the conservative Thatcher Tory government in Britain, but also by the social democratic Hawke Labor government in Australia. Johnson (1992b) argues that economic debates and policies within western democracies are still largely being shaped within the liberal continuum that Hall describes. The liberal meta-narrative is alive and well, and, as we suggested earlier, is epitomized by Fukuyama's claim that liberal democracy represents the highest evolutionary form for all societies and indeed therefore represents 'the end of history'. So much for the death of grand narratives or totalizing ideologies.[1]

Grand narratives continue to have influence not only in political economy, but also in other domains. Patriarchy, positivist science and the domination of nature by technological progress are ideological discourses which also have a contemporary relevance. There is no doubt that perspectives which challenge and undermine these do exist. The feminist critique of contemporary society has clearly had a discernible impact at all levels of society, from the structural to the personal. Nevertheless, despite changes, women are still underrepresented at the highest levels of employment; and are still doing the bulk of the housework and parenting despite working full-time. Although patriarchy has been significantly challenged, it remains largely intact. Moreover, while liberal feminism has successfully managed to gain a voice within some contemporary political debates, more radical feminist perspectives have been largely ignored and or marginalized.

THE STUDY AND LOCATION OF IDEOLOGY

While ideology remains an elusive concept, it becomes even more elusive when attempts are made to study it empirically. In empirical work, the question invariably becomes where does one look to find ideology? Given the Gramscian common-sense notion we have adopted for ideology, the answer must be in the everyday social world. We want to consider the different methods by which ideology has been researched thus far and the different contexts in which ideology has been located. It is important to point out, however, that some of the research we will be reviewing, especially of the social psychological variety, has rarely been viewed as research into ideology. Indeed, we will argue that research in certain areas of social psychology has 'unwittingly' uncovered ideological components in everyday thinking.

Ideology as consciousness

Traditionally, ideology has been treated as a cognitive construct which permeates human consciousness. From within this perspective ideology is to be found in the values, beliefs, attitudes and opinions which people hold. As Gaskell and Fraser (1990) suggest, one of the functions of widespread beliefs and values is that they may provide legitimacy to the socio-political structure of a society. In so doing, we would argue that such cognitions can be considered to be ideological in nature. As argued earlier, individualist values of achievement contribute significantly to the support of a capitalist socio-cultural system. Studies have found that as children grow older they are more likely to regard inequalities of wealth and income as inevitable and legitimate (Lewis, 1990; Stacey, 1982). They are also more likely to embrace equity principles of economic distribution rather than principles of equality (Bond, Leung and Wan, 1982; Sampson, 1975). That is, children learn to accept over time that resources within society are (and should be) distributed according to individual inputs (effort, abilities and skills). As Sampson (1975) argues, equity values encourage and legitimate individual competition and personal advancement at the expense of cooperation, communion and equality. Indeed, Sampson suggests that the forms of relations which dominate in the economic sphere tend to be adopted in other areas of human relationships.

Perhaps a classic example of ideological thinking which social psychology unwittingly discovered is the fundamental attribution 'error' or 'bias'. In contrast to the cognitive explanation which mainstream psychology has advanced for this bias, we have argued throughout this book that this bias demonstrates the dominance of dispositional explanations over situational explanations in western culture. Increasingly, it has been recognized that this attributional phenomenon is not a universal cognitive bias, but is culture-specific, reflecting an underlying ideological representation of the person as the centre of all action and process (Bond, 1983; Hewstone and Augoustinos, 1995; Ichheiser, 1949; Miller, 1984).

Stereotypes as ideological representations   Throughout this book we have demonstrated the centrality of the study of social stereotypes to social cognition research. While the existence and pervasiveness of social stereotypes was lamented earlier this century by social psychologists who viewed them largely as cognitive constructs used by people to justify prejudicial attitudes and discriminatory behaviour, increasingly stereotypes and the process of stereotyping have taken on a more benign status (Condor, 1988). Consistent with the dominant information processing approach to cognition, stereotypes are now seen to be an inevitable product of the need to categorize and simplify a complex social world. In this way, stereotyping is losing its negative connotations and is being viewed as servicing the cognitive needs of the individual. In contrast to this approach, we view stereotypes largely as ideological representations which are used to justify and legitimize existing social and power relations within a society. We propose that much of the research on stereotypes and stereotyping is largely a social psychological study of the role of ideology in everyday human thinking.

In a recent paper, Jost and Banaji (1994) argue that while social psychological theories have emphasized the ego- and group-justification functions of stereotypes, very little has been written about the role of stereotypes in system-justification. They define system-justification as 'the psychological process by which existing social arrangements are legitimized, even at the expense of personal and group interests' (1994: 2). This definition is very similar to the definition of ideology we have employed in stressing the way in which a particular world view is used to bolster and support existing societal arrangements. These authors draw on a number of empirical findings in the stereotype literature which an ego- and group-justification approach has significant difficulties in explaining. Foremost is the oft-found tendency for members of marginalized and minority groups to apply and internalize negative stereotypes to themselves and to their group as a whole. Negative self-stereotyping is certainly not self-serving, nor does it accord very well with social identity's maxim that groups will strive to maintain a positive ingroup identity or at least some degree of positive distinctiveness from outgroups. The favouritism toward dominant outgroups which is often associated with low-status groups is difficult to reconcile with the group-protecting and -enhancing principles of the theory. Nor can SIT explain adequately why social stereotypes are so consensual in content across different groups within society. It is for these reasons that Jost and Banaji (1994) put forward the long-needed view that stereotypes serve important ideological functions, which in effect support, rationalize and legitimate the status quo. In their words,

> stereotypes serve ideological functions, in particular that they justify the exploitation of certain groups over others, and that they explain the poverty or powerlessness of some groups and the success of others in ways that make these differences seem legitimate and even natural. . . . Based on theories of and data on self-perception, attribution, cognitive conservatism, the division of social roles, behavioral confirmation, and the belief in a just world, we stipulate a process whereby stereotypes are used to explain the existing social system and the positions and actions of self and others. (1994: 10)

In effect, what stereotypes do is to justify the dominant existing social relations within a society. Let's consider gender stereotypes for a moment. Despite the social, political and economic changes associated with the women's movement within the western world, the content of gender stereotypes continues to show 'traditional' elements, elements which reflect the traditional division of labour between men and women. The pervasiveness, sharedness and resilience of gender stereotypes has been explained by their capacity to rationalize and justify this division of labour (Hoffman and Hurst, 1990). Despite marked attitudinal changes these stereotypes persist because they are able to make sense of the dominant gender relations and existing social arrangements in society, that is, patriarchal relations of dominance.

Contrary to the view that stereotyping is fundamentally a product of individual motivational requirements (and, we would add, cognitive requirements), Jost and Banaji argue that the process of stereotyping is linked to the information processing needs of an 'ideological environment'. Thus the process of stereotyping is not simply an individual cognitive process; stereotypes are not rein-vented anew each time a person applies them. Stereotyping becomes a collective and ideological process linked to the power and social relations of a particular society within a particular historical context. Drawing from recent priming research Jost and Banaji suggest that the ideological environment is pervasive and insidious, so much so that stereotypes can emerge spontaneously and unconsciously, even among people who consciously embrace egalitarian values and beliefs (Devine, 1989a).

However, Jost and Banaji go much further than to argue for the ideological legitimating functions of stereotypes. They also argue that stereotypes reflect 'false consciousness'. When the oppressed engage in self-hate and deprecation, when people in general come to view existing social relations as natural and inevitable, when stereotypes mystify and obfuscate the real relations of dominance and exploitation within a society, then we have what Marx referred to as 'false consciousness'.[2] While we agree that stereotypes do indeed serve ideological functions, categorizing these cognitions and actions as 'false' is problematic. The Marxist concept of false consciousness assumes that one can arrive at a true or veridical version of reality. It is clear that Jost and Banaji operate very much from a positivist-empiricist approach to knowledge which, like traditional Marxism, assumes that a 'scientific', objective and true version of reality can be obtained. This epistemological approach is very different from the constructivist and discursive approaches we outlined in the previous chapter, both of which argue that all versions of reality, including scientific ones, are constructions.

While we would argue against equating ideology with false ideas or distorted knowledge we would not go so far, however, as to abandon realism altogether (but see Wetherell and Potter, 1992). One of the difficulties with a constructivist approach to reality is its inherent relativism. If there are no true and correct versions of reality, then how can we assess and evaluate the multiple constructions of reality that we come across? Some versions of reality are surely preferable to others, not only morally and politically, but, in some cases, epistemologically (see Eagleton, 1991).[3] Substantiating the truth or falsity of a statement may in some instances be an important way to undermine oppressive and discriminatory views and practices. However, substantiating the truth or falsity of the content of stereotypes is far from being simply an empirical issue.

As we pointed out in Chapter 9, in an effort to account for why stereotypes are so pervasive and resistant to change, many social psychologists have put forward the insidious 'kernel of truth' proposition regarding stereotypes. Because of their commitment to a realist epistemology, Jost and Banaji are forced to consider the relationship between stereotypes and social reality. Given Jost and Banaji's critical approach, it is not surprising that they argue against the notion that stereotypes are based on veridical perception. Implicitly, this invites others to empirically confirm or challenge their views of stereotypes as false. We saw in Chapter 9 how social psychologists have gone about evaluating the truth or falsity of stereotypes and the conceptual problems that this entails. How does one establish in an 'objective', disinterested way whether black American or Aboriginal Australians are 'really' lazy or whether men are 'really' aggressive and dominant? Such empirical concerns seem futile and simply lead to 'scientific' claims and counter-claims. 'Buying' into the kernel of truth argument is perhaps one of the most ideological issues confronting the research on stereotypes for there is no disinterested way of approaching this issue. The most cautious realist argument which has been advanced is that by Oakes et al. (1994), who argue that stereotypes are veridical to the extent that they reflect the nature of social intergroup relations within a society at a particular point in time.

For us, stereotypes are always ideological representations which serve important functions in legitimizing the dominant political, social and economic intergroup relations within a society. In arguing that they are ideological and system-serving, it is conceptually unnecessary to endow stereotypes or any other cognitive construct with the status of false consciousness. The notion of false consciousness suggests that ideology itself is a matrix of falsehoods, which not even the most orthodox of Marxists would argue today. Eagleton summarizes our view nicely:

.. in order to be truly effective, ideologies must make at least some minimal sense of people's experience, must conform to some degree with what they know of social reality from their practical interaction with it . . . ruling ideologies can actively shape the wants and desires of those subjected to them; but they must also engage significantly with the wants and desires that people already have, catching up genuine hopes and needs, reinflecting them in their own peculiar idiom, and feeding them back to their subjects in ways which render these ideologies plausible and attractive. They must be 'real' enough to provide the basis on which individuals can fashion a coherent identity, must furnish some solid motivations for effective action and must make at least some feeble attempt to explain away their own flagrant contradictions and incoherencies. In short, successful ideologies must be more than imposed illusions, and for all their inconsistencies must communicate to their subjects a version of reality which is real and recognizable enough not to be simply rejected out of hand. (1991: 15)

What we have attempted to do thus far in this chapter is to demonstrate the way in which liberalism and individualism, as particular constructions of reality, have become diffused throughout society and contributed to the stock of common-sense knowledge and truth which people draw upon to make sense of the world. We are not suggesting that liberalism as an ideological outlook is embraced and articulated as a coherent belief system, but that salient and central components become expressed in fragmentary ways. Indeed, we suggest that many of the system-justification and legitimating social psychological constructs which Jost and Banaji identify, such as stereotypes and just world beliefs, are underpinned by this moral-philosophical outlook. Such cognitive constructs and their system rationalizing effects emerge from historically specific ideological currents – currents which make sense of and justify the existing patterns of social relations. Ideology is not a system of falsehoods and illusions promulgated by dominant groups, but as Mepham (1972: 17) suggests, is 'firmly grounded in the forms of our social life' and thus has a material reality.

Ideology as discourse

There is little doubt that contemporary social theorists who have concerned themselves with the study of ideology have come increasingly to regard language and discourse as *the* location of ideology. The traditional arena for ideology, consciousness, has been replaced by the study of everyday discourse, ranging from the mundane to more institutional forms. As we demonstrated in the previous chapter, the study of everyday discourse is being adopted enthusiastically by an increasing number of social psychologists. Potter and Wetherell's (1987) book *Discourse and Social Psychology* reflects the wider paradigmatic shift from the study of 'consciousness' or cognition, to the study of discourse. Thompson describes the current fascination with language thus,

> . . . increasingly it has been realized that 'ideas' do not drift through the social world like clouds in a summer sky, occasionally divulging their contents with a clap of thunder and a flash of light. Rather, ideas circulate in the social world as utterances, as expressions, as words which are spoken or inscribed. Hence to study ideology is, in some part and in some way, to study language in the social world. (1984: 2)

As with social representations theory, everyday communication (the 'unceasing babble' to which Moscovici refers) is viewed as fundamental in producing and transmitting meaning in social life. Language is the medium by which relations of power are communicated and relations of domination are created and sustained. From this perspective, ideology is no longer an idealized set of cognitive objects, but a range of socially situated discursive practices which have material effects and consequences (Eagleton, 1991).

Ideology is to be located not only in the expression of ideas and values embodied in discourse, but also in the particular types of syntactic structures employed in language. For example, Kress and Hodge (1979) discuss the ways in which certain linguistic transformations can deny the agency and responsibility of actors. A simple sentence like 'South African police have burnt down a black township' can be transformed into a passive and agentless sentence such as 'A black township has burnt down' (Fairclough, 1989). Such transformations simplify information, but in so doing suppress, distort and mystify what is being communicated. Complex social processes can also be objectified – by representing them as 'things', or as persons (personification). For example, a complex economic process such as inflation is often described by the media and in everyday conversation as an adversary who can hurt and harm us: 'inflation has attacked the foundation of our economy', 'our biggest enemy right now is inflation', 'the dollar has been destroyed by inflation'. As Lakoff and Johnson (1980) explain, the metaphor of 'inflation as an adversary' lends legitimacy to government actions undertaken to deal with an economic process which, in many instances, is the direct result of government policy.

Many researchers have also demonstrated the powerful way in which sexist language such as the use of the generic 'he' in the English language can shape and mould social reality, especially for children, who interpret the world as essentially a male domain (Nilsen, 1977). Not only does gendered language reflect the prevailing relationships of gender dominance within society, but its continued use also serves to sustain those relationships.

Another way in which discourse reflects ideological undercurrents can be found in the kinds of categories people use to communicate about the social world. Categories are important because they communicate something of the 'taken-for-granted' or shared meanings that people have of the world. These shared meanings are likely to differ between different social groups in society so that variations in meaning are contested by different groups with conflicting interests. Categories not only make it easier to communicate by imposing order, but are also powerful in themselves, being able to define and control conceptions of reality. For example, take the conflicting categories of 'terrorist' or 'freedom fighter'. The label one uses to describe such individuals has clear political and evaluative connotations. As such, categories and systems of classification become the site of struggle between and within different interest groups in society (Thompson, 1984).

Ideology, however, is not simply reflected in linguistic utterances *per se*, in the content of language and its grammatical form. Rather, ideology is linked to the way in which language is used in specific discursive contexts to produce specific meanings and versions of reality. The discursive study of ideology examines the processes by which versions of reality are constructed, rationalized, legitimated and endowed with the status of 'truth', and the means by which some versions come to dominate, while others are undermined and disempowered. It is primarily interested in the discursive practices or interpretative repertoires that people use to argue, debate, convince, justify, their versions or accounts of the social world. While this approach to ideology has been seminal in poststructural theory and inquiry, it has attracted only a small number of researchers within the domain of social psychology. The most notable examples have been Wetherell and Potter's recent work on the ideological nature of racist discourse, much of which we discussed in the previous chapter, and Michael Billig's work on the rhetorical and ideological components in common-sense understandings of the world.

Wetherell and Potter argue that racist discourse is inextricably linked to ideology and power. Combining both Marxist accounts of ideology and a Foucauldian emphasis on the constitutive nature of discourse they demonstrate how the categories of 'race', 'nation' and 'culture' have been historically constructed in New Zealand and how these constructions have functioned ideologically in 'establishing, sustaining and reinforcing oppressive power relations' (1992: 70). But perhaps what is more central to their analysis is their demonstration of the ways in which liberal and social reformist principles are used adeptly to sustain racist positions, positions which ultimately legitimate the existing power relations. For example, many of their respondents spoke approvingly of the principles of equal opportunity, but this was usually qualified by the use of a specific *liberal* definition of equality. Individuals must earn their way legitimately by participating competitively within existing structures. 'Everyone should be treated equally' was a self-sufficient rhetorical argument that was used to argue against policies such as affirmative action. Many respondents argued that past injustices which had resulted in inequitable outcomes should not be righted by such 'unfair' policies and, besides, the present generation should not bear the brunt of past historical mistakes. The solution to existing inequities is to progress toward a better and more integrated society where all groups are united under one identity – a New Zealand 'national' identity.

Wetherell and Potter show that such arguments were used in a number of ways by respondents to avoid a racist identity and to justify and rationalize existing Maori–Pakeha relations. Their emphasis on particular discursive constructions demonstrate how racist claims can be 'communicated as fact and empowered as truth ' (1992: 59). Again here we are reminded of the inherent flexibility of liberalism, a philosophical outlook which can construct both an egalitarian version of reality and one which rationalizes, justifies and legitimates unequal and oppressive outcomes between groups.

Consistent with the discursive approach, Billig has long argued that traditional social psychology has failed to study the argumentative nature of human thinking; more specifically, the everyday use of rhetoric to criticize, justify and persuade. Every person is a rhetorician of some sort. Arguing, criticizing, blaming, justifying, are all common features of everyday life. According to Billig, the study of rhetoric is linked to the study of common sense, for one of the most effective means by which to argue and persuade is to present one's viewpoint as 'common-sensical' and 'obvious'. Moreover, for Billig, ideology is located in common sense itself, that which is taken for granted and which appears to be self-evident, natural and true. As for Gramsci and Moscovici, the stock of common sense from which people draw upon every day to understand the world is an important repository of knowledge and reasoning. It is not inferior knowledge and reasoning, as many scientists, especially psychologists, have assumed, but it is historically contingent. Unlike the image of the naïve and limited thinker central to cognitive social psychology,

The image of the subject in the rhetorical approach is very different. The rhetorical subject is a thinking and arguing subject. In this image, ideology, far from precluding thought, provides the resources for thinking in ordinary life and about ordinary life. Yet, in so doing, ideology can restrict the scope of thinking by setting the agenda for what is common-sensically thought and argued about. It is by adopting a historical and critical approach that this dimension of ideology can be examined, in order to see how its contingent history reaches down into the present micro-process of psychological thinking. In this sense, the rhetorical subject is subject to ideology, but not in a blind and unthinking manner. (Billig and Sabucedo, in press: 12)

For Billig, ideology can also be located in the process of argumentation itself. The inconsistencies, contradictions, gaps in knowledge, what is said as opposed to what is never mentioned, are aspects of argumentation which reflect the parameters within which ideology operates.

Importantly, Billig has argued that ideological components of common sense are not articulated in a highly consistent and integrated way. In contrast to cognitive accounts which look for coherent and consistent traces of ideology in consciousness, discursive and rhetorical accounts emphasize the fragmentary, fluid and flexible nature of ideology. In *Ideological Dilemmas*, Billig et al. (1988) point to the ways in which people apply contradictory themes in different contexts. Such inconsistencies and contradictions highlight the inherent *dilemmatic* quality of ideological thinking. People do not necessarily accept values uncritically and without conscious deliberation. Contradictory themes such as individualism/collectivism are expressed and articulated in variable and flexible ways in everyday life. As Susan Condor (1990) points out, people may not simply endorse or reject dominant views, but, rather, develop complex configurations of thought in which some dominant ideological elements find expression in conjunction with individual and group-based understandings.

Ideology as material practices

In addition to cognition and discourse, ideology may be reflected in the social practices that constitute everyday life. Gramsci's notion of hegemony emphasized that ideology was not only a 'system of ideas' but also referred to 'lived, habitual social practice[s]' (Eagleton, 1991: 115): everyday practices and rituals realized through contemporary social institutions such as the family, schools, the legal and political systems. For example, everyday economic practices such as banking, working, selling and buying may all contribute to legitimating the existing relations of production. Participating in a competitive educational system legitimates meritocracy, while traditional labour arrangements in the home perpetuate and reinforce patriarchal relations. Hegemony may also be exercised in more obvious ways by the dissemination of certain values and ideas by the mass media. Althusser (1970) emphasized the materialist base of ideology, grounding it to practices within contemporary institutions such as the family, schools, legal, political and state structures. For Althusser, ideology 'is a particular organization of signifying practices which goes to constitute human beings as social subjects, and which produces the lived relations by which such subjects are connected to the dominant relations of production in a society' (Eagleton, 1991: 18). While maintaining traces of economic determinism, Althusser argues that ideology does not simply reflect the nature of our 'lived relations', but that these lived relations themselves constitute our social identities. Ideology here is not just our beliefs, representations, discourses, but more like the behavioural and social practices that we engage in every day as we live out our lives. Moreover, Althusser suggests that our lived relations are largely unconscious and affective in nature. In this way ideology becomes a spontaneous, unconscious and affective way of responding to our lived relations, a way of being which has a strong affinity to the recent work on automaticity in social cognition. This reflects Althusser's rather determinist view that ideology is pervasive, inescapable, a view which, some would argue, underestimates the reflexive capacities of people to think and behave outside ideology.

In locating ideology in our behavioural and social practices, we need also to consider Foucault's view that modern power is capillary, touching all aspects of social life. For Foucault, relations of power and dominance are more likely to be maintained and perpetuated by the forms of our everyday micro-practices, rather than by our beliefs and cognitions (Fraser, 1989).[4] Foucault was primarily interested in the ways in which certain disciplines of knowledge were constructed historically, particularly the social sciences, and how this body of 'scientific' knowledge exercises power by regulating the behaviour and subjectivities of individuals throughout all layers of society. Foucault's notion of power is not one of coercion or repression. He argues that modern power is achieved largely through the self-regulation and self-discipline of individuals to behave in ways which are largely consistent with dominant discourses about what it is to be human. These discourses shape and mould our subjectivities, the people we ultimately become. For example, dominant psychological discourses about the self for a large part of this century have extolled the virtues of logical, rational thought, cognitive order and consistency, emotional stability and affective control, moral integrity, independence and self-reliance. These humanist discourses are powerful in that they have contributed to the shaping of certain behavioural practices, modes of thought and institutional structures which function to produce people possessing these valued qualities. Moreover, institutions and practices have emerged which rehabilitate, treat and counsel those who fail to become rational, self-sufficient, capable and emotionally stable individuals. Thus, psychology, as a body of knowledge and a 'scientifically' legitimated discipline, shapes and prescribes what it is to be a healthy and well-adjusted individual. While there has been considerable work deconstructing the ideological and legitimating functions of psychology as a discipline, Foucault's work also suggests that ideology can be studied at a micro-behavioural level by focusing upon the social and behavioural practices which regulate our everyday lives.

SUMMARY

We have argued in this chapter that there has been a dearth of social psychological work on the role and influence of ideology on what passes as everyday knowledge and practice and the ways in which ideology shapes and structures social reality for the ordinary person. We adopted a specific definition of ideology which referred to beliefs, values, representations, discourses, interpretative repertoires and behavioural practices which contribute to the legitimation and reproduction of existing institutional arrangements, power and social relations within a society. Asymmetries of power are not only socio-economic in nature but are related also to gender, race and ethnicity. The task for a social psychological theory of ideology is to understand the interface between social, economic and historic structural forces and the everyday functioning of individuals and groups. This can be contrasted with social cognitive theories which conceptualize thinking as primarily an individual phenomenon and also with some social theories which have the tendency to view people as being completely constituted and dominated by ideology. The study of ideology needs to be contextualized within a framework which sees the individual as being in a dialectical relationship with society, both as a product of society and as an active agent who can effect change in society.

The study of ideology, however, will require social psychologists to engage in wider debates about the nature of contemporary western culture and society. Critical theory, feminist social theory and postmodernism are intellectual movements which may contribute usefully to the future development of a social psychological theory of ideology. Furthermore, any efforts to study ideology must avoid the functionalist trap of simply seeking to explain the stability and reproducibility of social systems. The dynamics of challenge and resistance – the situations in which dominant representations or discourses become undermined or overhauled – needs to become an integral conceptual and empirical focus for the study of ideology. In this way we can achieve Moscovici's vision of studying 'social life in the making' (1988: 219). We believe that social psychology's contribution to the study of ideology is perhaps its most difficult, but greatest, challenge.

NOTES

1   Johnson (1992a, 1992b) is also critical of Habermas's argument that totalizing ideologies such as liberalism have been on the decline over the last century and are no longer essential in legitimating capitalism. Though coming from very different perspectives, Habermas here echoes Lyotard's view regarding the increasing fragmentation of contemporary life. Again, Johnson suggests that Habermas underemphasizes the extent to which liberal norms and values have been instrumental in the rhetorical construction of a political and ideological consensus.

2   In a related paper, Jost (1995) has suggested that much of what passes as social cognition – the errors, biases, distortions, found in human thinking – is essentially the social psychological study of 'false consciousness'.

3   Wetherell and Potter, however, do not see any inherent dangers with a relativist approach. They argue,

> The refusal to privilege some types of account on epistemological grounds – relativism, as it is often called – should not be seen as a morally or politically vacuous stance, or as rhetorically ineffective. There is still the imperative to establish the claims of some versions over others. . . . We do not, therefore see any contradiction between a view of discourse as constitutive and a view of discourse as ideological – where commitment to studying ideology is also a commitment to the critique of some positions, some of the ways in which power is exercised and some forms of argumentative practice. (1992: 69)

For an entertaining and witty defence of relativism see Edwards, Ashmore and Potter (in press).

4   Because the concept of ideology has often been associated with the Marxist notion of false consciousness, Foucault did not use the term 'ideology' in his analyses of modern power. Instead, he referred to dominant signifying and behavioural practices which sustained and legitimated relations of dominance as 'discourses'. This is similar to the way in which Parker uses the term in his approach to discourse analysis, which we discussed in Chapter 10.

REFERENCES

Abelson, R. (1981) Psychological status of the script concept. *American Psychologist*. 36: 715–29.

Abelson, R. P., Kinder, D. R., Peters, M. D. and Fiske, S. T. (1982) Affective and semantic components in political person perception. *Journal of Personality and Social Psychology*. 42: 619–30.

Abercrombie, N., Hill, S. and Turner, B. S. (eds) (1990) *Dominant ideologies*. London: Unwin Hyman.

Aboud, F. (1988) *Children and prejudice*. Oxford: Blackwell.

Abrams, D. (1990) *Political identity: Relative deprivation, social identity, and the case of Scottish nationalism*. ESRC 16–19 Initiative Occasional Paper No. 24, Social Statistics Research Unit, City University, London.

Abrams, D. and Hogg, M. A. (1988) Comments on the motivational status of self-esteem in social identity and intergroup discrimination. *European Journal of Social Psychology*. 18: 317–34.

Abrams, D. and Hogg, M. A. (eds) (1990a) *Social identity theory: Constructive and critical advances*. Hemel Hempstead: Harvester Wheatsheaf.

Abrams, D. and Hogg, M. A. (1990b) The context of discourse: Let's not throw out the baby with the bathwater. *Philosophical Psychology*. 3: 219–25.

Abramson, L. Y., Seligman, M. E. P. and Teasdale, J. D. (1978) Learned helplessness in humans: Critique and reformulation. *Journal of Abnormal Psychology*. 87: 49–74.

Abric, J.-P. (1984) A theoretical and experimental approach to the study of social representation. In R. M. Farr and S. Moscovici (eds), *Social representations*. Cambridge/Paris: Cambridge University Press/Maison des Sciences de l'Homme. pp. 169–83.

Adorno, T. W., Frenkel-Brunswik, E., Levinson, D. J. and Sanford, R. N. (1950) *The authoritarian personality*. New York: Harper & Row.

Agger, B. (1991) Critical theory, poststructuralism, postmodernism: Their sociological relevance. *Annual Review of Sociology*. 17: 105–31.

Ajzen, I. (1988) *Attitudes, personality, and behavior*. Milton Keynes: Open University Press.

Ajzen, I. (1989) Attitude structure and behavior. In A. R. Pratkanis, S. J. Breckler and A. G. Greenwald (eds), *Attitude structure and function*. Hillsdale, NJ: Erlbaum. pp. 241–74.

Ajzen, I. (1991) The theory of planned behavior. *Organizational Behavior and Human Decision Processes*. 50: 1–33.

Ajzen, I. and Fishbein, M. (1980) *Understanding attitudes and predicting behavior*. Englewood Cliffs, NJ: Prentice Hall.

Ajzen, I. and Madden, T. J. (1986) Prediction of goal-directed behavior: Attitudes, intentions, and perceived behavioral control. *Journal of Experimental Social Psychology*. 22: 453–74.

Ajzen, I., Dalto, C. A. and Blyth, D. P. (1979) Consistency and bias in the attribution of attitudes. *Journal of Personality and Social Psychology*. 37: 1871–6.

Ajzen, I., Timko, C. and White, J. B. (1982) Self-monitoring and the attitude–behavior relation. *Journal of Personality and Social Psychology*. 42: 426–35.

Allansdottir, A., Jovchelovitch, S. and Stathopoulou, A. (1993) Social representations: The versatility of a concept. *Papers on Social Representations*. 2: 3–10.

Allport, F. H. (1924) *Social psychology*. New York: Houghton Mifflin.

Allport, G. W. (1935) Attitudes. In C. Murchison (ed.), *A handbook of social psychology*. Worcester, MA: Clark University Press. pp. 798–844.

Allport, G. W. (1954) *The nature of prejudice*. Reading, MA: Addison-Wesley.

Altemeyer, R. W. (1981) *Right-wing authoritarianism*. Winnipeg: University of Manitoba Press.

Altemeyer, R. W. (1988) *Enemies of freedom: Understanding right-wing authoritarianism*. San Francisco: Jossey-Bass.

Altemeyer, R. W. (1994) Reducing prejudice in right-wing authoritarians. In M. P. Zanna and J. M. Olson (eds), *The psychology of prejudice: The Ontario symposium* (Vol. 7). Hillsdale, NJ: Erlbaum. pp. 131–48.

Althusser, L. (1970) Ideology and ideological state apparatuses. In L. Althusser (1971), *Lenin and philosophy and other essays*. London: New Left Books.

Andersen, S. M. and Klatzky, R. L. (1987) Traits and social stereotypes: Levels of categorization in person perception. *Journal of Personality and Social Psychology*. 53: 235–46.

Andersen, S. M., Klatzky, R. L. and Murray, J. (1990) Traits and social stereotypes: Efficiency differences in social information processing. *Journal of Personality and Social Psychology*. 59: 192–201.

Antaki, C. (1985) Ordinary explanation in conversation: Causal structures and their defence. *European Journal of Social Psychology*. 15: 213–30.

Apostilidis, T. (1992) Représentations sociales de la sexualité et responsabilisation de la contamination par le VIH. Paper presented at the First International Conference on Social Representations, Ravello, Italy.

Apostle, R. A., Glock, C. Y., Piazza, T. and Suelze, M. (1983) *The anatomy of racial attitudes*. Berkeley: University of California Press.

Aronson, E. (1968) Dissonance theory: Progress and problems. In R. P. Abelson, E. Aronson, W. J. McGuire, T. M. Newcomb, M. J. Rosenberg and P. H. Tannenbaum (eds), *Theories of cognitive consistency: A sourcebook*. Chicago: Rand-McNally. pp. 5–27.

Aronson, E. (1989) Analysis, synthesis, and the treasuring of the old. *Personality and Social Psychology Bulletin*. 15: 508–12.

Aronson, E., Wilson, T. D. and Akert, R. M. (1994) *Social psychology: The heart and the mind*. New York: HarperCollins.

Augoustinos, M. (1986) Psychiatric inpatients' attitudes toward mental disorder and the tendency to adopt a sick-role. *Psychological Reports*. 58: 495–8.

Augoustinos, M. (1989) Social representations and causal attributions. In J. Forgas and J. M. Innes (eds), *Recent advances in social psychology: An interactional perspective*. North Holland: Elsevier. pp. 95–106.

Augoustinos, M. (1990) The mediating role of representations on causal attributions in the social world. *Social Behaviour*. 5: 49–62.

Augoustinos, M. (1991a) Consensual representations of the social structure in different age groups. *British Journal of Social Psychology*. 30: 193–205.

Augoustinos, M. (1991b) Social representations and social cognition: A convergence of different traditions. Unpublished Doctoral Thesis, University of Adelaide, South Australia.

Augoustinos, M. (1993) The openness and closure of a concept: Reply to Allansdottir, Jovchelovitch & Stahopoulou. *Papers on Social Representations*. 2: 26–30.

Augoustinos, M. (1995) Social representations and ideology: Towards the study of ideological representations. In U. Flick and S. Moscovici (eds), *The psychology of the social: Language and social knowledge in social psychology*. Reinbek: Rowohlt. pp. 200–17.

Augoustinos, M. and Innes, J. M. (1990) Towards an integration of social representations and social schema theory. *British Journal of Social Psychology*. 29: 213–31.

Augoustinos, M., Ahrens, C. and Innes, J. M. (1994) Stereotypes and prejudice: The Australian experience. *British Journal of Social Psychology*. 33: 125–41.

Bagley, C., Verma, G. K., Mallick, K. and Young, L. (1979) *Personality, self-esteem and prejudice*. Aldershot: Gower.

Banaji, M. R. and Greenwald, A. G. (1994) Implicit stereotyping and prejudice. In M. P. Zanna and J. M. Olson (eds), *The psychology of prejudice: The Ontario symposium* (Vol. 7). Hillsdale, NJ: Erlbaum. pp. 55–76.

Bargh, J. A. (1984) Automatic and conscious processing of social information. In R. S. Wyer, Jr, and T. K. Srull (eds), *Handbook of social cognition* (Vol. 3). Hillsdale, NJ: Erlbaum. pp. 1–44.

Bargh, J. A. (1989) Conditional automaticity: Varieties of automatic influence in social perception and cognition. In J. S. Uleman and J. A. Bargh (eds), *Unintended thought*. New York: Guilford. pp. 3–51.

Bargh, J. A. (1994) The four horsemen of automaticity: Awarenesss, intention, efficiency, and control in social cognition. In R. S. Wyer, Jr, and T. K. Srull (eds), *Handbook of social cognition* (Vol. 1). Hillsdale, NJ: Erlbaum. pp. 1–40.

Bargh, J. A. and Pietramonaco, P. (1982) Automatic information processing and social perception: The influence of trait information presented outside of conscious awareness on impression formation. *Journal of Personality and Social Psychology*. 43: 437–49.

Baron, R. M. and Boudreau, L. A. (1987) An ecological perspective on integrating personality and social psychology. *Journal of Personality and Social Psychology*. 53: 1222–8.

Bartlett, F. (1932a) *A study in experimental and social psychology*. Cambridge: Cambridge University Press.

Bartlett, F. (1932b) *Remembering*. Cambridge: Cambridge University Press.

Bass, B. M. (1960) *Leadership, psychology, and organizational behavior*. New York: Harper & Row.

Baudrillard, J. (1983) *Simulations* (trans. P. Foss, P. Patton and P. Beitchman). New York: Semiotext(e).

Becker, H. W. (1963) *Outsiders: Studies in the sociology of deviance*. New York: Free Press.

Bell, D. (1960) *The end of ideology: On the exhaustion of political ideas in the fifties*. New York: Free Press of Glencoe.

Bem, D. (1967) Self-perception: An alternative interpretation of cognitive dissonance phenomena. *Psychological Review*. 74: 183–200.

Bem, D. (1970) *Beliefs, attitudes, and human affairs*. Belmont, CA: Brooks/Cole.

Bem, D. (1972) Self-perception theory. In L. Berkowitz (ed.), *Advances in experimental social psychology* (Vol. 6). New York: Academic Press. pp. 1–62.

Bem, S. L. (1981) Gender schema theory: A cognitive account of sex typing. *Psychological Review*. 88: 354–64.

Bennett, W. L. (1977) The growth of knowledge in mass belief studies: An epistemological critique. *American Journal of Political Science*. 21: 465–500.

Bentler, P. and Speckart, G. (1979) Models of attitude–behavior relations. *Psychological Review*. 86: 452–64.

Berger, P. and Luckmann, T. (1967) *The social construction of reality: A treatise in the sociology of knowledge*. Chicago: Aldine.

Berry, J. W., Kalin, R. and Taylor, D. M. (1977) *Multiculturism and ethnic attitudes in Canada*. Ottawa: Minister of Supply and Services.

Billig, M. (1976) *Social psychology and intergroup relations*. London: Academic Press.

Billig, M. (1982) *Ideology and social psychology*. Oxford: Blackwell.

Billig, M. (1987) *Arguing and thinking: A rhetorical approach to social psychology*. Cambridge: Cambridge University Press.

Billig, M. (1988) Social representation, objectification and anchoring: A rhetorical analysis. *Social Behaviour*. 3: 1–16.

Billig, M. (1991) *Ideology, rhetoric and opinions*. London: Sage.

Billig, M. and Sabucedo, J. (in press) Rhetorical and ideological dimensions of common-sense. In J. Siegfried (ed), *The status of common sense in psychology*. New York: Ablex.

Billig, M. and Tajfel, H. (1973) Social categorization and similarity in intergroup behaviour. *European Journal of Social Psychology*. 3: 27–52.

Billig, M., Condor, S., Edwards, M., Middleton, D. and Radley, A. (1988) *Ideological dilemmas: A social psychology of everyday thinking*. London: Sage.

Blanchard, F. A., Lilly, T., and Vaughn, L. A. (1991) Reducing the expression of racial prejudice. *Psychological Science*. 2: 101–5.

Block, J. and Funder, D. C. (1986) Social roles and social perception: Individual differences in attribution and 'error'. *Journal of Personality and Social Psychology*. 51: 1200–7.

Bobo, L. (1983) Whites' opposition to busing: Symbolic racism or realistic group conflict? *Journal of Personality and Social Psychology*. 45: 1196–1210.

Bocock, R. (1986) *Hegemony*. Chichester: Ellis Horwood.

Bodenhausen, G. V., Kramer, G. P. and Susser, K. (1994) Happiness and stereotypic thinking in social judgment. *Journal of Personality and Social Psychology*. 66: 621–32.

Bonacich, E. (1973) A theory of middleman minorities. *American Sociological Review*. 38: 583–94.

Bonacich, E. and Modell, J. (1980) *The economic basis of ethnic solidarity: Small business in the Japanese American community*. Berkeley: University of California Press.

Bond, M. (1983) Cross-cultural studies of attribution. In M. Hewstone (ed.), *Attribution theory: Social and functional extensions*. Oxford: Blackwell.

Bond, M., Leung, K. and Wan, K. C. (1982) How does cultural collectivism operate? The impact of task and maintenance on reward distribution. *Journal of Cross-Cultural Psychology*. 13: 186–200.

Bourhis, R. Y., Giles, H. and Tajfel, H. (1973) Language as a determinant of Welsh identity. *European Journal of Social Psychology*. 13: 321–50.

Bower, G. H., Black, J. B. and Turner, J. J. (1979) Scripts in memory for text. *Cognitive Psychology*, 11: 177–220.

Breakwell, G. and Canter, D. (eds) (1993) *Empirical approaches to social representations*. Oxford: Oxford University Press.

Breckler, S. J. (1984) Empirical validation of affect, behavior, and cognition as distinct components of attitude. *Journal of Personality and Social Psychology*. 47: 1191–205.

Breckler, S. J. and Wiggins, E. C. (1989) Affect versus evaluation in the structure of attitudes. *Journal of Experimental Social Psychology*. 25: 253–71.

Brewer, M. B. (1988) A dual process model of impression formation. In T. K. Srull and R. S. Wyer, Jr (eds), *Advances in social cognition* (Vol. 1). Hillsdale, NJ: Erlbaum. pp. 1–36.

Brewer, M. B. (1991). The social self: On being the same and different at the same time. *Personality and Social Psychology Bulletin*. 17: 475–82.

Brewer, M. B. and Campbell, D. T. (1976) *Ethnocentrism and intergroup attitudes: East African evidence*. New York: Halsted.

Brewer, M. B. and Silver, M. (1978) Ingroup bias as a function of task characteristics. *European Journal of Social Psychology*. 8: 393–400.

Brewer, M. B., Dull, V. and Lui, L. (1981) Perceptions of the elderly: Stereotypes as prototypes. *Journal of Personality and Social Psychology*. 41: 656–70.

Brigham, J. C. (1971) Ethnic stereotypes. *Psychological Bulletin*. 76: 15–33.

Brown, R. (1965) *Social psychology*. New York: Macmillan.

Brown, R. (1986) *Social psychology* (2nd edn). New York: Macmillan.

Brown, R. J. (1988) *Group processes: Dynamics within and between groups*. Oxford: Blackwell.

Brown, R. J. and Turner, J. C. (1979) The criss-cross categorization effect in intergroup discrimination. *British Journal of Social and Clinical Psychology*. 18: 371–83.

Brown, R. J., Hinkle, S., Ely, P. G., Fox-Cardamone, L., Maras, P. and Taylor, L. A. (1992) Recognizing group diversity: Individualist–collectivist and autonomous–relational social orientations and their implications for intergroup processes. *British Journal of Social Psychology*. 31: 327–42.

Bruner, J. S. (1958) Social psychology and perception. In E. E. Maccoby, T. M. Newcomb and E. L. Hartley (eds), *Readings in social psychology*. New York: Henry Holt. pp. 85–94.

Bruner, J. S., Goodnow, J. J. and Austin, G. (1956) *A study of thinking*. New York: Wiley.

Bulman, R. J. and Wortman, C. B. (1977) Attributions of blame and coping in the 'real world': Severe accident victims react to their lot. *Journal of Personality and Social Psychology*. 35: 351–63.

Burman, E. (1991) What discourse is not. *Philosophical Psychology*. 4: 325–42.

Buss, A. R. (1976) Galton and the birth of differential psychology and eugenics: Social, political, and economic factors. *Journal of the History of the Behavioral Sciences*. 12: 47–58.

Buss, A. R. (1979) Humanistic psychology as liberal ideology: The socio-historical roots of Maslow's theory of self-actualization. *Journal of Humanistic Psychology*. 19: 43–55.

Callan, V. J. (1986) *Australian minority groups*. Sydney: Harcourt Brace Jovanovich.

Callinicos, A. (1989) *Against postmodernism: A Marxist critique*. Cambridge: Polity Press.

Campbell, D. T. (1967) Stereotypes and the perception of group differences. *American Psychologist*, 22: 817–29.

Cano, I., Hopkins, N. and Islam, M. R. (1991) Memory for stereotype-related material – a replication study with real-life groups. *European Journal of Social Psychology*. 21: 349–57.

Cantor, N. and Mischel, W. (1977) Traits as prototypes: Effects on recognition memory. *Journal of Personality and Social Psychology*. 35: 38–48.

Cantor, N. and Mischel, W. (1979) Prototypes in person perception. *Advances in Experimental Social Psychology*. 12: 4–47.

Caplan, N. and Nelson, S. D. (1973) On being useful: The nature and consequences of psychological research on social problems. *American Psychologist*. 28: 199–211.

Cartwright, D. (1979) Contemporary social psychology in historical perspective. *Social Psychology Quarterly*. 42: 82–93.

Chamberlain, C. (1983) *Class consciousness in Australia*. Sydney: George Allen & Unwin.

Chombart de Lauwe, M. J. (1984) Changes in the representation of the child in the course of social transmission. In R. M. Farr and S. Moscovici (eds), *Social representations*. Cambridge/Paris: Cambridge University Press/Maison des Sciences de l'Homme.

Christie, R. and Jahoda, M. (eds) (1954) *Studies in the scope and method of the authoritarian personality*. Glencoe, IL: Free Press.

Clark, K. B. and Clark, M. P. (1947) Racial identification and preference in Negro children. In T. Newcomb and E. L. Hartley (eds), *Readings in social psychology*. New York: Holt. pp. 169–78.

Codol, J.-P. (1984) On the system of representations in an artificial social situation. In R. M. Farr and S. Moscovici (eds), *Social representations*. Cambridge/Paris: Cambridge University Press/Maison des Sciences de l'Homme. pp. 239–53.

Cohen, C. E. (1981) Person categories and social perception: Testing some boundaries of the processing effects of prior knowledge. *Journal of Personality and Social Psychology*. 40: 441–52.

Cohen, J. and Struening, E. L. (1962) Opinions about mental illness in the personnel of two large mental hospitals. *Journal of Abnormal and Social Psychology*. 64: 349–60.

Collier, G., Minton, H. L. and Reynolds, G. (eds) (1991) *Currents of thought in American social psychology*. New York: Oxford University Press.

Commins, B. and Lockwood, J. (1978) The effects on intergroup relations of mixing Roman Catholics and Protestants: An experimental investigation. *European Journal of Social Psychology*. 8: 383–6.

Condor, S. (1988) 'Race stereotypes' and racist discourse. *Text*. 8: 69–89.

Condor, S. (1990) Social stereotypes and social identity. In D. Abrams and M. Hogg (eds), *Social identity theory: Constructive and critical advances*. Hemel Hempstead: Harvester Wheatsheaf. pp. 230–49.

Connell, R. W. (1971) *The child's construction of politics*. Melbourne: Melbourne University Press.

Conover, P. J. and Feldman, S. (1984) How people organize the political world: A schematic model. *American Journal of Political Science*. 28: 95–126.

Converse, P. E. (1964) The nature of belief systems in mass publics. In D. E. Apter, *Ideology and Discontent*. New York: Free Press. pp. 206–61.

Cordua, G. D., McGraw, K. O. and Drabman, R. S. (1979) Doctor or nurse? Children's perception of sex-typed occupations. *Child Development*. 50: 590–3.

Corsaro, W. A. (1990) The underlife of the nursery school: Young children's social representations of adult rules. In G. Duveen and B. Lloyd (eds), *Social representations and the development of knowledge*. Cambridge: Cambridge University Press. pp. 11–26.

Costall, A. and Still, A. (eds) (1987) *Cognitive psychology in question*. Brighton: Harvester.

Craik, F. and Lockhart, R. S. (1972) Levels of processing: A framework for memory research. *Journal of Verbal Learning and Verbal Behavior*. 11: 671–84.

Crocker, J. and Luhtanen, R. (1990) Collective self-esteem and ingroup bias. *Journal of Personality and Social Psychology*. 58: 60–7.

Crosby, F., Bromley, S. and Saxe, L. (1980) Recent unobtrusive studies of black and white discrimination and prejudice: A literature review. *Psychological Bulletin*. 87: 546–63.

D'Alessio, M. (1990) Social representations of childhood: An implicit theory of development. In G. Duveen and B. Lloyd (eds), *Social representations and the development of knowledge*. Cambridge: Cambridge University Press. pp. 70–90.

Dandy, J. (1994) Academic achievement motivation: A cross-cultural study. Unpublished monograph, University of Adelaide, South Australia.

Dawes, R. M. and Smith, T. L. (1985) Attitude and opinion measurement. In G. Lindzey and E. Aronson (eds), *Handbook of social psychology* (3rd edn, Vol. 1). New York: Random House. pp. 509–66.

Deaux, K. and Emswiller, T. (1974) Explanations of successful performance on sex-linked tasks: What is skill for the male is luck for the female. *Journal of Personality and Social Psychology*. 29: 80–5.

de Rosa, A. S. (1987) The social representations of mental illness in children and adults. In W. Doise and S. Moscovici (eds), *Current issues in European social psychology* (Vol. 2). Cambridge/Paris: Cambridge University Press/Éditions de la Maison des Sciences de l'Homme. pp. 47–138.

Deschamps, J. C. (1977) Effects of crossing category membership on quantitative judgement. *European Journal of Social Psychology*. 7: 122–6.

Deschamps. J. C. (1984) The social psychology of intergroup relations and categorical identification, In H. Tajfel (ed.), *The social dimension* (Vol. 2). Cambridge: Cambridge University Press. pp. 541–59.

Deschamps, J. C. and Doise, W. (1978) Crossed category membership in intergroup relations. In H. Tajfel (ed.), *Differentiation between social groups*. London: Academic Press. pp. 141–58.

Devine, P. G. (1989a) Stereotypes and prejudice: Their automatic and controlled components. *Journal of Personality and Social Psychology*. 56: 5–18.

Devine, P. G. (1989b) Automatic and controlled processes in prejudice: The role of stereotypes and personal beliefs. In A. R. Pratkanis, S. J. Breckler and A. G. Greenwald (eds), *Attitude structure and function*. Hillsdale, NJ: Erlbaum. pp. 181–212.

Devine, P. G. and Ostrom, T. M. (1988) Dimensional versus information-processing approaches to social knowledge: The case of inconsistency management. In D. Bar-Tal and A. W. Kruglanski (eds), *The social psychology of knowledge*. Cambridge: Cambridge University Press. pp. 231–61.

Diehl, M. (1989) Dichotomy and discrimination: The effects of cross-categorizations on discrimination in a minimal group paradigm. *Zeitschrift für Sozialpsychologie*. 20: 92–102.

Di Giacomo, J.-P. (1980) Intergroup alliances and rejections within a protest movement (analysis of the social representations). *European Journal of Social Psychology*. 10: 329–44.

Dion, K. L. (1986) Responses to perceived discrimination and relative deprivation. In J. M. Olson, C. P. Herman and M. P. Zanna (eds), *Relative deprivation and social comparison: The Ontario symposium* (Vol. 4). Hillsdale, NJ: Erlbaum. pp. 159–80.

Doise, W. (1978) *Individuals and groups: Explanations in social psychology*. Cambridge: Cambridge University Press.

Doise, W. (1986) *Levels of explanation in social psychology*. Cambridge: Cambridge University Press.

Doise, W. and Sinclair, A. (1973) The categorization process in intergroup relations. *European Journal of Social Psychology*. 3: 145–57.

Doise, W., Clemence, A. and Lorenzi-Cioldi, F. (1993) *The quantitative analysis of social representations*. Hemel Hempstead: Harvester Wheatsheaf.

Doise, W., Deschamps, J. C. and Meyer, G. (1978) The accentuation of intracategory similarities. In H. Tajfel (ed.), *Differentiation between social groups* London: Academic Press. pp. 159–68.

Dornbusch, S. M. (1987) Individual moral choices and social evaluations: A research odyssey. *Advances in Group Processes*. 4: 271–307.

Dovidio, J. F. and Gaertner, S. L. (eds) (1986) *Prejudice, discrimination, and racism*. New York: Academic Press.

Dovidio, J. F., Evans, N. and Tyler, R. (1986) Racial stereotypes: The contents of their cognitive representations. *Journal of Experimental Social Psychology*. 22: 22–37.

Drabman, R. S., Robertson, S. J., Patterson, J. N., Jarvie, G. J., Hammer, D. and Cordua, G. (1981) Children's perceptions of media-portrayed sex roles. *Sex Roles*. 7: 379–89.

Duckitt, J. (1988) Normative conformity and racial prejudice in South Africa. *Genetic, Social, and General Psychology Monographs*. 114: 413–37.

Duckitt, J. (1991) The development and validation of a modern racism scale in South Africa. *South African Journal of Psychology*. 21: 233–9.

Duckitt, J. (1992) *The social psychology of prejudice*. New York: Praeger.

Duncan, B. L. (1976) Differential social perception and attribution of intergroup violence: Testing the lower limits of stereotyping of blacks. *Journal of Personality and Social Psychology*. 34: 590–8.

Durkheim, É. (1898) Représentations individuelles et représentations collectives. *Revue de Métaphysique et de Morale*. VI: 273–302.

Duval, S. and Wicklund, R. A. (1973) Effects of objective self-awareness on attributions of causality. *Journal of Experimental Social Psychology*. 9: 17–31.

Duveen, G. and de Rosa, A. S. (1992) Social representations and the genesis of social knowledge. *Papers on Social Representations*. 1: 94–108.

Duveen, G. and Lloyd, B. (eds) (1990) *Social representations and the development of knowledge*. Cambridge: Cambridge University Press.

Eagleton, T. (1991) *Ideology*. London: Verso.

Eagly, A. H. and Chaiken, S. (1993) *The psychology of attitudes*. Fort Worth, TX: Harcourt Brace Jovanovich.

Echabe, A. E. and Rovira, D. P. (1989) Social representations and memory: The case of AIDS. *European Journal of Social Psychology*. 19: 543–51.

Edwards, D. (1991) Categories are for talking: On the cognitive and discursive bases of categorization. *Theory and Psychology*. 1: 515–42.

Edwards, D. and Middleton D. (1986) Conversation with Bartlett. *The Quarterly Newsletter of the Laboratory of Comparative Human Cognition*. 8: 79–89.

Edwards, D. and Potter, J. (1992) *Discursive psychology*. London: Sage.

Edwards, D., Ashmore, M. and Potter, J. (in press) Death and furniture: The rhetoric, politics, and theology of bottom line arguments against relativism. *History of the Human Sciences*.

Eisen, S. V. (1979) Actor–observer differences in information inference and causal attribution. *Journal of Personality and Social Psychology*. 37: 261–72.

Eiser, J. R. (1986) *Social psychology: Attitudes, cognition and social behaviour*. Cambridge: Cambridge University Press.

Eiser, J. R. (1994) *Attitudes, chaos, and the connectionist mind*. Oxford: Blackwell.

Ellemers, N. (1993) The influence of socio-cultural variables on identity management strategies. *European Review of Social Psychology*. 4: 27–57.

Elms, A. C. (1975) The crisis of confidence in social psychology. *American Psychologist*. 30: 967–76.

Emler, N. (1987) Socio-moral development from the perspective of social representations. *Journal for the Theory of Social Behaviour*. 17: 371–88.

Emler, N. and Dickinson, J. (1985) Children's representation of economic inequalities: The effect of social class. *British Journal of Social Psychology*. 3: 191–8.

Emler, N., Ohana, J. and Dickinson, J. (1990) Children's representations of social relations. In G. Duveen and B. Lloyd (eds), *Social representation and the development of knowledge*. Cambridge: Cambridge University Press. pp. 47–69.

Erdley, C. A. and D'Agostino, P. R. (1988) Cognitive and affective components of automatic priming effects. *Journal of Personality and Social Psychology*. 54: 741–7.

Erikson, R. S., Luttbeg, N. R. and Tedin, K. L. (1980) *American public opinion: Its origins, content, and impact* (2nd edn). New York: Wiley.

Esses, V. M. and Zanna, M. P. (1989) Mood and the expression of ethnic stereotypes. Paper presented at the annual meeting of the American Psychological Association, New Orleans, LA.

Esses, V. M., Haddock, G. and Zanna, M. P. (1994) The role of mood in the expression of intergroup stereotypes. In M. P. Zanna and J. M. Olson (eds), *The psychology of prejudice: The Ontario symposium* (Vol. 7). Hillsdale, NJ: Erlbaum. pp. 77–101.

Etaugh, C. and Brown, B. C. (1975) Perceiving the causes of success and failure of male and female performers. *Developmental Psychology*. 11: 103.

Evans-Pritchard, E. E. (1976) *Witchcraft, oracles, and magic among the Azande*. Oxford: Clarendon Press.

Eysenck, H. J. (1975) The structure of social attitudes. *British Journal of Social and Clinical Psychology*. 14: 323–31.

Eysenck, H. J. and Wilson, G. D. (eds) (1978) *The psychological basis of ideology*. Lancaster: MTP Press.

Fairclough, N. (1989) *Language and power*. London: Longman.

Farina, A., Fisher, J. D., Getter, H. and Fisher, E. H. (1978) Some consequences of changing people's views regarding the nature of mental illness. *Journal of Abnormal Psychology*. 87: 272–9.

Farr, R. (1977) Heider, Harré and Herzlich on health and illness: Some observations on the structure of 'représentations collectives'. *European Journal of Social Psychology*. 7: 491–504.

Farr, R. (1987) Social representations: A French tradition of research. *Journal for the Theory of Social Behaviour*. 17: 343–69.

Farr, R. (1989) The social and collective nature of representations. In J. Forgas and J. M. Innes (eds), *Recent advances in social psychology: An international perspective*. North Holland: Elsevier. pp. 157–66.

Farr, R. (1990) Social representations as widespread beliefs. In C. Fraser and G. Gaskell (eds), *The social psychological study of widespread beliefs*. Oxford: Clarendon Press.

Farr, R. and Anderson, A. (1983) Beyond actor/observer differences in perspective: Extensions and applications. In M. Hewstone (ed.), *Attribution theory: Social and functional extensions*. Oxford: Blackwell. pp. 45–64.

Fazio, R. H. (1989) On the power and functionality of attitudes: The role of attitude accessibility. In A. R. Pratkanis, S. J. Breckler and A. G. Greenwald (eds), *Attitude structure and function*. Hillsdale, NJ: Erlbaum. pp. 153–79.

Fazio, R. H. and Williams, C. J. (1986) Attitude accessibility as a moderator of the attitude–perception and attitude–behavior relations: An investigation of the 1984 presidential election. *Journal of Personality and Social Psychology*. 51: 505–14.

Fazio, R. H. and Zanna, M. P. (1978a) Attitudinal qualities relating to the strength of the attitude–behavior relationship. *Journal of Experimental Social Psychology*. 14: 398–408.

Fazio, R. H. and Zanna, M. P. (1978b) On the predictive validity of attitudes: The roles of direct experience and confidence. *Journal of Personality*. 46: 228–43.

Fazio, R. H. and Zanna, M. P. (1981) Direct experience and attitude–behavior consistency. In L. Berkowitz (ed.), *Advances in experimental social psychology* (Vol. 14). New York: Academic Press. pp. 161–202.

Fazio, R. H., Zanna, M. P. and Cooper, J. (1977) Dissonance and self-perception: An integrative review of each theory's proper domain of application. *Journal of Experimental Social Psychology*. 13: 464–79.

Fazio, R. H., Sanbonmatsu, D. M., Powell, M. C. and Kardes, F. R. (1986) On the automatic activation of attitudes. *Journal of Personality and Social Psychology*. 50: 229–38.

Feagin, J. R. (1972) Poverty: We still believe that God helps those who help themselves. *Psychology Today*. 6: 101–29.

Feagin, J. R. (1975) *Subordinating the poor: Welfare and American beliefs*. Englewood Cliffs, NJ: Prentice Hall.

Feather, N. T. (1974) Explanations of poverty in Australian and American samples: The person, society or fate? *Australian Journal of Psychology*. 26: 199–216.

Feather, N. T. (1978) Reactions to male and female success and failure at sex-linked occupations: Effects of sex and socio-economic status of respondents. *Australian Journal of Psychology*. 30: 21–40.

Feather, N. T. (1985) Attitudes, values and attributions: Explanations of unemployment. *Journal of Personality and Social Psychology*. 98: 876–89.

Feather, N. T. and Simon, J. G. (1975) Reactions to male and female success and failure in sex-linked occupations: Impressions of personality, causal attributions, and perceived likelihood of different consequences. *Journal of Personality and Social Psychology*. 31: 20–31.

Featherstone, M. (1988) In pursuit of the postmodern: An introduction. *Theory, Culture and Society*. 5: 195–215.

Feldman-Summers, S. and Kiesler, S. B. (1974) Those who are number two try harder: The effects of sex on attributions of causality. *Journal of Personality and Social Psychology*. 30: 846–55.

Ferguson, L. (1973) Primary social attitudes of the 1960s and those of the 1930s. *Psychological Reports*. 33: 655–64.

Festinger, L. (1954) A theory of social comparison processes. *Human Relations*. 7: 117–40.

Festinger, L. (1957) *A theory of cognitive dissonance*. Stanford, CA: Stanford University Press.

Fiedler, K. (1982). Causal schemata: Review and criticism of research on a popular construct. *Journal of Personality and Social Psychology*. 42: 1001–13.

Fishbein, M. and Ajzen, I. (1975) *Belief, attitude, intention, and behavior: An introduction to theory and research*. Reading, MA: Addison-Wesley.

Fiske, S. T. (1982). Schema-triggered affect: Applications to social perception. In M. S. Clark and S.T. Fiske (eds), *Affect and cognition: The 17th Annual Carnegie Symposium on Cognition*. Hillsdale, NJ: Erlbaum. pp. 56–78.

Fiske, S. T. (1992) Thinking is for doing: Portraits of social cognition from Daguerreotypes to Laserphoto. *Journal of Personality and Social Psychology*. 63: 877–89.

Fiske, S. T. and Dyer, L. M. (1985) Structure and development of social schemata: Evidence from positive and negative transfer effects. *Journal of Personality and Social Psychology*. 48: 839–52.

Fiske, S. T. and Linville, P. W. (1980) What does the schema concept buy us? *Personality and Social Psychology Bulletin*. 6: 543–57.

Fiske, S. T. and Neuberg, S. L. (1990) A continuum of impression formation, from category-based to individuating processes: Influences of information and motivation on attention and interpretation. In M. P. Zanna (ed.), *Advances in experimental social psychology* (Vol. 23). New York: Academic Press. pp. 1–74.

Fiske, S.T. and Pavelchak, M. (1986) Category-based versus piecemeal-based affective responses: Developments in schema-triggered affect. In R. M. Sorrentino and E. T.

Higgins (eds), *Handbook of motivation and cognition: Foundations of social behavior*. New York: Guilford. pp. 167–203.

Fiske, S. T. and Taylor, S. E. (1984) *Social cognition*. Reading, MA: Addison-Wesley.

Fiske, S. T. and Taylor, S. E. (1991) *Social cognition* (2nd edn). New York: McGraw-Hill.

Fiske, S. T., Kinder, D. R., and Larter, W. M. (1983) The novice and the expert: Knowledge-based strategies in political cognition. *Journal of Experimental Social Psychology*. 19: 381–400.

Fleming, D. (1967) Attitude: The history of a concept. In D. Fleming and B. Bailyn (eds), *Perspectives in American history* (Vol. 1). Cambridge, MA: Charles Warren Center for Studies in American History. pp. 285–365.

Fletcher, G. J. O. and Ward, C. (1988) Attribution theory and processes: A cross-cultural perspective. In M. H. Bond (ed.), *The cross-cultural challenge to social psychology*. Newbury Park, CA: Sage. pp. 230–44.

Forgas, J. P. (1983) What is social about social cognition? *British Journal of Social Psychology*. 22: 129–44.

Forgas, J. P. (1985) Person prototypes and cultural salience: The role of cognitive and cultural factors in impression formation. *British Journal of Social Psychology*. 24: 3–17.

Foucault, M. (1977) *Discipline and punish: The birth of the prison* (trans. A. M. Sheridan-Smith). London: Allen Lane.

Foucault, M. (1980) *Power/knowledge: Selected interviews and other writings 1972–77*. (trans. C. Gordon). Hemel Hempstead: Harvester Wheatsheaf.

Frank, M. G. and Gilovich, T. (1989) Effect of memory perspective on retrospective causal attributions. *Journal of Personality and Social Psychology*. 57: 399–403.

Fraser, C. and Gaskell, G. (eds) (1990) *The social psychological study of widespread beliefs*. Oxford: Clarendon Press.

Fraser, N. (1989) *Unruly practices: Power, discourse and gender in contemporary social theory*. Minneapolis: University of Minnesota Press.

Friedrich, J., Kierniesky, N. and Cardon, L. (1989) Drawing moral influences from descriptive science: The impact of attitudes on naturalistic fallacy errors. *Personality and Social Psychology Bulletin*. 15: 414–25.

Fukuyama, F. (1992) *The end of history and the last man*. London: Hamish Hamilton.

Furnham, A. (1982a) Why are the poor always with us? Explanations for poverty in Britain. *British Journal of Social Psychology*. 21: 311–322.

Furnham, A. (1982b) Explanations for unemployment in Britain. *European Journal of Social Psychology*. 12: 335–52.

Furnham, A. (1982c) The perception of poverty amongst adolescents. *Journal of Adolescence*. 5: 135–147.

Furnham, A. (1982d) The Protestant work ethic and attitudes towards unemployment. *Journal of Occupational Psychology*. 55: 277–85.

Furnham, A. (1984) The Protestant work ethic: A review of the psychological literature. *European Journal of Social Psychology*. 14: 87–104.

Furnham, A. and Hesketh, B. (1988) Explanations for unemployment: A cross-national study. *Journal of Social Psychology*, 129: 169–81.

Fyock, J. and Stangor, C. (1994) The role of memory bias in stereotype maintenance. *British Journal of Social Psychology*. 33: 331–42.

Gaertner, S. L. and McLaughlin, J. P. (1983) Racial stereotypes: Associations and ascriptions of positive and negative characteristics. *Social Psychology Quarterly*. 46: 23–40.

Gallup, G. G., Jr (1977) Self-recognition in primates: A conceptual approach to the bidirectional properties of consciousness. *American Psychologist*. 32: 329–37.

Garland, H. and Price, K. H. (1977) Attitudes towards women in management and attributions for their success and failure in a managerial position. *Journal of Applied Psychology*. 62: 29–33.

Gaskell, G. and Fraser, C. (1990) The social psychological study of widespread beliefs. In C. Fraser and G. Gaskell, (eds), *The social psychological study of widespread beliefs*. Oxford: Clarendon Press. pp. 3–24.

Gaskell, G. and Smith, P. (1985) An investigation of youth's attributions for unemployment and their political attitudes. *Journal of Economic Psychology*. 6: 65–80.

Geertz, C. (1975) On the nature of anthropological understanding. *American Scientist*. 63: 47–53.

Gergen, K. J. (1967) Multiple identity: The healthy, happy human being wears many masks. *Psychology Today*. 5: 15–39.

Gergen, K. J. (1973) Social psychology as history. *Journal of Personality and Social Psychology.* 26: 309–20.

Gergen, K. J. (1985) The social constructionist movement in modern psychology. *American Psychologist.* 40: 266–75.

Gibbons, F. X. (1978) Sexual standards and reactions to pornography: Enhancing behavioral consistency through self-focused attention. *Journal of Personality and Social Psychology.* 36: 976–87.

Gibson, J. J. (1979) *The ecological approach to visual perception.* Boston: Houghton Mifflin.

Gilbert, D. C. and Levinson, D. J. (1956) Ideology, personality and institutional policy in the mental hospital. *Journal of Abnormal and Social Psychology.* 53: 263–71.

Gilbert, D. T. (1989) Thinking lightly about others: Automatic components of the social inference process. In J. S. Uleman and J. A. Bargh (eds), *Unintended thought.* New York: Guilford. pp. 189–211.

Gilbert, G. M. (1951) Stereotype persistence and change among college students. *Journal of Abnormal and Social Psychology.* 46: 245–54.

Gilbert, N. and Mulkay, M. (1984) *Opening Pandora's box.* Cambridge: Cambridge University Press.

Giles, H. and Coupland, N. (1989) Discourse: Realignment or revolution. *Language & Social Psychology.* 8: 63–8.

Goethals, G. R., Messick, D. M. and Allison, S. T. (1991) The uniqueness bias: Studies of constructive social comparison. In J. Suls and T. A. Wills (eds), *Social comparison: Contemporary theory and research.* Hillsdale, NJ: Erlbaum. pp. 149–76.

Goffman, E. (1963) *Stigma: Notes on the management of spoiled identity.* Englewood Cliffs, NJ: Prentice Hall.

Goodnow, J. J. (1976) Some sources of cultural differences in performance. In G. E. Kearney and D. W. McElwain (eds), *Aboriginal cognition: Retrospect and prospect.* Canberra: Australian Institute of Aboriginal Studies. pp. 19–28.

Gould, S. J. (1984) *The mismeasure of man.* Harmondsworth: Penguin.

Gramsci, A. (1971) *Selections from the prison notebooks* (trans. Q. Hoare and G. Nowell Smith). London: Lawrence and Wishart.

Graumann, C. F. (1986) The individualization of the social and the desocialization of the individual: Floyd H. Allport's contribution to social psychology. In C. F. Graumann and S. Moscovici (eds), *Changing conceptions of crowd mind and behavior.* New York: Springer-Verlag. pp. 97–116.

Greenberg, J. and Rosenfield, D. (1979) Whites' ethnocentrism and their attributions for the behaviour of blacks. A motivational bias. *Journal of Personality.* 47: 643–57.

Greenwald, A. G. and Pratkanis, A. R. (1984) The self. In R. S. Wyer, Jr, and T. K. Srull (eds), *Handbook of social cognition* (Vol. 3). Hillsdale, NJ: Erlbaum. pp. 129–78.

Guerin, B. (1992) Behavior analysis and the social construction of knowledge. *American Psychologist.* 47: 1423–32.

Guerin, B. (1993) Subtle gender bias in the abstractness of verbs and adjectives. Paper presented at the Meeting of Australian Social Psychologists, Newcastle, NSW.

Guerin, B. and Innes, J. M. (1989) Cognitive tuning sets: Anticipating the consequences of communication. *Current Psychology: Research and Reviews.* 8: 234–49.

Guimond, S. and Dube-Simard, L. (1983) Relative deprivation theory and the Quebec Nationalist Movement: The cognition–emotion distinction and the personal–group deprivation issue. *Journal of Personality and Social Psychology.* 44: 526–35.

Hagendoorn, L. and Henke, R. (1991) The effect of multiple category membership on intergroup evaluations in a north Indian context: Class, caste, and religion. *British Journal of Social Psychology.* 30: 247–60.

Hakmiller, K. L. (1966) Threat as a determinant of downward comparison. *Journal of Experimental Social Psychology.* 2 (Suppl. 1): 32–9.

Hall, S. (1986) Variants of liberalism. In J. Donald and S. Hall (eds), *Politics and ideology.* Milton Keynes: Open University Press. pp. 34–69.

Hamilton, D. L. (1979) A cognitive-attributional analysis of stereotyping. In L. Berkowitz (ed.), *Advances in experimental social psychology* (Vol. 12). New York: Academic Press. pp. 53–81.

Hamilton, D. L. and Sherman, J. W. (1994) Stereotypes. In R. S. Wyer, Jr, and T. K. Srull (eds), *Handbook of social cognition* (Vol. 2, 2nd edn). Hillsdale, NJ: Erlbaum.

Hamilton, D. L., Sherman, S. J. and Ruvolo, C. M. (1990) Stereotype-based expectancies: Effects on information processing and social behavior. *Journal of Social Issues.* 46: 35–60.

Harré, R. (1984) Some reflections on the concept of 'social representation'. *Social Research.* 51: 927–38.

Harré, R. and Secord, P. F. (1972) *The explanation of social behavior.* Oxford: Blackwell.

Hartstone, M. and Augoustinos, M. (1994) The minimal group paradigm: Categorization into two versus three groups. *European Journal of Social Psychology.*

Harvey, J. H., Town, J. P. and Yarkin, K. L. (1981) How fundamental is 'the fundamental attribution error'? *Journal of Personality and Social Psychology.* 40: 346–9.

Hasher, L., and Zacks, R. T. (1979) Automatic and effortful processes in memory. *Journal of Experimental Psychology: General.* 108: 356–88.

Haslam, S. A. and Turner, J. C. (1992) Context-dependent variation in social stereotyping 2: The relationship between frame of reference, self-categorization and accentuation. *European Journal of Social Psychology.* 22: 251–78.

Haslam, S. A., Turner, J. C., Oakes, P. J., McGarty, C. and Hayes, B. K. (1992) Context-dependent variation in social stereotyping 1: The effects of intergroup relations as mediated by social change and frame of reference. *European Journal of Social Psychology.* 22: 3–20.

Hass, R. G., Katz, I., Rizzo, N., Bailey, J. and Moore, L. (1992) When racial ambivalence evokes negative affect, using a disguised measure of mood. *Personality and Social Psychology Bulletin.* 18: 786–97.

Hastie, R. (1981) Schematic principles in human memory. In E. T. Higgins, C. P. Herman and M. P. Zanna (eds), *Social cognition: The Ontario symposium* (Vol. 1). Hillsdale, NJ: Erlbaum. pp. 39–88.

Hastie, R. and Kumar, P. A. (1979) Person memory: Personality traits as organizing principles in memory for behaviors. *Journal of Personality and Social Psychology.* 37: 25–38.

Hastie, R. and Park, B. (1986) The relationship between memory and judgment depends on whether the judgment task is memory-based or on-line. *Psychological Review.* 93: 258–68.

Hastorf, A. and Cantril, H. (1954) They saw a game: A case study. *Journal of Abnormal and Social Psychology.* 49: 129–34.

Hayes-Roth, B. (1977) Evolution of cognitive structure and processes. *Psychological Review.* 84: 260–78.

Headey, B. and Wearing, A. (1987) The sense of relative superiority – central to well-being. *Social Indicators Research.* 20, 497–516.

Heaven, P. (1994) The perceived causal structure of poverty: A network analysis approach. *British Journal of Social Psychology.* 33: 259–71.

Heider, F. (1944) Social perception and phenomenal causality. *Psychological Review.* 51: 358–74.

Heider, F. (1958) *The psychology of interpersonal relations.* New York: Wiley.

Heider, F. and Simmel, M. (1944) An experimental study of apparent behavior. *American Journal of Psychology.* 57: 243–9.

Herek, G. M. (1986) The instrumentality of attitudes: Toward a neofunctional theory. *Journal of Social Issues.* 42: 99–114.

Herek, G. M. (1987). Can functions be measured? A new perspective on the functional approach to attitudes. *Social Psychology Quarterly.* 50: 285–303.

Herzlich, C. (1973) *Health and illness: A social psychological analysis.* London: Academic Press.

Hewstone, M. (ed.) (1983) *Attribution theory: Social and functional extensions.* Oxford: Blackwell.

Hewstone, M. (1985) On common-sense and social representations: A reply to Potter and Litton, *British Journal of Social Psychology.* 24: 95–7.

Hewstone, M. (1986) *Understanding attitudes to the European Community: A social-psychological study in four member states.* Paris/Cambridge: Maison des Sciences de l'Homme/ Cambridge University Press.

Hewstone, M. (1988) Causal attribution: From cognitive processes to collective beliefs. *The Psychologist: Bulletin of the British Psychological Society.* 1: 323–7.

Hewstone, M. (1989a) *Causal attribution: From cognitive processes to collective beliefs.* Oxford: Blackwell.

Hewstone, M. (1989b) Représentations sociales et causalité. In D. Jodelet (ed.), *Les représentations sociales.* Paris: Presses Universitaires de France. pp. 252–74.

Hewstone, M. (1990) The 'ultimate attribution error'? A review of the literature on intergroup causal attribution. *European Journal of Social Psychology.* 20: 311–35.

Hewstone, M. and Augoustinos, M. (1995) Social attributions and social representations. In U. Flick and S. Moscovici (eds), *The psychology of the social: Language and social knowledge in social psychology*. Reinbek: Rowohlt. pp. 78–99.

Hewstone, M. and Brown, R. J. (1986) *Contact and conflict in intergroup encounters*. Oxford: Blackwell.

Hewstone, M. and Ward, C. (1985) Ethnocentrism and causal attribution in Southeast Asia. *Journal of Personality and Social Psychology*. 48: 614–23.

Hewstone, M., Hopkins, N. and Routh, D. A. (1992) Cognitive models of stereotype change: (1) Generalization and subtyping in young people's views of the police. *European Journal of Social Psychology*. 22: 219–34.

Hewstone, M., Jaspars, J. and Lalljee, M. (1982) Social representations, social attribution and social identity: The intergroup images of 'public' and 'comprehensive' schoolboys. *European Journal of Social Psychology*. 12: 241–69.

Hewstone, M., Johnston, L. and Aird, P. (1992) Cognitive models of stereotype change: (2) Perceptions of homogeneous and heterogeneous groups. *European Journal of Social Psychology*. 22: 235–49.

Higgins, E. T. and Bargh, J. A. (1987) Social cognition and social perception. *Annual Review of Psychology*. 38: 369–425.

Higgins E. T., King, G. A. and Mavin, G. H. (1982) Individual construct accessibility and subjective impressions and recall. *Journal of Personality and Social Psychology*. 43: 35–47.

Higgins, E. T., Kuiper, N. A. and Olson, J. M. (1981) Social cognition: A need to get personal. In E. T. Higgins, C. P. Herman and M. P. Zanna (eds), *Social cognition: The Ontario symposium* (Vol. 1). Hillsdale, NJ: Erlbaum. pp. 395–420.

Hilgard, E. R. (1980) The trilogy of mind: Cognition, affection, and conation. *Journal of the History of the Behavioral Sciences*. 16: 107–17.

Hilton, D. J. (1990) Conversational processes and causal explanation. *Psychological Bulletin*. 107: 65–81.

Hilton, D. J. and Slugoski, B. R. (1986) Knowledge-based causal attribution: The abnormal conditions focus model. *Psychological Review*. 93: 75–88.

Himmelfarb, S. (1993) The measurement of attitudes. In A. H. Eagly and S. Chaiken (eds), *The psychology of attitudes*. Fort Worth, TX: Harcourt Brace Jovanovich. pp. 23–87.

Hinkle, S. and Brown, R. J. (1990) Intergroup comparisons and social identity: Some links and lacunae. In D. Abrams and M. A. Hogg (eds), *Social identity theory: Constructive and critical advances*. Hemel Hempstead: Harvester Wheatsheaf. pp. 48–70.

Hoffman, C. and Hurst, N. (1990) Gender stereotypes: Perception or rationalization? *Journal of Personality and Social Psychology*. 58: 197–208.

Hofstede, G. (1980) *Culture's consequences*. Beverley Hills, CA: Sage.

Hofstede, G. (1983) National cultures revisited. *Behavior Science Research*. 18: 285–305.

Hogan, R. T. and Emler, N. P. (1978) The biases in contemporary social psychology. *Social Research*. 45: 478–534.

Hogg, M. A. and Abrams, D. (1988) *Social identifications: A social psychology of intergroup relations and group processes*. London: Routledge.

Hogg, M. A. and Abrams, D. (1990) Social motivation, self-esteem and social identity. In D. Abrams and M. A. Hogg (eds), *Social identity theory: Constructive and critical advances*. Hemel Hempstead: Harvester Wheatsheaf. pp. 28–47.

Hogg, M. A. and Hardie, E. A. (1991) Social attraction, personal attraction, and self-categorization: A field study. *Personality and Social Psychology Bulletin*. 17: 175–80.

Howard, J. W. and Rothbart, M. (1980) Social categorization and memory for in-group and out-group behavior. *Journal of Personality and Social Psychology*. 38: 301–10.

Hraba, J. and Grant, G. (1970) Black is beautiful: A re-examination of racial preference and identification. *Journal of Personality and Social Psychology*. 16: 398–402.

Hraba, J., Hagendoorn, L. and Hagendoorn, R. (1989) The ethnic hierarchy in the Netherlands: Social distance and social representation. *British Journal of Social Psychology*. 28: 57–59.

Hunter, E. M. (1991) *Aboriginal health and history: Power and prejudice in remote Australia*. Cambridge: Cambridge University Press.

Hunter, J. A. (1993) Social identity and social perception. Unpublished Doctoral Thesis, University of Ulster, Coleraine, Northern Ireland.

Hunter, J. A., Stringer, M. and Watson, R. P. (1991) Intergroup violence and intergroup attribution. *British Journal of Social Psychology*. 30: 261–6.

Huston, A. (1983) Sex typing. In P. H. Mussen (ed.), *Handbook of child psychology: Socialization, personality and social development* (Vol. 4. 4th edn). New York: Wiley. pp. 387–467.

Ibañez, T. (1994) Constructing a representation or representing a construction? *Theory and Psychology.* 4: 363–81.

Ichheiser, G. (1949) *Misunderstandings in human relations: A study in false social perception.* Chicago: University of Chicago Press.

Innes, J. M. and Ahrens, C. (1991) Positive mood, processing goals and the effects of information on evaluative judgment. In J. Forgas (ed.), *Emotion and social judgments.* Oxford: Pergamon. pp. 221–39.

Innes, J. M. and Fraser, C. (1971) Experimenter bias and other possible biases in psychological research. *European Journal of Social Psychology.* 1: 297–310.

Jahoda, G. (1988) Critical notes and reflections on 'social representations'. *European Journal of Social Psychology.* 18: 195–209.

Jaspars, J. M. F. (1986) Forum and focus: A personal view of European social psychology. *European Journal of Social Psychology.* 16: 3–15.

Jaspars, J. and Fraser, C. (1984) Attitudes and social representations. In R. M. Farr and S. Moscovici (eds), *Social representations.* Cambridge/Paris: Cambridge University Press/ Maison des Sciences de l'Homme. pp. 101–23.

Jennings, M. K. and Markus, G. B. (1984) Partisan orientations over the long haul: Results from the three wave political socialization panel study. *American Political Science Review.* 78: 1000–18.

Jodelet, D. (1984) The representation of the body and its transformations. In R. M. Farr and S. Moscovici (eds), *Social representations.* Cambridge/Paris: Cambridge University Press/ Maison des Sciences de l'Homme. pp. 211–38.

Jodelet, D. (ed.) (1989) *Les représentations sociales.* Paris: Presses Universitaires de France.

Jodelet, D. (1991) *Madness and social representations.* Hemel Hempstead: Harvester Wheatsheaf.

Joffe, H. (1992) Blame and AIDS: A study of South African and British social representations. Paper presented at the First International Conference on Social Representations, Ravello, Italy.

Johnson, C. (1992a) Fragmentation versus Fukuyama: An essay on the unexpected longevity of grand narratives. Paper presented to the Annual Conference of the Australian Sociological Association, Adelaide, South Australia.

Johnson, C. (1992b) Applying Habermas to Australian political culture. *Australian Journal of Political Science.* 27: 55–70.

Johnston, L. and Hewstone, M. (1992) Cognitive models of stereotype change: (3) Subtyping and the perceived typicality of disconfirming group members. *Journal of Experimental Social Psychology.* 28: 360–86.

Jonas, K. and Hewstone, M. (1986) The assessment of national stereotypes: A methodological study. *Journal of Social Psychology.* 126: 745–54.

Jones, E. E. (1985) Major developments in social psychology during the past five decades. In G. Lindzey and E. Aronson (eds), *Handbook of social psychology* (3rd edn, Vol. I). New York: Random House. pp. 47–107.

Jones, E. E. and Davis, K. E. (1965) From acts to dispositions: The attribution process in person perception. In L. Berkowitz (ed.), *Advances in experimental social psychology* (Vol. 2). New York: Academic Press. pp. 219–66.

Jones, E. E. and Harris, V. A. (1967) The attribution of attitudes. *Journal of Experimental Social Psychology.* 3: 1–24.

Jones, E. E. and Nisbett, R. E. (1972) The actor and the observer: Divergent perceptions of the causes of behavior. In E. E. Jones, D. E. Kanouse, H. H. Kelley, R. E. Nisbett, S. Valins and B. Weiner (eds), *Attribution: Perceiving the causes of behavior.* Morristown, NJ: General Learning Press. pp. 79–94.

Jones, J. (1972) *Prejudice and racism.* Reading, MA: Addison-Wesley.

Jost, J. T. (1995) Negative illusions: Conceptual clarification and psychological evidence concerning false consciousness. *Political Psychology,* 16: 397–424.

Jost, J. T. and Banaji, M. R. (1994) The role of stereotyping in system-justification and the production of false consciousness. *British Journal of Social Psychology.* 33: 1–27.

Judd, C. M. and Park, B. (1993) Definition and assessment of accuracy in social stereotypes. *Psychological Review.* 100: 109–28.

Jussim, L. (1986) Self-fulfilling prophecies: A theoretical and integrative review. *Psychological Review*. 93: 429–45.

Jussim, L. (in press) Self-fulfilling prophecies and the maintenance of social stereotypes: The role of dyadic interactions and social forces. In N. Macrae, C. Stangor and M. Hewstone (eds), *The foundations of stereotypes and stereotyping*. New York: Guilford.

Kahneman, D. and Tversky, A. (1972) Subjective probability: A judgment of representativeness. *Cognitive Psychology*. 3: 430–54.

Kahneman, D. and Tversky, A. (1973) On the psychology of prediction. *Psychological Review*. 80: 237–51.

Karlins, M., Coffman, T. L. and Walters, G. (1969) On the fading of social stereotypes: Studies in three generations of college students. *Journal of Personality and Social Psychology*. 13: 1–16.

Kashima, Y. and Triandis, H. C. (1986) The self-serving bias in attributions as a coping strategy. *Journal of Cross-Cultural Psychology*. 17: 83–97.

Kashima, Y., Siegal, M., Tanaka, K. and Kashima, E. S. (1992) Do people believe behaviours are consistent with attitudes? Towards a cultural psychology of attribution processes. *British Journal of Social Psychology*. 31: 111–24.

Katz, D. (1960) The functional approach to the study of attitudes. *Public Opinion Quarterly*. 6: 248–68.

Katz, D. and Braly, K. (1933) Racial stereotypes in one hundred college students. *Journal of Abnormal and Social Psychology*. 28: 280–90.

Katz, D. and Braly, K. (1935) Verbal stereotypes and racial prejudice. *Journal of Abnormal and Social Psychology*. 30: 175–93.

Katz, I. and Hass, R. G. (1988) Racial ambivalence and American value conflict: Correlational and priming studies of dual cognitive structures. *Journal of Personality and Social Psychology*. 55: 893–905.

Katz, P. A. and Taylor, D. A. (1988) Introduction. In P. A. Katz and D. A. Taylor (eds), *Eliminating racism: Profiles in controversy*. New York: Plenum Press. pp. 1–16.

Kawakami, K. and Dion, K. L. (1993) The impact of salient self-identities on relative deprivation and action interpretations. *European Journal of Social Psychology*. 23: 525–40.

Kawakami, K. and Dion, K. L. (1994) Social identity and affect as determinant of collective action: Toward an integration of relative deprivation and social identity theories. Manuscript in submission.

Kearins, J. (1976) Skills of desert Aboriginal children. In G. E. Kearney and D. W. McElwain (eds), *Aboriginal cognition*. Canberra: Australian Institute of Aboriginal Studies. pp. 199–212.

Kelley, H. H. (1967) Attribution theory in social psychology. In D. Levine (ed.), *Nebraska Symposium on Motivation* (Vol. 15). Lincoln, NE: University of Nebraska Press. pp. 192–238.

Kelley, H. H. (1972) Causal schemata and the attribution process. In E. E. Jones, D. E. Kanouse, H. H. Kelley, R. E. Nisbett, S. Valins and B. Weiner (eds), *Attribution: Perceiving the causes of behavior*. Morristown, NJ: General Learning Press. pp. 151–74.

Kelley, H. H. (1973) The processes of causal attribution. *American Psychologist*. 28: 107–28.

Kelley, H. H. and Stahelski, A. J. (1970) The social interaction basis of cooperators' and competitors' beliefs about others. *Journal of Personality and Social Psychology*. 16: 66–91.

Kelly, C. (1993) Group identification, intergroup perceptions and collective action. *European Review of Social Psychology*. 4: 59–83.

Kelvin, P. (1984) The historical dimension of social psychology. The case of unemployment. In H. Tajfel (ed.), *The social dimension: European developments in social psychology* (Vol. 2). Cambridge/Paris: Cambridge University Press/Maison des Sciences de l'Homme. pp. 405–24.

Kerlinger, F. N. (1984) *Liberalism and conservatism: The nature and structure of social attitudes*. Hillsdale, NJ: Erlbaum.

Kernis, M. H., Cornell, D. P., Sun, C.-R., Berry, A. and Harlow, T. (1993) There's more to self-esteem than whether it is high or low: The importance of stability of self-esteem. *Journal of Personality and Social Psychology*. 65: 1190–204.

Kinder, D. R. and Sears, D. O. (1981) Prejudice and politics: Symbolic racism versus racial threats to the good life. *Journal of Personality and Social Psychology*. 40: 414–31.

Kinder, D. R. and Sears, D. O. (1985) Public opinion and political action. In G. Lindzey and E. Aronson (eds), *Handbook of social psychology* (3rd edn, Vol. 2). New York: Random House. pp. 659–741.

King, G. W. (1975) An analysis of attitudinal and normative variables as predictors of intentions and behavior. *Speech Monographs*. 42: 237–44.

Kleinman, A. (1980) *Patients and healers in the context of culture*. Berkeley, CA: University of California Press.

Kothandapani, V. (1971) Validation of feeling, belief, and intention to act as three components of attitude and their contribution to prediction of contraceptive behavior. *Journal of Personality and Social Psychology*. 19: 321–33.

Krech, D., Krutchfield, R. S. and Ballachey, E. L. (1962) *Individual in society: A textbook of social psychology*. New York: McGraw-Hill.

Kress, G. and Hodge, R. (1979) *Language as ideology*. London: Routledge and Kegan Paul.

Krosnick, J. A. (1989) Attitude importance and attitude accessibility. *Personality and Social Psychology Bulletin*. 15: 297–308.

Kruglanski, A. W. (1975) The endogenous–exogenous partition in attribution theory. *Psychological Review*. 82: 387–406.

Kruglanski, A. W. (1979) Causal explanation, teleological expansion: On the radical particularism in attribution theory. *Journal of Personality and Social Psychology*. 37: 1447–57.

Kruglanski, A. W. (1989) *Lay epistemics and human knowledge*. New York: Plenum Press.

Kruglanski, A. W. and Ajzen, I. (1983) Bias and error in human judgment. *European Journal of Social Psychology*. 13: 1–44.

Kuhn, M. H. (1960) Self-attitudes by age, sex, and professional training. *Sociological Quarterly*. 9: 39–55.

Kuhn, M. H. and McPartland, T. S. (1954) An empirical investigation of self-attitudes. *Sociological Review*. 19: 68–76.

Kuiper, N. A. (1978) Depression and causal attributions for success and failure. *Journal of Personality and Social Psychology*. 36: 236–46.

Lakoff, G. (1987) *Women, fire and dangerous things: What categories reveal about the mind*. Chicago: University of Chicago Press.

Lakoff, G. and Johnson, M. (1980) *Metaphors we live by*. Chicago: University of Chicago Press.

Lalljee, M. and Abelson, R. P. (1983) The organization of explanations. In M. Hewstone (ed.), *Attribution theory: Social and functional extensions*. Oxford: Blackwell. pp. 65–80.

Lalljee, M., Brown, L. B. and Ginsburg, G. P. (1984) Attitudes: Dispositions, behaviour or evaluation? *British Journal of Social Psychology*. 23: 233–44.

Lalljee, M., Watson, M. and White, P. (1982) Explanations, attributions and the social context of unexpected behaviour. *European Journal of Social Psychology*. 12: 17–29.

Langer, E. J. (1989) *Mindfulness*. Reading, MA: Addison-Wesley.

LaPiere, R. T. (1934) Attitudes vs. actions. *Social Forces*. 13: 230–7.

Larrain, J. (1979) *The concept of ideology*. London: Hutchinson.

Larrain, J. (1983) *Marxism and ideology*. London: Macmillan.

Lash, S. and Urry, J. (1987) *The end of organised capitalism*. Cambridge: Polity.

Latour, B. (1991) The impact of science studies on political philosophy. *Science, Technology and Human Values*. 16: 3–19.

Lau, R. R. and Hartman, K. A. (1983) Common-sense representations of common illnesses. *Health Psychology*. 2: 167–85.

Lau, R. R. and Russell, D. (1980) Attributions in the sports pages. *Journal of Personality and Social Psychology*. 39: 29–38.

Lau, R. R., Bernard, T. M. and Hartman, K. A. (1989) Further explorations of common-sense representations of common illnesses. *Health Psychology*. 8: 195–219.

Lemaine, G. (1966) Inegalité, comparison et incomparabilité: Esquisse d'une théorie de l'originalité sociale. *Bulletin de Psychologie*. 20: 24–32.

Lemaine, G., Kastersztein, J. and Personnaz, B. (1978) Social differentiation. In H. Tajfel (ed.), *Differentiation between social groups: Studies in the social psychology of intergroup relations*. London: Academic Press. pp. 269–300.

Lerner, M. (1980) *The belief in a just world: A fundamental delusion*. New York: Plenum Press.

Lerner, M. and Miller, D. (1978) Just world research and the attribution process: Looking back and ahead. *Psychological Bulletin*. 85: 1030–51.

Levine, R. A. and Campbell, D. T. (1972) *Ethnocentrism: Theories of conflict, ethnic attitudes, and group behavior*. New York: Wiley.

Lewin, K. (1951) *Field theory in social science*. New York: Harper.

Lewinsohn, P. M., Mischel, W., Chaplin, W. and Barton, R. (1980) Social competence and depression: The role of illusory self-perceptions. *Journal of Abnormal Psychology*. 89: 203–12.

Lewis, A. (1990) Shared economic beliefs. In C. Fraser and G. Gaskell (eds), *The social psychological study of widespread beliefs*. Oxford: Clarendon Press. pp. 192–209.

Lippmann, W. (1922) *Public opinion*. New York: Harcourt, Brace.

Lipset, S. (1960) *Political man*. London: Heinemann.

Litson, J. (1990) The Placido effect. *The Australian Magazine: Supplement to The Weekend Australian* (25–6 August).

Litton, I. and Potter, J. (1985) Social representations in the ordinary explanation of a 'riot'. *European Journal of Social Psychology*. 15: 371–88.

Lloyd, B. and Smith, C. (1985) The social representation of gender and young children's play. *British Journal of Developmental Psychology*. 3: 65–73.

Lloyd, B., Duveen, G. and Smith, C. (1988) The social representation of gender and young children's play: A replication. *British Journal of Developmental Psychology*. 6: 85–8.

Locke, V., MacLeod, C. and Walker, I. (1994) Automatic and controlled activation of stereotypes: Individual differences associated with prejudice. *British Journal of Social Psychology*. 33: 29–46.

Locksley, A., Borgida, E., Brekke, N. and Hepburn, C. (1980) Sex stereotypes and social judgment. *Journal of Personality and Social Psychology*. 39: 821–31.

Long, K. M., Spears, R. and Manstead, A. S. R. (1994) The influence of personal and collective self-esteem on strategies of social differentiation. *British Journal of Social Psychology*. 33: 313–29.

Lord, C. G., Lepper, M. R. and Ross, L. (1979) Biased assimilation and attitude polarization: The effects of prior theories on subsequently considered evidence. *Journal of Personality and Social Psychology*. 37: 2098–109.

Luhtanen, R. and Crocker, J. (1991) Self-esteem and intergroup comparisons: Toward a theory of collective self-esteem. In J. Suls and T. A. Wills (eds), *Social comparison: Contemporary theory and research*. Hillsdale, NJ: Erlbaum. pp. 211–34.

Luhtanen, R. and Crocker, J. (1992) A Collective Self-Esteem Scale: Self-evaluation of one's social identity. *Personality and Social Psychology Bulletin*. 18: 302–18.

Lukes, S. (1973) *Individualism*. Oxford: Blackwell.

Lukes, S. (1975) *Émile Durkheim, his life and work: A historical and critical study*. Harmondsworth: Penguin.

Lyotard, J.-F. (1984) *The postmodern condition: A report on knowledge* (trans. G. Bennington and B. Massumi). Manchester: Manchester University Press.

McArthur, L. Z. and Baron, R. (1983) Toward an ecological theory of social perception. *Psychological Review*. 90: 215–38.

McArthur, L. Z. and Post, D. L. (1977) Figural emphasis and person perception. *Journal of Experimental Social Psychology*. 13: 520–35.

McCauley, C. and Stitt, C. L. (1978) An individual and quantitative measure of stereotypes. *Journal of Personality and Social Psychology*. 36: 929–40.

McCauley, C., Stitt, C. L. and Segal, M. (1980) Stereotyping: From prejudice to prediction. *Psychological Bulletin*. 87: 195–208.

McClosky, H. (1964) Consensus and ideology in American politics. *American Political Science Review*. 58: 361–82.

McClure, J. (1991) *Explanations, accounts, and illusions: A critical analysis*. Cambridge: Cambridge University Press.

McClure, J., Lalljee, M., Jaspars, J. and Abelson, R. P. (1989) Conjunctive explanations for success and failure: The effect of different types of causes. *Journal of Personality and Social Psychology*. 56: 19–26.

McConahay, J. B. (1986) Modern racism, ambivalence, and the modern racism scale. In J. F. Dovidio and S. L. Gaertner (eds), *Prejudice, discrimination, and racism*. New York: Academic Press. pp. 91–125.

McConahay, J. B., Hardee, B. B. and Batts, V. (1981) Has racism declined in America? *Journal of Conflict Resolution*. 25: 563–79.

McDougall, W. (1921) *The group mind*. London: Cambridge University Press.

McGarty, C. and Penny, R. E. C. (1988) Categorization, accentuation, and social judgement. *British Journal of Social Psychology*. 27: 147–57.

McGarty, C., Turner, J. C., Hogg, M. A., David, B. and Wetherell, M. S. (1992) Group polarization as conformity to the prototypical group member. *British Journal of Social Psychology*. 31: 1–20.

McGuire, W. J. (1973) The yin and yang of progress in social psychology. *Journal of Personality and Social Psychology*. 26: 446–56.

McGuire, W. J. (1985) Attitudes and attitude change. In G. Lindzey and E. Aronson (eds), *Handbook of social psychology* (3rd edn, Vol. 2). New York: Random House. pp. 136–314.

McGuire, W. J. (1986) The vicissitudes of attitudes and similar representational constructs in twentieth-century psychology. *European Journal of Social Psychology*. 16: 89–130.

Mackie, D. M. and Hamilton, D. L. (eds) (1993) *Affect, cognition, and stereotyping: Interactive processes in group perception*. San Diego: Academic Press.

McKinlay, A. and Potter, J. (1987) Social representations: A conceptual critique. *Journal for the Theory of Social Behaviour*. 17: 471–8.

McLellan, D. (1986) *Ideology*. Milton Keynes: Open University Press.

Macpherson, C. B. (1962) *The political theory of possessive individualism: Hobbes to Locke*. Oxford: Clarendon Press.

Macrae, C. N., Milne, A. B. and Bodenhausen, G. V. (1994) Stereotypes as energy saving devices: A peek inside the cognitive toolbox. *Journal of Personality and Social Psychology*. 66: 37–47.

Macrae, K. and Foddy, M. (1993) Rethinking Hazel Markus' self schema theory. Paper presented at the 22nd Meeting of Australian Social Psychologists, Newcastle, NSW.

Manicas, P. T. and Secord, P. F. (1983) Implications for psychology of the new philosophy of science. *American Psychologist*. 38: 399–413.

Mann, J. F. and Taylor, D. M. (1974) Attributions of causality: Role of ethnicity and social class. *Journal of Social Psychology*. 94: 3–13.

Mann, M. (1970) The social cohesion of liberal democracy. Reprinted (1982) in A. Giddens and D. Held (eds), *Classes, power and conflict: classical and contemporary debates*. London: Macmillan.

Manstead, A. S. R., Proffitt, C. and Smart, J. L. (1983) Predicting and understanding mothers' infant-feeding intentions and behavior: Testing the theory of reasoned action. *Journal of Personality and Social Psychology*. 44: 657–71.

Maracek, J. and Metee, D. R. (1972) Avoidance of continued success as a function of self-esteem, level of esteem-certainty, and responsibility for success. *Journal of Personality and Social Psychology*. 22: 98–107.

Marcus, G. E., Tabb, D. and Sullivan, J. L. (1974) The application of individual differences scaling in the meaurement of political ideologies. *American Journal of Political Science*. 18: 405–20.

Marjoribanks, K. and Jordan, D. F. (1986) Stereotyping among Aboriginal and Anglo-Australians. *Journal of Cross-Cultural Psychology*. 17: 17–28.

Markova, I. and Wilkie, P. (1987) Representations, concepts and social change: The phenomenon of AIDS. *Journal for the Theory of Social Behaviour*. 17: 389–409.

Marks, G. (1984) Thinking one's abilities are unique and one's opinions are common. *Personality and Social Psychology Bulletin*. 10: 203–8.

Marks, G. and Miller, N. (1987) Ten years of research on the false-consensus effect: An empirical and theoretical review. *Psychological Bulletin*. 102: 72–90.

Markus, H. (1977). Self-schemata and processing information about the self. *Journal of Personality and Social Psychology*. 35: 63–78.

Markus, H. and Kunda, Z. (1986) Stability and malleability of the self-concept. *Journal of Personality and Social Psychology*. 51: 858–66.

Markus, H. and Nurius, P. (1986) Possible selves. *American Psychologist*. 41: 954–69.

Markus, H. and Wurf, E. (1987) The dynamic self-concept: A social psychological perspective. *Annual Review of Psychology*. 38: 299–337.

Markus, H., Crane. M., Bernstein, S. and Siladi, M. (1982) Self-schemas and gender. *Journal of Personality and Social Psychology*. 42: 38–50.

Marx, K. and Engels, F. (1947) *The German ideology* (1846). New York: International Publishers.

Mead, G. H. (1934) *Mind, self, and society*. Chicago: University of Chicago Press.

Mepham, J. (1972) The theory of ideology in capital. *Radical Philosophy*. 2: 12–19.

Merton, R. K. (1948) The self-fulfilling prophecy. *Antioch Review* (Summer): 193–210.

Meyer, D., Leventhal, H. and Guttman, M. (1985) Common sense models of illness: The example of hypertension. *Health Psychology*. 4: 115–35.

Michael, M. (1991) Some postmodern reflections on social psychology. *Theory & Psychology*. 1: 203–21.

Michotte, A. E. (1963) *The perception of causality*. New York: Russell and Russell.

Middleton, R. (1976) Regional differences in prejudice. *American Sociological Review*. 41: 94–117.

Miles, R. (1989) *Racism*. London: Routledge.

Miller, A. G., Jones, E. E. and Hinkle, S. (1981) A robust attribution error in the personality domain. *Journal of Experimental Social Psychology*. 17: 587–600.

Miller, D. T. (1976) Ego involvement and attributions for success and failure. *Journal of Personality and Social Psychology*. 34: 901–6.

Miller, D. T. and Norman, S. A. (1975) Actor–observer differences in perceptions of effective control. *Journal of Personality and Social Psychology*. 31: 503–15.

Miller, G. A. (1969) Psychology as a means of promoting human welfare. *American Psychologist*. 24: 1063–75.

Miller, J. G. (1984) Culture and the development of everyday social explanation. *Journal of Personality and Social Psychology*. 46: 961–78.

Mills, J. (1958) Changes in moral attitudes following temptation. *Journal of Personality*. 26: 517–31.

Molinari, L. and Emiliani, F. (1990) What is an image? The structure of mothers' images of the child and their influence on conversational styles. In G. Duveen and B. Lloyd (eds), *Social representations and the development of knowledge*. Cambridge: Cambridge University Press. pp. 91–106.

Morgan, D. L. and Schwalbe, M. L. (1990) Mind and the self in society: Linking social structure and social cognition. *Social Psychology Quarterly*. 53: 148–64.

Moscovici, S. (1961) *La Psychoanalyse, son image et son public*. Paris: Presses Universitaires de France.

Moscovici, S. (1963) Attitudes and opinions. *Annual Review of Psychology*. 14: 231–60.

Moscovici, S. (1972) Society and theory in social psychology. In J. Israel and H. Tajfel (eds), *The context of social psychology: A critical assessment*. London: Academic Press. pp. 17–68.

Moscovici, S. (1973) Foreword. In C. Herzlich, *Health and illness: A social psychological analysis*. London: Academic Press.

Moscovici, S. (1981) On social representations. In J. P. Forgas (ed.), *Social cognition: Perspectives on everyday understanding*. London: Academic Press. pp. 181–209.

Moscovici, S. (1982) The coming era of representations. In J.-P. Codol and J.-P. Leyens (eds), *Cognitive analysis of social behaviour*. The Hague: Martinus Nijhoff.

Moscovici, S. (1984a) The phenomenon of social representations. In R. M. Farr and S. Moscovici (eds), *Social representations*, Cambridge/Paris: Cambridge University Press/ Maison des Sciences de l'Homme. pp. 3–69.

Moscovici, S. (1984b) The myth of the lonely paradigm: A rejoinder. *Social Research*. 51: 939–67.

Moscovici, S. (1985) Comment on Potter and Litton. *British Journal of Social Psychology*. 24: 91–2.

Moscovici, S. (1988) Notes towards a description of social representations. *European Journal of Social Psychology*. 18: 211–50.

Moscovici, S. (1989) Des représentations collectives aux représentations sociales: Éléments pour une histoire. In D. Jodelet (ed.), *Les représentations sociales*. Paris: Presses Universitaires de France. pp. 62–86.

Moscovici, S. and Hewstone, M. (1983) Social representations and social explanation: From the 'naive' to the 'amateur' scientist. In M. Hewstone (ed.), *Attribution theory: Social and functional extensions*. Oxford: Blackwell. pp. 98–125.

Moskowitz, G. B. and Roman, R. J. (1992) Spontaneous trait inferences as self-generated primes: Implications for conscious social judgment. *Journal of Experimental Psychology*. 106: 226–54.

Mulkay, M. J. (1979) *Science and the sociology of knowledge*. London: Allen and Unwin.

Mullen, B. and Goethals, G. R. (1990) Social projection, actual consensus, and valence. *British Journal of Social Psychology*. 29: 279–82.

Mullen, B., Brown, R. and Smith, C. (1992) Ingroup bias as a function of salience, relevance and status: An integration. *European Journal of Social Psychology*. 22: 103–22.

National Inquiry into Racist Violence in Australia (1991) *Racist violence: Report of the National Inquiry into Racist Violence in Australia*. Canberra: Australian Government Publishing Service.

Neuberg, S. L. (1994) Expectancy-confirmation processes in stereotype-tinged social encounters: The moderating role of social goals. In M. P. Zanna and J. M. Olson (eds), *The psychology of prejudice: The Ontario symposium* (Vol. 7). Hillsdale, NJ: Erlbaum. pp. 103–30.

Nevid, J. S. and Morrison, J. K. (1980) Attitudes toward mental illness: The construction of the Libertarian Mental Health Ideology Scale. *Journal of Humanistic Psychology*. 20: 72–85.

Nicholls, J. G. (1975) Causal attribution and other achievement-related cognitions: Effects of task outcome, attainment value, and sex. *Journal of Personality and Social Psychology*. 31: 379–89.

Nilsen, A. P. (1977) Sexism in children's books and elementary teaching materials. In A. P. Nilsen, H. Bosmajian, H. L. Gershuny and J. P. Stanley (eds), *Sexism and language*. Urbana, IL: National Council of Teachers of English. pp. 161–80.

Nisbett, R. and Ross, L. (1980) *Human inference: Strategies and shortcomings of social judgement*. Englewood Cliffs, NJ: Prentice Hall.

Nisbett, R. E., Caputo, C., Legant, P. and Maracek, J. (1973) Behavior as seen by the actor and as seen by the observer. *Journal of Personality and Social Psychology*. 27: 154–64.

Noble, W. (1987) Perception and language: Towards a complete ecological psychology. In A. Costall and A. Still (eds), *Cognitive psychology in question*. Brighton: Harvester. pp.128–41.

Oakes, P. J. (1987) The salience of social categories. In J. Turner, M. A. Hogg, P. J. Oakes, S. D. Reicher and M. S. Wetherell (eds), *Rediscovering the social group: A self-categorization theory*. Oxford: Blackwell. pp. 117–41.

Oakes, P. J., Haslam, S. A. and Turner, J. C. (1994) *Stereotyping and social reality*. Oxford: Blackwell.

Oatley, K. and Johnson-Laird, P. N. (1987) Toward a cognitive theory of emotion. *Cognition and Emotion*. 1: 29–50.

Opton, E. M., Jr (1971) It never happened and besides they deserved it. In N. Sanford and C. Comstock (eds), *Sanctions for evil*. San Francisco: Jossey-Bass. pp. 49–70.

Orne, M. T. (1969) Demand characteristics and the concept of design controls. In R. Rosenthal and R. L. Rosnow (eds), *Artifact in behavioral research*. New York: Academic Press. pp. 143–79.

Orpen, C. (1975) Authoritarianism revisited: A critical examination of 'expressive' theories of prejudice. In S. Morse and C. Orpen (eds), *Contemporary South Africa: Social psychological perspectives*. Johannesburg: Juta and Co. pp. 103–11.

Ostrom, T. M. (1969) The relationship between the affective, behavioral, and cognitive components of attitude. *Journal of Experimental Social Psychology*. 5: 12–30.

Ostrom, T. M. (1989) Three catechisms for social memory. In P. R. Solomon, G. R. Goethals, C. M. Kelley and B. R. Stephens (eds), *Memory: Interdisciplinary approaches*. New York: Springer-Verlag. pp. 201–20.

Páez, D., Echebarria, A., Valencia, J., Romo, I., San Juan, C. and Vergara, A. (1991) AID's social representations: Contents and processes. *Journal of Community and Applied Social Psychology*. 1: 89–104.

Parker, I. (1987) Social representations: Social psychology's (mis)use of sociology. *Journal for the Theory of Social Behaviour*. 17: 447–69.

Parker, I. (1990) Discourse: Definitions and contradictions. *Philosophical Psychology*. 3: 189–204.

Parker, I. (1991) *Discourse dynamics: Critical analyses for social and individual psychology*. London: Routledge.

Peevers, B. H. and Secord, P. F. (1973) Developmental changes in attributions of descriptive concepts to persons. *Journal of Personality and Social Psychology*. 27: 120–8.

Pepitone, A. (1976) Toward a normative and comparative biocultural social psychology. *Journal of Personality and Social Psychology*. 34: 641–53.

Pepitone, A. (1981) Lessons from the history of social psychology. *American Psychologist*. 36: 972–85.

Perdue, C. W. and Gurtman, M. B. (1990) Evidence for the automaticity of ageism. *Journal of Experimental Social Psychology*. 26: 199–216.

Perdue, C. W., Dovidio, J. F., Gurtman, M. B. and Tyler, R. B. (1990) Us and them: Social categorization and the process of intergroup bias. *Journal of Personality and Social Psychology*. 59: 475–86.

Pereira de Sa, C. (1992) On the relationship between social representations, socio-cultural practices and behavior. Paper presented at the First International Conference on Social Representations, Ravello, Italy.

Peterson, C. and Seligman, M. E. P. (1984) Causal explanations as a risk factor for depression: Theory and evidence. *Psychological Review*. 91: 347–74.

Petta, G. and Walker, I. (1992) Relative deprivation and ethnic identity. *British Journal of Social Psychology*. 31: 285–93.

Pettigrew, T. F. (1958) Personality and socio-cultural factors in intergroup attitudes: A cross-national comparison. *Journal of Conflict Resolution*. 2: 29–42.

Pettigrew, T. F. (1959) Regional differences in anti-Negro prejudice. *Journal of Abnormal and Social Psychology*. 59: 28–36.

Pettigrew, T. F. (1960) Social distance attitudes of South African students. *Social Forces*. 38: 246–53.

Pettigrew, T. F. (1961) Social psychology and desegregation research. *American Psychologist*. 16: 105–12.

Pettigrew, T. F. (1967) Social evaluation theory. In D. Levine (ed.), *Nebraska Symposium on Motivation*. Lincoln, NE: University of Nebraska Press. pp. 241–311.

Pettigrew, T. F. (1979) The ultimate attribution error: Extending Allport's cognitive analysis of prejudice. *Personality and Social Psychology Bulletin*. 5: 461–76.

Pill, R. and Stott, N. C. H. (1982) Concepts of illness causation and responsibility: Some preliminary data from a sample of working-class mothers. *Social Science and Medicine*. 16: 43–52.

Pill, R. and Stott, N. C. H. (1985) Choice or chance: Further evidence on ideas of illness and responsibility for health. *Social Science and Medicine*. 20: 981–91.

Potter, J. and Billig, M. (1992) Re-presenting representations – Discussion of Raty and Snellman. *Papers on Social Representations*. 1: 15–20.

Potter, J. and Litton, I. (1985) Some problems underlying the theory of social representations. *British Journal of Social Psychology*. 24: 81–90.

Potter, J. and Wetherell, M. (1987) *Discourse and social psychology: Beyond attitudes and behaviour*. London: Sage.

Potter, J., Wetherell, M., Gill, R. and Edwards, D. (1990) Discourse: Noun, verb or social practice? *Philosophical Psychology*. 3: 205–17.

Pratkanis, A. R. (1989) The cognitive representation of attitudes. In A. R. Pratkanis, S. J. Breckler and A. G. Greenwald (eds), *Attitude structure and function*. Hillsdale, NJ: Erlbaum. pp. 71–98.

Pratkanis, A. R. and Greenwald, A. G. (1989) A sociocognitive model of attitude structure and function. In L. Berkowitz (ed.), *Advances in experimental social psychology* (Vol. 22). New York: Academic Press. pp. 245–85.

Preston, C. E. and Harris, S. (1965) Psychology of drivers in traffic accidents. *Journal of Applied Psychology*. 49: 284–8.

Rabbie, J. M. and Horwitz, M. (1988) Categories versus groups as explanatory concepts in intergroup relations. *European Journal of Social Psychology*. 18: 117–23.

Rabkin, J. G. (1972) Opinions about mental illness: Overview. *Psychological Bulletin*. 77: 153–71.

Reed, E. (1987) Why do things look as they do? The implications of James Gibson's *The ecological approach to visual perception*. In A. Costall and A. Still (eds), *Cognitive psychology in question*. Brighton: Harvester. pp. 90–114.

Reeder, G. D. and Brewer, M. B. (1979). A schematic model of dispositional attribution in interpersonal perception. *Psychological Review*. 86: 61–79.

Reeder, G. D. and Fulks, J. L. (1980) When actions speak louder than words: Implicational schemata and the attribution of ability. *Journal of Experimental Social Psychology*. 16: 33–46.

Regan, D. T. and Fazio, R. H. (1977) On the consistency between attitudes and behavior: Look to the method of attitude formation. *Journal of Experimental Social Psychology*. 13: 38–45.

Resnick, L. B., Levine, J. M. and Teasley, S. D. (eds) (1991) *Perspectives on socially shared cognition*. Washington, DC: American Psychological Association.

Ring, K. (1967) Experimental social psychology: Some sober questions about some frivolous values. *Journal of Experimental Social Psychology*. 3: 113–23.

Rojahn, K. and Pettigrew, T. (1992) Memory for schema-relevant information: A meta-analytic resolution. *British Journal of Social Psychology*. 31, 81–109.

Rokeach, M. (1960) *The open and closed mind*. New York: Basic Books.

Rosch, E. (1975) Cognitive reference points. *Cognitive Psychology.* 7: 532–47.

Rosch, E. (1978) Principles of categorization. In E. Rosch and B. B. Lloyd (eds), *Cognition and categorization.* Hillsdale, NJ: Erlbaum. pp. 27–48.

Rosch, E., Mervis, C., Gray, W., Johnson, D. and Boyes-Braem, P. (1976) Basic objects in natural categories. *Cognitive Psychology.* 8: 382–439.

Rosenberg, M. J. and Hovland, C. I. (1960) Cognitive, affective, and behavioral components of attitudes. In C. I. Hovland and M. J. Rosenberg (eds), *Attitude organization and change.* New Haven, CT: Yale University Press. pp. 1–14.

Rosenthal, R. (1966) *Experimenter effects in behavioral research.* New York : Appleton-Century-Crofts.

Rosenthal, R. (1969) Interpersonal expectations: Effects of the experimenter's hypothesis. In R. Rosenthal and R. L. Rosnow (eds), *Artifact in behavioral research.* New York: Academic Press. pp. 181–277.

Rosenthal, R. (1974) *On the social psychology of the self-fulfilling prophecy: Further evidence for Pygmalion effects and their mediating mechanisms.* M.S.S. Medviar Publications.

Rosenthal, R. and Jacobson, L. (1968) *Pygmalion in the classroom: Teacher expectation and pupils' intellectual development.* New York: Holt.

Ross, L. (1977) The intuitive psychologist and his shortcomings: Distortions in the attribution process. In L. Berkowitz (ed.), *Advances in experimental social psychology* (Vol. 10). New York: Academic Press. pp. 173–220.

Ross, L. and Lepper, M. R. (1980) The perseverance of beliefs: Empirical and normative considerations. In R. A. Schweder (ed.), *New directions for methodology of behavioral science: Fallible judgment in behavioral research.* San Francisco: Jossey-Bass.

Ross, L. and Nisbett, R. E. (1991) *The person and the situation: Perspectives of social psychology.* New York: McGraw-Hill.

Ross, L., Amabile, T. M. and Steinmetz, J. L. (1977) Social roles, social control, and social perception processes. *Journal of Personality and Social Psychology.* 35: 485–94.

Ross, L., Greene, D. and House, P. (1977) The false consensus phenomenon: An attributional bias in self-perception and social perception processes. *Journal of Experimental Social Psychology.* 13: 279–301.

Ross, M. and Sicoly, F. (1979) Egocentric biases in availability and attribution. *Journal of Personality and Social Psychology.* 37: 322–37.

Rothbart, M. (1981) Memory processes and social beliefs. In D. Hamilton (ed.), *Cognitive processes in stereotyping and intergroup behavior.* Hillsdale, NJ: Erlbaum. pp. 145–82.

Rothbart, M., Evans, M. and Fulero, S. (1979) Recall for confirming events: Memory processes and the maintenance of social stereotypes. *Journal of Experimental Social Psychology.* 15: 343–55.

Rubin, Z. and Peplau, A. (1975) Who believes in a just world? *Journal of Social Issues.* 31: 65–89.

Ruble, D. N. and Stangor, C. (1986) Stalking the elusive schema: Insights from developmental and social-psychological analyses of gender schemas. *Social Cognition.* 4: 227–61.

Ruble, D. N., Feldman, N. S., Higgins, E. T. and Karlovac, M. (1979) Locus of causality and use of information in the development of causal attributions. *Journal of Personality.* 47: 595–614.

Rumelhart, D. E. (1984) Schemata and the cognitive system. In R. S. Wyer, Jr, and T. K. Srull (eds), *Handbook of social cognition* (Vol. 1). Hillsdale, NJ: Erlbaum. pp. 161–88.

Rumelhart, D. E. and Norman, D. A. (1978) Accretion, tuning and restructuring: Three modes of learning. In J. W. Cotton and R. Klatzky (eds), *Semantic factors in cognition.* Hillsdale, NJ: Erlbaum.

Runciman, W. G. (1966) *Relative deprivation and social justice.* Berkeley, CA: University of California Press.

St Claire, L. and Turner, J. C. (1982) The role of demand characteristics in the social categorization paradigm. *European Journal of Social Psychology.* 12: 307–14.

Sampson, E. E. (1975) On justice as equality. *Journal of Social Issues.* 31: 45–64.

Sampson, E. E. (1977) Psychology and the American ideal. *Journal of Personality and Social Psychology.* 35: 767–82.

Sampson, E. E. (1981) Cognitive psychology as ideology. *American Psychologist.* 86: 730–43.

Sampson, E. E. (1988) The debate on individualism: Indigenous psychologies of the individual and their role in personal and societal functioning. *American Psychologist.* 43: 15–22.

Sampson, E. E. (1993) Identity politics: Challenges to psychology's understanding. *American Psychologist*. 48: 1219–30.

Sarbin, T. R. and Mancuso, J. C. (1970) Failure of a moral enterprise: Attitudes of the public toward mental illness. *Journal of Consulting and Clinical Psychology*. 35: 159–73.

Scarborough, E. (1990) Attitudes, social representations, and ideology. In C. Fraser and G. Gaskell (eds), *The social psychological study of widespread beliefs*. Oxford: Clarendon Press. pp. 99–117.

Schank, R. C. and Abelson, R. P. (1977) *Scripts, plans, goals and understanding: An inquiry into human knowledge structures*. Hillsdale, NJ: Erlbaum.

Schiffman, R. and Wicklund, R. A. (1992) The minimal group paradigm and its minimal psychology. *Theory and Psychology*. 2: 29–50.

Schlenker, B. R. and Leary, M. R. (1982) Audiences' reactions to self-enhancing, self-denigrating, and accurate self-presentations. *Journal of Experimental Social Psychology*. 18: 89–104.

Schlenker, B. R. and Miller, R. S. (1977) Egocentrism in groups: Self-serving biases or logical information processing? *Journal of Personality and Social Psychology*. 35: 755–64.

Schlozman, K. L. and Verba, S. (1979) *Injury to insult: Unemployment, class and political response*. Cambridge, MA: Harvard University Press.

Schmidt, C. F. (1972) Multidimensional scaling of the printed media's explanations of the riot of the summer of 1967. *Journal of Personality and Social Psychology*. 24: 59–67.

Schneider, W. and Shiffrin, R. M. (1977) Controlled and automatic human information processing: I. Detection, search, and attention. *Psychological Review*. 84: 1–66.

Schwartz, S. H. (1978) Temporal instability as a moderator of the attitude–behavior relationship. *Journal of Personality and Social Psychology*. 36: 715–24.

Schwartz, S. H. and Tessler, R. C. (1972) A test of a model for reducing measured attitude–behavior discrepancies. *Journal of Personality and Social Psychology*. 24: 225–36.

Sears, D. O. (1988) Symbolic racism. In P. A. Katz and D. A. Taylor (eds), *Eliminating racism: Profiles in controversy*. New York: Plenum Press. pp. 53–84.

Secord, P. F. (1959) Stereotyping and favorableness in the perception of negro faces. *Journal of Abnormal and Social Psychology*. 59: 309–15.

Secord, P. F., Bevan, W. and Katz, B. (1956) The negro stereotype and perceptual accentuation. *Journal of Abnormal and Social Psychology*. 53: 78–83.

Sedikides, C. (1990) Effects of fortuitously activated constructs versus activated communication goals on person impressions. *Journal of Personality and Social Psychology*. 58: 397–408.

Semin, G. R. (1985) The 'phenomenon of social representations': A comment on Potter and Litton. *British Journal of Social Psychology*. 24: 93–4.

Semin, G. R. (1989) Prototypes and social representations. In D. Jodelet (ed.), *Les représentations sociales*. Paris: Presses Universitaires de France. pp. 239–51.

Semin, G. R. and Fiedler, K. (1988) The cognitive functions of linguistic categories in describing persons: Social cognition and language. *Journal of Personality and Social Psychology*. 54: 558–68.

Semin, G. R. and Fiedler, K. (1989) Relocating attributional phenomena within a language–cognition interface: The case of actors' and observers' perspectives. *European Journal of Social Psychology*. 19: 491–508.

Shavitt, S. (1989) Operationalizing functional theories of attitude. In A. R. Pratkanis, S. J. Breckler and A. G. Greenwald (eds), *Attitude structure and function*. Hillsdale, NJ: Erlbaum. pp. 311–38.

Shavitt, S. (1990) The role of attitude objects in attitude functions. *Journal of Experimental Social Psychology*. 26: 124–48.

Shaw, M. E. (1971) *Group dynamics: The psychology of small group behaviour*. New York: McGraw-Hill.

Sheppard, B. H., Hartwick, J. and Warshaw, P. R. (1988) The theory of reasoned action: A meta-analysis of past research with recommendations for modifications and future research. *Journal of Consumer Research*. 15: 325–43.

Sherif, C. W., Sherif, M. and Nebergall, R. E. (1965) *Attitude and attitude change: The social judgment–involvement approach*. Philadelphia, PA: Saunders.

Sherif, M. (1966) *In common predicament: Social psychology of intergroup conflict and cooperation*. Boston: Houghton Mifflin.

Sherif, M. and Sherif, C. W. (1956) *An outline of social psychology* (rev. edn). New York: Harper & Row.

Sherif, M., Harvey, O. J., White, B. J., Hood, W. and Sherif, C. (1961) *Intergroup conflict and cooperation: The Robbers cave experiment*. Norman, OK: University of Oklahoma Institute of Intergroup Relations.

Shotter, J. (1984) *Social accountability and selfhood*. Oxford: Blackwell.

Shotter, J. (1992) Social constructionism and realism: Adequacy or accuracy? *Theory and Psychology*. 2: 175–82.

Shrauger, J. S. (1975) Responses to evaluation as a function of initial self-perceptions. *Psychological Bulletin*. 82: 581–96.

Shweder, R. A. and Bourne, E. J. (1982) Does the concept of the person vary cross-culturally? In A. J. Norsello and G. M. White (eds), *Cultural conceptions of mental health and therapy*. Boston: Reidel Publishing Company. pp. 97–137.

Simpson, G. E. and Yinger, J. M. (1985) *Racial and cultural minorities: An analysis of prejudice and discrimination* (5th edn). New York: Plenum Press.

Singh, S. and Vasudeva, P. (1977) A factorial study of the perceived reasons for poverty. *Asian Journal of Psychology and Education*. 2: 51–6.

Slugoski, B. R., Lalljee, M., Lamb, R. and Ginsburg, G. P. (1993) Attribution in conversational context: Effect of mutual knowledge on explanation-giving. *European Journal of Social Psychology*. 23: 219–38.

Smetana, J. G. and Adler, N. E. (1980) Fishbein's value x expectancy model: An examination of some assumptions. *Personality and Social Psychology Bulletin*. 6: 89–96.

Smith, H., Spears, R. and Oyen, M. (1994) 'People like us': The influence of personal deprivation and group membership salience on justice evaluations. *Journal of Experimental Social Psychology*. 30: 277–99.

Smith, M. and Walker, I. (1991) Evaluating the British version of the Attitudes toward Women Scale. *Australian Journal of Psychology*. 43: 7–10.

Smith, M. and Walker, I. (1992) The structure of attitudes to a single object: Adapting Criterial Referents Theory to measure attitudes to 'woman'. *British Journal of Social Psychology*. 31: 201–14.

Smith, M. B. (1945) Social situation, social behavior, social group. *Psychological Review*. 52: 224–9.

Smith, M. B. (1947) The personal setting of public opinions: A study of attitudes toward Russia. *Public Opinion Quarterly*. 11: 507–23.

Smith, M. B., Bruner, J. S. and White, R. W. (1956) *Opinions and personality*. New York: Wiley.

Smith, P. and Gaskell, G. (1990) The social dimension in relative deprivation. In C. Fraser and G. Gaskell (eds), *The social psychological study of widespread beliefs*. Oxford: Clarendon Press. pp. 179–91.

Sniderman, P. M. and Tetlock, P. E. (1986a) Symbolic racism: Problems of motive attribution in political analysis. *Journal of Social Issues*. 42: 129–50.

Sniderman, P. M. and Tetlock, P. E. (1986b) Interrelationship of political ideology and public opinion. In M. G. Hermann (ed.), *Political psychology: Contemporary problems and issues*. San Francisco: Jossey-Bass. pp. 62–96.

Snyder, M. (1984) When belief creates reality. In L. Berkowitz (ed.), *Advances in experimental social psychology* (Vol. 18). New York: Academic Press. pp. 248–306.

Snyder, M. (1992) Motivational foundations of behavioral confirmation. In M. P. Zanna (ed.), *Advances in experimental social psychology* (Vol. 25). Orlando, FL: Academic Press. pp. 67–114.

Snyder, M. and Kendzierski, D. (1982) Acting on one's attitudes: Procedures for linking attitude and behavior. *Journal of Experimental Social Psychology*. 18: 165–83.

Snyder, M. and Swann, W. B. (1978) Behavioral confirmation in social interaction: From social perception to social reality. *Journal of Experimental Social Psychology*. 14: 148–62.

Snyder, M., Tanke, E. D. and Berscheid, E. (1977) Social perception and interpersonal behavior: On the self-fulfilling nature of social stereotypes. *Journal of Personality and Social Psychology*. 35: 656–66.

Sousa, E. and Leyens, J.-P. (1987) *A priori* versus spontaneous models of attribution: The case of gender and achievement. *British Journal of Social Psychology*. 26: 281–92.

Spence, J. T. and Helmreich, R. (1972) The Attitudes toward Women Scale: An objective instrument to measure attitudes toward the rights and roles of women in contemporary society. *JSAS Catalog of Selected Documents in Psychology*. 2: 66.

Spence, J. T. and Helmreich, R. L. (1978) *Masculinity and femininity: Their psychological dimensions, correlates and antecedents*. Austin: University of Texas.

Sperber, D. (1984) Anthropology and psychology: Towards an epidemiology of representations. *Man.* 20: 73–89.

Sperber, D. (1990) The epidemiology of beliefs. In C. Fraser and G. Gaskell (eds), *The social psychological study of widespread beliefs.* Oxford: Clarendon Press. pp. 25–44.

Sprott, W. J. H. (1958) *Human groups.* Harmondsworth: Pelican.

Stacey, B. G. (1982) Economic socialization in the pre-adult years. *British Journal of Social Psychology.* 21: 159–73.

Stacey, B. G. and Singer, M. S. (1985) The perception of poverty and wealth among teenagers. *Journal of Adolescence.* 8: 231–42.

Stacey, B. G., Singer, M. S. and Ritchie, G. (1989) The perception of poverty and wealth among teenage university students. *Adolescence.* 24: 193–207.

Stangor, C. and Lange, J. E. (1994) Mental representations of social groups: Advances in understanding stereotypes and stereotyping. In M. P. Zanna (ed.), *Advances in experimental social psychology* (Vol. 26). San Diego, CA: Academic Press. pp. 357–416.

Stangor, C. and McMillan, D. (1992) Memory for expectancy-congruent and expectancy-incongruent information: A review of the social and social-developmental literatures. *Psychological Bulletin.* 111: 42–61.

Stangor, C., Sullivan, L. A. and Ford, T. E. (1991) Affective and cognitive determinants of prejudice. *Social Cognition.* 9: 359–80.

Stephan, W. G. (1977) Stereotyping: The role of ingroup–outgroup differences in causal attribution for behavior. *Journal of Social Psychology.* 101: 255–66.

Stephan, W. G. (1985) Intergroup relations. In G. Lindzey and E. Aronson (eds), *Handbook of social psychology* (3rd edn, Vol. 2). New York: Random House. pp. 599–658.

Stephan, W. G., Ageyev, V., Stephan, C. W., Abalakina, M., Stefanenko, T. and Coates-Schrider, L. (1993) Measuring stereotypes: A comparison of methods using Russian and American samples. *Social Psychology Quarterly.* 56: 54–64.

Stephenson, G. M. (1981) Intergroup bargaining and negotiation. In J. C. Turner and H. Giles (eds), *Intergroup behaviour.* Oxford: Blackwell. pp. 168–98.

Still, A. and Costall, A. (1987) In place of cognitivism. In A. Costall and A. Still (eds), *Cognitive psychology in question.* Brighton: Harvester. pp. 1–12.

Stone, W. F. and Schaffner, P. E. (1988) *The psychology of politics.* New York: Springer-Verlag.

Stone, W. F., Lederer, G. and Christie, R. (eds) (1993) *Strength and weakness: The authoritarian personality today.* New York: Springer-Verlag.

Storms, M. D. (1973) Videotape and the attribution process: Reversing actors' and observers' points of view. *Journal of Personality and Social Psychology.* 27: 165–75.

Stouffer, S. A., Suchman, E. A., De Vinney, L. C., Star, S. A. and Williams, R. M., Jr (1949) *The American soldier: Adjustment during army life* (Vol. 1). Princeton, NJ: Princeton University Press.

Stryker, S. and Statham, A. (1985) Symbolic interaction and role theory. In G. Lindzey and E. Aronson (eds), *Handbook of social psychology* (3rd edn, Vol. 1). New York: Random House. pp. 311–78.

Svenson, O. (1981) Are we all less risky and more skillful than our fellow drivers? *Acta Psychologica.* 47: 143–8.

Swann, W. B., Jr, and Read, S. J. (1981) Self-verification processes: How we sustain our self-conceptions. *Journal of Experimental Social Psychology.* 17: 351–70.

Sweeney, P. D., Anderson, K. and Bailey, S. (1986) Attributional style in depression: A meta-analytic review. *Journal of Personality and Social Psychology.* 50: 974–91.

Tajfel, H. (1969) Cognitive aspects of prejudice. *Journal of Social Issues.* 25: 79–97.

Tajfel, H. (1970) Experiments in intergroup discrimination. *Scientific American.* 223: 96–102.

Tajfel, H. (1972) Experiments in a vacuum. In J. Israel and H. Tajfel (eds), *The context of social psychology: A critical assessment.* London: Academic Press. pp. 69–119.

Tajfel, H. (1978a) The structure of our views about society. In H. Tajfel and C. Fraser (eds), *Introducing social psychology.* Harmondsworth: Penguin. pp. 302–21.

Tajfel, H. (ed.) (1978b) *Differentiation between social groups: Studies in the social psychology of intergroup relations.* London: Academic Press.

Tajfel, H. (1981) *Human groups and social categories.* Cambridge: Cambridge University Press.

Tajfel, H. (1982) Social psychology of intergroup relations. *Annual Review of Psychology.* 33: 1–39.

Tajfel, H. and Turner, J. C. (1979) An integrative theory of intergroup conflict. In W. G. Austin and S. Worchel (eds), *The social psychology of intergroup relations*. Monterey, CA: Brooks/Cole. pp. 33–48.

Tajfel, H. and Turner, J. C. (1986) The social identity theory of intergroup relations. In S. Worchel and W. G. Austin (eds), *Psychology of intergroup relations*. Monterey, CA: Brooks/Cole. pp. 7–24.

Tajfel, H. and Wilkes, A. L. (1963) Classification and quantitative judgement. *British Journal of Psychology*. 54: 101–14.

Tajfel, H., Sheikh, A. A. and Gardner, R. C. (1964) Content of stereotypes and the inference of similarity between members of stereotyped groups. *Acta Psychologica*. 22: 191–201.

Tajfel, H., Billig, M. G., Bundy, R. P. and Flament, C. (1971) Social categorization and intergroup behaviour. *European Journal of Social Psychology*. 1: 149–78.

Taylor, D. M. and Brown, R. J. (1979) Towards a more social social psychology. *British Journal of Social and Clinical Psychology*. 18: 173–80.

Taylor, D. M. and Jaggi, V. (1974) Ethnocentrism and causal attribution in a South Indian context. *Journal of Cross-Cultural Psychology*. 5: 162–71.

Taylor, S. E. (1982) Social cognition and health. *Personality and Social Psychology Bulletin*. 8: 549–62.

Taylor, S. E. and Crocker, J. (1981) Schematic bases of social information processing. In E. T. Higgins, C. P. Herman and M. P. Zanna (eds), *Social cognition: The Ontario symposium* (Vol 1). Hillsdale, NJ: Erlbaum. pp. 89–134.

Taylor, S. E. and Fiske, S. T. (1975) Point of view and perceptions of causality. *Journal of Personality and Social Psychology*. 32: 439–45.

Taylor, S. E. and Fiske, S. T. (1978) Salience, attention, and attribution: Top of the head phenomena. In L. Berkowitz (ed.), *Advances in experimental social psychology* (Vol 11). New York: Academic Press. pp. 249–88.

Taylor, S. E., Peplau, L. A. and Sears, D. O. (1994) *Social psychology* (8th edn). Englewood Cliffs, NJ: Prentice Hall.

Taylor, S. E., Fiske, S., Etcoff, N. L. and Ruderman, A. J. (1978) Categorical and contextual bases of person memory and stereotyping. *Journal of Personality and Social Psychology*. 36: 778–93.

Terborg, J. R. and Ilgen, D. R. (1975) A theoretical approach to sex discrimination in traditionally masculine occupations. *Organizational Behavior and Human Performance*. 13: 352–76.

Tesser, A. (1986) Some effects of self-evaluation maintenance on cognition and action. In R. M. Sorrentino and E. T. Higgins (eds), *Handbook of motivation and cognition: Foundations of social behavior*. New York: Guilford. pp. 435–64.

Tesser, A. (1988) Toward a self-evaluation maintenance model of social behavior. In L. Berkowitz (ed.), *Advances in experimental social psychology* (Vol. 21). New York: Academic Press. pp. 181–227.

Thomas, W. I. and Znaniecki, F. (1918–20) *The Polish peasant in Europe and America* (5 vols). Boston, MA: Badger.

Thompson, J. B. (1984) *Studies in the theory of ideology*. Cambridge: Polity Press.

Thurstone, L. L. (1928) Attitudes can be measured. *American Journal of Sociology*. 38: 529–54.

Tougas, F. and Veilleux, F. (1988) The influence of identification, collective relative deprivation, and procedure of implementation on women's response to affirmative action: A causal modelling approach. *Canadian Journal of Behavioral Science*. 20: 15–28.

Tougas, F. and Veilleux, F. (1990) The response of men to affirmative action strategies for women: The study of a predictive model. *Canadian Journal of Behavioural Science*. 22: 424–32.

Townsend, P. (1979) *Poverty in the United Kingdom: A survey of household resources and standards of living*. Harmondsworth: Penguin.

Triandis, H. C., Bontempo, R., Villareal, M. J., Asai, M. and Lucca, N. (1988) Individualism and collectivism: Cross-cultural perspectives in self–ingroup relationships. *Journal of Personality and Social Psychology*. 54: 323–8.

Triandis, H., Lisansky, J., Setiadi, B., Chang, B-H., Marin, G. and Betancourt, H. (1982) Stereotyping among Hispanics and Anglos: The uniformity, intensity, direction, and quality of auto- and heterostereotypes. *Journal of Cross-Cultural Psychology*. 13: 409–26.

Trope, Y. (1986) Identification and inferential processes in dispositional attribution. *Psychological Review*. 93: 239–57.

Trope, Y. and Cohen, O. (1989) Perceptual and inferential determinants of behaviour-correspondent attributions. *Journal of Experimental Social Psychology*. 25: 142–58.

Turner, J. C. (1985) Social categorization and the self-concept: A social-cognitive theory of group behavior. In E. J. Lawler (ed.), *Advances in group processes: Theory and research* (Vol. 2). Greenwich, CT: JAI Press. pp. 77–122.

Turner, J. C. and Oakes, P. J. (1989) Self-categorization theory and social influence. In P. B. Paulus (ed.), *Psychology of group influence* (2nd edn). Hillsdale, NJ: Erlbaum. pp. 233–75.

Turner, J. C., Hogg, M. A., Oakes, P. J., Reicher, S. D. and Wetherell, M. S. (1987) *Rediscovering the social group: A self-categorization theory*. Oxford: Blackwell.

Tversky, A. and Kahneman, D. (1973) Availability: A heuristic for judging frequency and probability. *Cognitive Psychology*. 5: 207–32.

Vallone, R. P., Ross, L. and Lepper, M. R. (1985) The hostile media phenomenon: Biased perception and perceptions of media bias in coverage of the 'Beirut Massacre'. *Journal of Personality and Social Psychology*. 49: 577–85.

van Dijk, T. A. (1987) *Communicating racism: Ethnic prejudice in thought and talk*. Newbury Park, CA: Sage.

van Dijk, T. A. (1988) Social cognition, social power and social discourse. *Text*. 8: 129–57.

Vanbeselaere, N. (1987) The effects of dichotomous and crossed social categorizations upon intergroup discrimination. *European Journal of Social Psychology*. 17: 143–56.

Vaughan, G. M. (1978a) Social categorization and intergroup behaviour in children. In H. Tajfel (ed.), *Differentiation between social groups: Studies in the social psychology of intergroup relations*. London: Academic Press. pp. 339–60.

Vaughan, G. M. (1978b) Social change and intergroup preferences in New Zealand. *European Journal of Social Psychology*. 8: 297–314.

Walker, I. (1994) Attitudes to minorities: Western Australians' attitudes to Aborigines, Asians, and women. *Australian Journal of Pychology*, 46: 137–43.

Walker, I. and Mann, L. (1987) Unemployment, relative deprivation, and social protest. *Personality and Social Psychology Bulletin*. 13: 275–83.

Walker, I. and Pettigrew, T. F. (1984) Relative deprivation theory: An overview and conceptual critique. *British Journal of Social Psychology*. 23: 301–10.

Weary, G. (1981) Role of cognitive, affective, and social factors in attribution biases. In J. H. Harvey (ed.), *Cognition, social behavior, and the environment*. Hillsdale, NJ: Erlbaum. pp. 213–25.

Weber, R. and Crocker, J. (1983) Cognitive processes in the revision of stereotypic beliefs. *Journal of Personality and Social Psychology*. 45: 961–77.

Weiner, B. (1985) 'Spontaneous' causal thinking. *Psychological Bulletin*. 97: 74–84.

Weiner, B. (1986) *An attributional theory of motivation and emotion*. New York: Springer-Verlag.

Weinstein, N. D. (1980) Unrealistic optimism about future life events. *Journal of Personality and Social Psychology*. 39: 806–20.

Wells, A. (1987) Social representations and the world of science. *Journal for the Theory of Social Behaviour*. 17: 433–45.

Wertsch, J. V. (1991) A sociocultural approach to socially shared cognition. In L. B. Resnick, J. M. Levine and S. D. Teasley (eds), *Perspectives on socially shared cognition*. Washington, DC: American Psychological Association. pp. 85–100.

Wetherell, M. (1982) Cross-cultural studies of minimal groups: Implications for the social identity theory of intergroup relations. In H. Tajfel (ed.), *Social identity and intergroup relations*. Cambridge: Cambridge University Press. pp. 207–40.

Wetherell, M. and Potter, J. (1992) *Mapping the language of racism: Discourse and the legitimation of exploitation*. Hemel Hempstead: Harvester Wheatsheaf.

Wheeler, L. (1991) A brief history of social comparison theory. In J. Suls and T. A. Wills (eds), *Social comparison: Contemporary theory and research*. Hillsdale, NJ: Erlbaum. pp. 3–21.

White, P. A. (1988) Causal processing: Origins and development. *Psychological Bulletin*. 104: 333–48.

White, P. A. and Younger, D. P. (1988) Differences in the ascription of transient internal states to self and other. *Journal of Experimental Social Psychology*. 24: 292–309.

Wicker, A. W. (1969) Attitudes versus actions: The relationship of verbal and overt behavioral responses to attitude objects. *Journal of Social Issues*. 25: 41–78.

Wicklund, R. A. and Gollwitzer, P. M. (1982) *Symbolic self-completion*. Hillsdale, NJ: Erlbaum.

Wilder, D. A. and Thompson, J. E. (1988) Assimilation and contrast effects in the judgments of groups. *Journal of Personality and Social Psychology*. 54: 62–73.

Wiley, M. G., Crittenden, K. S. and Birg, L. D. (1979) Why a rejection? Causal attributions of a career achievement event. *Social Psychology Quarterly*. 42: 214–22.

Williams, G. A. (1960) Gramsci's concept of egemonia. *Journal for the History of Ideas*. XXI: 586–99.

Williams, J. (1984) Gender and intergroup behaviour: Towards an integration. *British Journal of Social Psychology*. 23: 311–16.

Wills, T. A. (1981) Downward comparison principles in social psychology. *Psychological Bulletin*. 90: 245–71.

Wilson, T. D. and Linville, P. W. (1985) Improving the performance of college freshmen with attributional techniques. *Journal of Personality and Social Psychology*. 49: 287–93.

Wilson, T. D., Kraft, D. and Dunn, D. S. (1989) The disruptive effects of explaining attitudes: The moderating effect of knowledge about the attitude object. *Journal of Experimental Social Psychology*. 25: 379–400.

Wittgenstein, L. (1953) *Philosophical investigations*. Oxford: Basil Blackwell.

Word, C. O., Zanna, M. P. and Cooper, J. (1974) The non-verbal mediation of self-fulfilling prophecies in interracial interaction. *Journal of Experimental Social Psychology*. 10: 109–20.

Zajonc, R. B. (1960) The process of cognitive tuning and communication. *Journal of Abnormal and Social Psychology*. 61: 159–67.

Zajonc, R. B. (1980) Feeling and thinking: Preferences need no inferences. *American Psychologist*. 35: 151–75.

Zajonc, R. B. (1989) Styles of explanation in social psychology. *European Journal of Social Psychology*. 19: 345–68.

Zajonc, R. B. and Adelman, P. K. (1987) Cognition and communication: A story of missed opportunities. *Social Science Information*. 26: 3–30.

Zanna, M. P. and Rempel, J. K. (1988) Attitudes: A new look at an old concept. In D. Bar-Tal and A. W. Kruglanski (eds), *The social psychology of knowledge*. Cambridge: Cambridge University Press. pp. 315–34.

Zanna, M. P., Olson, J. M. and Fazio, R. H. (1980) Attitude–behavior consistency: An individual difference perspective. *Journal of Personality and Social Psychology*. 38: 432–40.

Zuckerman, M. (1979) Attribution of success and failure revisited, or: The motivational bias is alive and well in attribution theory. *Journal of Personality*. 47: 245–87.

Zurcher, L. (1977) *The mutable self: A self concept for social change*. Beverly Hills, CA: Sage.

INDEX

Compiled by Meg Davies (Society of Indexers)